SEP 9 '9X

SO-ADP-966

Organising
Knowledge

8-9-10-11   12-14

Organising Knowledge

An Introduction to Information Retrieval

Jennifer E Rowley

Gower

© Jennifer E. Rowley, 1987
All rights reserved. No part of this publication may be reproduced, stored in a
retrieval system, or transmitted in any form or by any means, electronic,
mechanical, photocopying, recording or otherwise without the prior permission of
Gower Publishing Company Limited.

Published by
Gower Publishing Company Limited
Gower House
Croft Road
Aldershot
Hants GU11 3HR
England

Gower Publishing Company
Old Post Road
Brookfield
Vermont 05036
U.S.A.

Reprinted 1988, 1989

British Library Cataloguing in Publication Data
Rowley, J.E.
    Organising knowledge: an introduction to
    information retrieval.
    1. Information storage and retrieval
    systems
    I. Title
    025.5'24   Z699

ISBN 0-566-03574-X (Hbk)
ISBN 0-566-03486-7 (Pbk)

Printed in Great Britain by
Billing & Sons Ltd, Worcester

Contents

Figures

Acknowledgements

It would be impossible to list all of those to whom I owe a debt of some kind in the creation of this book, and invidious to select only a group for special mention. Of course, the ideas gathered here have been drawn from those of many other writers in this field, and my first debt is to all of those who have contributed to the development of the field that can be called the Organisation of Knowledge. I am grateful to all the publishers, authors and systems suppliers who have permitted me to make use of extracts from their works. These are individually acknowledged at the point at which they are included in the work. The plan of this work owes much to Christopher Needham's *Organising Knowledge in Libraries,* and I am particularly grateful for the inspiration and education that this framework has provided, although I think I now understand why Christopher Needham did not wish to prepare a futher edition of his work! My students and my colleagues at Birmingham Polytechnic deserve a mention. Several of my colleagues were responsible for introducing me to the art (as opposed to the science) of cataloguing, although they should not be held responsible for my interpretation of their teaching. My students have had, patiently, year by year, to bear the refining of some of these ideas. David Butcher was invaluable in sharing my enthusiasms and in offering much needed encouragement. Above all, however, I am grateful to my husband Peter for his support through one of the most exhausting projects that I have yet undertaken.
April 1984

List of Abbreviations

Note: This is a list of the more common abbreviations used in this text. On occasions it has proved difficult to discriminate between acronyms and abbreviations, but, in general, acronyms are not included. For information on acronyms the reader should consult the index under the appropriate acronym. Key data bases, hosts, software packages and co-operatives are included, but the coverage in these areas is not comprehensive, since to produce such a complete list would take more space than such a list merits.

AA Code	Anglo-American cataloguing code 1908
AACR	Anglo-American Cataloguing Rules
AACR1	Anglo-American Cataloguing Rules, first edition
AACR2	Anglo-American Cataloguing Rules, second edition
ADP	Automatic Data Processing Inc.
AGRIS	Agricultural Information System
ALA	American Library Association
ALA Code	American Library Association code 1949
ASSASSIN	Agricultural System for Storage and Subsequent Selection of Information
BC	Bibliographic Classification Scheme (Bliss)
BC2	Bibliographic Classification Scheme, second edition
BCM	British Catalogue of Music
BCOP	Birmingham Libraries Cooperative
BELINDIS	Belgian Information and Dissemination Service
BIBDES	Bibliographic Data Entry System
BIOSIS	Biosciences Information
BL	British Library
BLAISE	British Library Automated Information Service
BLBSD	British Library Bibliographic Services Division
BLCMP	formerly Birmingham Libraries Cooperative Mechanisation Project
BM	British Museum
BNB	British National Bibliography
BRS	Bibliographic Retrieval Services Inc.

BSI	British Standards Institution
BSO	Broad System of Ordering
BTI	British Technology Index
BUCOP	British Union Catalogue of Periodicals
CAB	Commonwealth Agricultural Bureau
CAG	Cooperative Automation Group
CAS	Chemical Abstracts Services
CBI	Cumulative Book Index
CC	Colon Classification Scheme
CIP	Cataloguing-in-Publication
CIS	Cataloguing-in-Source
COM	Computer Output Microform
COMARC	Cooperative Machine Readable Cataloguing
COMPENDEX	Computerised Engineering Index
CONSER	Conversion of Serials
COPOL	Council of Polytechnic Libraries
CRG	Classification Research Group
CTI	Current Technology Index
DBMS	Database Management System
DC	Dewey Decimal Classification Scheme
DC18	Dewey Decimal Classification Scheme, 18th edition
DC19	Dewey Decimal Classification Scheme, 19th edition
DC20	Dewey Decimal Classification Scheme, 20th edition
DIANE	Direct Information Access Network for Europe
Ei	Engineering Index
EMMA	Extra MARC Material
ESA	European Space Agency
ESRO	European Space Research Organisation
EURONET	European Network System
FID	Fédération International de Documentation
GMD	General Materials Designation
ICCP	International Conference on Cataloguing Principles
IFLA	International Federation of Library Associations
IIB	Institut International de la Bibliographie
INIS	International Nuclear Information System
INSPEC	Information Service–Physics, Electrical + Electronics and Computers and Control
IPSS	International Packet Switch Stream

IRRD	International Road Research Documentation System
IRS	Information Retrieval Service (of ESA)
ISBD	International Standard Bibliographic Description
ISBD(CM)	ISBD for Cartographic Materials
ISBD(CP)	ISBD for Component Parts
ISBD(G)	ISBD for General framework
ISBD(M)	ISBD for Monographs
ISBD(NBM)	ISBD for Nonbook Materials
ISBD(PM)	ISBD for Printed Music
ISBD(S)	ISBD for Serials
ISBN	International Standard Book Number
ISI	Institute for Scientific Information
ISO	International Standards Organisation
ISSN	International Standard Serial Number
JSC	Joint Steering Committee (for the revision of AACR)
KWIC	Keyword in Context
KWOC	Keyword out of Context
LASER	London and South East Region
LC	Library of Congress
LCC	Library of Congress Classification Scheme
LCSH	Library of Congress Subject Headings
LIBRIS	Library Information System
LIS	Lockheed Information Systems
LOCAS	Local Catalogue Service
MARC	Machine Readable Cataloguing
MARC(S)	Machine Readable Cataloguing (Serials)
MEDLARS	Medical Literature Analysis and Retrieval System
MEDLINE	MEDLARS On-Line
MeSH	Medical Subject Headings
MULS	Minnesota Union List of Serials
MUMS	Multiple Use MARC System
NEMROC	Newcastle Media Resources Organisation Committee
NPAC	National Program for Acquisitions and Cataloguing
NSDC	National Serials Data Centre
NTIS	National Technical Information Service
NUC	National Union Catalog
OCLC	Online Computer Library Centre

PMEST	Personality-Matter-Energy-Space-Time
PRECIS	Preserved Context Indexing System
PSS	Packet Switch Stream
PTT	Post, Telephone and Telegraph Authority
RECON	Retrospective Conversion
RLG	Research Libraries Group
RLIN	Research Libraries Information Network
SCOLCAP	Scottish Libraries Cooperative Automation Project
SCONUL	Standing Conference of National and University Libraries
SCORPIO	Subject Content Oriented Retriever for Processing Information Online
SDC	Systems Development Corporation
SDI	Selective Dissemination of Information
SHE	Subject Headings for Engineering
SHEMROC	Sheffield Media Resources Organisation Committee
SLA	School Library Association
SLIC	Selective Listing in Combination
SWALCAP	South West Area Libraries Cooperative Automation Project
UBC	Universal Bibliographic Control
UDC	Universal Decimal Classification Scheme
UKCSO	United Kingdom Central Statistical Office
UKLDS	United Kingdom Library Database System
UNESCO	United Nations Educational, Scientific and Cultural Organisation
UNIBID	UNISIST International Centre for Bibliographic Description
UNIMARC	Universal MARC format
UNISIST	United Nations Information Systems in Science and Technology
UTLAS	University of Toronto Library Automation System
VDU	Visual Display Unit
WLN	Washington Library Network
WPI	World Patents Index

Periodicals

Textbooks are prone to date. This text attempts to reflect the state of the art at the time that it was written. However, in order to make sure that he is adequately aware of new developments, the reader is urged to scan periodicals in which contributions relevant to the Organisation of Knowledge are to be found. Some of the periodicals which might be appropriate are:

Aslib Proceedings
Catalogue and Index
The Electronic Library
The Indexer
Information processing and management
Information technology and libraries
Information storage and retrieval
International cataloguing
International classification
Journal of Documentation
Journal of Information Science
Journal of the American Society for Information Science
Library Resources and Technical Services
Online
Online Review
Program
Special Libraries
Software review
Vine

Many other periodicals also include contributions on special aspects of the organisation of knowledge.

Introduction

This is an introductory text on information retrieval and the organisation of knowledge. It updates C.D. Needham's *Organising Knowledge in Libraries*, and takes its inspiration for its framework from this earlier text. Since this earlier work was published computers and information technology have had far-reaching effects on the organisation of knowledge and information retrieval, and this text is therefore essentially a new work. The text covers both cataloguing and classification and indexing techniques, all of which have been influenced by the application of computers. The level of treatment is designed to be appropriate to students on undergraduate and postgraduate courses in librarianship.

The objective of any catalogue, index or data base is to enable one to retrieve records or documents that have been stored and organised by the indexing process. The indexing process creates a description of a document or information, and successful retrieval hangs on the ability of the searcher to reconstruct that document description. Thus, it is important that all information workers understand the skills and tools associated with the organisation of knowledge, whether they will be engaged in their creation or are more likely to participate in their exploitation.

The book reflects the author's approach to the subject which is that many information retrieval systems have common elements, and that they differ one from another in the ways in which they select from the range of possible formats and facilities. Thus the main sections are: records, access points, including authors' names, subject terms and titles. Finally there is a part on the systems that incorporate these features, and a brief part gathering together some aspects of user perspectives. Some topics, such as evaluation, which might have been included have been omitted in order to restrict the length of the text. This omission of evaluation as a separate topic is not to imply that an evaluative approach to all of the topics considered in this text should not be encouraged.

No attempt has been made to give comprehensive details of individual sources. The purpose of this text is to fit these sources into their broader context, and to make comparisons. The text assumes that the student will have the opportunity to examine for himself the basic tools which are mentioned in this text.

1 Bakewell, K.G.B., *A manual of cataloguing practice*, Pergamon: London, New York, 1972.
2 Chan, L.M., *Cataloguing and classification*, McGraw-Hill: New York, London, 1981.
3 Anthony, L.J. ed., *Handbook of special librarianship and information*, 5th edition, Aslib: London, 1982.
4 Horner, J., *Cataloguing*, Association of Assistant Librarians: London, 1970.
5 Hunter, E.J., *Cataloguing: a guidebook*, Bingley: London, 1974.
6 Hunter, E.J. and Bakewell, K.G.B., *Cataloguing*, 2nd edition, Bingley: London, 1983.
7 Knight, G.N., *Indexing, the art of*, Allen & Unwin: London, 1979.
8 Needham, C.D., *Organizing knowledge in libraries: an introduction to cataloguing and classification*, Deutsch: London, 1971.
9 Salton, G. and McGill, M.J., *Introduction to modern information retrieval*, McGraw-Hill: Auckland, London, 1983.
10 Van Rijsbergen, C.J., *Information retrieval*, 2nd edition, Butterworth: London, 1979.
11 Vickery, B.C., *Information systems*, Butterworth: London, 1973.
12 Vickery, B.C. *Techniques of information retrieval*, Butterworth: London, 1970.

A relatively comprehensive bibliography covering many of the topics considered in this text is:

Wellisch, H.H., *Indexing and abstracting: an international bibliography*, ABC-Clio: Santa Barbara, California and Oxford, 1980.

Part I   Records

1   The tools of information retrieval and the organisation of knowledge

Introduction

The organisation of knowledge is a process that has been recognised as necessary for thousands of years. As the quantity of knowledge expands the need to organise it becomes more pressing. In those branches of librarianship or information work which are concerned with knowledge or information and its use for recreation, education or commercial gain, the organisation of knowledge .is an essential preliminary to the effective exploitation of that information. A vast number of different means of organising knowledge have been devised and exploited since the earliest of times, although many of the systems in use today have evolved over the past one hundred or so years. During the last twenty years the variety of approaches to the organisation of knowledge has proliferated with the introduction of computer-based methods.

Any attempt to organise knowledge must, in order to justify the effort of organisation, have an objective. Some people like order for its own sake, but it is rarely an economic proposition to engage in organising large collections of knowledge without some more explicit purpose. In general terms, the objective of the organisation of knowledge is to permit that information or knowledge to be found again on a later occasion. Thus the organisation of knowledge and its later retrieval, sometimes known as information retrieval, are very much part of the same process. Poor organisation makes it difficult to find something later, whereas if everything has a place, and is located in that place when it is not in use, when that thing is required it can be picked out immediately. This principle applies as much to objects, such as the tools in a workshop, as to units of knowledge or information. There is another principle which can be identified from our analogy with the organisation of objects. If someone else puts your things away, and that someone else has no familiarity with your usual system, then the objects become organised, but that does not mean that you can find things. Organisation in itself has little value. The organisation must be sensible, according to some criterion, and preferably familiar to or at least expected by the user. Thus it becomes yet plainer that it is not possible to divorce the organisation of knowledge from information retrieval. This simple observation also goes some of the way to wards explaining the variety of tools, methods and systems which are encountered in the organisation of knowledge. Each set of knowledge, with its own set of users may require a different system, although this diversity must be tempered by the fact that any one user when interacting with various different collections of knowledge would obviously find it easier if each set were organised in a manner which was at least consistent with that which he had encountered in other systems.

Before advancing to a more detailed consideration of specific tools, it will be useful to consider some definitions of the basic concepts which have been introduced in this section. *The Oxford English Dictionary* proposes the following definitions for the four words which have been used previously.

To organise is to 1. furnish with organs, make organic, make into living being or tissue; become organic. 2. form into an organic whole; give orderly structure to, frame and put into working order; make arrangements for.

Knowledge is knowing, familiarity gained by experience; person's range of information; a theoretical or practical understanding of; the sum of what is known.

To retrieve is to 1. recover by investigation or effort of memory, restore to knowledge or recall to mind; regain possession of. 2. rescue from bad state, revive, repair, set right.

Information is 1. informing, telling; thing told, knowledge, items of knowledge, news.

Notice that the definitions of information and knowledge are both closely intertwined. The definitions of to organise and to retrieve are both active, and in particular the element which says 'to put into working order' is particularly appropriate.

Now we are concerned in this work with the organisation of knowledge and information retrieval in a specific context. In particular we are concerned with those techniques which are of interest to librarians and information workers. These will include techniques and tools found and used in libraries, but other tools which impinge on the process of information work must also be considered. However, one important feature to note about such systems is that many of them do not in fact organise knowledge or retrieve information. Many are actually concerned with the organisation and retrieval of documents, or references to documents. True information retrieval systems are beginning to impinge upon libraries, but many of the techniques that have been labelled information retrieval techniques do not provide direct access to information, but rather offer an avenue to the documents which contain that information. These ideas will be explored later. This chapter now goes on to introduce some of the more basic tools used in the organisation of knowledge.

1.1 The tools of the organisation of knowledge

In order to organise knowledge librarians and information workers create a variety of tools. Traditionally the tools of information retrieval have been catalogues, bibliographies and printed indexes. Now computer-held data bases and their indexes are also important in the organisation of knowledge and are gradually replacing the traditional tools in a number of applications. At this point in time both the traditional tools and the computer-based tools are components in a unified approach to the organisation of knowledge.

This section introduces some definitions of common terms concerned with the tools for the organisation of knowledge. These definitions are the first elements of a language concerning information retrieval which will be used subsequently in this work.

A *catalogue* is a list of the materials or items in a library (or, traditionally, a list of the books in a library), with the entries representing the items arranged in some systematic order. A catalogue may be held as a card catalogue, microfilm catalogue or as a computer data base.

A *bibliography* is a list of materials or items which is restricted in its coverage by some feature other than the materials being gathered in one library collection. A bibliography may list the materials published in a certain country, or on a given subject, or in a given form, or its coverage may be restricted by a number of other factors. Many bibliographies are printed, but machine-held equivalents can be identified.

A *printed index* is a pointer, or indicator, or more fully, a systematic guide to the items contained in, or concepts derived from a collection. Another dictionary definition is that an index is an alphabetical list of references, usually at the end of a book.

A *computer-held data base* is a little more difficult to define simply and effectively. A data base is a collection of similar records, with relationships between the records. According to this definition catalogues and indexes are data bases, and this is indeed the case. A computer-held data base is held in machine readable format. A catalogue data base may indeed be regarded as one type of computer-held data base. There are also other types of bibliographic data bases. A bibliographic data base comprises a set of records which refer to documents (such as books, films, periodical articles or reports). Other data bases, which may be described as non-bibliographic, and are sometimes known as data banks, store actual facts and figures and text. Data bases may contain references to documents, or actual information on various subjects. Access to the contents of data bases is via some computer-searching technique, often using an online terminal.

These four types of information retrieval tools have a number of common features. To start with, most catalogues, indexes, data bases and bibliographies provide access to information or documents. This access is achieved by organising the tools so that a user may search under a specific access point or heading or index term, for example, subject term, author name, title, date. Similar types of headings or access points are evident in all four of the categories of tools. In addition to similar access points, all categories of tool include some description (however abbreviated) of the documents or information which they serve to organise. Thus, the remainder of this work discusses access points and description in general terms, and many points are equally relevant to a variety of the devices used for the organisation of knowledge.

The various tools are also intertwined in their production. Although some catalogues, indexes and bibliographies are generated traditionally, many have been derived from a computer data base. Figure 1.1 summarises simply the production of many printed indexes and catalogues. Data in various forms (according to the type of product required subsequently) may be put into a computer data base, reorganised by the computer system, and used to produce printed products. The same data base may also be examined directly by online access.

Figure 1.1 Production of the tools for the organisation of knowledge

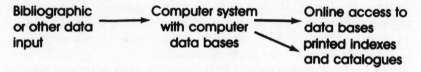

Bibliographic or other data input → Computer system with computer data bases → Online access to data bases / printed indexes and catalogues

1.2 Basic characteristics of the tools of information retrieval

1.2.1 Catalogues

Any catalogue comprises a number of entries each entry representing or acting as a surrogate for a document. There may be several entries per document, or merely one. Figure 1.2 shows an entry or a record in a catalogue.

Figure 1.2 A simple sample catalogue entry

Judge, Arthur William

Car maintenance and repair/by Arthur W Judge.—6th edition.—London: Chapman and Hall, 1972.—466p.:ill;19cm.—(Motor Manuals;4).— ISBN 0412 01050

The entry shown in Figure 1.2, like all other catalogue entries, comprises two sections: the heading (which is the author's name in this example), and the description (starting in this example with the title 'Car maintenance . . .'). Variations in the extent of the description between a set of entries account to a large extent for the distinction between main, added and unit entries. These ideas are explored more fully in Chapter 2.

Headings determine the order of the catalogue sequence. The entries in an author catalogue will have authors' names as headings, and the catalogue will be organised alphabetically according to the authors' names. Similarly a subject catalogue will have headings which represent the subject content of the document. The entry in Figure 1.2, then, could be filed in an author catalogue. The types of catalogue commonly found in libraries are:

Author catalogues which contain entries with authors' names as the heading. Authors may be persons or corporate bodies, and the term author is normally extended to include writers, illustrators, performers, producers, translators, and others with some intellectual or artistic responsibility for a work.

Title catalogues contain entries with titles as the heading. Some libraries and information units make title entries for all items being indexed, but in other situations title entries are made selectively for only some materials.

Author/title catalogues contain both title and author entries. Since both titles and authors' names are alphabetical it is easy to interfile authors' names and titles as headings.

Subject catalogues have an indication of the subject of the documents being indexed as their headings. The entries are arranged in an appropriate systematic order. There are two significantly different types of subject catalogue:

Alphabetical subject catalogues have headings which are words or index terms designed to summarise the subject content of the document, for example, Cars, Lawyers. These entries are arranged alphabetically, according to the subject heading.

Classified subject catalogues have headings on entries which are classification symbols, for example 682.9, QC275, which have been drawn from a classification scheme (see Chapter 14). In a classification scheme each subject is allocated a piece of notation, and that notation is used to represent the subject. The headings will be arranged according to the filing sequence of the notation (for example, alphabetically for letters or numerically for numbers).

The catalogues that have been identified so far are single sequence. A catalogue for a complete library collection will normally combine a number of these single sequence catalogues.

A classified catalogue is a catalogue with three or four separate sequences: an author/title catalogue or index (or separate author and title catalogues), a classified subject catalogue, and a subject index to the classified catalogue. Figure 1.3 shows the entries in a classified catalogue for a book which presents relatively few cataloguing problems.

A dictionary catalogue is a catalogue with only one sequence which contains author, title and alphabetical subject entries interfiled. Since all of the headings are alphabetical words, it is possible to interfile entries regardless of the nature of their heading.

Classified v dictionary catalogues. Figure 1.3 shows the different entries to be included in the classified and the dictionary catalogue. The distinction between these two types of catalogue represents two opposing approaches to the subject approach to information: classified and alphabetical headings. Both the classified, or ordered approach to subjects, and the alphabetical, or direct approach to subjects are important in any situation where consideration is being given to the organisation of knowledge. For instance, even a dictionary catalogue uses the symbols of a classification scheme to indicate the shelf location of documents. The documents themselves, especially if they are non-fiction, are likely to have been arranged in accordance with a

Figure 1.3 Entries in classified and dictionary catalogues

Classified Catalogues	Dictionary Catalogues
1. Brown, R. How to play chess/R Brown. Macmillan, 1983.-66p. 794.1	Brown, R How to play chess/R Brown. Macmillan, 1983.-66p. 794.1
2. How to play chess/R Brown. Macmillan, 1983.—66p. 794.1	How to play chess/R Brown. Macmillan, 1983.—66p. 794.1
3. 794.1 How to play chess/R Brown. Macmillan, 1983.—66p. 794.1	Chess How to play chess/R Brown. Macmillan, 1983.—66p. 794.1
4. Chess 794.1	

classification scheme. A classified catalogue, on the other hand, must be supported by an alphabetical subject index which serves to translate the user's normal language into the notation of the classification scheme. The dictionary and classified catalogues do not represent attempts to avoid the alternative device, be it classified or alphabetical subject headings, but rather show different emphases.

The purpose of a subject catalogue can be seen to have two elements:

1. To obtain documents on a specific subject.
2. To note documents on related subjects.

Both components are important, but whereas the dictionary catalogue is designed to give priority to the first objective, the classified catalogue recognises the importance of the second objective. Figure 1.4 tabulates a comparison of the classified and dictionary catalogues.

With computerisation the distinction between the types of catalogue has become less significant. A library is no longer constrained to choose either a classified or a dictionary catalogue. For very little additional cost it is possible to print (on paper or microfilm) as many catalogue sequences as are deemed appropriate for a given application.

1.2.2 Printed indexes

It is perhaps fortunate that the array of terms that are used to describe indexes is a little more restricted than the variety of terms used in respect of catalogues.

Two basic types of index are common: author indexes and subject indexes. A subject index has alphabetical terms or words as headings; these terms represent concepts or subjects. Entries are arranged in alphabetical order according to the letters in the heading. Where the works of a number of authors are listed in one index, an author index will provide access via authors' names. The index is arranged alphabetically according to the authors' names. The 'descriptive part' of the entry in an index will vary considerably depending upon the information or document collection being indexed. Indeed, in order to discuss indexes any further it is necessary to introduce some of the contexts in which indexes are to be found.

A *book index* is an alphabetically arranged list of words or terms leading the reader to the numbers of pages on which specific topics are considered, or on which specific names appear. Many non-fiction books and directories include an index. Many book indexes are predominantly lists of subject terms. Some indexes also include the names of bodies or persons in the same sequence. Occasionally a separate author index might be created, in for instance, an extensive bibliography or reading list. Many of the principles which apply to the construction of alphabetical subject descriptors in

Figure 1.4 Relative merits of classified and dictionary catalogues

Classified catalogue

1. Provides collocation of related subjects.
2. The subject index collocates distributed relatives, that is draws together related subjects which are otherwise scattered by the classified order.
3. Shelf order is reproduced.
4. Subject index to shelf enquiries are rapid, and can bypass the more complex classified subject catalogue.
5. Convenient for the generation of lists of documents in given subject areas, such as reading lists and simple bibliographies.
6. The notation avoids language problems. Whatever a user's native language, the same notation can be used to represent a subject.
7. It is easy to make use of effective guiding which groups entries into broad subject categories.

Dictionary catalogue

1. The single alphabetical sequence is easy to understand.
2. The sequence, headings and references are independent of a classification scheme, and may thus avoid the pitfalls of any specific classification scheme.
3. Leads direct to a given subject (which has a known name) at one referral.
4. Some collocation of related subjects occurs, by accident (if subjects have names which are alphabetically close to one another).
5. There is no organised structure of relationships.
6. References help to indicate relationships, and are more explicit statements of relationships than are found in a classified catalogue.
7. The alphabetical approach is widely used in printed indexes and data bases.

catalogues are also relevant to the construction of book indexes. Generally, the terms used in a book index will be more specific than those encountered in an alphabetical subject catalogue. An extract from a book index is shown in Figure 1.5.

A *periodical index* is an index to a specific periodical title (for example, *Proceedings of the London Mathematical Society, Library Association Record*). Usually indexes are generated at intervals to cover several issues. For instance, an annual index, covering all issues within one year is quite common. Annual indexes may also cumulate to, say five- or ten-yearly cumulations. Periodical indexes are very similar to book indexes. The major difference is that a periodical index relates to a number of issues and to contributions from a number of different authors. This means that the location of information on a subject needs to be indicated by giving a volume or date of issue in addition to page numbers. More significantly, an author index may be useful. Periodicals may, then, have either subject or author, or even title indexes, or any combination of these three.

Indexing journals (and the indexes to printed abstracting journals) are alphabetical indexes to the literature of a subject area. Usually, many of the entries relate to periodical literature, but monographs, conference proceedings, reports and other literature may also be covered. The key component in an indexing journal is an alphabetical subject index, in which the headings are terms representing the subject concepts covered in the documents listed in the indexing journal. The 'description' is the bibliographical citation which gives details of the document. Many indexing journals also include an author index, which permits the literature of a subject area to be approached via authors' names.

1.2.3 Current awareness services

Current awareness services are not necessarily to be regarded as tools for the organisation of knowledge, but since they are important in the dissemination of information, and many of the techniques discussed in other sections of this work are of relevance in their production, some simple definitions are introduced here.

A current awareness service is a service designed to alert information users to new information in a specific field which they have previously decided is of interest to them. Current awareness services can be derived from large external data bases such as are discussed in Chapter 19, or they

Figure 1.5 An extract from a book index

Cabbage	60
Cabbage, Red	63
Carrot	64
Cauliflower	65
Caustic lime	17
Celery	68
Celery, self-blanching	68
Celery, Non self-blanching	69
Circular greenhouses	29
Cloches	37
Cropping table	14
Cucumber	72

may be one product of an in-house information retrieval system of the type considered in Chapter 20. Thus some current awareness services can be purchased from external vendors, whilst others may be offered by a library or information unit to its particular group of users. Current awareness services are not specifically intended to have any archival value, although the data base from which they might be generated can have a valuable retrospective function.

There are a number of formats in which current awareness services can be encountered. Two basic forms are possible: bulletins and selective dissemination of information (or SDI). A bulletin will be a printed list, or set list for consultation on a VDU, which is published and distributed to a number of users on a specific subject area, say, building products or cancer research. Most such bulletins list titles or abstracts, together with citations of relevant new documents in the subject area. Some bulletins offer a digest of the information, and others actually include extracts from the documents which are announced (particularly if the documents being covered are newspaper articles). Usually a new bulletin will be issued at intervals, for example, monthly, weekly or daily. The other form of current awareness service is the SDI service. In an SDI service the user specifies his own individual interests in detail, and these are then expressed in terms of a user interest profile. The user then receives, on a regular basis, notifications of new documents or information which fall within the topic specified in his profile. Most SDI systems use the computer to perform the selection of announcements, and are thus able to offer this individualised service to many users. SDI can be printed, or can be made available for online viewing, in which case the user goes to the terminal to view the new notifications at regular intervals. Other options are Standard and Group SDI. These services are not individualised, but rather are based either on a set of standard profiles (Standard SDI) from which the user can choose, or on a group profile which bridges the interests of a group of people.

1.2.4 Bibliographies

Bibliographies are lists of books and other materials, restricted by some other feature than their physical presence in a library. Such a list can be limited by geography, for example the *British National Bibliography* covers all books with a British imprint, or by language, with for example, the *Cumulative Book Index* covering books in the English language, or by subject, such as is evident in the *London Bibliography of the Social Sciences*. Lastly the bibliography may concentrate on a specific physical form, as the *British National Film Catalogue* seeks to cover films. In the sense that both bibliographies and catalogues are lists of bibliographic records, all of the arrangements that have been discussed for catalogues may be equally applicable in a bibliography, and in general, there is no reason why the same principles that are used in catalogue compilation should not be used in compiling a bibliography. To go further, the catalogues of major libraries, or the union catalogues of a large co-operative can be important bibliographical tools in their own right. Thus the British Museum's *General Catalogue of Printed Books* is both a catalogue and a bibliographical tool, and the *National Union Catalog* (US) is a major catalogue which has an important role beyond that of a catalogue.

1.2.5 Computer data bases

The records in computer data bases are structured in order to suit the information that is being stored for various applications. Bibliographic data bases provide references to documents, in a similar way to printed abstracting or indexing journals or catalogues. Typical records are shown in Figure 6.3 on p.90. This shows a record in an abstracts based bibliographic data base. One type of bibliographic data base is the catalogue record data base. These data bases store catalogue records which libraries can copy and add to their own catalogue data base.

A computer data base is structured within the computer, but this structure is not particularly important to the user. Records can be retrieved by character strings (that is, sequences of letters and numerals). What is retrieved and how it may be retrieved are more important to the user. Obviously, what can be retrieved depends upon what is in the data base in the first place, and the way in which the information has been structured. Typically some parts of records can be searched and their elements used as search keys. Retrieval facilities will vary between systems, but it is usual to be able to search bibliographic data bases by authors' names, subject words in the title, classification numbers, assigned subject terms, and combinations of these. Retrieval from a computer data base offers more options than retrieval from a printed index. The search keys, and the combinations of search keys that are possible are more numerous in a computer data base. Also, several options normally exist with respect to the proportion of the record which is displayed or printed on any particular occasion.

It is worth briefly observing a general approach to the creation of a data base. In general, if we wish to add the details concerning the document, as shown in Figure 1.6(a) to a data base, we follow steps, some by the human indexer, and others by the computer:

1. Analysis of the document, and decisions concerning the elements that are to be used to represent the document.
2. Fill these elements onto a paper form or on to some type of form via an online terminal. This form will be set up to reflect the fields in a record of the type to be entered in this particular data base (see Chapters 19 and 20 for more details).

Figure 1.6(a) Fields in a simple bibliographic record

Title: Local current awareness services in industrial libraries
Author: Rowley, J E
Source: Aslib Proceedings 31 (10) October 1979, 476-484.
Index terms: Current awareness services, SDI, Special libraries.
Abstract: Considers the results of a survey of the current
                 awareness services offered by industrial libraries to ....
Language   English

Figure 1.6 (b) Sample entries from an online dictionary

Term	Postings	Addresses
Currency (TI)	4	456, 718, 986, 1312
Current (TI)	1	876
Current awareness (TI)	3	173, 999, 1534
Current awareness services (IT)	32	345, 346, 588, 999, 1345 ...
Curriculum (IT)	2	45, 867.

3. The record can then be checked, and converted into machine-readable form, if the original record is on paper, a reference number allocated, and input into the computer.

4. Once the records are available in machine-readable form, the computer can automatically identify all the searchable elements of the record. The extent of searchable elements will vary from one data base to another. In the example in Figure 1.6 the searchable elements might be:

from title (TI)   local, current awareness, services, industrial
                                  libraries.
from the author (AU)   Rowley, JE
from the source (SO)   Aslib Proceedings, 1979
from the index terms
   (IT)   current awareness services, SDI, special
                                  libraries
from the abstract (AB)   results, survey, current awareness, services,
                                  industrial libraries . . .
from the language (LA)   English

5. Once identified, all of these searchable elements are merged into an existing file or dictionary of searchable elements. An entry in this dictionary consists of the term to be searched, the number of records containing the term (known as the number of postings), and the reference number of those records. Some sample entries are shown in Figure 1.6(b). This file is sometimes referred to as the inverted file.

6. Full records will be contained in another file, and the reference number used to link entries between the two files. Thus the record for a given document can be retrieved, by the user specifying the search element, the computer identifying the reference number of a record containing that search element, and using this to identify the record itself. Once this is done, the full record can, if desired, be displayed or printed.

Whilst the nature and application of data bases is considered in various other places in this work it is perhaps important to establish that the data base can be the source of many other printed products, since it is possible to rearrange data which are input into a computer data base into a variety of different formats and selections to meet different requirements. Figure 1.7 provides a brief résumé of some of the products that may be generated from a computer data base.

1.3 Data bases versus printed indexes and catalogues

Having established that in one sense the data base can be used as a basis for the generation of a variety of tools for the organisation of knowledge it may appear rather strange that this chapter has not started with the data base, and moved on to its products. Rather the earlier definitions relate to catalogues, bibliographies and printed indexes. This order is partly historical, reflecting the development of the tools of the organisation of knowledge, and is partly borne of a belief that these earlier definitions remain central in defining the end product, and as such are preliminary to an understanding of data base design. A data base must be designed in order to support the end products that are to be derived from it, and thus these

Figure 1.7 Some data base products

Selective Dissemination of Information (SDI)
Group SDI
Standard SDI
Online SDI
Printed abstracting and indexing journals and their indexes
Batch retrospective searching (for example, Bibliographies)
Online retrospective searching
Magnetic tape services (that is, those which buy or lease tapes)
Review services
Thesauri
Classification schemes
Lists of journals covered
Reports (of tests, evaluations and practice)
Computer software

products must be described and understood before the data bases from which they can be derived can be considered.

There is an uneasy truce between data bases and printed indexes. Online access to catalogues and other data bases is becoming increasingly widely available, and a user or librarian frequently has the choice between a printed product and its online equivalent. It is difficult to generalise as to the relative merits of the two types of tool, and this discussion is returned to in more specific terms elsewhere in this work. However, Figure 1.8 is a reasonably simple attempt to draw some broad comparisons.

The advances in online access to all types of computer data base in the future lead to a completely different approach to cataloguing and indexing. This hypothesis is considered further later in this text.

1.4 Functions of document and information organisation tools

The description of the tools for the organisation of knowledge in the earlier sections of this chapter goes some way towards identifying the purpose of these tools.

As early as 1876, Charles Ammi Cutter defined the purpose of a catalogue, and in so doing outlined the purpose of any tool for the organisation of knowledge, if his functions are broadly interpreted. Cutter defined the functions of a catalogue thus:

(i) To enable a person to find a document of which
   (a) the author, or
   (b) the title, or   is known.
   (c) the subject
(ii) To show what the library has
   (d) by a given author
   (e) on a given subject (and related subjects)
   (f) in a given kind (or form) of literature.
(iii) To assist in the choice of a document
   (g) as to its edition (bibliographically)
   (h) as to its character (literary or topical).

Not all catalogues or other tools for the organisation of knowledge aim to fulfil all these functions, but this list shows the range of functions.

The first function concentrates on the identification and location of documents from a variety of pieces of information that a user might bring to the catalogue or index. In a printed catalogue or index a user is constrained to look under the headings in the catalogue. Whatever information the user brings to the retrieval device it is important that he should be able to identify documents by being supplied with details of the documents which match the information being brought to the catalogue. Having been alerted to the

Figure 1.8 Printed indexes v. online indexes

Printed Indexes

1. Basically pre-coordinate, and headings and terms for searching are set prior to searching.

2. More restricted search strategies.

3. Modifications in search pattern lead to laborious searching under alternative terms.

4. May be in the same physical form as the documents that they index.

5. Mostly uses controlled-language indexing.

6. Output from index must be determined in advance, and necessitates considerable clerical manipulation.

7. Additional access points are shown by see and see also references.

8. Portable if not too bulky.

9. Coverage may be broad or narrow, local or national.

10. Cost is per copy, regardless of number of consultations.

11. Tedious to search many sources if there are only one or two items that are relevant, and neither data nor author is known.

12.

Online Indexes

May be pre- or post-coordinate, with terms and links between them established either before or during searching, or a combination.

Choice available in search strategy.

Search strategy is flexible; it is easy to modify a search.

Until documents are also stored extensively in machine-readable form, the index will be a different physical form from the documents that are indexed.

Free or controlled-language indexing, or both, are possible.

Great flexibility of output from data base, e.g. bibliographies, selective lists.

Additional access points are suggested by thesaurus-type displays and other aids.

Needs online terminals which must be relatively fixed.

Current coverage includes many large data bases, also an increasing number of smaller ones.

Cost is related to number of consultations and time spent searching.

Becoming increasingly easy to search a number of data bases.

Printed indexes are one product of computerized data bases. ●

From: **The Indexer**, Vol. 13 April 1983 p. 189

existence of a document, the user needs information concerning the actual location of the document, in order that the document may be read. In a library catalogue, the classification number, which indicates the position of a document on the library shelves, makes it possible to find the document. In a bibliographic data base there may be no direct information as to the whereabouts of the document, or the user may be referred to a document delivery service or a major library.

The second function of the catalogue is concerned with the housekeeping activity of keeping a record of the library stock. A catalogue must show the extent of a collection, and make it possible to assess the quality of a collection in respect to its authors, subjects and forms.

The third function is achieved primarily by the description in an index, catalogue or data base. By giving details such as the title, edition, publisher and pagination, the description facilitates the choice of the document, both by distinguishing the document from others and by indicating the nature (for example, subject, quality) of the document.

1.5 Catalogues, indexes, data bases and document arrangement

The tools of the organisation of knowledge have not been exhaustively listed until document arrangement has been considered. All of the devices considered so far arrange and provide access to surrogates or representations of documents. As identified in the previous section, an important component of the retrieval process is the location of the document. Document arrangement aids the direct retrieval of the documents themselves. In some collections and libraries documents have been arranged in a serial number order or some other simple order. However, normally documents will be arranged in some systematic order which facilitates the examination of a collection, either with or without the intercession of an index or catalogue. The significance of document arrangement means that it warrants a separate chapter, Chapter 22.

Nevertheless, although important, document arrangement has two fundamental limitations:

1. Documents (in any printed form) can be arranged in only one order (perhaps by author, title or subject). For example, if a set of documents has been arranged according to subjects then the reader who wishes to identify all the books by a given author will need to sift the entire collection.
2. Each document can be put in only one place, in any given sequence. For example, a document with several authors or many subjects cannot be arranged in accordance with more than one author's name or subject label, unless there are multiple copies of the work in the collection.

Catalogues, indexes and data bases overcome these two limitations.

Chapter 1 Readings

A. Catalogues

1 Bryant, P., 'The catalogue', *Journal of documentation*, 36(2), 1980, 133–63
2 Grose, M.W. and Line, M.B., 'On the construction and care of white elephants', *Library Association Record*, 70(1), 1968, 2–5
3 Line, M.B., 'White elephants revisited', *Catalogue and Index* (13), 1969, 4–6
4 Malinconico, S.M. and Fasana, P.J., *The future of the catalog: the library's choices*, Knowledge Industry Publications: White Plains, N.Y., 1979.
5 Maltby, A., *UK Catalogue use survey*, Library Association: London, 1973.
6 Rowley, J.E., 'Cataloguing: here today, gone tomorrow?', *Catalogue and Index* (67), 1982, 7–8.

B. Other tools

7 Housman, E.M., 'Selective dissemination of information', *Annual review of information science and technology*, 8, 1973, 221–41
8 Kemp, A., *Current awareness services*, Bingley: London, 1979. (Outlines of modern librarianship)
9 Leggate, P., 'Computer-based current awareness services', *Journal of documentation*, 31(2), 1975, 93–115
10 Mauerhoff, G.R., 'Selective dissemination of information', *Advances in librarianship*, 4, 1974, 25–62
11 Rowley, J.E. 'Locally produced current awareness services', *Aslib Proceedings*, 31(6), 1979, 284–295
12 Rowley, J.E., 'Printed versus online indexes', *The Indexer*, 13(3), 1983, 188–9
13 Whitehall, T., *Personal current awareness services: a handbook of techniques for manual SDI*. British Library: London, 1980. (BL R & D Report 5502)

2 Records in printed indexes and catalogues

Chapter 1 reviewed the types of index, catalogue and data base. It is evident that in a printed index there may be different types of records or entries. Entries may vary in their headings, but also in the nature and quantity of the description. This chapter reviews the different types of entries to be found in indexes and catalogues.

2.1 Entries

In catalogues there are two possible approaches to the provision of multiple entries for one work. One of these is the use of main and added entries. The main entry is the complete catalogue record of the document. The main entry for a work may be made under a classification number, an author's name or under a title. In the dictionary catalogue, the main entry will be an author entry (see Figure 2.2). In the classified catalogue the main entry will be one of those in the classified sequence (see Figure 2.1).

In a catalogue using main and added entries, all other entries beside the one main entry are added entries. Added entries provide a range of access points. Figure 2.1, which shows an extract from the *British National Bibliography*, shows added entries. Added entries may have subject labels, authors' names or titles as headings.

In an author index, for example, added entries may be expected under:

1. Personal names of: collaborating authors, writers, editors and compilers, translators, illustrators, and other persons implicated in the creation of a work.
2. Corporate body names, where such a body is prominently named in a work.

In other sequences added entries may be made under titles, if the title has not been used as the heading in a main entry. Added entries under series titles are to be expected. Additional subject headings or classification numbers may also be used as headings on added entries.

The second approach to the provision of multiple entries is the unit entry approach. The unit entry approach uses the same unit or entry

Figure 2.1 British National Bibliography extracts

701'.1'8— Visual arts. Criticism

Stephenson, Lionel. The arts observed : a study of recent trends in art criticism / by Lionel Stephenson.— London : Stonehart, c1980.— (59)p : 26cm
£1.25 (corrected : pbk)   B83-12862

701'.1'80943— Arts. Historiography

Podro, Michael. The critical historians of art.— London : Yale University Press, Nov. 1982.— (244)p
ISBN 0-300-02862-8 : £15.00 : CIP entry
                                          B83-02222

702— VISUAL ARTS. MISCELLANY

702'.3'41—Great Britain. Visual arts—Career guides

Ball, Linda, 1950-. Careers in art and design.— 2nd ed.—London : Kogan Page, May 1983. — (100)p
Previous ed: 1981
ISBN 0-85038-686-1 (cased) : £6.95 : CIP entry
ISBN 0-85038-687-x (pbk) : £2.50   B83-09388

Green, Peter, 1933-. Working in art and design. — London: Batsford, Apr. 1983.— (128)p
ISBN 0-7134-2539-3 : £5.95 : CIP entry
                                          B83-07111

702'.5'41— Great Britain. Visual arts— Directories

Waddell, Heather. The artist's directory/ Heather Waddell and Richard Layzell.— London : Art Guide Publications, 1982.— 156p : ill : 21cm
ISBN 0-9507160-5-7 (pbk) : £5.95 : CIP rev.
                                          B82-09314

Continued

Figure 2.1 Continued

704— VISUAL ARTS. SPECIAL ASPECTS

704'.03924'074— Jewish visual arts, 1900–1978—
Catalogues
Jewish art : paintings and sculpture by 20th century
Jewish artists of the French and British schools.—
(Glasgow) (Kelvingrove, Glasgow G3): Glasgow
Museums and Art Galleries, c1979.—24p : ill (some
col.), ports : 21 × 22cm Published to accompany
an exhibition at the Art Gallery and Museum,
Glasgow, 1979.—
Text on inside cover
Unpriced (pbk)   B83-00289

704.9'423— English visual arts, 1833–1881. Special
subjects: Prose in English. Carlyle, Thomas—
Catalogues
Ormond, Richard. Thomas Carlyle 1795–1881/
Richard Ormond and John Cooper.— London :
National Portrait Gallery, c1981.— 27p : ill, ports :
21cm
Published to accompany an exhibition held at the
National Portrait Gallery, 1981–Jan. 1982
ISBN 0-904017-44-3 (unbound) : Unpriced
                                               B83-04090

704.9'482— Orthodox Eastern Church. Decorative arts,
ca 1000–ca 1100. Semiotic aspects
Walter, Christopher, 1925–. Art and ritual of the
Byzantine Church/ Christopher Walter : preface by
Robin Cormack.— London : Variorum, 1982.—
xxiv, 279, xxxiip of plates: ill : 24cm.— (Birmingham
Byzantine series ; 1)
Bibliography: p251–258.—Includes index.
ISBN 0-86078-104-6 : £28.00 : CIP rev.
                                               B82-21398

Continued

Figure 2.1 Continued

707— VISUAL ARTS. STUDY AND TEACHING

707—Art studies, to 1982

Bellony-Rewald, Alice. Imagination's chamber: artists
and their studies.— London :
Fraser, Apr. 1983.— (240)p
ISBN 0-86092-070-4 : £15.50 : CIP entry

B83-07664

**707'.1041—Great Britain. Schools. Curriculum subjects:
Ethnic visual arts—Conference proceedings**

Arts education in a multi-cultural society.— London
(10-12 Allington St, SW1E 5ER) : Commission for
Racial Equality, 1981.— 23p ill, port ; 42cm
Conference papers.— Includes bibliographies
£1.00 (unbound)   B83-11419

708—VISUAL ARTS. GALLERIES. MUSEUMS, PRIVATE COLLECTIONS

**708.2'254—East Sussex. Hove. Museums: Museums of
Art (Hove)—Visitors' guides.**

Museum of Art (Hove). Hove Museums and Art
Gallery : a brief guide to the collections.— Hove
((Town Hall, Hove BN3 4AH)) : Hove Borough
Council, (1982?)).— 16p : ill; 21 cm
Unpriced (pbk)   B83-06346

Subject Index

Continued

Figure 2.1 Continued

Newport-on-Tay. Fife Region. Scotland
Social life, 1900–1966— Personal observations
941.2'92

News media 302.2'34
Reporting of terrorism 070.4'4932242

News reporting services. Television services. Great
Britain Independent Television News. Editing, 1956–
1968—
Personal observations 070.1'9'0924

News reporting services. Welfare services for blind
people.
Bromley (London Borough)
Bromley and District Talking Newspaper Association, to 1980 070.4'8

Newspaper publishing industries. Great Britain & United
States
Owners, 1830–1980— Biographies 338.7'6107'0922

Newspaper publishing industries. Sheffield. South
Yorkshire (Metropolitan County)
Sheffield Newspapers. Fair trading practice— Inquiry
reports 338.8'261072821

Newspapers. Bentilee. Stoke-on-Trent. Staffordshire
Community newspapers: UBB. Involvement of Young
Volunteer Force Foundation 361.7'63

Newspapers. Great Britain
Reporting of economic conditions, 1960–1981
070.4'49330941

Newspapers. Scotland
Reporting of crime 070.4'493649411

Author/Title Index

Malet Lambert local history originals : v.10
Local jottings, persons and events in the Borough of
Kingston upon Hull in the 18th and 19th centuries/
by John Richardson.— Malet Lambert High School
(pbk) Unpriced
942.8'37'07 B83-07321

Continued

Figure 2.1 Continued

Malevich, Kazluir

Malevich/(compiled by) Larissa A. Zhadova: (translated from the Russian by Alexander Lieven).— Thames and Hudson. £20.00
709'.2'4   B83-11721   ISBN 0-500-09147-1

Malevich: suprematism and revolution in Russian art, 1910-1930/(compiled by) Larissa A. Zhadova : (translated from the Russian by Alexander Lieven).— Thames and Hudson. £20.00
709'.2'4   B83-11721   ISBN 0-500-09147-1

Maley, Alan

Drama techniques in language learning.—2nd ed.— Cambridge University Press (cased). £9.95: CIP entry
418'.007   B83-02254   ISBN 0-521-24907-4

Malgadi days/ R.K. Narayan.—Heinemann. £7.50
823(F)   B83-05336   ISBN 0-434-45028-6

Malherbe, Madelaine

Accreditation in social work.—Central Council for Education and Training in Social Work (spiral). £1.25
361.3'023'41   B83-00863

Malignant skin tumours/edited by Anthony J. J. Emmett, Michael G.E. O'Rourke.— Churchill Livingstone. Unpriced : CIP rev.
616.99'477   B82-09717   ISBN 0-443-02263-2

Figure 2.2 Cumulative Book Index - an extract

James, Epistle of See Bible. N.T. James
James, Jude, 2 Peter. Sidebottom, E.M. pa 1982 Eerdmans; Marshall, Morgan & Scott Publs.
Janáček, Leoš, 1854-1928
  Kátá Kabanová
  —Leoš Janáček, Kátá Kabanová. 1982 Cambridge Univ. Press (Cambridge).

Continued

Figure 2.2 Continued

Janeway, Elizabeth
 Cross sections from a decade of change. Q 320p 1982 Morrow
  ISBN 0-688-01024-5   LC 82-3485
Jannott, Paul F.
 Teller world. 2nd ed Q 125p il pa $19.95 1983 Bankers
  ISBN 0-87267-040-6   LC 82-18497
Janowitz, Morris
 (ed) See The Political education of soldiers
Japan
                    Bibliography
An Introductory bibliography for Japanese studies. v4 ptl 1982
 University of Tokyo Press
     Distr. in USA by Columbia Univ. Press $12.50
                  Foreign relations
                    United States
 Lee, C.J. U.S. policy toward Japan and Korea. $19.95; pa $7.95
 1982 Praeger Pubs.
                      History
           Tokugawa period, 1600-1868
Hall, J.W. Tanuma Okitsugu, 1719-1788. lib bdg 1982 Greenwood
 Press
                     1912-1945
Dollinger, H. The decline and fall of Nazi Germany and imperial
 Japan. 1982 Bonanza Bks; for sale by Crown
                 Juvenile literature
Davidson, J. Japan. lib bdg $9.95 Dillon Press
               Politics and government
                       1945-
Burks, A.W. The government of Japan. 2nd ed 1982 Greenwood Press
Japanese cloisonné. Coben, L.A. 1982 Weatherhill (NY)
Jasieński, Bruno, 1901-1939
 Kolesnikoff, N. Bruno Jasieński. 1982 Wilfrid Laurier Univ. Press
   Distri. in USA by Humanities Press. $17
Jaws
                    Radiography
Poyton, H.G. Oral radiology. $35 1982 Williams & Wilkins
                 Wounds and injuries
Symposium on dentofacial trauma. 1982 Saunders (Philadelphia)
Jay, Michael
 Spacecraft. (Easy-read fact book) 32p col il 1983 Watts (NY)
  ISBN 0-86313-012-7 (UK); 0-531-04512-9 (US)
  LC 82-51005

wherever a given work is listed. The same entry appears in all sequences, with only different headings superimposed in order to distinguish one entry from another. Thus, in a unit entry catalogue all entries contain the same quantity of detail. The unit entry approach was popular in card and sheaf catalogues and indexes, because the physical reproduction of entries to be inserted in different sequences was simpler if the same basic record could be inserted in the various sequences. With the fading significance of these physical forms some of the rationale for unit entries has disappeared. Others might argue that the unit entry approach is similar to access to a record in a computer data base. Here the same record may be accessed with a number of search keys. Proponents of this point of view believe that in time it will no longer be necessary to distinguish between main and added entries.

Currently it is still necessary to distinguish between main and added entries. This is in part due to the different stages of development reached by different libraries. Yet, even with further advances the distinction between main and added entries remains important because:

1. One entry systems will continue in some form; here it is important to identify which of the many entries that could usefully be made, should, in fact, be made.
2. The main entry contributes to the document arrangement sequence. For example in a classified catalogue the classification notation which is used for the main entry determines the position of the document on the shelves.
3. Printed catalogues and indexes are likely to continue to need to distinguish between main and added entries in the interests of economy (that is, so that some sequences when printed can be shortened by the use of added entries).
4. The use of references rests on the designation of a main entry.

2.2 References

A reference is not generally as helpful to the user of a catalogue or index as an entry might be. This is because a reference provides little direct information about a document, but rather refers the user to another location or entry where this information can be found. Nevertheless, references are common in indexes and catalogues. References represent economy of cataloguing effort when compared with an added entry.

There are two types of reference: 'see' and 'see also' references. These references operate in a similar fashion whether they are used to link authors' names or subject headings.

A 'see' reference directs the user from a name, title or subject or other term which has not been used as a heading in an entry to an alternative term which does serve as a heading or descriptor. 'See' references may link two subject terms with similar meanings, for example, Currency see Money; or variant author names, for example, Council for the Education and Training of Health Visitors see Great Britain. Council for the Education and Training of Health Visitors; or different titles, for example, Cookery course see *Delia Smith's Cookery Course*.

A 'see also' reference connects headings or index terms which are in some way related, where both of the headings are regarded as acceptable for use as headings for entries. For example, the following 'see also' reference:

Monasteries see also Abbeys

links two headings under which entries may be found. The searcher is recommended to examine entries under both index terms if it is likely that documents might prove to be relevant. A 'see also' reference may be used between different headings for the same person, when some of that person's works have been entered under each of the headings linked by 'see also' references. 'See also' references can be used between the names of related, but independently entered corporate bodies, and also to connect the titles of related works.

Explanatory references may be either 'see' or 'see also' references, which give a little more explanation than merely the direction to look elsewhere. An example might be:

Devon, Sarah
    For works of this author published under other names see
    Murray, Jill   Treves, Kathleen.

Some libraries make more extensive use of references, in preference to added entries, than others. A reference is always shorter than an added entry, but in some circumstances the economies which accrue from the use of a reference instead of an added entry mean that it is normal practice to employ a reference. In these instances a reference is not only shorter than an added entry, but removes the need to make multiple added entries. For example, added entries could be made under both I.L.E.A. and the Inner London Education Authority. If this practice is adopted then two new entries will be necessary for every new document to be entered under the name of this corporate body. A reference:

I.L.E.A. see Inner London Education Authority

once inserted in an index or catalogue will suffice for any subsequent documents to be entered under the name of this corporate body; only one added entry with respect to this name need be made for each new document added to the index. Although author names have been used to illustrate this point, it is important to recognise that the same arguments are equally applicable to references under subject terms.

3   Description of documents: principles and monographs

The description of a document as part of a catalogue entry acts as a document surrogate. A description represents the document in various catalogues, indexes and data bases. Headings serve to determine where the record will be filed, or how it may be retrieved, but the description is necessary to make it possible to locate and retrieve the document.

Document descriptions may be drafted for a wide variety of different kinds of library material, but some common principles can be established. This chapter identifies some central principles and practices appertaining to description, and goes on to exemplify these principles and practices with reference to descriptive cataloguing practices for monographs.

Documents need to be described wherever they need to be represented by a surrogate for the purposes of the organisation or retrieval of information or documents. Descriptions may be included in catalogues, bibliographies and other listings of documents. The different applications may place different demands upon the description to be included and, therefore, the practices pertaining to the description of documents may vary.

3.1 Purpose of the description

Note: Throughout this chapter the term 'document' is used to refer to any item which might be found in a library or information centre or data base, including books, periodicals, magnetic tapes, video cassettes, microforms and so on.

The description may have three possible purposes:

1. to *identify* or individualise the document being catalogued or indexed, or to give sufficient information for the reader to be able uniquely to identify the edition of the work being catalogued.

2. to *characterise* the document, or to give information whose purpose is to assist in the choice of a document, by indicating aspects of its character such as its subject, authorship, style, physical format, level and date.

3. to *place an entry* in its most useful position under a chosen heading, or to act as a subsidiary component in determining filing order.

All the elements in any bibliographic description are intended to contribute to one or more of these purposes. Any framework for description must determine:

1. What information should be given in the description, and the extent of the detail to be given in the description.
2. In what order the information should be given, and preferably,
3. the punctuation which is to be used to divide and distinguish between the elements of the description.

3.2 Standards and bibliographic description

There are a number of standards for bibliographic description. Some of these standards are more widely applied than others, and in some types of application a greater degree of standardisation can be expected than in others. The area in which standards for bibliographic description have had the most impact is in catalogues and catalogue record data bases. Catalogues, then, are easy to examine as a group because there is a good deal of standardisation with respect to the document records that they contain. We will therefore consider the standards used in catalogues at some length.

Exchange of machine-readable records in an attempt to economise on and streamline the cataloguing process has made the use of standard records highly desirable. The programme of International Standard Bibliographic Descriptions (ISBDs) which was developed during the 1970s has been an important component of successful standardisation. The International Standard Bibliographic Description for Monographs (ISBD(M)) was adopted by the International Federation of Library Associations (IFLA) committee on Cataloguing in 1971, and was followed by International Standard Bibliographic Descriptions for other categories of materials, amongst which are numbered: the ISBD(S) for serials, the ISBD(PM) for printed music, the ISBD(CM) for cartographic materials and the ISBD(NBM) for non-book materials. Since these standards were evolved by different committees with the proliferation of standards to cover different types of materials it was becoming increasingly difficult to ensure that no inconsistencies arose between the standards. Hence in 1976 the general framework ISBD(G) was agreed. The International Standard Bibliographic Descriptions offer a framework for bibliographic description and satisfy the three points at the end of section 3.1. Although they identify the components of the description, their preferred order and the necessary punctuation, they offer no assistance on how each of the components that are to be included are to be chosen or presented. To provide this type of guidance is the function of a cataloguing code. However, in order that a cataloguing code be helpful in this respect it is plain that its recommendations must not conflict with the framework for bibliographic description specified by the ISBDs. The Anglo-American Cataloguing Rules (AACR2) (see Chapters 8 and 9 for fuller details) do indeed follow the recommendations of the ISBD programme, and one reason for the first edition being supplanted by a second edition was the adjustments necessary in order to make AACR consistent with the ISBDs. AACR then also shows the components to be included in a bibliographic description, their order and punctuation. In addition, AACR provides guidelines on how to handle more intractable situations, and will help in, for instance, deciding which of six authors' names to record in a description, or which date to give when there are a variety of copyright and reprint dates but no imprint date.

Bibliographic descriptions in lists and data bases other than library catalogues such as, for instance, in printed abstracting and indexing journals, or the data bases which are related to them, are less likely to be entirely consistent with any one standard, although users might view standardisation as desirable. Most data base producers have in-house guidelines for bibliographic description, and aim to achieve consistency of citation within their products. There is a good deal of common ground between the bibliographic descriptions used in these various lists, but practices vary in specific details, such as the extent of the detail given, and the order in which elements are to be cited.

However, although data base producers choose to adhere to in-house practices, there are international standards which can be applied, and indeed do influence practice. First, the ISBDs and cataloguing codes such as AACR2 can be applied to some documents, such as monographs, conference proceedings, reports and other complete works. These guides do however lack a satisfactory solution for the description of parts of documents. In particular, a data base may be concerned to list separately individual periodical articles and single papers in conference proceedings. (More discussion is to be found on this topic in Chapter 4.) Another important standard in this area is ISO 690–1975 Bibliographical references – Essential and Supplementary Elements. This offers general suggestions on bibliographic citation, which may be applied to books, periodicals and other materials, and parts of these documents. This standard is not always consistent with recommendations given in AACR2. ISO 690-1975 will be considered more fully in Chapter 4 since in practice its most valuable guidance is in respect of periodical articles.

3.3 Principles of description

In preparing the description of a document it is necessary to make certain preliminary decisions if the same record is to be derived from one document by different cataloguers, even if it is agreed that the description should perform a recognised function. These general considerations include:

1. *The source of the information* for the description. In order that all cataloguers use the same basis for the information for the description it is necessary to designate a chief source of information. Normally this will be a segment of the document itself. Preference is normally given to information within the document itself in order to facilitate matching the record and its document on subsequent occasions. When the information available in the document is not sufficiently complete to form a helpful record, it may be necessary to supplement information from within the document with information from other sources. For books the chief source of information for some elements of the description is the title page. Thus, for instance, a title statement will be extracted from a title page, and not from the cover or the spine. Plainly some elements of the description cannot be found on the title page, and must be taken from wherever in the document they can be identified. Pagination, for instance, can only be discovered by examining the work. Figure 3.1 gives the chief sources of information according to AACR2.

2. *Organisation of the description* Having decided upon the essential elements for a catalogue record, as discussed in 3.4, it is important to adopt a consistent order for citing them. This order is demonstrated by Figure 3.2.

3. *Punctuation* must be established and be adopted consistently. Punctuation is essential to partition the components of the description. An international standard which makes recommendations for punctuation, such as the ISBDs, is important in international exchange of records.

4. *Levels of detail in the description* Different applications demand different quantities of detail in the description. In a small general library simple records are adequate, whereas a large special collection will require that works with similar titles, and different editions of the same work be distinguished from one another. AACR2 identifies three distinct levels of quantity of detail. If libraries and other cataloguing or indexing agencies adopt one of these levels of detail the interchange of bibliographic records may be facilitated. It is important to recognise that although these three levels cater for the majority of applications, some libraries will opt for rather less detail than specified even in level 1 (maybe just title, publisher and date), and others may opt for full descriptive cataloguing which extends beyond that specified in level 3. Figure 3.3 shows the components to be included in the three levels of description. The main components are discussed more fully in the next section. Figure 3.4 shows how these levels may be applied to one example.

Figure 3.1 Chief sources of information according to AACR2

Type of Material	Source
Books, pamphlets, and printed sheets	Title page
Cartographic materials	a. Cartographic item itself b. Container or case, the cradle and stand of a globe, etc.
Manuscripts	Title page Colophon
Music	Title page
Sound recordings	
Disc	Label
Tape (open reel-to-reel)	Reel and label
Tape cassette	Cassette and label
Tape cartridge	Cartridge and label
Roll	Label
Sound recording on film	Container and label
Motion pictures and videorecordings	Film itself and its container (if integral part of item)
Graphic materials	Item itself including any labels and the container
Machine-readable data files	Internal user label
Three-dimensional artefacts and realia	Object itself with any accompanying textual material and container
Microforms	Title frame
Serials (printed)	Title page

From: Chan, L M Cataloguing and Classification: An Introduction, McGraw-Hill, 1981.

Figure 3.2 The ISBD(G)

Area	Prescribed Preceding (or Enclosing) Punctuation for Elements		Element

Note: Each area, other than the first, is preceded by a point, space, dash, space (.—).

1. Title and statement of responsibility area		1.1	Title proper
	( )	1.2	General material designation
	=	1.3	Parallel title
	:	1.4	Other title information
		1.5	Statements of responsibility
	/		First statement
	;		Subsequent statement
2. Edition area		2.1	Edition statement
	=	2.2	Parallel edition statement
		2.3	Statements of responsibility relating to the edition
	/		First Statement
	;		Subsequent statement
	,	2.4	Additional edition statement
		2.5	Statements of responsibility following an additional edition statement
	/		First statement
	;		Subsequent statement
3. Material (or type of publication) specific details area			

Area	Prescribed Preceding (or Enclosing) Punctuation for Elements		Element
4. Publication, distribution, etc., area		4.1	Place of distribution, distribution, etc.
			First place
	;		Subsequent place
	:	4.2	Name of publisher, distributor, etc.
	( )	4.3	Statement of function of publisher, distributor, etc.
	,	4.4	Date of publication, distribution, etc.
	(	4.5	Place of manufacture
	:	4.6	Name of manufacturer
	,)	4.7	Date of manufacture
5. Physical description area		5.1	Specific material designation and extent of item
	:	5.2	Other physical details
	;	5.3	Dimensions of item
	+	5.4	Accompanying material statement
6. Series area		6.1	Title proper of series
	=	6.2	Parallel title of series
Note: A series statement is enclosed by parentheses. When there are two or more series statements, each is enclosed by parentheses.	:	6.3	Other title information of series
		6.4	Statements of responsibility relating to the series
	/		First statement
	;		Subsequent statement

Continued

Figure 3.2 Continued

Area	Prescribed Preceding (or Enclosing) Punctuation for Elements		Element
	,	6.5	International Standard Serial Number of series
	;	6.6	Numbering within series
	.	6.7	Enumeration and/or title of subseries
	=	6.8	Parallel title of subseries
	:	6.9	Other title information of subseries
		6.10	Statements of responsibility relating to the subseries
	/		First statement
	;		Subsequent statement
		6.11	International Standard Serial Number of subseries
	;	6.12	Numbering within subseries
7. Note area			
8. Standard number (or alternative) and terms of availability area		8.1	Standard number (or alternative)
	=	8.2	Key title
	:	8.3	Terms of availability and/or price
	( )	8.4	Qualification (in varying positions)

Source: International Federation of Library Associations. Working Group on the General International Bibliographic Description. **ISBD(G): General International Standard Bibliographic Description: Annotated Text.** London: IFLA International Office for UBC, 1977.-

Figure 3.3 The three levels of description as in AACR2

1.0D1. First level of description. For the first level of description, include at least the elements set out in this schematic illustration:

> Title proper/first statement of responsibility, if different from main entry heading in form or number or if there is no main entry heading.—Edition statement.—Material (or type of publication) specific details.—First publisher, etc., date of publication, etc.—Extent of item.—Note(s).—Standard number.

> See 1.1B, 1.1F, 1.2B, 1.3, 1.4D, 1.4F, 1.5B, 1.7, 1.8B.

1.0D2. Second level of description. For the second level of description, include at least the elements set out in this schematic illustration:

> Title proper (general material designation)=parallel title: other title information/first statement of responsibility; each subsequent statement of responsibility.—Edition statement/first statement of responsibility relating to the edition.—Material (or type of publication) specific details.—First place of publication, etc.: first publisher, etc., date of publication, etc.—Extent of item: other physical details; dimensions.—(Title proper of series/statement of responsibility relating to series, ISSN of series; numbering within the series. Title of subseries, ISSN of subseries; numbering within subseries).—Note(s).—Standard number.

1.0D3. Third level of description. For the third level of description, include all elements set out in the following rules that are applicable to the item being described.

3.4 Components of the description

The ISBD(G) identifies eight main areas within a bibliographic description. This section explores the reasons for the inclusion of each of these areas and discusses some of the common problems that pertain to each area.

Title and statement of responsibility area

The title of a work is well established as the first component of the description. This is because the title of a work is the primary individualising element for a given document, and distinguishes one work from another by the same author. The purpose of the title, in bibliographic description, is then:

Figure 3.4 An example of the application of different levels of description

First level of description

Oil statistics/ (Organisation for Economic Co-operation and Development).-O.E.C.D., 1975.-295p.-ISBN 92-64-01565-5

Second level of description

Oil statistics=Statistiques petrolières: supply and disposal=approvisionnement et consommation /(Organisation for Economic Co-operation and Development).-Paris: O.E.C.D., 1975.-295p. :col.- ill; 27cm.-ISBN 92-64-01565-5

Third level of description

Oil statistics=Statistiques petrolières: supply and disposal=approvisionnement et consommation /(Organisation for Economic Co-operation and Development).-Paris: O.E.C.D., (London): (H.M.S.O.) 1975.-1976.-295p.: col. ill; 27cm.- Fold sheet 3p. as insert.-ISBN 92-64-01565-5.

(a) to indicate the nature and content of the document. For example, with non-fiction the title summarises the subjects covered by the document, and may indicate the level or approach to the subject.

(b) to identify the document uniquely. The title, taken together with the author's name is sufficient to identify a work uniquely (although not to distinguish between editions of the same work).

(c) to determine the position of the description amongst other descriptions with the same heading (for example, to distinguish works by the same author, and entered under the same author heading).

Where there are a number of titles associated with different editions or versions of a work, it may be necessary to identify a uniform title for use where the title is used as a heading. This topic is explored more fully in Chapter 11.

With a limited number of exceptions (see AACR2 1.1B) the 'title proper is transcribed exactly as to order, wording and spelling'. This practice ensures that a later match can be achieved between the document and its description.

The statement of authorship is also transcribed as it appears in the work. Obviously, there will be a number of instances where the author statement will add no additional information about authorship than that which can be gleaned from the author heading. AACR2 permits omission of the author statement in such cases. If, however, the author statement can give additional information, such as the relationship between the author and his work (for example, illustrated by, edited by, surveyed by, composed by) or additional names (for example, the names of multiple authors, illustrators, translators) then it is important that it be included. The function of the author statement is to:

(a) indicate the relationship between authors and their work.
(b) further uniquely identify the work.
(c) indicate, particularly with well-known authors, the likely quality or style of a work. This function is particularly significant with fiction.

Edition area

The edition statement is given if stated in the document, in the form that it is given in the document. It is normally taken to indicate that the document has been revised if a work has progressed to a second or subsequent edition. A work which has gone into a number of editions is likely to have proved its worth and may be a standard text. It is useful to note that first editions are rarely specified as such and that edition statements are normally only to be found in second and subsequent editions. For a user it is often important to be able to identify the current edition of a work, especially if the text has been revised significantly between editions.

Editors and compilers of editions of works are recorded together with the edition statement (for example, third edition, second revised edition), in the edition area. Responsibility for the edition must be distinguished from responsibility for the work.

Material (or type of publication) specific details area

This is a special area that has been reserved for items of important information which are necessary for certain categories of material. This section has different contents for different types of material. It is especially useful for serials and maps. For serials the volume and part numbers and the dates of issue are included here. For maps this area is available for recording the scale. For many categories of material nothing will be recorded in this area.

Publication, distribution etc area

The primary components in this area are place of publication, publisher's name and date of publication (that is, the date of the edition). For some categories of materials it can be difficult to distinguish publishers from distributors and/or producers. AACR2 allows for the inclusion of the place of distribution and the distributor's name, if this is required. For example, in various graphic materials, such as slide sets, film strips and motion pictures the roles of publishers and distributors may not be as well defined as in traditional mongraph publishing.

The imprint is given in the language of the document. The place of publication usually indicates the location of the main offices of the publishers, and is intended to help in identifying the publisher. The place of publication may also warn of biases in approach or differences in terminology that arise in the text. For example, a work on law published by a Canadian publisher is likely to emphasise Canadian law and legal practice, and therefore may have little value for a student of United States law. Works from international publishing houses may be more difficult to characterise in this way.

The name of the publisher obviously aids in the identification of the origins of a document, and indicates the agents who have prepared a work for the marketplace. The publisher's name may also be some indication of the quality of a document. Various publishers have reputations for specific styles, subject areas or works for specific audiences. The publisher's name is given in the briefest form in which it can be understood.

The date of the edition is arguably the most important part of the imprint or distribution, publication area. The date may serve to distinguish distinct editions of the same work which are not otherwise labelled. The date of the edition is generally taken to indicate the approximate date of the information contained in the work, and is important in indicating the currency of the document. Currency is more important in subjects where developments are rapid, than in more stable areas. If no edition or imprint date can be ascertained, then an attempt is made to provide a date from amongst any other dates given on the work, such as copyright dates, and reprint dates. In the absence of any date the cataloguer is encouraged to estimate a date, and give this, indicating that this is an estimate.

Physical description area

The physical description is the area of the description that varies most with the particular type of material. Nevertheless, the four fundamental areas can be seen to be similar for all types of material.

The first component of the physical description for all items except one volume monographs is an indication of the specific medium designation which states the nature of the item for example, 1 map, 1 jigsaw puzzle, 4v. The next component indicates the extent of the item, or its size. For monographs this statement gives the number of pages, and, if appropriate, the number of plates. For a slide set the number of slides in the set is the equivalent. The extent of an item is important in selection. Obviously a book on the chemistry of mercury which runs to 200 pages will give less detail than one which runs to 600 pages.

The other physical details to be given will depend upon the features that are important for the type of material under consideration. These points will be discussed further in Chapter 4 on the cataloguing of non-book materials. In the case of monographs these other physical details include the illustration statement. This indicates whether a work is illustrated, whether the illustrations are coloured or black and white, and the type of illustrations to be found in the work, for example maps. Books on some subjects need illustrations. For example, it is expected that an art book will be illustrated and that a geography book will contain some maps. The dimensions of the item may also be important. For a monograph the height of the book is normally given, in centimetres. If the book has an unusual shape then both the height and the width of the book will be given. The height of a book is of minor importance, except in that it indicates the overall size of the text. For other materials size may be more significant, since the size may determine the nature of the equipment to be used in association with the item.

Series area

The series area includes the series title, an indication of the responsibility for the series (often series editors), and the number of the individual work within the series, if the work is one of a numbered series. To the user who recognises a series and has seen other works in the same series, the series statement may provide a useful indication of the style and level of a document. In general, the series statement is a source of information about the authority, approach and intention of the content of a document. In certain special cases, as with report series, government publications and standards the series statement is important in placing the individual document in the context of other works in the series.

Note area

The elements to be included in the previous areas of the description are carefully controlled if the recommendations of AACR2 are followed. The note area is the part of the description where it is permitted to include any additional information which the cataloguer feels may be of value to the user. The items that are recorded in the note area, and the style in which they are recorded, is at the discretion of the cataloguer.

Notes may perform one of the following two functions:

(a) elucidate or develop the existing description, such as information given in notes relating to earlier editions, the nature of illustrations, and performers of musical works, might succeed in doing.

(b) characterise the document more fully by adding information on the subject matter (content or level) and possibly the document's relationship to other documents.

Notes should be made in the most succinct form possible without loss of clarity. Notes may relate to any of the previous elements of the description, i.e. title, authorship, edition, editorship, publisher area, physical description area or series area. In addition notes may be made on: the relationship between the document and other publications, the nature, scope, language or literary form of the work's contents, or partial contents (that is, highlighting significant sections). AACR2 recommends that notes be given in the order reflected in the preceding description.

Standard number and terms of availability area

In this section standard numbers, such as International Standard Book Numbers (ISBNs) or International Standard Serial Numbers (ISSNs) are the first element to be recorded. These form a brief and unique identification of a specific title and are important in control. Price and other terms of availability are also given. These details are primarily useful as a record of expenditure or to organisations or individuals contemplating the purchase of a work.*

Chapter 3 Readings

Maltese, D., 'A standard for bibliographic citations: a proposal for the use of the ISBD', *International cataloguing*, 11(2), 1982, 19–21.

Note: Many of the items cited in the Reading lists to Chapters 8 and 9 include comments on bibliographic description.

*Note: Examples of descriptions of monographs can be found in Figures in Chapters 1 and 2.

4

More on bibliographic description – nonbook materials, periodicals and analytical cataloguing

The preceding chapter has introduced the essential characteristics of bibliographic descriptions. General points have been illustrated with reference to the cataloguing of books. This chapter takes the opportunity to look at an assortment of other aspects of bibliographic description. First, the cataloguing of nonbook materials is considered, and later special attention is focused on periodicals and analytical cataloguing.

4.1 The cataloguing and bibliographic description of nonbook materials

Much attention was focused specifically on the cataloguing and organisation of nonbook materials in the early 1970s. It is a matter of opinion whether nonbook materials merit separate discussion in respect of cataloguing practices, or whether it is sufficient to establish general principles for description which can then be applied across the spectrum of many different materials. Current trends favour cataloguing practices which can be applied to a variety of library materials. This section aims to summarise some of the special problems of nonbook materials, and to indicate the interpretation of cataloguing principles in respect of nonbook materials.

The term 'nonbook materials' reflects the context in which the consideration of these types of materials in libraries arose. When the term was coined the predominant information and text-carrying medium in libraries was the book. Thus any new media could be grouped into a contrasting category of nonbook. Increasingly a significant proportion of the stock of libraries, resource and information centres are nonbooks. Collections are increasingly likely to embrace a number of different media, and eventually in a true multi-media environment the distinction between books and nonbooks will become of historical interest only.

Nonbook materials, then, may include any library information or resource centre materials, other than books or monographs. Some of these items will be audio-visual, such as sound recordings, filmstrips, motion pictures and video-recordings. Other items are print and these include maps, charts, posters, and others are non-print. The term nonbook may extend to pamphlets, microforms and serials, or these items may be classified as books. In the last analysis the definition of nonbook is best made pragmatically in relation to the specific organisational problem under examination.

4.1.1 General problems of nonbook materials cataloguing

It is convenient to outline some of the general problems concerning the cataloguing of nonbook materials, at the same time as introducing the description of nonbook materials. This broader consideration of cataloguing problems serves to set a context for the consideration of descriptive cataloguing problems associated with nonbook materials.

Nonbook materials differ from books and from each other chiefly in their physical format and in the means by which they are created and marketed. The range of subjects that may be represented in nonbook materials, and the range of types of names that can be associated with the creation of nonbook materials are not all that different from their equivalents for books. Both the author and the subject approach for nonbook materials can be regarded as broadly similar for all media. Many of the particular problems in cataloguing nonbook materials arise in the preparation of bibliographic descriptions for these materials.

The subject approach to all types of nonbook materials can be very similar in principle. General classification schemes, such as the Dewey Decimal Classification scheme can be and are applied where appropriate, and standard lists of subject headings, such as the Library of Congress List of Subject Headings or Sears' List of Subject Headings, may be used in an alphabetical catalogue or bibliography listing nonbook material. In addition to these general schemes there are also special classification schemes and subject headings lists which have been designed for: special categories of material, for example, the British Classification of Music, or for special collections such as a collection of pictures, local history materials or photographs. Further comments on various of these topics are to be found in the chapters on the subject approach. The subject approach required for different collections and categories of nonbook materials will vary with the nature of the collection and its users. It is frequently the case, for example, that the subject categories needed to organise a collection of materials in a school resource centre will be relatively broad. Topics for portfolios might be no more specific than: the motor industry, the Brontës, computers, the environment. Although these topics are covered in general classification schemes and lists of subject headings they may not be represented in the most appropriate form for a collection of nonbook materials.

Equally, the author approach has features which are more or less common to all types of materials. The question of authorship, or intellectual responsibility can be more difficult to identify neatly than with books, and intellectual responsibility may need to be established for each medium. For example, the composer is normally regarded as the author of musical works, but if there is both a composer and a lyricist (writer of the words of a song), then which is to be given priority? In the creation of a motion picture there is a team of people, any of whom may be regarded as intellectually responsible for the content. These could include: the author of the script, producer, director, actors, musical arrangers and so on. So, undoubtedly, the assignment of intellectual responsibility may present fresh considerations for each new kind of medium. However, once responsibility has been allocated, the types of names that can arise in headings will be the same for all types of materials. All names will either be the names of corporate bodies or persons, and will represent the same range of problems with regard to form of name as any other medium.

4.1.2 Basic decisions for nonbook materials cataloguing

Certain fundamental decisions concerning the strategy for nonbook materials cataloguing need to precede detailed consideration of cataloguing practices. The first decision centres on the extent of integration of entries for different materials into one sequence. A number of choices exist, for example, the following:

1. to produce a catalogue which integrates entries for all library or resource centre materials.
2. to produce two catalogues, one of which contains all the entries pertaining to books, and the other all the entries concerning nonbook materials.
3. to produce as many different catalogues as there are types of material represented in any library or resource centre collection.

The integration of catalogue entries for different types of materials into one catalogue sequence facilitates common access to information, regardless of the physical form in which it is recorded. A common catalogue encourages users to regard the different information carrying media as part of a range of media. For example, in a school resource centre an integrated catalogue brings a variety of media to the attention of the teacher or the pupil at one consultation. Equally, integration removes the need to decide how to categorise media in determining the different catalogue sequences. For example, can one catalogue cover all graphic materials, or would it be advisable to opt for one catalogue for filmstrips, another for posters, and a third for slides? The chief limitation of integrated cataloguing of different media is the constraint that this approach places upon cataloguing practices. For an integrated catalogue to be successful it is essential that headings be the same for all types of material, for example, classification numbers. In addition, compatible practices for the description of library materials are desirable for both staff and users. Practice as regards integration varies considerably. In reality the extent of integration for catalogue entries for different media depends on administrative considerations, such as which section of the library is responsible for the compilation of catalogues for the various media. Some cataloguing may be conducted by a technical services department, whilst other cataloguing may be executed in the local studies department, or the children's library.

The second major decision in respect of nonbook cataloguing is the selection of a cataloguing code. Some cataloguing codes have been specifically designed to cater for one type of material. Other codes attempt to offer an integrated or consistent approach across all or many nonbook materials.

The following catalogue codes are typical of the codes drafted and published in the early 1970s, when it became apparent that the available cataloguing codes did not deal adequately with these types of materials. Most of these codes reflect the resource centre approach and attempt to integrate cataloguing of all types of materials.

1. Nonbook materials cataloguing rules/prepared by the Library Association Media Cataloguing Rules Committee. – London: National Council for Educational Technology, 1973. – (Working Paper; no. 11).

2. Nonbook materials: the organisation of integrated collections/Jean Riddle Weihs, Shirley Lewis, Janet Macdonald. – 1st edition. – Ottawa: Canadian Library Association, 1973.

3. Standards for cataloguing nonprint materials: an interpretation and practical application/by Alma Tillin and William J Quinly.–4th edition. –Washington: Association for Educational Communication and Technology [1976].

4.1.3 Headings and nonbook materials

This topic is not considered in any detail in this section, although it is obvious that entries for nonbook materials require headings in order to place the description of a nonbook item relative to descriptions of other works. Similar principles may be applied in the formulation and assignment of headings irrespective of the physical form of the document. These principles are reviewed in some detail in Parts II and III. Certain nonbook materials need special treatment in respect of some types of headings. Thus, for example, music requires the formulation of special types of uniform titles.

4.1.4 *Some special descriptive cataloguing problems with nonbook materials*

There is only space to review briefly the special problems associated with the descriptive cataloguing of nonbook materials. The general ISBD(G) framework certainly provides an outline, and the components which constitute a bibliographic description have been introduced in Chapter 3. Nevertheless, each group of materials presents unique problems, in the way in which the general framework is to be interpreted, and thus AACR2 allots a separate chapter for each category of material. In order to demonstrate some of the problems which arise from the variety of formats some key features of the descriptive cataloguing of various materials are identified below. First, however, it is necessary to establish the source of the information to be used in the description, or to identify the chief source of information. Figure 4.1 lists the chief source of information for a number of different categories of material.

4.2 Cartographic materials

Cartographic materials are, according to AACR2, all the materials that represent, in whole or in part, the earth or any celestial body. This will include two- and three-dimensional maps and plans; aeronautical, navigational and celestial charts; atlases; globes; block diagrams; sections; aerial photographs with a cartographic purpose and bird's eye views, and so on.

One of the main problems with descriptive cataloguing of maps is the fact that maps are often sold as part of a series. For instance, the Ordnance Survey of Great Britain one inch to one mile map: seventh series, constitutes a number of maps, covering separate areas, such as Birmingham or Cambridge and Newmarket. These maps can be bought as a series or as individual titles. The map cataloguer has to decide whether to treat these maps as separate works, or as parts of a series. This dilemma is illustrated more fully in section 4.3 which considers the concept of a distinct work and explores the styles of analytical cataloguing.

Another important component to be included is the mathematical data area; this is inserted in the materials specific area, after the statement of responsibility. The mathematical data area includes the statement of scale, and the statement of projection if it is given. Scales are normally given as a representative fraction expressed as a ratio, but provision is made for other statements of scale, where there is uncertainty or variation. Some examples are:

Scale 1:6,360

Figure 4.1 Some examples of nonbook materials catalogue records

Music score:
>Dvorak, Antonin
>(Concertos, cello, orchestra, op. 104, B minor)
>Konzert h-moll für Violoncello und Orchester, Opus 104/ Antonin Dvorak; herausgegeben von Max Pommer.—Leipzig; London: Peters, 1976.—1 miniature score (86p.); 15cm.

Sound recordings:
>Bruch, Max
>>(Concertos, violin, orchestra, no. 1, op. 26, G minor)
>>Violin concerto no. 1 in G minor, op. 26.—London:
>Ace of Clubs, 1953.—on 1 side of 1 sound disc (20 min.): 33 1/3 rpm, mono.; 12 in.—ACL 64
>>Violin: Campoli. London Symphony Orchestra, Anatole Fistoulari, conductor.
>>With: Havanaise; Introduction and rondo capriccioso, op. 28/ Saint-Saëns.

Maps

Deutschland (cartographic material).—
>Scale 1:800,000.—Stuttgart:
>R.V. 1967
>1 map: col.; 98 × 76cm.

>Road map route numbers, distances and showing places of tourist interest.

Ordnance Survey one-inch tourist map
>(cartographic material)
>Scale 1:63,360.— Southampton:
>Ordnance Survey

>The Peak District. 90 × 75cm.
>folded to 23 × 12cm. 1963.

Scale ca 1:500,000
Scale 1:10,000–1:20,000
Scale varies

The physical description of maps also merits special attention. This will include:
the number of physical units of a cartographic item, for example:

1 globe
3 maps
10 plans

other physical details such as the number of maps in an atlas, material, colour, mounting, for example:

3 maps: col.
1 globe: col., wood
1 map: col., mounted on cloth.

dimensions, that is, height × width in centimetres, for example:
1 map: col.; 35 × 50 cm.
1 map: col; on sheet 55 × 63 cm.
1 plan; 25 × 60 cm on sheet 31 × 130 cm.
1 map; 80 × 57 cm folded to 21 × 10 cm.

In the note area, contents notes can be particularly appropriate. To be specific, parts, insets and maps on the verso of other maps need to be indicated. For example:

Insets: social and political conditions.—Air distances from New York.—
Includes 7 insets
Includes key to 250 place names.

In addition, where two or more significant maps are on the same sheet or in the same volume 'with' notes may be used to link separate entries for the individual maps on the same sheet.

4.3 Music

Music can include a variety of forms, such as works about musicians and music, music scores and recordings. The cataloguing of music involves many special problems, both in description and headings. An effective music cataloguer needs to understand the various formats in which music can be published, and to have an appreciation of the various contexts in which music is used.

One of the most daunting aspects of music cataloguing arises from the fact that music and music recordings have international value. The user is not concerned whether the text on a music score or a record sleeve is in a foreign language and thus the music cataloguer is more likely than cataloguers of other materials to be handling items with text in a variety of languages.

A further problem which is particularly apparent in music cataloguing is the definition of a 'work'. One musical theme can be rewritten for different instruments, or different parts can be written for different instruments in an ensemble or orchestra. The same theme may be used by a single instrument, accompanied by a voice or several voices, used to accompany a film, to name but a few of the options. It is a considerable problem to relate all connected pieces of music to one another in a faithful and helpful manner.

When the cataloguer turns to the description of a piece of music a common problem will be the absence of a title page to be used as the chief source of information. Figure 3.4 shows some of the solutions to this problem for some of the formats in which music is encountered.

Provided that these considerable problems with music cataloguing can be negotiated, the description of books about music and musicians and music scores has much in common with the cataloguing of monographs. The description of books about musicians and music can be approached with the aid of Chapters 1 and 2 of AACR2, whilst special attention is focused on music scores in Chapter 5. Careful treatment of the presentation of uniform and conventional titles is necessary.

Sound recordings are dealt with in Chapter 6 of AACR2. A few comments on the cataloguing of sound recordings might be helpful. Chapter 6 covers discs, tapes, piano rolls and sound recordings on film. The first stage is the definition of the chief source of information for each separate medium. Another special feature is that the trade name or brand name may be used as the name of the publisher, if this is provided.

The physical description of sound recordings must include as many of the following elements as are appropriate:
extent, or number of physical units, for example:

1 sound cassette
2 sound cartridges

total playing time, for example:

on 1 side of 1 sound disc (13 min)

other physical details, including, as appropriate, type of recording, playing speed, groove characteristics, track configuration, number of tracks, number of sound channels, recording and reproduction characteristics, for example:

   1 sound cassette (60 min): 17/8 ips, stereo, Dolby processed.
   1 sound disc (7 min): 78 rpm, microgroove.

dimensions, according to medium. For example:

   sound discs: diameter in inches, for example, 1 sound disc: 12 in
   sound cassettes: height × width, and width of tape if other than standard,
   for example, 1 sound cassette (65 min); $7\frac{1}{4} \times 3\frac{1}{2}$ in, $\frac{1}{4}$ in tape.

Moving on from the physical description of sound recordings there are elements of the notes which are especially important. Notes are common for names of performers and the medium in which they perform (if this information has not already been given elsewhere in the entry). Contents notes are expected in respect particularly of collections of well-known works. A list of the titles of the individual works, possibly accompanied by statements of responsibility, is useful.

4.4 Periodical article citation

Periodical article citation could be regarded as one type of analytical entry. With periodical article citation details and access are given in respect of a part of a serial or periodical, that is, the individual article.

The components of a full citation for a periodical article are typically:

1. Document identification number
2. Author(s) names
3. Title
4. Source reference

Sometimes the following additional data or a subset of these elements is also given:

5. Sponsoring agency, and its report reference number
6. Contract number
7. Original language and/or source of a translation
8. Any other additional descriptive notes.

Different agencies engaged in preparing citations to periodical articles have different standards. Typically such citations are to be found in current awareness services, computer data bases and indexing and abstracting services. There are standards which can be applied in citing periodical articles, but these are not always applied in practice. Each agency must establish its own practices in accordance with its own specific requirements.

For articles in periodicals there are a number of International Standards Organisation standards which provide guidance. ISO 690-1975 Documentation – Bibliographical references – Essential and supplementary elements, gives some suggestions concerning the structure of a bibliographic reference for periodical articles. The parallel BS 1629: 1976 Recommendations for bibliographical references provides guidance for the presentation of references to books and other separately issued publications, serials, contributions, articles and patents. BS 5605: 1978 Recommendations for citing publications by bibliographical reference gives concise guidance for authors and editors on the preferred methods of arranging references in books and journal articles.

Some comments on each of the four primary components of the periodical article citation are in order. The document identification number is the number which provides the unique identification of the document in the data base or publication where the document is cited. The number will not usually be standard for the work, but will be assigned to the periodical article when its record is added to the data base. Author(s) name(s) provide rapid identification of an article. The name(s) may be entered in an author index, or merely given as part of the description. Despite the advantages to be gained by standardisation various practices regarding the form of the author(s) name(s) persist. There will be increasing numbers of instances in which it would be desirable to match the entries on different data bases. Author(s) name(s) must be an important element in the matching process, and common practices between different data bases would make matching simpler. Cataloguing codes such as AACR2 provide systematic guidelines on the citation of author(s) name(s), but these are not always heeded.

The title of an article is another important identifier, and also indicates the subject content. In the interests of document identification, the title is normally quoted verbatim in order that the document record can be successfully and confidently matched with the document at a later stage. Uninformative or unclear titles may be augmented by additional words; these words are usually enclosed in square brackets in order to distinguish them from the authentic title. Titles of foreign language publications are generally cited in both the original language and the translation language.

The description of the source of a periodical article comprises: periodical title, date of issue, volume number, issue number and pagination. The first element, the periodical title, will often appear in an abbreviated form. Standards exist to cover periodical title abbreviation. ISO-4-1972 presents an international code for the abbreviation of titles of periodicals. ISO 833-1974 and ISO 832-1975 both contribute specifically by listing abbreviations to be adopted for certain title worlds. ISO 833-1974 gives an international list of periodical title word abbreviations, and ISO 832-1975 provides abbreviations of typical words in bibliographic references. The international list of periodical title word abbreviations is maintained by the International Serials Documentation System (ISDS) International Centre in Paris. This centre is responsible for the publication of amendments and revisions to ISO 833-1974. Many organisations work from their own standard list of abbreviations. Journal titles will normally be accompanied by an indication of the issue in which a specific article is contained. Volume and issue and part numbers will serve this purpose. These may be presented in a variety of ways, for example, volume 6, number 8, or 6(8). In addition it is common to give the date of an issue, for example, March 1984. The date of the issue is cited as fully as is necessary to identify the issue and usually in the form given in the publication, for example, May 1983 or 3 May 1983. Page numbers are also necessary and may be inserted in one of many positions. Page numbers should be cited in accordance with the exact pages on which the text of the article appears, for example, 56–58, 61, 68–73. Pagination should be inclusive and should show full page numbers (that is 234–246, not 234–46).

Punctuation will be present in the citation, and should serve to distinguish one component from its neighbour. Figure 4.2 shows some examples of periodical article citations.

4.5 Serials and their records

Serials cataloguing and the maintenance of adequate records of serials stock present two distinct categories of problems. One area has already been tackled in the last section, namely, the citation of individual parts of serials. The other area is the maintenance of appropriate records of serials collections and the bibliographic control of serials titles. This is considered in this section.

The cataloguing of serials is an area which has presented many problems, too many of which remain only partially resolved. With the improved bibliographical control over serial titles in the past few years the situation has been eased, but serials cataloguing has not advanced to the same extent as monographs cataloguing.

The first problem which faces the serials cataloguer is the definition of a serial. The International Serials Data System (ISDS), Paris, defines a serial to be 'a publication issued in successive parts and intended to be continued indefinitely'. The definition continues 'serials include periodicals, newspapers, annuals, journals, memoirs, proceedings, transactions etc. of societies, and monographic series. A serial can be in print or near print form and its parts usually have numerical or chronological designations'. In practice, this definition coincides reasonably well, but certainly could not be

Figure 4.2 Some periodical citations—samples

Engineering index

077925 Solid-phase pressure forming for profit. This paper describes the solid-phase pressure forming (SPPF) technique which has been developed for mass production of containers for food and beverage. Unlike melt-phase thermoforming, SPPF forms solid plastic sheet at a temperature below the polymer's melting point. Whereas melt-phase forming of polypropylene takes place at temperatures ranging from 165 to 175°C, SPPF is performed at temperatures of 150 to 160°C (usually around the middle section to high end of the range, which is below its crystalline melting point of 166°C). Because solid plastic sheet is transformed into biaxially stressed containers or other hollow shapes by the application of a rapidly descending shaped plug, followed immediately by high-pressure air (100 psi for polypropylene), the containers are stiffer, have greater impact, tensile, and yield strength, develop transparency and gloss, as well as gas and water-vapor barrier properties, and are more uniform from piece to piece. Economic advantages of the new system are outlined.

Ryder, Leonard B. (Ryder Assoc Inc. Whippany, NJ, USA). Plast Eng v 37 n 8 Aug 1981 p 17-20

077929 International update on materials used in thermoforming.An international update has been presented on materials used in the thermoforming process. Many thermoplastic materials are available to control color, flexibility, and clarity among many other important properties. Tables shown indicate that, if necessary, other considerations can be made such as thermal and dimensional stability as well as heat sealing properties in selection of the most suitable thermoforming film to meet specific end requirements. Should a single polymer have deficiencies to meet the required specifications, then combinations of polymer materials or laminates are available and may be used to produce a satisfactory thermoformed article. Extended property data for several thermoplastics available are tabulated. 4 refs.

Landfield, H. (Abbott Lab, Chicago, Ill, USA). Polym Plast Technol Eng v 14 n 1 1980 p 63-73.

077924 Sheet co-extrusion after 15 years - A 1981 status report. Feed block co-extrusion has now been commercially practiced in sheet for well over ten years. Starting with simple two layer structures, the market has now developed a tremendous variety of ingenious and useful structures. This paper presents details of some of these and describes their applications and methods of production. Some details on extruders and die designs are given.

Nissel, Frank R. (Welex Inc, Blue Bell, Pa, USA). Adv Plast Technol v 1 n 4 Oct 1981 p 14-19.

Lead abstracts

L83-2295/04918

CC=421; DT=11; LC=Fr

Degradation of TEL in seawater.

Charlou, J.L., Caprais, M.P., Blanchard, G. and Martin, G. Environmental Technol.
Letters (UK), Sept. 1982 3 (9), 415-424. 9 figs, 3 tables.

The geochemical behaviour of tetraethyl lead and its chloride by-products is studied in laboratory conditions. The influence of sunlight and u.v. radiations is examined in permuted water, running water and seawater. The degradation compounds obtained in the solid, liquid and gas phases are identified and the evolution of some of them is described. 26 references.

L83-2296/04926

CC=421; DT=11; LC=En

The analytical chemist in studies of metal pollution in sediment cores.

Farmer, J.G. Anal. Proceedings (UK), June 1981, 18 (6), 249-252. 1 fig.

Analysis of sediment cores can throw much light on anthropogenic metal pollution and on other properties. Findings of a study of the history of metal pollution in Scottish coastal and freshwater sediments are discussed is terms of present shortcomings with regard to sample collection and critical verification of results. Studies of chemical speciation and partitioning of elements among various sedimentary phases are also reported. Some data are presented for lead and zinc concentrations in sediment cores from a loch. The need for international standard reference materials is considered. 13 references.

L83-2297/04930

CC=421; DT=12; LC=EN

Accumulative phases for heavy metals in limnic sediments.

Fošjurstner, U. Hydrobiologia (Netherlands), July 1982, 91, 269-284. 5 figs., 5 tables.

Data from mechanical concentrates of recent sediments indicate that clay-rich aggregates and heavy minerals are the major carriers of heavy metals in detrital sediment fractions. Hydrous Fe Mn oxides and carbonates and sulphides, in their specific environment, are the predominant accumulative phases for heavy metals in autochthonous fractions. Sequential chemical extraction techniques permit the estimation of characteristic heavy metal bonding forms: exchangeable metal cations, easily reducible, moderately reducible, organic and residual metal fractions, whereby both diagenetic processes and the potential availability of toxic compounds can be studied. The data from lakes affected by acid precipitation indicates that zinc, cobalt, and nickel are mainly released from the easily reducible sediment fractions.

Continued

Figure 4.2 Continued

Current technology index

Cummins calls the Shotts in Scotland. G. Montgomorie. Comm. Mot., 158 (5 Nov 83) p. 50-1.

C.a.d./c.a.m.—they are together, at last. (Cambridge Interactive Systems Ltd.) B. Kellock. Machinery Prod. Engng., 141 (7/21 Dec 83) p. 38+

Asbestos out: M13011 in new liner for '84. G. Montgomorie. Comm. Mot., 158 (29 Oct 83) p. 33-4.

In-cycle gauging down to half a micron. (Jones & Shipman plc) (Thomas Marcer Ltd.) Tooling. 37 (Oct 83) p. 20-1.

Anbar management abstracts

ZB

3 The Chief Executive Goes On-Line

J. F. Rockart + M. E. Treacy in Harvard Business Review (USA), Jan/Feb 82: p. 82 (6½ pages, charts)

Acknowledges that most managers see the use of electronic aids as a violation of their traditional management style, but quotes examples to show increasing use of terminals, initially to access a financial database, and ultimately to handle analytical work. Doesn't quote figures for the proportions of terminal time spent playing Space Invaders. ★

ZB

4 Technology as a Competitive Weapon

A. L. Frohman in Harvard Business Review (USA), Jan/Feb 82: p. 97 (8 pages chart)

From a study of methods of managing technological products in unnamed companies, concludes that success depends on (1) a technical orientation of the part of top management, (2) project criteria, and (3) linking the development effort to the needs of the business.

said to be identical with the definition that many individual libraries assign to the term 'serial'.

Serials, then, are distinguished from monographs by their ongoing nature. Any serials control system will have fewer titles to handle, but must record more detail for each title, and can expect a greater number of transactions per title. Usually, serials control systems operate separately from monograph systems, but still need to cover the three funtions of ordering and acquisitions, cataloguing and circulation control. For serials, however, much of the record keeping may centre upon the acquisitions subsystem, as opposed to, say, the circulation control subsystem which may be viewed as more central for books. Obviously, central to any such systems is some type of record to represent each serial title. Before proceeding to consider this aspect, however, it is worth first considering some underlying features of serials control, and then reviewing some of the organisational factors which to some extent determine the nature of records for serials.

Five key issues which are unique to serials present problems with cataloguing and other serials control subsystems. These are:

(a) Successive issues are received at regular or irregular intervals, and it is important to note and respond to the arrival or non-arrival of individual issues.

(b) Subscriptions must be renewed at regular intervals.

(c) Catalogue records must describe both the serial and the library's holdings of the serial.

(d) Serials change their titles, are published under variant titles (for example, translated titles) and may change their frequency of publication, editor, format and other features.

(e) Serials need to be cumulated and bound.

In general, a large amount of data needs to be recorded for each serial title, and amendments to individual records will be common.

Various standards have emerged in recent years for bibliographic records for serials. One agency to be responsible for such a standard is the International Serials Data System (ISDS) whose International Centre is in Paris. This is an international registry of serial publications and serves to contribute to the standardisation of serial citations, partly by the maintenance of common principles, cataloguing rules, and a machine-readable format. There are forty-six centres in twenty-five countries participating in the scheme. In the United Kingdom, the British Library is responsible for the serials published in the UK. This National Serials Data Centre (NSDC) acquires information about changes in serial publication patterns from publishers, organisations, existing catalogues and legal deposit. Its function, together with other centres, is to

1. provide identification and bibliographical control of the entire serials population
2. assign ISSNs
3. register serials published within respective countries and send records to Paris, and amend and update records
4. build and maintain files
5. take part in standardisation programmes and activities relation to serials and their bibliographical control.

All serials entered in the ISDS are assigned a key title and an ISSN.

The three main objectives of the ISDS centred on the provision of bibliographic control, and were:

1. the building and maintaining of an international register of serials from all countries and all disciplines with sufficient information for the unambiguous identification of serials.
2. to make this information available to all countries, organisations and individuals.
3. to establish a network of communications between libraries, secondary information services, publishers of serial literature and international organisations.

The ISDS has now been in operation for over ten years.

Another trend in the movement towards bibliographical control of serials was the formulation of the International Standard Bibliographic Description for Serials ISBD(S), which was issued in 1974. This was developed separately from the ISDS outlines for identification and there are a number of differences between them, which derive from their differing objectives. The ISDS record was developed independently of cataloguing rules but the ISBD(S) was developed with cataloguing in mind, and is thus rather fuller than the ISDS format. This latter does not, for example, have a title proper or edition area. The particular area of conflict is the title area. For the ISDS the key title is constructed according to the rules in the 'Guidelines for ISDS' but the ISBD(S) dictates that the title proper must be transcribed. This has caused particular problems with generic titles (for example, Annual Report, Bulletin) because the rules used to form the ISDS key title and those used to form the title in the ISBD(S) are slightly different. A major problem is that the ISBD(S) does not provide precise advice on what constitutes a major or minor title change; minor title changes may be disregarded for the ISBD, whilst under the provisions of the ISDS they would require a new record, including a new ISSN and a new key title. This, in turn, leads to the situation where several ISSNs and key titles can apply to one ISBD(S). Conversely, the ISDS rule that a publication in several formats (for example, microfilm and paper) can keep the same ISSN, leads to one ISDS record having several ISBD(G) records.

Figure 4.3 Sample records for serials

From 'Serials in the British Library'

Library administrator's digest.—Vol. 18, no. 1 (Jan. 1983).—South
    San Francisco : R. S. Alvarez, 1983-. — v. — Monthly except
    July and August. — Continues: Administrator's digest (South
    San Francisco). — Description based on: Vol. 18, no. 2 (Feb.
    1983)
    XY/N-1: Vol. 18(2), Feb. 1983-
       *A=1*E=5188.160*F=8304

Look in pop annual.—(No. 1)-. — London : ITV Books, 1982-.
    — v. : ill (some col.), ports (some col.) ; 29cm.
    £2.25
    CA/U-1: (No. 1)-
       *A=1*F=8308

London environmental bulletin.— Vol. 1, no. 1 (summer 1983).- —
    London : Greater London Council, 1983-. — v. ; 30cm. —
    Quarterly. — Prepared by: Pollution Monitoring Group,
    Scientific Services Branch. — Supplement: London
    environmental supplement
    ISSN 0264-5904=London environment bulletin : Unpriced
    Abbreviated key-title: Lond. environ. bull.
    XY/N-1: Vol. 1, 1983-
       *A=1*E=5293.3506*F=8307

From 'New Serial Titles'

International Federation for Documentation.
    FID directory . . . —   — The Hague,
    Netherlands : International Federation for Documentation.
       v. ; 21 cm. — (FID 575)
    Biennial.
    Description based on: 1979-1980; title from cover.
    Continues: FID yearbook.
    1. International Federation for Documentation—Directo-
    ries. I. Title. II. Series: FID publication : 575.
    Z1008.1659a   025'.06'01   82-641930
    CLU   CaAEU   DLC   IU   MB   MdU   N   NNC
    NjR   NmU   PPD   WaU   AACR2

Continued

Figure 4.3 Continued

Instrument manufacturing. — Vol. 20, no. 1 (Jan.-
Feb. 1952)-v. 23, no. 6 (Nov.-Dec. 1955). —
(Pittsburgh, Pa. : Instruments Pub. Co., c1952-
c1955)
4 v. : ill. ; 30 cm.
Bimonthly.
Title from cover.
Some volumes include: Instrument manufacturing. The . . .
buyers' guide, issued separately in some years.
Continues: Instrument maker.
Absorbed by: Instruments and automation.
ISSN 0096-2619=Instrument manufacturing.
TA165.157   47-40674
DLC   InU   AACR 2
                    (830lr83)rev3

International abstracts in operations research.   v.
1-   Nov. 1961-
Amsterdam (etc.) North Holland Publishing Co.
    v. 23 cm.
Five no. a year (irregular) Nov. 1961-   ; quarterly
1961-June 1970 published by the Operations Research Society
of America; Aug. 1970-72 published by International
Federation of Operational Research Societies; 1973-
published for International Federation of Operation Research
Societies by Operations Research Society of America.
    Indexes:
Vols. 5-8, in v.8.
    Other title: O.R. International abstracts in operations research
1. Operations research—Abstracts.   I. International
Federation of Operational Research Societies.   II. Operations
Research Society of America.
    (DNLM: 1. Administrative Management—abstracts   2.
Human engineering—abstracts.   3. Research—abstracts)
Q500.I5   65-53605
DLC

International Conference on Pattern Recognition.
Proceedings / International Conference on Pattern
Recognition. — 5th (1980) -   —New
York : Institute of Electrical and Electronics Engineers,
1980-
v. : ill ; 28 cm.
Annal.
Cover title: IEEE . . . pattern recognition
Continues: International Joint Conference on Pattern
Recognition. Proceedings, 1-4 (1973-1978)
I. Title

sn 83-10019
CU-A   IU   InLP   NIC   NRU   AACR 2

There have been attempts to make the two systems compatible. In 1981, the Directors of the ISDS Centres passed a resolution endorsing the need to achieve the greatest possible compatibility between ISDS and ISBD(S), which suggested identical punctuation, terminology and definitions, identical formulations for the same rules and the elimination of needless differences. It is hoped that a new ISDS manual and guidelines for bibliographic description will be published in 1986.

Obviously, ISBD(S) has been incorporated into AACR2. However, AACR2 has provided additional problems with choice of entry or access points for serials. Serials with generic or non-distinctive titles were entered under the corporate body issuing them according to AACR1. This practice led to inconsistencies with ISDS practice, and resulted in changes in the recommendations for entry of serials for AACR2, so that now almost all serials are entered under title, see Figure 4.3. These changes have meant modifications, some very time-consuming, to serials catalogues in libraries. One of the outcomes of entry under title has been the proliferation of serials titles. For example, one record in Serials in the British Library may include four titles: a uniform title as heading, a title proper at the beginning of the descriptive part of the record, a key title in the notes and an abbreviated key title in the notes.

A further contribution to the international bibliographical control of serials was the CONSER Project (Conversion of Serials). Begun in 1973, CONSER was concieved by an *ad hoc* discussion group on Serials Data Bases of American and Canadian librarians. They aimed to create a consolidated data base, with OCLC acting as host. The twelve original participants began to convert their records into machine-readable form, using the Minnesota Union List of Serials (MULS) and the Library of Congress MARC(S) file as a base. CONSER's guidelines on standards, the

'Agreed-upon-Practices' stated that the requirements of ISSN, ISBD(S), AACR, US MARC, Canadian MARC and the ALA catalog code be met. This inevitably created some problems, and one serial may be represented by more than one record. These records are now available through the Library of Congress MARC(S) records and from 1982, CONSER took over responsibility for producing New Serial Titles. CONSER is the ISDS centre for the United States, and is becoming the US national serials data base.

Other co-operatives and libraries also have serials records. Those of BLCMP union serials list have been used as part of the basis of a national data base. Newcastle University Library uses a record for serials which includes elements which pertain to both catalogue or holdings records, and ordering data. The elements of these records are:

1. Title (sub-title) and issuing body	2. ISSN
3. Holdings	4. Shelf location
5. Class number	6. Notes
7. University departments interested in title	8. Agent from whom purchased
9. Price code	10. Control number

4.6 Analytical cataloguing

Most of the cataloguing conducted by libraries and other cataloguing agencies is concerned to produce records pertaining to individual works. This emphasis upon 'the work' reflects the packaging of text, information, music, graphics, and so on, and indicates to the subsequent user what packages are available for use or consultation. In the sense that libraries lend works as units, and publishers and distributors also make works available as entire units, this approach is understandable. Nevertheless, the conventional approach of bibliographic listings in listing individual works has limitations. One of the most obvious of the limitations of this approach is that it is difficult to decide what constitutes a separate work. Is the individual monograph in a monograph series the work, or should the series be seen as the work? With a set of Ordnance Survey maps, should the entire set be treated as one map, or should the individual components covering the various areas of the country be regarded as distinct works? The definition of a 'work' has eluded cataloguers for many years, and AACR2 has not found a solution. AACR2 has been criticised on the grounds that it does not identify the cataloguing unit to which the rules refer. The need to identify the cataloguing unit is becoming more pressing as the variety of media expands and as computerised cataloguing systems offer new opportunities.

Unfortunately, these factors simultaneously make the resolution of the situation more intractable.

Analytical cataloguing aims to emphasise the content of documents, rather than relying entirely upon cataloguing whole works. Obviously with the definition of what constitutes an entire work still pending it is not easy to define analytical cataloguing precisely. Perhaps it is sufficient to say that analytical cataloguing identifies the components of works to a greater extent than would be the case in normal cataloguing practice. The intention is to provide access to specific parts of works. Analytical cataloguing is valuable in respect of any type of media, but many of the ideas have been tested most thoroughly in the context of monographs and serials. To take a simple example, analytical cataloguing would aim to make the text of *Hamlet* equally accessible whether it had been published as a separate volume or whether it was available in a volume containing a collection of Shakespeare's works. Similarly, there is no reason why a substantial chapter in a book on Asia, which deals with China, should not be as valuable as a separate leaflet on China. Analytical cataloguing seeks to overcome physical packaging.

Analytical cataloguing is practised to varying extents in libraries. To some extent it is left to the abstracting and indexing services and associated data bases to provide access to the contents of works, but some libraries also feel that it is appropriate to indulge in some local analytical cataloguing. The constraint which prevents extensive analytical cataloguing, despite its attraction to users, is that analytical cataloguing represents an extra burden on the processing facilities of a library. Any analytical entries which are made must be made in addition to the standard catalogue entries for complete works. Each library must make policy decisions concerning whether it will indulge in analytical cataloguing, and to which categories of works analytical cataloguing will be applied.

Recommendations relating to analytical cataloguing practices concern themselves primarily with the way in which the part of a document or work to be accessed is described. Obviously the headings for analytical entries are also important, but there is little need for separate comment upon these headings, as they must be consistent with the headings used for the catalogue entries for complete works. In other words, in a catalogue with author and subject sequences analytical entries will have either author's names or subject terms or notation as headings. No special provision need be made for analytical entries.

The format of the description in an analytical entry requires careful consideration. The style of description may depend on the nature of the relationship between the part and the whole. The parts to be described may be individual volumes in a series, or parts of individual volumes. This distinction is not necessarily relevant to the literary or information content of the document, but will influence the appropriate form for the analytical entry.

There are two tools which discuss the compilation of analytical entries and which must be introduced here: AACR2 and the ISBD(CP), where CP stands for component parts.

4.7 AACR2 and analytical cataloguing

In Chapter 13 AACR2 identifies the following categories of analytical entry:

Analytics of monographic series and multipart monographs

If an item is part of a monographic series or a multipart monograph and has a title not dependent on that of the whole item, an analytical entry may be prepared in terms of a complete description of the part, by using the series area. For example:

English costume 1890–1910/R M Small.-
Oxford: Heather Press, 1984. - xx, 325p.: ill.; 23 cm.-
(A History of English costume; v. 8).-

Note area

If a comprehensive entry for a larger work is made, this entry may contain a display of parts in the note area (normally in a contents note). For example:

The Wimsey family/edited by C W Scott-Giles.-
London: Victor Gollancz, 1977.-87.: ill.; 23 cm.-
Contents: The Search for Wimseys/by C W Scott-Giles.- The Early Wimseys/by R M Brown.- The Barons/by C R Overton.- The Earls of Denver/by N M Howe.- The Dukes of Denver/ by R S Teem.

Analytical added entries

If a comprehensive entry for a larger work is made that shows the part in either the title and statement of responsibility area or the note area, an added entry may be made for the heading appropriate to the part. This can give direct access to a part of a document without resorting to an additional bibliographic record for the part. For example, the record above could be entered under Overton, C R.

In analytics

If more bibliographic description is needed for the part than can be obtained by displaying it in the note area the 'in' analytic entry may be considered. This consists of two parts: the description of the part, and a short citation of the whole item in which the part is to be found. For example:

The discovery of New Zealand/M R Costa.-
p. 210–306; 23 cm.
In: Rom, R S Australasia; discovery and early history.-Sydney:
Downunder Press, 1984.

Multi-level description

Multi-level description is normally used by national bibliographies and cataloguing agencies that prepare entries needing complete identification of both parts and comprehensive whole, in a single record that shows as its primary element the description of the whole. The descriptive information is divided into two or more levels: first level for the multi-part item as a whole, and second level, for information relating to a group of parts or to the individual part. For example:

Sources for a history of the Sparry family/extracted by Stella & Erle Sparry. – Trowbridge (Victoria Rd., Trowbridge, Wilts. [BA14 7LD]): R.E. Sparry
Vol. 1: Sparry wills 1600–1699 – [1982]. – 94 leaves in various foliations; 20 cm

ISBD(CP)

Draft 5 of the recommendations for the International Standard Bibliographic Description for Component Parts (ISBD(CP)) was published in 1981. In the draft a component part is defined as:

Any document that for the purposes of bibliographic identification or access requires reference to a host document of which it forms a part. Component parts include articles in journals, illustrations and maps in printed text, an aria in a music score, or a music score issued with a sound recording.

The ISBD(CP)'s recommendations are very similar in principle to those for AACR2's 'in' analytics, except for slight changes in punctuation and order. More explicitly, the main differences for monographs are:

1. the description of the component part is separated from that of the host document by a double slash.

2. parts of the physical description of the component part are given after the physical description of the host document. This is adopted in the belief that it is in line with general preference, although AACR's approach does have the merit of keeping information about the part and the whole separate from one another.

For example:
The discovery of New Zealand/M R Costa.//In: Rom R S Australasia; discovery and early history. – Sydney: Downunder Press, 1984. – 293p. – p. 210–306.

4.8 Subject analysis

Subject analysis can be very helpful in special departments of public or academic libraries, especially where unique collections exist or for combatting the problem of scatter, for example, where there is a conference paper on adoption in the proceedings of a conference concerned with the 'making of laws'. Subject analytical entries can be made according to all of the styles outlined in AACR2, by making use of classification notation or subject headings as the entry points or headings for the records. For example:

ART, GREEK.
Topics in art history/Dunbarton Art Panel. – Glasgow [etc.]:
Blackie.
In 6 vols.
Egyptian, Greek and Roman art. – 1977. – 32p: ill, map, plans,
ports; 21x27cm.
Bibl: p.32. – List of filmstrips: p.32.
ISBN 0-216-90270-3 Sd: £1.30
The 20th century: 1880 to the present. – 1977. – 32p.: ill; 21x27cm.
Bibl.: p.32. – List of filmstrips: p.32.
ISBN 0-216-90275-4 Sd: £1.30

The foregoing discussion concerning analytical entries assumes implicitly a conventional catalogue format, that is, card, microform or other printed catalogue. The role of analytical entries in an online catalogue is less clear. Access to different fields in a computer held data base offers considerably more flexibility in access points. This point is explored more extensively in Chapter 23. However, it is important to note that although an online catalogue improves the range of access points to catalogue entries, it is necessary that full details be included in records in order that the full potential of online catalogues can be exploited. A future with online catalogues will still require analytical entries, to the extent that records will need to contain notes of contents of works if individual components of works are to be identifiable via the catalogue.

Chapter 4 Readings

A. Nonbook materials

1 Andrewes, R., 'AACR2 and printed music'. in: *Seminar on AACR2: proceedings*, Library Association: London, 1980, 19–25.

2 Butchart, I., 'AACR2 and the cataloguing of audio-visual material', in: *Seminar on AACR2: proceedings*, Library Association: London, 1980, 25–32.

3 Clarke, A., 'A new non-code for films: AACR2 chapter 7', *Audiovisual Librarian*, 6(4), 1980, 128–33.

4 Fairclough, R.H., 'Map cataloguing and AACR2' in: *Seminar on AACR2: proceedings*, Library Association: London, 1980, 42–9.

5 Hagler, R., 'Nonbook materials: chapter 7 through 11', in: *International conference on AACR2, Florida State University, 1979, The making of a code* . . . American Library Association: Chicago, 1980, 72–87.

6 Hinton, F., 'Cartographic materials, manuscripts, music and sound recordings' in: *International conference on AACR2, Florida State University, 1979, The making of a code* . . . American Library Association: Chicago, 1980, 60–71.

7 Horner, J., *Special cataloguing*, Bingley: London, 1976.

8 Nichols, H., *Map librarianship*, Bingley: London, 1976.

9 Redfern, B. *Organising music in libraries, vol.2: Cataloguing*, Bingley: London, 1979.

10 Richmond, S., 'Problems in applying AACR2 to music materials', *Library Resources and Technical Services*, 26(2), 1982, 204–11.

11 Roberts, E., 'AACR2 and serials', *Cataloguing Australia* 6(3), 1980, 65–70.

12 Shrifrin, M., *Information in the school library: an introduction to the organisation of nonbook materials*, Bingley: London, 1973.

13 'Study into the effects of AACR2 on music MARC catalogue', BRIO 16(2), 1979, 38–41.

B. Serials

14 Anderson, D., 'Compatibility of ISDS and ISBD(S) records in international exchange: the background', *International Cataloguing*, 12(2), 1983, 14–17.

15 'Automation and serials': proceedings of the UK Serials Group Conference 1980/ ed. Margaret E. Graham, UK Serials Group, 1981.

16 Bourne, R., 'Building a serials file', *Program*, 12(2), 1978, 78–86.

17 Bourne, R., *Serials librarianship*, Library Association: London, 1980.

18 Bourne, R., 'AACR2: cataloguing of serials' in: *Seminar on AACR2: proceedings*, Library Association: London, 1980, 50–60.

19 Fasana, P., 'Serials data control: current problems and prospects', *Journal of Library Automation*, 9(1), 1976, 19–33.

20 Frazmeir, G., 'The miraculous multiplication of serial titles' *International Cataloguing*, 11(1), 1982, 9.

21 Jeffrey, A.G., 'Newcastle library serials catalogue', *Program* 12(4), 1978, 175–84.

22 Peregoy, M., 'AACR II and serials cataloguing', *Serials Librarian*, 3(1), 1978, 15–30.

23 Soper, M.E., 'Description and entry of serials in AACR2', *Serials Librarian*, 4(2), 1979, 167–76.

24 Standard practices in the preparation of bibliographic records, IFLA UBC: London, 1982.

25 Szilvassy, J., 'ISDS and ISBD(S) records in international exchange: compatibility issues', *International Cataloguing*, 12(4), 1983, 38–41.

26 Turner, A., 'The effects of AACR2 on serials cataloguing', *Serials Librarian* 4(2), 1979, 177–86.

27 Woodward, D., 'The National Serials Data Centre', *Program*, 9(3), 1975, 158–65.

C. Analytical cataloguing

28 ISBD (CP) (component parts), International Office for UBC: London, 1981. (Draft 5)

5 Summaries and full text data bases

5.1 Introduction

The previous chapters have considered the statement of the source of a document in some detail. So far, the description of documents by bibliographic records has been considered in detail. This chapter does little to adjust the balance. Libraries and information centres are indeed primarily concerned with bibliographic data bases but even many bibliographic data bases contain more than the type of bibliographic description outlined in the previous three chapters. Bibliographic data bases which concern themselves with references to documents may include document summaries for some or all of the records present in the data bases. Cataloguing data bases may include brief annotations, but the data bases associated with abstracting and indexing tools, and commonly used for information retrieval, will often contain abstracts or other document summaries.

A non-bibliographic data base or data bank which provides the searcher with direct access to information can be expected to contain text, such as extracts from legal texts or directories, statistical data in the form of numbers and other factual information. Currently the possibilities for storing graphical information, for example, drawings, pictures and diagrams, are limited, but this is another possibility that will be important in the future.

5.2 Document summaries in bibliographic data bases

There are a number of different kinds of document summary. We will now consider some of the more common options:

1. An *abstract* is a concise and accurate representation of the contents of a document, in a style similar to that of the original document. An abstract covers all of the main points made in the original document, and usually follows the style and arrangement of the parent document. Abstracts, unless specifically intended to be so, are non-critical. Criticism is not appropriate in a style which aims to report, but not comment upon the content of the original document. Abstracts are self-contained and complete. They assume only that the reader has some knowledge of the subject, so that the abstract

can be understood. No reference to the original should be necessary for the comprehension of the abstract.

2. An *annotation* is a note added to the title and/or other bibliographic information concerning a document, by way of comment or explanation. In cataloguing the term annotation is often used to refer to the notes section of a standard bibliographic description, as introduced in Chapter 3. Annotations such as may be encountered in bibliographies may be less stylised, and are more likely to concentrate on conveying more of the subject content of a document. Although there are some similarities between annotations and abstracts, the objectives of an annotation are generally more limited than those of an abstract, and hence the annotation will tend to be briefer.

3. An *extract* is one or more portions of a document selected to represent the whole document. Plainly such representative sections may not be present in many documents, but sometimes an extract from the results, conclusions or recommendations of a document may serve to identify the key issues covered by the entire document. Extracts are unlikely to offer a balanced account of the content of a document, but may be valuable to the reader for whom an emphasis on the outcome of a study is appropriate.

4. A *summary* is a restatement, within the document, of the salient findings and conclusions of a document. A summary at the end of a document is intended to complete the orientation of the reader, and to identify the significant ideas for the reader to remember. A summary at the beginning of a document serves to prepare the reader to proceed to the remainder of the text. A summary differs from an abstract in that it assumes that the reader will have the opportunity to peruse the accompanying text. Hence, certain elements essential to a complete understanding of the text, such as the sections on background, purpose and methodology tend to be absent from a summary.

5. Many other terms are used to denote a regurgitation or abbreviation of document content. An *abridgement* is usually taken to be a condensation that necessarily omits a number of secondary points. Abridgement is a relatively general term. A *précis* is an account which restricts itself to the essential points in an argument. A *paraphrase* is an interpretation of the concepts featured in a document, written in the language of the writer of the paraphrase. A *digest* should be a methodically arranged presentation of the main arguments in a document. A *synopsis* is one type of résumé prepared by the author of a work.

The definitions given above are intended to help in recognising document summaries. The wide array of such terms serves to demonstrate the range of perspectives on document summaries, and emphasises that any one document can be summarised by a number of different summaries. Whilst one writer of a summary may look for a balanced account of the key points, another writer may emphasise conclusions almost to the point of exclusion of all else; a further writer may deal only with a specific element of the methodology (for example, catalyst used in a chemical process, questionnaire used in a survey), and yet another writer may be more concerned with the impact that a given document may have on the subject field to which it contributes, than on the details of the content of the document. It is also important to recognise, that whilst some definitions are given above which represent common usage of the terms, different groups may well define the terms differently. In practice the distinction beween one term and the next is not very clear.

5.3 More on abstracts

Probably the most important of the document summaries identified in section 5.2 is the abstract. Abstracts are widely used as an aid to the reader in assessing the contents of a document, that is, as an aid in the selection of documents for further consultation. Abstracts are found in primary publications generally accompanying reports of research and other developments in both the published and unpublished report literature, in journal articles, in reports of professional, scientific and technical meetings and conferences, theses, books and patent applications and specifications. In a journal most formal items including articles, essays, discussions and reviews can be expected to be accompanied by an abstract. Although such abstracts are valuable, they are not directly relevant to the systems for the organisation of knowledge (although, obviously these abstracts do contribute to the organisation of knowledge).

Abstracts have for some years been a major component in published abstracting services, literature reviews and bibliographies. Large bibliographic data bases also use abstracts as the primary means of document representation. It follows naturally that many retrospective search services and current awareness services derived from or associated with these data bases also feature abstracts. Wherever abstracts are found they are included to save the user's time in information gathering and selection.

There are a number of types of abstracts or labels that can be applied to abstracts. The most appropriate type of abstract must be chosen in accordance with the requirements of each individual application. The most appropriate type of abstract will be a function of the nature of the original document (for example, language, length, audience level), and intended audience of the abstract, and the resources of the abstracting agency. Some of the different types of abstracts are worth examining since they demonstrate in more detail the various functions of abstracts.

Informative abstracts present as much as possible of the quantitative or qualitative information contained in a document. The objective is to aid the assessment of document relevance, and, at the same time, to offer a substitute for the document when only a superficial knowledge of document content is required. Thus an informative abstract actually conveys some of the information in the original, rather than restricting itself to reporting what information is available in the original. Informative abstracts tend to be relatively lengthy. Abstracts of journal articles merit 100 to 250 words, whilst abstracts of lengthy theses or reports may extend to 500 words. Informative abstracts are appropriate for texts describing experimental work, and documents with a central theme. A fully informative abstract may often be impossible to write for a wide-ranging discussion paper or review, since these documents are likely to cover a large number of separate concepts. To cover each of these concepts informatively would lead to an excessively long abstract. A working guide is to seek to make any abstract as informative as possible within the constraints of time, length and audience.

Indicative abstracts are suitable for discussions and review article books, and in some circumstances, conference proceedings, reports without conclusions, essays and bibliographies. An indicative abstract restricts itself to indicating the content of an item and makes general statements about the document. Indicative abstracts abound in phrases such as 'is discussed' or 'has been surveyed', but do not record the outcome of the discussion or survey. An indicative abstract is merely a sophisticated selection aid. An indicative abstract can be written more quickly than an informative abstract, and requires less perception and subject expertise on the part of the abstractor.

Indicative-informative abstracts are more common than either the purely indicative or the purely informative abstract. Parts of the abstract are written in the informative style, whilst those points which are of less significance are treated indicatively. When used by skilled abstractors this mixture of styles can achieve the maximum transmission of information, within a minimum length.

Although *critical abstracts* are unusual they are often favoured by users (until they discover the cost!). A critical abstract evaluates a document and the work that it records. Typically a critical abstract will note the depth and extent of the work, commenting upon the experimentation and methodology, the assumed background of the intended audience, and the significance of the contribution to the development of knowledge. A critical approach to abstracts permits the abstractor to highlight particularly worthwhile documents, and to dismiss those that have little new to say. In practice critical abstracts are rare, and certainly do not usually feature in published secondary services. In order to prepare effective critical abstracts the abstractor needs a sound knowledge of the subject field, and of the literature of the subject field, in addition to abstracting skills. Such abstractors are expensive to employ.

There are a number of types of abstract which will be grouped under the term '*mini-abstracts*'. To start with it should be remembered that a title is a fair indication of document content, and many indexes and current awareness services rely almost entirely upon titles. Short abstracts comprising only one or two sentences may be valuable in current awareness services where speed is essential, such as newsletters for local government officers, and commercial current awareness services. Telegraphic abstracts are written in a note form or in a telegram style. Keywords or indexing terms may serve as a crude indicator of subject scope of a document.

Statistical, tabular and numerical abstracts are a means of summarising numerical data, which may be presented in its original format in a tabular form. Normally the most effective way of summarising a table is to produce a simplified table. Such abstracts can be useful for various types of economic, social and business information.

There are other kinds of abstracts, but this introduction should demonstrate some of the possibilities. The examples in Figure 5.1 make possible some useful comparisons between the different types of abstracts.

5.4 Manual files

Files of small documents such as leaflets and newspaper cuttings are a means of storing full text. Such files are important means of storing small

Figure 5.1 Some examples of types of abstracts

Informative abstract

A Future for printed indexes? J E Rowley
Aslib Proceedings, 35(4), May 1983, 234-238.

Printed indexes are still common despite the increasing scope of online information retrieval systems. Printed indexes are currently used as book indexes, periodical indexes, indexes to directories and other quick reference sources and indexing services and the indexes to abstracting services. Particularly with regard to this last category online information retrieval offers an attractive alternative. To what extent is the printed index likely to be superseded in the future? In book and periodical indexes an important factor in the future of the printed index will be the desirability of keeping the index in the same physical form as the document(s) which it indexes. Printed indexes in directories will persist as long as the directories themselves are still available in the printed form. Indexing services and indexes to abstracting services are likely to be more threatened by online information retrieval systems, although economic factors are important.

Continued

Figure 5.1 Continued

Indicative abstract

A Future for printed indexes? J E Rowley
Aslib Proceedings, 35(4) May 1983, 234-238.

The present applications of printed indexes in books, periodicals, quick reference sources and indexing and abstracting publications are considered, and the future for printed indexes in each of these spheres is examined. The printed index is often a supplement to the document which it indexes. For each of the four categories of printed index two questions are explored: whether the documents indexed will continue in printed form; and whether it will continue to be unacceptable to have the index and document in different physical forms.

Extract

A Future for printed indexes? J E Rowley
Aslib Proceedings, 35(4), May 1983, 234-238.

The availability of machine-readable indexes will have some impact on whether printed indexes cease to be important, but also, on the style and comprehensiveness of the future printed index.

Short abstract

A Future for printed indexes? J E Rowley
Aslib Proceedings, 35(4), May 1983, 234-238.

The present applications of printed indexes in books, periodicals, quick reference sources and indexing and abstracting publications are considered, and the future for printed indexes in each of these spheres is examined.

Keywords

A Future for printed indexes? J E Rowley
Aslib Proceedings, 35(4), May 1983, 234-238.

Printed indexes; book indexes; periodical indexes; indexing services; abstracting services; online information retrieval; data bases.

items, and in some senses can be regarded as the forerunners of full text data bases. These manual files are still important in the organisation of small collections of materials, both in libraries and in personal collections.

Physical form of files

Accessibility to the documents stored in files is an important factor, so the physical storage is important. A number of relatively straightforward possibilities exist:

1. Drawers of standard filing cabinets, with folders or pockets, or both. Folders allow a set of papers to be kept together when a set on a given topic is removed from the file. Pockets maintain a space for each category.
2. File boxes can be used and filed on shelves, if appropriate, interfiled with the books. This arrangement may facilitate browsing across different kinds of materials.
3. Upright divider filing is a variation on filing cabinets.
4. Guard book or scrapbook type arrangement, with possibly a loose-leaf format, is suitable for organising and keeping cuttings, letters and other small items. The drawbacks of this form are its limited flexibility, and the time taken in maintenance.
5. Small documents, such as cuttings, can alternatively be mounted on catalogue cards.
6. Aperture cards, where the full text of the document is kept in a special index card in the form of a microfiche, have been used for various collections of, for instance, patents and technical drawings.

Headings

Each file will be labelled with a heading which corresponds with the material to be organised. The possible types of headings are various, but in many files the headings will be subject headings of some kind. These headings may be drawn from an alphabetical list of subject headings or from a classification scheme. Apart from the names of subjects, the names of corporate bodies, persons, chemicals, trade products, and trade names are some other possibilities. For example a set of slides for use by teachers may be indexed according to alphabetical subject headings. A set of government publications could be filed alphabetically by the issuing bureau, and then by title of the particular series in numerical order.

The principles for the construction of headings for use in files are the same as those principles for the construction of similar types of headings in other indexes, with the exception that the limitations listed below may pose some problems.

Leaving aperture cards aside, all files have some limitations in common:

1. Files only work effectively for a limited number of documents. If the number of categories becomes large, cross-references will be necessary between individual files. If the number of items in one category becomes large, then the user must scan a larger number of items in order to identify relevant items.
2. Items in a file can only be stored in one place, and in one sequence. It follows that only a limited number of relationships can be displayed, and retrieval tends to be inflexible.
3. Files are difficult to publish or disseminate in any form.

Figure 5.2 Data on NEXIS

```
    CLIENT:HICKORY CAST IRON-ACQUISITION
      DATE:MARCH 26, 1981
   LIBRARY:NEXIS General & Business Information
                 Stories From Newspapers,
                 Magazines, & Wire Services
      FILE:MAGS -Combined file of magazine
                 stories

Your search request is:
WOOD W/7 STOVE OR BURN!|
AND ENVIRONMENT! W/12 WOODLAND OR FOREST OR TREE

Number of STORIES found with your search request through:
  LEVEL 1...   129  LEVEL 2...   4

If you want to save and resume your research on this problem later
today (until 02:00 A.M. Eastern Time), press the Y key (for YES) and
then the TRANSMIT key. If you do not, press the N key (for NO) and
then the TRANSMIT key.

After you exercise one of the above options, the time used in this
research session will be displayed.

If you do not want to end this research session, press the SIGN-OFF
key again. For further explanation, press the H key (for HELP) and
then the TRANSMIT key.
```

Continued

Against these limitations, it must be remembered that files are quick to compile, and give direct retrieval (no index is necessary as an intermediate guide). The approach or basic arrangement of the file can be supplemented by additional approaches in supplementary indexes.

5.5 Full text computer data bases or data banks

Over the past two to three years the number of full text data bases and data banks has started to escalate considerably. Many reference sources which were once available only in hard copy are now available either in hard copy (sometimes both microform and paper), or to be consulted by online access to a computer-held data base. As was earlier the case with

Figure 5.2 Continued

LEVEL 2-1 OF 4 STORIES

Copyright (c) 1980 Congressional Quarterly;
Editorial Research Reports--The Report

November 21, 1980

PAGE: Vol. II; No. 19; Pg. 843

LENGTH: 8680 words
HEADLINE: AIR POLLUTION CONTROL: PROGRESS AND PROSPECTS

BYLINE: by William Sweet

BODY:
... a regulated pollutant, with nitrous oxides, which are harmless products of plant respiration. Gus Speth, chairman of the president's Council on Environmental Quality (CEQ), pointed out that soil bacteria -- not trees --are the primary source of nitrous oxides. Calling Reagan's remarks "strange and bewildering," Speth said that human sources emit sulfur ...

... states, the Northwest and even the Southwest to heat their homes with wood. More than one-third of the households in New England now burn wood for

Above: How the research material is displayed on NEXIS for easy browsing—screen by screen

(from Mead Data Central)

bibliographic data bases, such as those related to abstracting and indexing journals, the creation of a data base is a step in the creation of the printed product, and it makes sense to make this directly available, especially since the communications technology exists in order to make it possible to offer such facilities. Standard reference works, such as *Ulrich's Periodicals Directory* are now available online in full text (although this might also be referred to as a bibliographic data base).

Other full text data bases include the *Bowker Biographical Data base*, which offers citations and abstracts for 1971 to 1981, and full text records from 1982. This includes on the data base, *American Men and Women of Science*. *Harvard Business Review Online* covers not only the text of the *Review*, but also references cited in articles. In this sense, this is a partly bibliographic and partly full text data base.

LEXIS and NEXIS are two important full text data bases from Mead Data Central. Together they constitute the world's largest data base. LEXIS is a retrieval system for legal documents. In addition to its coverage of reported cases since 1945, there are twenty-nine series of law reports, including:

All England Law Reports
Building Law Reports
Criminal Appeal Reports
Local Government Reports
Patent Cases
Weekly Law Reports.

NEXIS covers various financial, business and economic newspapers, such as *American Banker, Bond Buyer, Washington Post*, and various magazines, including *ABA Banking Journal, Bank Administration, Business Week, Chemical Engineering, Dun's Business Month*, and the *Oil and Gas Journal*. Since 1983, NEXIS has covered material previously available through the *New York Times* Information bank. (See Figure 5.2.)

Martindale is a large directory of drugs produced by the Pharmaceutical Society of Great Britain. Figure 5.3 shows a search in *Martindale Online*, the online version of the directory, and the record which results from the search. The full text of the directory is available online.

Other full text data bases are mentioned in 19.7.

5.6 Videotex and teletext

Videotex and teletext systems could be regarded as full text. They normally give information, such as statistics, or addresses or other factual information on the topics that they cover. However, it is possible for

Figure 5.3 Martindale Online

QUESTION:	What nomenclature information is there in Martindale Online on the compound with CAS Registry Number 51-30-9?
SEARCH:	51-30-9
RESULT:	1

PRINT SUMMARY: AN 2074-h.
    TI   Isoprenaline Hydrochloride (B.P.).
    RF Drug Definition and Description.
    LE 1271 Characters.
    ED Jan. 1983.

PRINT: AN 2074-h.
    TI   Isoprenaline Hydrochloride (B.P.).
    RF Drug Definition and Description.
    LE 1271 Characters.
    ED Jan. 1983.
    SY Isoprenalini Hydrochloridum;
          Isoproterenol Hydrochloride (U.S.P.);
          Isopropylarterenol Hydrochloride;
          Isopropylnoradrenaline
          Hydrochloride.
          1-(3, 4-Dihydroxyphenyl)-2-
          isopropylaminoethanol hydrochloride.
    MO $C_{11}H_{17}NO_3.HCl$ (247.7).
    RN 7683-59-2 (isoprenaline);
          51-30-9 (hydrochloride).
    PC In Arg., Br., Braz., Chin., Hung., Int., Roum., Turk., and U.S.
    TX A white or almost white, odourless or almost odourless, crystalline powder with a slightly bitter taste. It gradually darkens on exposure to air and light. M.p. 165 degrees to 170 degrees with decomposition. Soluble 1 in less than 1 of water and 1 in 50 to 55 of alcohol; less soluble in dehydrated alcohol; practically insoluble in chloroform and ether. A 1% solution in water has a pH of about 5. Solutions are sterilised by filtration and stored in ampoules, the air in which is

Continued

Figure 5.3 Continued

DE   replaced by nitrogen or other suitable gas. Solutions become pink to brownish-pink on standing exposed to air and almost immediately so when made alkaline. Store in airtight containers. Protect from light.

DE   isoprenaline, des, pharm, deterioration, stability, light, phase-change-point, solubility, solution, ph, filtration-sterilisation, storage, packaging.

This sample question shows a drug definition and description record and a search with a CAS number.

---

bibliographic data bases to be made available through videotex systems. For example the library catalogue may be made available through a videotex. system.

Videotex systems were conceived as a means of providing easy access to information held on a central computer. Access is via a modified television set, a telephone (and its connections) and a simple keypad. Prestel is British Telecom's videotex service, and was started in 1979. Although the original aim of British Telecom was to penetrate the domestic market, most of the terminals are in the business sector. Many public libraries participated in various of the Prestel trials. The information available on Prestel changes as the information providers come and go. The information is provided by around three hundred information providers which gives around 160,000 screens of information that can be viewed. Information providers pay a fee to British Telecom, and may then charge users for each frame that they consult. Access to frames is through a menu-based system, whereby the user is offered a number of options on each screen and must choose the appropriate label for the information that he wishes to retrieve by keying the appropriate number. Videotex services are being made available in other countries, including Canada, Finland, France, the Netherlands, Switzerland and West Germany. Closed user groups, for organisations such as the travel trade have been popular, and some large organisations are establishing their own videotex systems.

Teletext services are broadcast information services which may be accessed in a non-interactive mode. These services may be accessed with a television and a telephone line, but tend to be limited in the quantity of information that they can carry, and so may be mainly restricted to summary financial and business statistics, news (international, national and local), weather, and so on.

5.7 The electronic journal

With teleconferencing and the availability of various compilations of data and text online, the natural proposal is for an electronic journal, which makes use of telecommunications networks and computer storage to enable scientists and others to interact and communicate research in a new technology-based mode. Thus the electronic journal is a concept where scientists are able to input ideas and text to a computer data base for their colleagues to view, and similarly to view the work of others. Various modes of operation are possible for such a journal, and the precise operation will depend upon the type of information being conveyed. Some possibilities are: chit-chat, work messages, news about the electronic journal network, an enquiry answer system between experts, a bulletin, an annotated abstracts journal, discussion and questions on papers, a poster papers journal and a referred journal. These options obviously range from the very informal to the very formal.

Two major projects in this area have been conducted to date. The first electronic journal was established with funding from the National Science Foundation on the EIES network and ran from 1976 to 1980. More recently, the BLEND project was established by the British Library as a co-operative effort between Birmingham University and Loughborough University. The topic of the journal was Computer Human Factors. This started in 1980, and has around forty members who receive some support to cover telephone charges. The journal is a traditional referred journal. So contributions are input to the data base, then referred, and any suggestions made by the referee are communicated through the data base to the editor. Then these suggestions can be picked up by the editor, and communicated to the author. Communication can continue through the same medium until eventually the paper is accepted. This process has the advantage of retaining the refereeing and editing processes whilst streamlining communication, and removing the need for the costly stages of journal production such as printing, publishing, marketing and distribution. When the basic feasibility and desirability of the electronic journal has been assessed it will be necessary to consider the organisation and indexing of contributions in these journals, and the bibliographic control of such journals. However, it must be stressed that these problems are still in the future.

5.8 Some comparisons

It will be a long time before all documents are available in machine-readable form, and even then it is likely that documents will continue to be available in more than one form. Improvements in document delivery services, via the further application of techniques such as facsimile transmission will also have an important role to play. Figure 5.4 attempts to summarise some of the strengths of the two alternatives.

Figure 5.4 A comparison of full text data bases against hard copy

Full text data base	Hard paper copy
1. Pay-as-you-go costs, therefore, cheap for occasional use.	Pay once only, and make investment. Cheaper for extensive multiple use by an uncontrolled public.
2. Updated regularly, sometimes continuously or every day or week.	Updated less frequently, for example, monthly, annually, or even five-yearly.

3. Even where the frequency of updating is the same, the time lag in availability of information will usually be less for the electronic version.

4. Users may be able to edit, modify and otherwise contribute to the data base.	Publication and printing fixes the information. Note that sometimes this stability is welcome.
5. Greater range of retrieval facilities are possible, for example free text searching.	Retrieval is limited by the printed indexes which are offered.
6. More options for formatting output - any printed copy is controlled by the user.	Format of output is determined.
7. Portability and convenience limited.	Very portable, depending on whether it belongs to the user only.
8. Terminals must be available.	No terminals, networks or other technology are necessary.

Chapter 5 Readings

A. Abstracts

1 American National Standards Institute, *American national standard for writing abstracts.* ANSI: New York, 1971.
2 American Petroleum Institute, *API abstracts of refining literature: abstractors' manual.* API: New York, 1969.
3 American Psychological Association, *Guide for volunteer abstractors.* APA: Washington, DC. (undated)

4 Ashworth, W. 'Abstractors', in *Handbook of special librarianship and information work*, 3rd edition. Aslib: London 1967, 453–81. 4th edition. Aslib: London, 1975, 124–52.

5 Ashworth, W., 'Abstracting as a fine art', *Information Scientist*, 7, 1973, 43–53.

6 Borko, H. and Bernier, C.L. *Abstracting concepts and methods*. Academic Press: New York, 1975.

7 Borko, H. and Chatman, S., 'Criteria for acceptable abstracts: a survey of abstractors' instructions', *American Documentation*, 14, 1963, 149–60.

8 Chemical Abstracts Service, Directions for abstractors, 1971, revision, Ohio State University: Ohio, 1971.

9 International Organisation for Standardisation, Documentation: abstracts for publication and documentation. ISO: Geneva, 1976.

B. Other tools

10 Carr, R., 'Prestel in the test trial: an academic library user looks back', *Journal of Librarianship*, 12(3), 1980, 145–58.

11 Clarke, K.E. and Childs, G.H.L. 'The future of videotex', *Electronic publishing review*, 1(1), 1981, 43–51.

12 Fedida, S. and Malik, R., *The viewdata revolution*. Associated Business Press, 1979.

13 Lancaster, F.W., *Towards paperless information systems*, Academic Press: New York, 1978.

14 Martyn, J., 'Prestel and public libraries: an LA/Aslib experiment', *Aslib Proceedings*, 31(5), 1979, 216–36.

15 Money, S.A., *Teletext and Viewdata*, Newnes: London, 1980. (Technical aspects).

16 Plakias, M., 'New electronic media: the future and co-operation', *RQ* 20(1), 1980, 66–9.

17 Shackel, B. *et al.*, 'The BLEND-LINC project on electronic journals ater two years', *Aslib Proceedings*, 35(2), 1982, 77–91.

18 Singleton, A., 'The electronic journal and its relatives', *Scholarly Publishing*, 13(1), 1981, 3–18.

19 *Videotext: the coming revolution in home/office information retrieval*, eds E. Sigel *et al.*, Knowledge Industry Publications: White Plains, N.Y.: 1980.

6   Computerised record formats

6.1 Record formats

The information which is stored in data bases and data banks must be organised in a way that makes it easy to retrieve. A data base is comprised of a series of records. A *record* is the information contained in a data base relating to one document, for example, all the cataloguing information pertaining to a specific document. Records are composed of a number of fields. The type of fields used, their length, and the number of fields in a record must be chosen in accordance with a specific application. For a bibliographic data base, a field will generally be provided for each important element of the bibliographic record, for example, classification number, author, title, edition, indexing terms.

There are two types of field. A *fixed length field* is a field which has the same length, that is, contains the same number of characters in each record. With this degree of consistency, it is not necessary to signal to the computer the beginning and end of any given field. The lengths of the fields are determined when the data base is designed, and notified to the computer just once. Fixed length fields then are economical on storage space, and records using fixed length fields are quick and easy to code. The drawback of fixed length fields is their rigidity. Fixed length fields are entirely satisfactory when the length of the unit of information to be inserted is predictable, and the field length can be set to coincide with the length of the data. Fixed length fields are acceptable, therefore, particularly for codes, for example, ISBNs, dates, language codes, journal codes, identity numbers, membership numbers. For many other types of information fixed length fields can be inconvenient. For example, if a title field is defined to be sixty characters in length, any title exceeding sixty characters will be truncated after the sixtieth character, and the end of the title will not be stored or displayed. With variable length data a *variable length field* is more appropriate. A variable length field takes different lengths in different records. Thus a name field might contain thirty characters in one record, and forty-five in the next record. Obviously, the computer cannot recognise when one field ends and the next starts – the computer merely sees the whole record as a series of characters. Since the fields are of different lengths in different records it is necessary that the beginning and end of fields be flagged in some way.

Bibliographic data bases often use a variety of fixed and variable length fields. The formats discussed below demonstrate the use of a mixture of field types.

Within fields, individual data elements or units of information may be designated as *subfields*. Subfields can only be identified if similar data elements can be expected within a given field across a number of records. Thus, in a name field it is easy to recognise that the data elements – family name, and forename – will occur in many records, and these two data elements can be identified as possible subfields of the same field. Subfields are also usually flagged in some way.

In order to pursue this discussion further, it is necessary to consider some specific examples of record formats. The next sections describe a variety of record formats.

6.2 The MARC record format

The large cataloguing record data bases are structured according to a format known as the MARC format. MARC stands for *Ma*chine *R*eadable *C*ataloguing. The Library of Congress, the British Library and national cataloguing agencies in countries such as Canada, Australia, West Germany and France all produce catalogue records in the MARC format. These national catalogue record data bases are used by libraries in catalogue creations. Records for the stock of a specific library are downloaded from the national data bases and added to the data base of catalogue records for the individual library. Thus, libraries using the national catalogue record data bases will either use the MARC format for their catalogue records, or use 'stripped down' versions of MARC or other modifications of the MARC record format. Thus, with respect to catalogue records the MARC record format is important.

The MARC record format was designed by the Library of Congress and the British Library with the aim of constructing bibliographic records in a machine-readable form which facilitated re-formatting for a wide variety of purposes. Early trials around 1966, conducted by the Library of Congress, used the MARC I format, but this was superseded by MARC II or MARC in 1967. As the number of countries using the MARC format expanded, the variations on the basic MARC format proliferated. These variations led to a need for the UNIMARC format in order that catalogue records could be exchanged on an international basis. National agencies creating MARC records use national standards within their own country, and re-format records to UNIMARC for international exchange. The comments that follow relate to UK MARC. Both UK MARC and UNIMARC comply with ISO 2709, the international standard for bibliographic record interchange on magnetic tape.

The MARC format includes up to sixty-one data elements, of which twenty-five are directly searchable. The format is compatible with the second edition of AACR and the nineteenth edition of the Dewey Decimal Classification Scheme (DDC 19) and will be modified to accommodate new editions of these standard cataloguing tools.

The MARC format comprises two sections: section 1 which gives information describing the bibliographic data and section 2 which holds the bibliographic data itself. Thus a segment of magnetic tape for three records could be imagined as:

Record 1		Record 2		Record 3	
Section 1	Section 2	Section 1	Section 2	Section 1	Section 2

Section 2 is comprised entirely of variable length fields. In order to signal the beginning of each field each field is identified by a three character *tag* followed by two numeric indicators. Each field also ends with a special delimiter, which signals the end of the fields. Tags consist of three numerals within the range 000–945. The tags have a mnemonic structure; the numerical value of the tags is consistent with the order of the components of a catalogue record, and the tags for added entries headings follow those for main entry headings. Some of the chief tags are:

100 Personal author main entry heading
110 Corporate name main entry heading
240 Uniform title
245 Title and statement of responsibility
250 Edition and statement of edition author, editor and so on.
260 Imprint
300 Collation
440 Series statement
5-- Notes.

Now, consistency is exhibited between tags in that, for instance, '00' will always appear in the second and third positions in a tag if the field contains a personal name. So

100 is used for a main entry personal author heading
600 is used for a subject entry personal name heading
700 is used for an added entry personal author heading.

In addition to a tag, each of the main fields also has two field *indicators*; indicators are used to distinguish between the different types of information that can be entered in the same field. Indicators might suggest the need for title added entries, show the number of characters to be dropped in filing titles, and signal whether information such as edition and imprint statements relate to a part or the whole of a multi-part work. To take an example, in the field for main entry under a corporate author heading, the following indicators are used in conjunction with the tag 110:

110.10 Name of government
110.20 Corporate name excluding name of government.

Many fields in a catalogue record contain smaller distinct units, known as subfields. For example the imprint field includes subfields for the place of publication, the publisher and the date of publication. All subfields are preceded by a subfield code, which consists of a single symbol, for example $ followed by a single letter, for example b. Thus an imprint field might be coded as:

260.00 $a London $b Mitchell Beazley $c 1983

with tag, indicators and subfield codes. Subfield codes are re-defined for each field. For example the subfield code b will signal different subfields in different fields. Nevertheless, where consistent subfield codes are appropriate, the same codes will be used in different fields. Thus, for instance, the subfield code used to designate the forename part of a personal name heading is always the same, whether the heading is in respect of a main entry, an added subject, or author entry.

Section 1 includes the record label, the directory and the control fields. Only the control fields are input by the cataloguer; the other two components are supplied by the computer. The control fields contain coded data such as the record control number, for example ISBN, language of the text, an intellectual level code, a country of publication code. These fields control the access to the main record and are all fixed length fields. Each record commences with a label and a directory. The label contains information about the record, indicating, for instance, its length, status (for example, new, amended), type and class. The directory is a finding list which lists for every field its tag, the number of characters in the field, and the starting character position of the field within the record.

Figures 6.1 and 6.2 show some screen formats and records for catalogue data bases.

6.3 Bibliographic record formats in non-cataloguing applications

Most of the centralised and shared cataloguing projects take account of and probably use the MARC record format. This degree of standardisation is not the pattern outside of this specific area of application. Essentially there are two different categories of systems which may be encountered: external data bases such as those discussed in Chapter 19, and local systems supported by software packages, such as those discussed in Chapter 20.

For the large data bases, there has been little pressure to accept a standard format, and each data base producer has in general chosen a record format to suit his particular data base. A review of the variety of citation practices which may be encountered in abstracting and indexing services for referring to periodical articles should be sufficient to demonstrate the differences between the elements to be included in a record between different agencies (see Chapter 4). As demonstrated by Figure 6.3 which

Figure 6.1 An online record from BLCMP online cataloguing, including general and local records

General record

```
LEADER        1 am 2200325  B      g
001         013550855×+
008 0       800829s1979  uk ak    00011    eng +
100 0 10   `aYourdon`hEdward+
245 0 00   `aManaging the structured techniques`d(by) Edward Yourdon+
250 0 00   `2nd ed+
260 0 00   `aEnglewood Cliffs`aLondon (etc.)`bPrentice-Hall`c1979+
300 0 00   `avi,266p`bill, form`c24 cm+
350 0 00   `a£16.20+
440 0 00   `aPrentice-Hall software series+

General record from UNION          Local record from UNION
LIBCODES SH MP KP PP
```

Local record

```
001      001    (013550855x)    Local Monograph Format

Leader   Lea    Status (r)    Title a/e (1)    CA Exclu ( )    Sp Coll( )
                Retro ( )      No of copies (01)

008   008   WIP ( )  Loan ( )  Wants ( )  Sp class ( )  How obt ( )
            Dept sugg ( )  Phys form ( )  Bind Code ( )  Sp coll ( )
            UC Code ( )  Bib int ( )  Stat Anal ( )

009 1 00  `a0123456 0123457+
009 2 00  `a0123458+
030 1 00  `aJD+
030 2 00  `aBB+
060 0 00  `a658.91+
065 0 00  `aYOU+
```

Figure 6.2 Catalogue input formatted screens from ADLIB, from LMR Information Systems

```
NEXT (    )  SCREEN (1REC)  TASK (alter )            REF. 50000101
KEY (01655515                                    )

                    COPY RECEIPT LOGGING SCREEN


Title                    Journal of Information Science
                         Jourof
                         01655515        Copy no 1


Enter details of next expected issue here:
Vol no (5  )     Part no (9  )    Date (SEPT83  )    Due 01/10/83

If issue received is in the table below, enter the date received:

Vol   Part  Date of issue Date due    Received  Circd   Claimed

(5  ) (8  ) (AUG83    )  (01/09/83) (15/09/83)
(5  ) (7  ) (JUL83    )  (01/08/83) (13/08/83)   Y
(5  ) (6  ) (JUNE83   )  (01/07/83) (14/06/82)   Y
(5  ) (5  ) (MAY83    )  (01/06/83) (14/06/83)   Y
(5  ) (4  ) (APRL83   )  (01/05/83) (15/05/83)   Y
(5  ) (3  ) (MAR83    )  (01/04/83) (14/04/83)   Y

If this issue is not indicated above, enter details here:
Vol no ( )          Part no ( )          Date( )       Recvd ( )
```

```
NEXT (   )      SCREEN (2MRC)      TASK (find )      REF. 37
KEY (layzell/                                   )
                CATALOGUE INPUT/EDIT—MARC FORMAT
Title:
  245.(  ) $a (Introductory guide to research in librarianship and     )
           (Information studies in the UK.                             )
           (                  Local record                            )
Personal author(s):
  100.(  ) $a (Layzell-Ward, P (editor)           )
  700.(  ) $a (Burkett, J (editor)                )
  700.(  ) $a (Whiteman, P (editor)               )

Corporate author:
  110.(  ) $a (                                                        )
Publication details:
  260.(  ) $a (                                                        )
Edition:
  250.(  ) $a (                                                        )
Collation:
  300.00 $a (80pp                                                      )
Language: 008 $1 (           )         ISBN: 021.10 $a (0853650586)
Class no: 082.00 $a (025.4            )
Notes:
  513.(  ) $a (LA pamphlet no 37                                       )
```

89

Figure 6.3 BRS

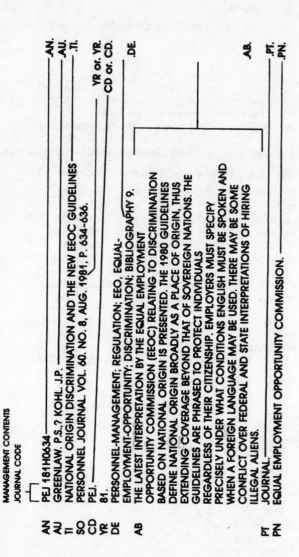

BRS
Bibliographic Retrieval Service

MANAGEMENT CONTENTS
JOURNAL CODE

AN	PEJ 181H0634	AN.
AU	GREENLAW. P.S.,? KOHL. J.P.	AU.
TI	NATIONAL ORIGIN DISCRIMINATION AND THE NEW EEOC GUIDELINES	.TI.
SO	PERSONNEL JOURNAL. VOL. 60. NO. 8, AUG. 1981, P. 634-636.	
CD	PEJ.	YR or. YR. / CD or. CD.
YR	81.	
DE	PERSONNEL-MANAGEMENT; REGULATION; EEO. EQUAL-EMPLOYMENT-OPPORTUNITY; DISCRIMINATION; BIBLIOGRAPHY 9.	DE.
AB	THE LATEST INTERPRETATION BY THE EQUAL EMPLOYMENT OPPORTUNITY COMMISSION (EEOC) RELATING TO DISCRIMINATION BASED ON NATIONAL ORIGIN IS PRESENTED. THE 1980 GUIDELINES DEFINE NATIONAL ORIGIN BROADLY AS A PLACE OF ORIGIN, THUS EXTENDING COVERAGE BEYOND THAT OF SOVEREIGN NATIONS. THE GUIDELINES ARE PHRASED TO PROTECT INDIVIDUALS REGARDLESS OF THEIR CITIZENSHIP. EMPLOYERS MUST SPECIFY PRECISELY UNDER WHAT CONDITIONS ENGLISH MUST BE SPOKEN AND WHEN A FOREIGN LANGUAGE MAY BE USED. THERE MAY BE SOME CONFLICT OVER FEDERAL AND STATE INTERPRETATIONS OF HIRING ILLEGAL ALIENS.	AB.
PT	JOURNAL.	.PT.
PN	EQUAL EMPLOYMENT OPPORTUNITY COMMISSION.	.PN.

Continued

BRS FILE NAME: MGMT

PARAGRAPH NAME	PARAGRAPH QUALIFICATION	EXAMPLE
Abstract	AB.	EEOC SAME CITIZENSHIP .AB.
Accession Number	AN.	PEJ81H0634
Author	AU.	KOHLAU.
Journal Code	CD or .CD.	.LIMIT/N CD EQ PEJ or PEJ .CD.
Proper Names	PN.	EQUAL ADJ EMPLOYMENT .PN.
Publication Type	PT.	JOURNAL .PT.
Publication Year	YR or .YR.	.LIMIT/N YR=81 or 81 .YR.
Source	I	DISPLAY ONLY
Special Feature	DE.	BIBLIOGRAPHY .DE.
Subject Descriptors	DE.	REGULATION .DE.
Title	TI.	DISCRIMINANTS WITH GUIDELINES .TI.
Update	UP or .UP.	.LIMIT/N UP 8110

91

Figure 6.3 Continued

92

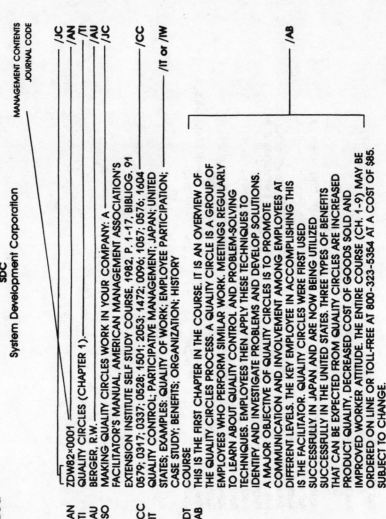

SDC
System Development Corporation

MANAGEMENT CONTENTS
JOURNAL CODE

AN ZDW82×0001 ———————————— /JC
TI QUALITY CIRCLES (CHAPTER 1). ——————— /AN
AU BERGER, R.W. ———————————————— /TI
SO MAKING QUALITY CIRCLES WORK IN YOUR COMPANY: A —— /AU
    FACILITATOR'S MANUAL, AMERICAN MANAGEMENT ASSOCIATION'S —— /JC
    EXTENSION INSTITUTE SELF STUDY COURSE, 1982, P. 1-17, BIBLIOG. 91
    0579; 0317; 0337; 0528; 1501; 2053; 1472; 0096; 1057; 0576; 1604
CC QUALITY CONTROL; PARTICIPATIVE MANAGEMENT; JAPAN; UNITED ———— /CC
IT STATES; EXAMPLES: QUALITY OF WORK; EMPLOYEE PARTICIPATION;
    CASE STUDY; BENEFITS; ORGANIZATION; HISTORY ——————— /IT or /IW
DT COURSE
AB THIS IS THE FIRST CHAPTER IN THE COURSE. IT IS AN OVERVIEW OF
    THE QUALITY CIRCLES PROCESS. A QUALITY CIRCLE IS A GROUP OF
    EMPLOYEES WHO PERFORM SIMILAR WORK. MEETINGS REGULARLY
    TO LEARN ABOUT QUALITY CONTROL AND PROBLEM-SOLVING
    TECHNIQUES. EMPLOYEES THEN APPLY THESE TECHNIQUES TO
    IDENTIFY AND INVESTIGATE PROBLEMS AND DEVELOP SOLUTIONS.
    A MAJOR OBJECTIVE OF QUALITY CIRCLES IS TO PROMOTE
    COMMUNICATION AND INVOLVEMENT AMONG EMPLOYEES AT
    DIFFERENT LEVELS. THE KEY EMPLOYEE IN ACCOMPLISHING THIS
    IS THE FACILITATOR. QUALITY CIRCLES WERE FIRST USED
    SUCCESSFULLY IN JAPAN AND ARE NOW BEING UTILIZED
    SUCCESSFULLY IN THE UNITED STATES. THREE TYPES OF BENEFITS
    THAT CAN BE EXPECTED FROM QUALITY CIRCLES ARE INCREASED
    PRODUCT QUALITY, DECREASED COST OF GOODS SOLD AND
    IMPROVED WORKER ATTITUDE. THE ENTIRE COURSE (CH. 1-9) MAY BE
    ORDERED ON LINE OR TOLL-FREE AT 800-323-5354 AT A COST OF $85.
    SUBJECT TO CHANGE. ———————————————————— /AB

SDC FILE NAME: MANAGEMENT

ELEMENT NAME	QUALIFIER	EXAMPLE
Abstract	/AB	STRS/AB: WORKER: ATTITUDE:
Accession Number	/AN	ZDW82X0001/AN
Author	/AU	ALL BERGER, R:/AU
Category Code	/CC	1604/CC
Index Terms	/IT or /IW	QUALITY CONTROL/IT
Journal Code	/JC	ZDW/JC
Journal Name	/JC	/JC MAKING AND QUALITY:
Publication Year	–	n AND 82-82
Source	–	DISPLAY ONLY
Title	/TI	ALL QUALITY:/TI AND CIRCLES/TI
Update Code	/UP	8211/UP

93

Figure 6.3 Continued

DIALOG

JC=   MANAGEMENT CONTENTS DOCUMENT CODE

DIALOG ACCESSION NUMBER   252973   IRL8320283

OSHA'S GENERAL DUTY CLAUSE: AN ANALYSIS OF ITS USE AND ABUSE.   TI=or/TI

AU=   MORGAN, D.L.; DUVALL, M.N.

JN=   INDUSTRIAL RELATIONS LAW JOURNAL. VOL. 5, NO. 2, 1983.

P. 283-321., JOURNAL. BIBLIOG. 25   PY=

SECTION 5(A)(1) OF THE OCCUPATIONAL SAFETY AND HEALTH ACT   SF=
(OSHA) KNOWN AS THE GENERAL DUTY CLAUSE, REQUIRES
EMPLOYERS TO FURNISH EMPLOYMENT AND AN EMPLOYMENT PLACE
FREE FROM RECOGNIZED HAZARDS. AN OVERVIEW OF THE ACT AND
THE LEGISLATIVE HISTORY OF THE GENERAL DUTY CLAUSE INDICATES

DT=   THAT THE INTENT OF CONGRESS IN ITS ENACTMENT WAS TO
SUBORDINATE THE CLAUSE TO SPECIFIC STANDARDS PROMULGATED
AND ENFORCED BY OSHA. IT IS CONTENDED THAT INSTEAD OSHA HAS
OVERUSED THE CLAUSE BECAUSE OF ITS OWN INEFFICIENCIES. TO
CURE THIS ABUSE, OSHA IS URGED TO PROMULGATE PERFORMANCE
STANDARDS AND ADVISORY GUIDELINES.   /AB

JU=   JURISDICTION: UNITED STATES

CN=   INDUSTRIAL UNION DEPT., AFL-CIO V. AMERICAN PETROLEUM INST.,

448 U.S. 607 (1980)   CC=

SN=   OCCUPATIONAL SAFETY AND HEALTH ACT OF 1971 (OSHA) PUBL.NO.   SO=

91-596, 84 STAT. 1590.29 U.S.C. SECS. 651-678 (1976)

DESCRIPTORS: OCCUPATIONAL SAFETY AND HEALTH ADMIN.::   /DE or /DF

WORKING CONDITIONS; PERFORMANCE; STANDARDS; SAFETY;

GUIDELINES; OSHA; 0042; 0420; 0249; 2205; 0042; 1593; 0042   DC=

DIALOG FILE NAME: 75

FIELD NAME	SUFFIX PREFIX	EXAMPLE
Abstract	/AB	S OCCUPATIONAL/AB
Author	AU=	S AU=MORGAN, D.L.
Case Citation	CC	S CC 448 U.S. 607?
Case Name	CN	S CN INDUSTRIAL?
Descriptor	/DE or /DF	S STANDARDS/DF
Descriptor Code	DC	S DC 2205
Document Type	DT=	S DT=JOURNAL
Journal Code	JC=	S JC=IRL
Journal Name	JN=	S JN=INDUSTRIAL RELATIONS?
Jurisdiction	JU=	S JU=UNITED STATES
Publication Year	PY=	S PY=1983
Special Feature	SF=	S SF=BIBLIOG.
Statute Citation	SO=	S SO=PUB. L. NO. 91-596?
Statute Name	SN=	S SN=OCCUPATIONAL?
Title	/TI	S GENERAL (1W) CLAUSE/TI
Update	UD=	S UD=8308

95

shows one record from Management Contents, in the form in which it appears for the different hosts, even one data base may emerge in different record formats according to the host on which it is mounted. In Dialog, one of the international on-line hosts offering access to a wide variety of data bases, across a number of data bases a very large number of different searchable fields may be identified. Figure 6.4 shows an extract from the

Figure 6.4 Some of the searchable fields available on a Dialog data base

Abbreviations for searchable fields

AA   Asset amount, author affiliation

AB   Abstract, note

AC   Legislative authority code, country of patent application, area code, activity code, assignee code

AG   Asset greater than, grant greater than

AI   Alloys index

AL   Asset less than, grant less than

AM   Grant amount, contract amount

AN   ·Assignee name, accession number, agency name, abstract number

AP   Approach

AR   Authority record

AS   Agency state, agency state code, agency/service abbreviation

AT   Asset type, article type

AU   Personal author, inventor

AV   Availability on microfiche, availability

BC   Biosystematic code, branch city

BN   Biosystematic name, branch name, bureau number, book number, ISBN

BS   Branch state

BZ   Branch zip code

CA   Card alert, cited author, call number

CC   Concept code, corporate source, category code, country code, contractor company code, class code, geographic code

CF   Cosati field

CG   Contributions greater than, corporate source location

CH   Clearinghouse code

CL   Patent classification number, classification code, contributions less than, classification group, conference location

CM   Community code

alphabetical list of searchable fields for Dialog. Yet another variable factor is the growing presence of full text data bases. They will naturally demand a somewhat different record format from bibliographic records if the information is to be appropriately displayed. However, although separate formats have been created for different systems, there are some standards. Various large abstracting and indexing co-operative ventures or networks have developed their own formats. Thus there are groups of organisations with common subject interests which exchange data and co-operate in the creation of international data bases. Amongst these can be numbered: INIS (International Nuclear Information System), IRRD (International Road Research Documentation System), CAS (Chemical Abstracts Services), BIOSIS (BioSciences Information Services Inc.) and AGRIS (Agricultural Information System). All these networks have standard record formats, although it is regrettable that they all operate to different standards.

The record formats to be encountered in local systems which are supported by the type of software package discussed in Chapter 20 are many and various. Some of these software packages offer cataloguing systems which will work in a MARC record format, or which produce records which are compatible with the MARC record format. Others do not offer such an option. Virtually all software packages offer the purchaser the opportunity to evolve a record format which suits a specific application. Figure 6.2 shows two catalogue record formats in ADLIB, which is available from LMR Information Systems. Frequently it is necessary for the librarian or information worker to make choices concerning record size and field size. The smaller microcomputer-based systems may impose limits on either field size or record size or both. For example, with MicroQUERY no field can exceed seventy characters in length. If the library or information worker is offered a choice in the design of record format, it will be necessary to decide upon the types of records to be maintained, and to settle which fields are to be included in each record, and the length of each field. Sometimes there will also be options concerning the use of fixed and variable length fields. Thus, in local systems there may well be great variability in record format, as designs are implemented within the parameters set by the various software packages.

6.4 The UNISIST reference manuals and UNIBID

The UNISIST Reference Manual for Machine-Readable Bibliographic Descriptions, and the record format that it proposes, UNIBID, is an attempt to offer a standard record format for use by abstracting and indexing services, independent of any existing description or cataloguing rules. The first edition of the manual was prepared by the UNISIST/ICSU-AB Working Group on Bibliographic Description, and was published in 1974.

Figure 6.5 Records according to the UNIBID reference record format

Figure 6.5 Records according to the UNIBID reference record format

Example 1

SERIAL ARTICLE (A/S)

Mavaddat, F. and Parhami, B. (Department of Mathematics and Computer Science, Arya-Mehr University of Technology, Tehran, Iran). A data structure for family relations. Computer Journal, 22(2). May 1979. ISSN 0010-4620, pp. 110-113.
Abstract:- A data structure is proposed which enables efficient determination of family relations of common interest with the minimum amount of information on each individual.

Implementation codes
Character position 6: Type of bibliographic entity: S
Character position 9: Bibliographic level: A

Data fields

AØ1	ØØ@ØØØ1Ø-462Ø	ISSN
AØ3	Ø5@1Computerƀournal	Title of serial (Key title)
AØ5	ØØ@222	Volume number
AØ6	ØØ@22	Part number
AØ8	Ø1@1Aƀdataƀstructureƀforƀfamilyƀrelations	Title of analytic
A11	Ø1@1Mavaddat.ƀF.	Author - analytic
A11	Ø1@1Parhami,ƀB.	Author - analytic
A14	ØØ@1Arya-MehrƀUniversityƀofƀTechnology+DepartmentƀofƀMathematicsƀandƀComputerƀScience@2Tehran@3IR	Affiliation - analytic
A2Ø	ØØ@111Ø-113	Pagination - article
A21	ØØ@11979Ø5ØØ	Date of publication
*A22	Ø3@11977Ø6ØØ	Date received by journal
A23	ØØ@ØENG	Language of document (coded)
*A44	ØØ@1Aƀdataƀstructureƀisƀproposedƀwhichƀenablesƀefficientƀdeterminationƀofƀfamilyƀrelationsƀofƀcommonƀinterestƀwithƀtheƀminimumƀamountƀofƀinformationƀonƀeachƀindividual	Abstract
A51	ØØ@ØGB	Country of publication code

Example 3

MONOGRAPH IN A SERIES (M/S)

> Wellisch, Hans H. The Conversion of Scripts - Its Nature,
> History, and Utilization. New York, Wiley, 1978. xviii,
> 509p. (Hayes, Robert M.; Becker, Joseph (eds). Information
> Science Series). Bibliography; pp.441-461. ISBN Ø-471-
> Ø162Ø-9.

Implementation codes
Character position 6: Type of bibliographic entity: M
Character position 9: Bibliographic level: M

Data fields

AØ9	Ø1@1TheβConversionβofβScri ptsβ-βItsβNature,βHist oryβandβUtilization	Title - monograph
AØ3	Ø1@1InformationβScienceβSe ries	Title - serial
A12	Ø1@1Wellisch,βHansβH.	Author - monograph
*A13	Ø2@1Hayes,βRobertβM.	Editor - serial
*A13	Ø2@1Becker,βJoseph	Editor - serial
*A15	Ø1@1UniversityβofβMaryland	Affiliation - monograph
A21	ØØ@11978ØØØØ	Date of publication
A23	ØØ@ØENG	Language of document
A25	ØØ@1Wiley@2NewβYork	Publisher
A26	ØØ@ØØ-471-Ø162Ø-9	ISBN
A29	ØØ@1xviii,β509	Collation - monograph
A51	ØØ@ØUS	Country of publication code
*A7Ø	ØØ@Øpp.441-461	Bibliography note

Information Sciences Series

Editors

ROBERT M. HAYES
University of California
Los Angeles, California

JOSEPH BECKER
President
Becker and Hayes, Inc.

Consultant

CHARLES P. BOURNE
University of California
Berkeley, California

Details of the series

June 1981

From: *Reference Manual for machine-readable bibliographic descriptions.*
2nd rev. ed. Compiled and edited by Harold Dierickx and Alan
Hopkinson, Paris, Unesco, 1981.

In 1976 the UNISIST International Centre for Bibliographic Descriptions (UNIBID) was established by the British Library in collaboration with Unesco, and revision of the manual was undertaken, which led to the publication of the second edition in 1981. Also published, in 1982, was the reference manual for machine-readable descriptions of research projects and institutions. A pilot project is under way to develop and complete portable software to support the applications of both manuals. Software already exists to support the record format, specifically, Unesco's CDC/ISIS and the International Development Research Centre, Canada, MINISIS, but neither of these packages is portable across many machines, although both are available internationally. This software is important to the further implementation of the record format, especially in developing countries.

Figure 6.5 shows two records coded according to the UNIBID reference record format. It may be profitable to compare further UNIBID with UNIMARC. UNIBID has less redundancy and covers more types of bibliographic material than UNIMARC, whereas the latter probably has more entry points for catalogue headings. While the UNIBID format is used by a number of national and international information systems, UNIMARC, in itself, so far has not been implemented, although plans exist for interchange between MARC-oriented national bibliographic agencies and it is intended to be a universal exchange format suitable for any type of library or information system. Publication, after testing, is imminent. CCF is likely to be compatible with UNIMARC and the UNIBID format.

Chapter 6 Readings

1 Avram, H.D., *MARC: its history and implications*, Library of Congress: Washington DC, 1975.
2 Cataloguing practice notes for UKMARC records – Notes 1–20. BLAISE: London, 1982–.
3 Dierickx, H. and Hopkinson, A., *Reference manual for machine-readable bibliographic descriptions*, 2nd rev. edition, Unesco/General Information Programme and UNISIST: Paris, 1981. (PG1/81/WS/22).
4 Dierickx, H., 'The UNISIST reference manuals and UNIBID standardisation for development' *Program*, 17(2), 1983, 68–85.
5 IFLA Working Group on Content Designators: UNIMARC-Universal MARC format. IFLA Office for UBC: London 1977.
6 Library of Congress, MARC Development Office, *Information on the MARC system*, 4th edition, Library of Congress: Washington, DC, 1974.
7 MARC Task Force, *Canadian MARC*, National Library of Canada: Ottawa, 1972.
8 National Library of Australia, *Australian MARC specification*, 3rd edition, NLA: Canberra, 1980.

9 *Reference manual for machine-readable bibliographic descriptions.* 2nd rev. edition/compiled and edited by H. Dierickx and A. Hopkinson for UNIBID, Unesco: Paris, 1981.

10 *UKMARC manual,* 1st standard edition. British Library Bibliographical Services Division: London, 1975.

11 UNIMARC, *Universal MARC format,* 2nd rev. edition, IFLA International Office for UBC: London, 1980.

12 US Library of Congress, MARC Development Office, *Books: a MARC format,* 5th edition. USGPO: Washington, DC, 1972.

Note: Various of the items listed in the readings at the end of Chapters 19 and 20 will introduce ideas on record formats for specific systems.

Part II   Authors and titles

7   Problems in author cataloguing and indexing

7.1   The purpose of the author approach

Chapter 1 describes author catalogues and indexes and cites authors' names as one access point in a computer data base. Obviously the author's name has provided an important access key to documents in both computer data bases and earlier in card, microfiche and printed indexes for many years. The author of a document is the person or organisation responsible for its creation, that is, the writer of a text, the illustrator in respect of illustrations and others responsible for the intellectual content of a work. Generating author indexes or catalogues involves creating headings from authors' names, that is the names of persons or organisations.

Listings other than author indexes or catalogues also involve the arranging of entries according to the names of persons or organisations, and some of the problems that author cataloguing codes and practices attempt to handle are also evident in other environments. A significant example is a telephone directory. These are often alphabetical arrangements of the names of persons and organisations. Equally, various trade directories and other lists need to list and organise names in a form that will enable a searcher to find information about an organisation or person. The use of persons' and organisations' names as headings has been explored thoroughly in catalogues. Thus, cataloguing practices will be considered in detail in this section, and may form a basis for practice in other listings of names of persons and organisations.

Author catalogues have always been important in libraries. Indeed, many libraries have kept author catalogues where no other catalogue sequences have been provided. The author catalogue can be regarded as a basic record of stock. Authors' names are important search keys in trying to retrieve documents. In particular, they have been accepted as one of the more specific and memorable search keys for the retrieval of specific known documents. In contrast, the choice of a subject heading or notation presents many varied problems of interpretation. Although, as will be demonstrated later in this chapter, there may be differences of opinion as to the most appropriate author heading for a work, it is more difficult to achieve consistency in selection of subject labels between the indexer and searcher. More recently, the introduction of the International Standard Book Number (ISBN) has provided a more specific search key than the author's name and this is used for retrieval in many computerised housekeeping systems. However, in general, it is unreasonable to expect a user to know the ISBN of a book (except where the number is available to him through other bibliographical listings, such as might be the case in book selection). The author approach remains an important means of tracing a specific document. This approach is especially appropriate for fiction which tends to be known by its author. The subject approach is also useful for non-fiction, but has little value for fiction. In the author approach there is a clear emphasis on document retrieval as distinct from information retrieval.

To be a little more precise, there are two basic reasons why users make an approach to documents through authors' names. These remain the same as they were in the days of Charles Ammi Cutter (see 1.3):

1. To enable a person to find a document of which the author is known.
2. To show what the library has by a given author.

Unfortunately, these two objectives are not necessarily fulfilled by one and the same set of solutions to the creation of author headings. Problems arise when an author uses different names in different documents. An author may change his name or use different pseudonyms for different works. There are two basic policies open to the cataloguer:

1. Enter all of the works of one author under one standard name, which may be any one of: the earliest name used by the author, the best-known name used by the author, the briefest name of the author, or the most formal name used by the author.
2. Enter each work under the name on the title page of that work.

The adoption of the first of these policies will lead to all the author's works being collocated or grouped together in the catalogue. This will satisfy the second objective of an author catalogue, in that it becomes easy to review the extent of a library's collection of works by a specific author. The first objective, however, is best satisfied by the second policy. This would result in the different works of one author being entered under different headings, and thus making it difficult to assess the extent of the collection in respect of the works of any given author. Thus, it can be seen that the cataloguer is presented with two options, one of which must be selected, and which, when chosen, can only fully satisfy either objective 1 or 2, but not both. Naturally, references would be made to allow for the objective which was not primarily fulfilled, but nevertheless the basic conflict remains. To take an example, John Creasey has used his real name in some works and in others he has used pseudonyms which include: Gordon Asshe, Michael Halliday, J J Marric,

Anthony Morton and Jeremy York. If each work were entered under the name on the title page of the work this author's works would be found under a plethora of different names. Any searcher wishing to assemble all books by John Creasey would need to be aware of all the pseudonyms under which John Creasey wrote, or be offered this information through references. On the other hand, if all John Creasey's works were entered under Creasey, John, a searcher who had been recommended a book by, say Anthony Morton, would find no entry for the book under Morton, Anthony. In a good catalogue or index, a reference of the form:

Morton, Anthony see Creasey, John.

would assist the reader.

Objective 1 results in what is known as a direct catalogue, because it gives direct access to a specific document. Its prime purpose is the finding of specific documents, and consequently this type of catalogue has been labelled a finding list catalogue or an inventory catalogue.

Objective 2 results in what could be described as a collocative catalogue, because a catalogue based on this principle collocates the writings of a particular author. Because this style of catalogue attempts to group documents which are related to each other by having the same author this type of catalogue is sometimes referred to as a bibliographic catalogue.

In practice, many cataloguers favour the direct catalogue partly because it is simpler for the cataloguer to compile. The cataloguer merely accepts the name on the title page as the heading. If new information about the author's identity or the use of his name later comes to light then new names can be covered by references linking works entered under different headings. In a collocative catalogue new information about an author might require tedious revision of headings and entries. Nevertheless, modern cataloguing practices often represent some amalgam of the collocative and the direct approaches.

This section has begun to demonstrate some of the problems associated with the author approach. Author catalogues and indexes can be designed to meet different objectives. No one catalogue can satisfy all the requirements of all users simultaneously. The user may come to the catalogue relatively ignorant of the heading under which a work is to be found. The cataloguer must take account of this situation. Good author cataloguing depends not only upon a knowledge of established codes and rules, but also on an appreciation of the bibliographic history and context of the works being catalogued. Even within rules a cataloguer is frequently required to exercise judgement.

7.2 The concept of authorship

What is an author? Can the British Broadcasting Corporation or the Library of Congress be an author? Who is to be regarded as the author of a motion picture? Can an illustrator be regarded as the author of a book which has little text and is comprised primarily of pictures? These questions, and the many others posed in later sections of this chapter serve to demonstrate that the concept of authorship and the definition of the term 'author' need to be carefully considered. If sought headings are to be established it is important to evolve a clear and applicable definition of the concept of authorship.

However, the definition of an 'author' has taxed cataloguers for many years. Figure 7.1 shows some of the definitions of cataloguing codes of recent years. AACR2 defines authorship in terms of the intellectual responsibility for a work. An illustrator, composer, adapter, editor, and others may be regarded as the author of a work in appropriate circumstances.

Personal authorship has been accepted for some time, and indeed reflects the scholarly practice of the Western world. Personal authors are important as identifying elements of works.

The concept of corporate authorship has had a more chequered history. Until the mid-nineteenth century the concept of authorship was confined to personal authors. Even today a recent study (see n.3 of Chapter 10) of corporate headings in catalogues, national bibliographies and cataloguing codes revealed a chaotic state. 'Among the great number of cataloguing codes recognising corporate authorship, it is scarcely possible to find even two which interpret the concept in the same way.' Efforts are being made in the direction of an international consensus on the definition and treatment of corporate authorship. The uncertainty over the concept of corporate authorship is amply illustrated by the change in the application of corporate headings between the first and second editions of AACR. The rules in AACR2 lead to fewer works being entered under corporate bodies as main entries than the equivalent rules in AACR1.

AACR2 defines a corporate body thus: 'A corporate body is an organisation or group of persons that is identified by a particular name and that acts, or may act, as an entity'.

Corporate authors present difficulties essentially because a corporate body cannot think or write. Therefore, in the traditional sense, a corporate body cannot be an author. Nevertheless, a corporate body (or the group of individuals that comprise that body) can be intellectually responsible for the creation of a work, and in addition, the name of that body may be the information that users bring to a catalogue or index. There is no ready solution to the problems associated with the 'concept of corporate bodies as authors', but current cataloguing practices have to offer some pragmatic solutions. These issues are reviewed more thoroughly in Chapter 10.

Figure 7.1 Some definitions of 'author'

Cutter:
Author, in the narrower sense, is the person who writes a book; in a wider sense it may be applied to him who is the cause of the book's existence by putting together the writings of several authors (usually called the editor, more properly to be called the collector). Bodies of men (societies, cities, legislative bodies, countries) are to be considered the authors of their memoirs, transactions, journals, debates, reports, etc.

ALA 1908:
1. The writer of a book, as distinguished from translator, editor, etc.
2. In a broader sense, the maker of the book or the person or body immediately responsible for its existence. Thus, a person who collects and puts together the writings of several authors (compiler or editor) may be said to be the author of a collection. Corporate bodies may be considered the authors of publications issued in their name or by their authority.

ALA 1949:
1. The writer of a work, as distinguished from the translator, editor, etc. By extension, an artist, composer, photographer, cartographer, etc.
2. In the broader sense, the maker of the work or the person or body immediately responsible for its existence. Thus, a person who collects and puts together the writings of several authors (compiler or editor) may be said to be the author of a collection. A corporate body may be considered the author of publications issued in its name or by its authority.

AACR 1
The person or corporate body chiefly responsible for the creation of the intellectual or artistic content of a work, e.g., the writer of a book, the compiler of a bibliography, the composer of a musical work, the artist who paints a picture, the photographer who takes a photograph.

AACR 2:
A personal author is the person chiefly responsible for the creation of the intellectual or artistic content of a work.

From: Chan, L.M. Cataloguing and Classification.—McGraw-Hill, 1981.

7.3 Problems of author cataloguing

The compilation of an author catalogue or index presents four basic questions which need to be answered:

1. How many entries to make.
2. Which of these entries should be regarded as the main entry?
3. What form should the headings take?
4. Which references should be made from other possible headings which have not been used as headings to entries?

For some documents these four questions are relatively easy to answer. For example, without any external guidelines the answers to the four questions for the following work might, on the basis of common sense, be:

The Odessa File/Frederick Forsyth
1. One
2. Frederick Forsyth
3. Forsyth, Frederick
4. None.

A glance at the title page in Figure 7.2 should be sufficient to convince the reader that the selection of author headings is not always as straightforward as with our first example. Unfortunately documents which present dilemmas in the selection of author headings are present in even the smallest library collections.

Figure 7.3 shows short extracts from the text of a number of documents, and shows a number of authorship situations. Answers to the basic questions could be produced on the basis of common sense, in each individual instance. This might produce reasonably sought headings for each individual document, and would certainly facilitate fast cataloguing, but would probably lead to inconsistencies in the way in which different documents might be catalogued. For example, a user might reasonably expect two documents both produced by the Communications Research Centre of the University of London to be found under the same heading (for instance University of London. Communications Research Centre), and not one under that heading and the other under Communications Research Centre. Cataloguing codes are important to establish some consistency in cataloguing practices between:

(i) different catalogues
(ii) different cataloguers
(iii) different documents
(iv) the cataloguer's and the user's approaches.

Figure 7.2 Example of a title page

INTERNATIONAL COMMITTEE OF HISTORICAL SCIENCES
COMITE INTERNATIONAL DES SCIENCES HISTORIQUES
LAUSANNE—PARIS

INTERNATIONAL BIBLIOGRAPHY
OF HISTORICAL SCIENCES

INTERNATIONALE BIBLIOGRAPHIE DER GESCHICHTSWISSENSCHAFTEN
BIBLIOGRAFIA INTERNACIONAL DE CIENCIAS HISTORICAS
BIBLIOGRAPHIE INTERNATIONALE DES SCIENCES HISTORIQUES
BIBLIOGRAFIA INTERNAZIONALE DELLE SCIENZE STORICHE

VOLUME XLVII—XLVIII
1978—1979

Edited with the Contribution of the National Committees
by Michel François† and Michael Keul

Published with the assistance of Unesco
and under the patronage of the
International Council for Philosophy and Humanistic Studies

K·G· SAUR   MÜNCHEN · NEW YORK · LONDON · PARIS

Codes are sets of rules which indicate how different types of documents are best catalogued, if sensible and consistent headings are to be established in author catalogues and indexes. Some of the major codes are considered in more detail in Chapter 8.

7.4 Conditions and cases

AACR and other recent cataloguing codes have been drafted upon the 'condition' approach to formulating cataloguing rules. A 'condition' is a relevant code problem, such as 'change of author's name' or 'dependent documents'. A 'case' is a class of documents or organisations in which that problem is found. The condition approach to drafting catalogue rules has led to a more analytical approach to cataloguing. Attempts are made to treat similar problems in a similar way, regardless of the type of documents (for example, serial or dictionary) or organisation (for example, government department, conference) in which it arises. The alternative approach which is evident in earlier codes is to enumerate all cases, that is, all classes of documents, organisations and so on, which give rise to problems and make a rule for each.

The condition approach is more satisfactory in that:

1. It tends to lead to a more detailed and thorough analysis of the problems, and provides a framework within which otherwise hidden problems might be revealed.
2. It helps in consistency between related cases, since principles are established, and removes the need for separate rules for the different types

Figure 7.3 Some extracts from the text of title pages illustrating a variety of authorship conditions

1. **Outlines of a critique of technology** / Ink Kinks Ltd.
2. **The micro revolution** / by Peter Large
3. **Sweden in world society** / Swedish Secretariat for Future Studies
4. **Dubrovnik, Italy and the Balkans in the late Middle Ages.** Facsimile reprints of 21 articles, originally published between 1952 and 1979. Various authors.
5. **Ethics and problems of the 21st century** / edited by K E Goodposter and K M Sayre.
6. **Millennium and charisma among Pathans** / by Akbar Salahudin Ahmed.
7. **Some personal views** / by Margaret Mead; edited by Phoda Metraux.

8. **The organisation** / by M J Newell, I A Todd, M G Woodley.

9. **To be human** / by Alexander Alland Jr.

10. **The analysis of social skill** / edited by W T Singleton, P Spurgeon and R B Stammers.—Proceedings of the analysis of social skill (conference), London, 1979.

11. **Social theories of the press** / by Hanno Hardt; foreword by James W Carey.

12. Report of the Social Sciences Research Council.

13. **The Freud-Jung letters: the correspondence between Sigmund Freud and C G Jung** / edited by Willian McGuire; translated by Ralph Manheim and R F C Hull; Abridged edition / abridged by Alan McGlasham.

14. **Animal models in alcohol research**; proceedings of the international conference on animal models in alcohol research, Helsinki, 1979.

15. **Medicine in the tropics** / edited by A W Woodruff.

16. Department of Health and Social Security; **Notes on the diagnosis of occupational diseases: prescribed under the industrial injuries provisions of the Social Security Act.**

17. **Progress in allergy** Volume 27 / editors Kimishige Ishizaka ... et al.; and various other contributors.

18. **Essential malariology** / Leonard Jan Bruce-Chwatt.

19. **Imperial eggs** / by Hermione Waterfield and Christopher Forbes; illustrated with works from the Forbes Magazine Collection, New York.

20. **The plan for restoration and adaptive use of the Frank Lloyd Wright home and studio** / The Restoration Committee of the Frank Lloyd Wright Home and Studio Foundation.

21. **Eva Hesse 1936-1970: sculpture** / edited by Nicholas Serote; catalogue of an exhibition held at the Whitechapel Art Gallery, London, 4 May-17 June 1979, RijksMuseum Kröller-Müller, Otterlo, 30 June-5 August 1979.

22. **Oxford and Cambridge**; photographs by Richard Gloucester, Duke of Gloucester; text by Hermione Hobhouse.

23. **Architecture: form, space and order** / by Francis Fai-Kam Ching.

24. **English heritage monitor** / Planning and Research Services, English Tourist Board.

25. **Religious buildings** / by the editors of **Architectural Record.**

26. **The natural superiority of the left hander** / by James T de Kay; second edition / edited by N M Close.

27. **Red dagger.**—London: D C Thompson.—No. 1—

28. **Olympaidd** / testun gan Goscinny; illuniau gan Uderzo; troswyd o'r Ffrangeg gan Alun Jones.

of material. One general rule with dependent special rules is more likely to lead to a consistent approach than a number of individual and unrelated rules covering a series of separately treated cases.

3. The condition approach should require less enumeration of rules for different types of materials, and therefore should require fewer rules.

4. New cases will not require new rules, with a condition approach, and so the rules can remain relatively stable. Occasionally a new authorship condition will arise and this will need to be recognised by the code, but a new condition is not as frequent an occurrence as a new case.

In general then, the analytical approach is to be preferred, but it does have two limitations:

1. The practice that should be adopted for individual cases may not be clearly identified, and there may be scope for variations in the interpretation of rules, which, in the absence of any clearer advice, will lead the cataloguer to catalogue in accordance with one or two examples rather than by rules.

2. As with any categorisation, the categories are likely to be imperfectly defined. Some documents will be difficult to fit into any specific condition.

These limitations are partially tackled by AACR2 by resorting to rules for special cases; details of these instances are considered in Chapters 9 and 10.

8   Cataloguing codes – purpose and development

8.1 Purpose of cataloguing codes

Chapter 7 has amply demonstrated the need for catalogue codes. As soon as it is accepted that consistency in dealing with documents which are similar or the same in some sense is desirable, it becomes evident that some guidelines or rules must be drafted in order to indicate how consistency is to be achieved. Without such guidelines each document would need to be assessed individually, and inconsistencies would be inevitable. So, to a definition:

> A catalogue code is a systematic arrangement of laws and statutes so as to avoid inconsistency and duplication in catalogues.

There are a number of features of a catalogue or index which benefit from some standardisation. Part I had occasion to refer to the use of catalogue codes in compiling descriptions for documents. A more complete list of the possible areas of concern for catalogue codes might be:

1. Author main entries
2. Number and type of added entries for authors
3. Number and type of references for authors' names
4. Title entries
5. Description
6. Subject headings
7. Filing
8. Abbreviations, glossary, punctuation

Such a list might well lead to the question: why then are we dealing with catalogue codes in this part of this work, since it would seem that catalogue codes impinge on many aspects of catalogues? In practice modern day catalogue codes are concerned primarily with description and author headings. The recommendations in cataloguing codes concerning description need to be considered alongside other standards for description and so it makes sense to consider this topic in its totality in Part I. Some early codes included recommendations for filing practices and subject headings, but these are usually now the subject of a separate list or set of rules. Thus, potentially the scope of a catalogue code is wide, but in practice most codes are restricted to 1, 2, 3, 4, 5 and 8 above. In this chapter a review of the development of cataloguing codes is given in order to explain and place in context the nature of modern cataloguing codes. This review also illustrates some of the issues which cataloguers have discussed over the years, and demonstrates other solutions to standards in cataloguing than those embodied in modern cataloguing codes. An appreciation of alternative approaches is particularly important in this field where trends towards standardisation are the norm.

8.2 Early cataloguing codes

Some of the early codes had an important influence upon subsequent cataloguing practices, if only because they established ideas about cataloguing against which all subsequent suggestions concerning cataloguing practices could be matched. Three codes are sufficiently important to merit specific mention.

The oldest code of importance in English is the British Museum Rules, which was first published in 1841. Sometimes known as Panizzi's ninety-one rules, this code covered author and title headings and description. Its influence is evident in the British Museum catalogue and in the codes of other national and academic libraries, including, for example, the Bodleian Library (University of Oxford).

The code was designed to meet the needs of a single large library, and the choice of heading is influenced by the difficulties inherent in any changes in a large catalogue. For example, when an author changes his name, the code recommends that all entries be under the earlier name, thus avoiding any change in headings. In spite of its inherent conservatism, the BM code favours direct entry. The basic rule is that headings should be chosen from information found in the book, and further, pseudonyms and initials are allowed as main entry headings if they reflect the information found in the book. Two remarkable features of the BM code are its acceptance of corporate authorship, and its use of form headings. The concept of corporate authorship was first formulated in the BM code and has been adopted in all subsequent English language codes. Other codes in other languages were slower to accept this concept, and prefer to regard works by corporate authors as anonymous. Form headings (such as congresses, dictionaries, directories) were recommended by the BM code, and caused some problems later.

It is hardly fair to assess the BM code by modern standards for catalogue codes, but there are obvious areas in which it would now be regarded as lacking. The code is very limited in its analysis of cataloguing situations, and the structure is not particularly logical.

Another early code which has had an immense influence is *Cutter's Rules for a Dictionary Catalog*, which was first published in 1876. The code embraced author, title, subject and form entry, description and the filing of entries. Because of its great scope, *Cutter's Rules* had a significant influence upon all aspects of the dictionary catalogue, and forms the point of departure for both author and subject cataloguing in the United States. Cutter's contribution to subject headings is developed further in Chapters 16 and 17.

Cutter's approach to cataloguing was basically pragmatic, and many of his recommendations can be seen to be clearly reflected in current cataloguing codes. Alternative rules are suggested in several instances and three styles of cataloguing are suggested: short, medium and full. Where it is difficult to provide an absolute ruling, 'the convenience of the public is to be the final guide', and the choice of the 'best-known name' is recommended. This reflects the general preference for a direct catalogue. Rules for corporate authorship are relatively detailed. General preference is for entry under name of organisation, but there are many exceptions. Cutter recognised the value of a structured approach to cataloguing rules and this has been accepted by subsequent codifiers. Cutter also recognised the distinction between cases and conditions which is taken up in later codes, and the structure of the code identified two key cataloguing problems. Part A considered Entry, or where to enter, and Part B, Style, is concerned with how to enter.

In Germany and more widely in Europe an important early code was the *Prussian Instructions*, published in 1898. The *Prussian Instructions* were revised in 1908 with some simplification, and through the German Union Catalogue, based at the Prussian State Library, libraries in Germany and Austria were drawn into conformity with the rules. The *Prussian Instructions* were also widely adopted in Hungary, Sweden, Switzerland, and to a lesser extent Denmark, Holland and Norway. Thus this code was important in catalogues on the mainland of Europe. The reason for its popularity was largely that it was based upon a principle of conformity in essentials, and freedom in details. One major feature of the *Prussian Instructions* was the treatment of the works of corporate bodies as anonymous if no personal author was identifiable. Also, title entries were ordered by grammatical arrangement, rather than in natural word order. The keyword was the first noun, and this was followed by other words in correct grammatical word order. This type of subject approach is reasonably successful in the German language but presents problems in the English language. The *Prussian Instructions* were used, with further revisions, until the mid-1960s.

8.3 The Anglo-American or Joint Code (1908)

Variously known as the Anglo-American Code, the AA Code, the Joint Code and the 1908 Code, this code had an important impact upon cataloguing practices in the United States and the United Kingdom, and endured for over half a century. Certainly in the United Kingdom, and to a lesser extent in the United States, there was no serious rival to the 1908 Code until the publication of the first edition of the *Anglo-American Cataloguing Rules* in 1967. In the absence of any serious rival, the code was widely used in producing bibliographic records in catalogues and bibliographies, despite some well-recognised weaknesses.

The 1908 Code was the result of the combined efforts of the Library Association (UK) and the American Library Association. Its objective was to establish a unity of practice throughout the English-speaking world.

There are 174 rules covering author and title headings and description. Arrangement is in two broad sections: Entry and heading (1–135) and Description (136–174). Rules for author headings are in two subsections: personal authors and corporate authors. There were differences between the approaches adopted by the American and UK Committees, but these only pertain to eight rules. These discrepancies are associated with the problem of 'authors having more than one name'. Americans tend to prefer collocation of an author's works under latest name or tend to advocate 'best known' name, in keeping with Cutter's recommendations, whereas the British prefer collocation under earliest name.

By the 1920s the 1908 Code was already receiving criticism. As is the way with these things there were two conflicting criticisms levelled at the 1908 Code. Some considered the rules over-complicated and fussy, whereas others were of the opinion that more detail was required. Both these general criticisms stemmed from more specific problems with the code. These could be listed as:

1. *The analysis into conditions and cases is not complete.* There is frequent enumeration of types of document (libretti, concordances, and so on) and types of organisation (alumni, associations, churches). This leads to an approach which is insufficiently analytical, and which relies too heavily upon enumeration. Enumeration can lead to inconsistencies between separate rules for different but related types of materials, excessive numbers of rules, and omissions in both types of organisations and types of documents covered.

2. *Inadequate definitions.* Some of the terms are vague. For example, although the distinction between 'societies' and 'institutions' lies at the heart of the code, these terms are only defined by example.

3. *Examples* are generally poor or obscure (often in Latin or German). Many of the rules for government publications have only American examples.

4. *Tendency to ignore the author's identity as found in the document,* and to prefer instead a real name to a pseudonym.

5. *Form headings* are sometimes suggested – for example, in the case of laws and treaties.

6. *Corporate authors* present many problems. The code makes a primary division into governments, societies and institutions which results in the overlooking of problems which arise in both categories, such as change of name and subordinate bodies. The main rules call for entry of societies under name and institutions under place. Since this general rule does not always lead to the sought name being chosen in a heading, many exceptions to the main rules have to be enumerated. The rules for government bodies, both local and central, also pose problems, with some categories of organisation not being considered and some of the recommended headings being far from sought.

Eventually, in the 1930s the Committees of the American Library Association and the Library Association began to discuss revision of the 1908 code. On the outbreak of war in 1939, the Library Association was forced to withdraw from deliberations and the American Library Association continued alone. The ALA produced a draft code in 1941 and the final code in 1949.

8.4 The American Library Association or ALA Code (1949)

Although the 1949 code was much longer than its predecessor, the 1908 Code, it only contained rules pertaining to headings. Thus the descriptive part of catalogue entries had to wait until 1967 and the production of the *Anglo-American Cataloguing Rules*, when a new code was drafted to cover this area.

The 1949 Code was essentially a greater elaboration of the 1908 Code in an attempt to rectify the omissions of the 1908 Code. Any reliance on principles alone is rejected, and an attempt is made to codify 'experience'. In the sense that the 1949 Code makes no attempt to identify or incorporate principles, it is only a limited improvement on the 1908 Code.

The 1949 Code does boast some improvements on the 1908 Code. The sequence of rules is rearranged in some areas so that the order is more logical. There are more and better examples. The listing of types of literature and the rules for government publications are extended. Some of the specific rules have also been modified from the 1908 Code. Amongst these are rules relating to: joint authorship, librettos, thematic catalogues, encyclopaedias and dictionaries, pseudonyms and anonymous classics. Obviously any of the American alternatives in the 1908 Code are reflected in the 1949 Code. The 1949 Code was adopted to a fair extent in the United States.

8.5 Lubetzky and catalogue code revision 1949–1967

As early as 1951, the American Library Association invited Seymour Lubetzky, consultant on bibliography and cataloguing policy to the Library of Congress, to 'prepare a general analysis of the 1949 Code . . . with special consideration of the rules for corporate authors and a discussion of the objectives and principles which should underlie a revision of the rules'. Lubetzky's report was published in 1953, and formed the basis of the analytical approach to catalogue code construction which has since been accepted and expected. The report introduced a range of ideas which have influenced subsequent code construction. In particular, Lubetzky proposed that a direct catalogue was to be preferred, with any necessary collocation achieved by references. He also proposed a set of authorship conditions which could form the basis for a code. These conditions are reflected in subsequent codes.

The ALA accepted Lubetzky's report, and began work on a new code. Meanwhile in 1951, the Library Association reconstituted its Catalogue Code Revision Committee and started discussions. By 1960 a draft code had been produced, and from this time on, British and American Committees co-operated closely. In 1961 an International Conference on Cataloguing Principles was held in Paris, and a statement of principles emerged, which became known as the Paris Principles. After much subsequent discussion, and the publication of a series of interim reports, a new code was published in 1967 as the *Anglo-American Cataloguing Rules*.

8.6 Anglo-American Cataloguing Rules or AACR (1967)

The first edition of the *Anglo-American Cataloguing Rules* (AACR1) was published in 1967 in two texts: the British text published by the Library Association, and the North American text published by the American Library Association. Complete agreement had not been possible, but the numbers of rules where divergent practices were evident is limited. The need for two separate texts arose largely from the reluctance of large libraries, in particular the Library of Congress, to accept new principles and rules when these might require extensive recataloguing.

This chapter does not consider the principles underlying AACR, nor does it review the structure of the code to any significant extent. Aspects of these topics are developed elsewhere in this work. Instead, the place of AACR in the historical development of cataloguing codes will be examined here.

AACR represented a significant element in the progress towards rational and standard cataloguing practices. Timing was important. An agreed standard towards which cataloguing practice could begin to adhere was important with the first trials of the MARC (Machine Readable Cataloguing) format in 1966. Both the Library of Congress and the British National Bibliography were aiming to produce machine-readable cataloguing records which would be acceptable in a large number of libraries. A standard for cataloguing practice was a necessary prerequisite. Without AACR it is doubtful whether computerised cataloguing would have been implemented so relatively painlessly and successfully. Libraries have sufficiently different requirements of catalogues to make standardisation of practice difficult, without being hampered by the absence of a code from which they can select their own practice, and make their own deviations. On the other hand, it is not difficult to argue that the success of AACR1 owes less to the carefully identified principles, than to the obvious economic benefits of libraries adopting a standard code. Whatever viewpoint is taken, it is difficult to dispute the significance of AACR1. The code was widely accepted by libraries of all types and sizes in the English-speaking world and beyond.

AACR1 is a weighty code, not because it contains extensive enumeration, but rather because of its comprehensive coverage. The code has three main parts:

Part I: Entry and heading
Part II: Description
Part III: Nonbook materials

Throughout, the code is based upon clearly stated principles. In particular, the intention is to produce a more direct form of entry based on information found in the document, and there is a consistent attempt to distinguish between conditions and cases (see Chapter 7).

As part of the revision and review of AACR1 three amendment bulletins were published in 1970, 1971 and 1975. All three bulletins proposed modifications, but most of these were minor, with the exception of the amalgamation of the rules for collections and works produced under editorial direction (see section 9.2 for further details). In 1974 a revision of 'Chapter 6: Separately published monographs and other non-serial publications' concerned with the description of these materials, was published. This revised chapter modified the code in keeping with the recently agreed ISBD(M) (see Chapter 3), and proposed a slightly different description for monographs. Specifically, an internationally agreed set of punctuation was established for use in description. Other revised chapters were also published. Chapter 12 Revised, covering audio-visual media and special instructional material, was published in 1975, and Chapter 14 for sound recordings was revised in 1976.

Two criticisms were quickly formulated in respect of AACR1. The flush of success with AACR1 gave the code compilers and cataloguers the confidence to criticise the new code with the object of further refining it. The two early criticisms were:

(a) a lack of adequate definition of the nature of authorship and responsibility, both personal and corporate.

(b) an occasional unwillingness to accept the consequences of its decisions on principles. For example in rule 43 the cataloguer is advised always to give full forenames, even though this might not always result in a sought heading for authors who habitually use initials (for example, C S Lewis).

A code such as AACR could only be tested thoroughly by extensive application in different types of libraries, with different requirements, and different materials. Other criticisms emerged. The main body of criticism centred upon the treatment of nonbook materials. The rules for nonbook materials cataloguing had not been as carefully considered by the Revision Committee – monograph cataloguing needed and was given priority. Nevertheless the early 1970s saw the escalation in the variety of nonbook media in libraries and resource centres, and the need for a satisfactory cataloguing code for these materials became more pressing. Part III of AACR1 enjoyed little popularity, and during the early 1970s several possible codes were drafted and some of these were published. Typically these referred to AACR1 Parts I and II where appropriate, and they thus acknowledged the contribution of Parts I and II. Some of these codes have been mentioned in Chapter 4. It was expected that most of these codes would be superseded by AACR's second edition.

Thus there was a need to opt for revision. A revised text could make full allowance for the expansion in the range of media in today's libraries, whilst at the same time taking into account various effects of computerisation in library housekeeping systems. Equally important was the desire to achieve a single text. The Council on Library Resources agreed to fund the revision, and a Joint Steering Committee for Revision of AACR met in 1974 and settled the five authors. These were to be: the American Library Association, The British Library, The Canadian Committee on Cataloguing, The Library Association, and the Library of Congress. National committees were established to consider issues and proposals for revision.

8.7 Anglo-American Cataloguing Rules or AACR2 (1978)

The second edition of AACR was published in 1978, amidst some dispute as to whether it was either necessary or desirable. Many librarians viewed AACR1 as such a significant improvement upon its predecessors, that they were content. Besides, any second edition threatened to require some recataloguing. Nevertheless, AACR2 is now widely accepted, and the second edition does differ from the first in various important aspects. AACR2 was adopted by the Library of Congress and the British Library, the National Library of Australia and the National Library of Canada in January 1981. At an earlier stage, the Library of Congress had decided to retain certain pre-AACR headings, in order to avoid the expense of extensive recataloguing. The Library of Congress has now reconsidered the position, and abandoned what was known as its compatible headings policy from September 1982.

The most obvious changes between the first and second editions of AACR are:

1. Finally it has been possible to agree upon one code (there are no longer two texts).

2. The second edition has a completely different organisation and structure.

AACR2 recognised that a cataloguing code of the 1980s must treat all media as equal. Thus AACR2 has two parts:

Part I Description
Part II Entry and Heading

Part II deals with entry and heading for all types of materials. Where possible general rules which can be applied to all media are proposed. In addition some special rules are included for special types of materials, for example, sound recordings. Part I comprises a series of chapters. Chapter 1 establishes general rules, and each subsequent chapter deals with a specific part of the media in more detail. For example, Chapter 2 tackles books, pamphlets and printed sheets, and Chapter 3 is dedicated to cartographic materials. The intention is to establish a general framework, and then to give exceptions or further explanation and examples for each area in turn. Although this is generally successful, this approach does necessitate the consultation of two chapters when considering the cataloguing of any given medium.

Figure 8.1 shows a comparative table of descriptive rules in AACR1 and AACR2. Figure 8.2 gives an outline of the main chapters and rules of AACR2. AACR2 also incorporates rather more options in terms of alternative rules than AACR1, and also allows for and identifies three levels of detail which might be adopted in descriptive cataloguing (see Chapter 3). This flexibility represents an attempt to make the code amenable to use in a variety of different library environments, rather than as in AACR1 emphasising the needs of major research libraries.

Although AACR2 is widely adopted, criticisms have been voiced. These can be broadly categorised into the following two groups:

Figure 8.1 Comparative table of the structure of descriptive rules in AACR1 and AACR2

AACR1 Part II	AACR2 Part I
Chapter 6 Separately published monographs and other (printed) non-serial publications	Chapter 2 Books, pamphlets and printed sheets
— Rule 156, Analytical entries	Chapter 13 Analysis
Chapter 7 Serials (ie printed serials)	Chapter 12 Serials
— Rule 168, Analytical entries	Chapter 13 Analysis
Chapter 8 Incunabula	Chapter 2 Books, pamphlets and printed sheets
Chapter 9 Photographic and other reproductions	Chapter 2 Books, pamphlets and printed sheets
— Macroform	
— Microform	Chapter 11 Microforms
— of serials	Chapter 12 Serials

AACR1 Part III

Chapter 10 Manuscripts	Chapter 4 Manuscripts (including manuscript collections)
Chapter 11 Maps, relief models, globes and atlases	Chapter 3 Cartographic materials
Chapter 12 Motion pictures and filmstrips	Chapter 7 Motion pictures and video recordings
— Rule 229, Continuations	Chapter 12 Serials
Chapter 13 Music	Chapter 5 Music
Chapter 14 Phonorecords	Chapter 6 Sound recordings
Chapter 15 Pictures, designs, and other two-dimensional representations	Chapter 8 Graphic materials
— Rule 271, 'In' analytical note	Chapter 13 Analysis
— Rule 269A4, Microfilm reproductions	Chapter 11 Microforms

Chapters in AACR2 Part 1 without equivalents in AACR1

Chapter 1 General chapter

Chapter 9 Machine-readable data files

Chapter 10 Three-dimensional artefacts and realia

Figure 8.2 The Anglo-American Cataloguing Rules, second edition, 1978

An outline of the main chapters and rules

Contents

Part 1 - Description

1 General rules for description
2 Books, pamphlets, and printed sheets
3 Cartographic materials
4 Manuscripts (including manuscript collections)
5 Music
6 Sound recordings
7 Motion pictures and videorecordings
8 Graphic materials
9 Machine-readable data files
10 Three-dimensional artefacts and realia
11 Microforms
12 Serials
13 Analysis

Part II - Headings, uniform titles and references

21 Choice of access points
22 Headings for persons
23 Geographic names
24 Headings for corporate bodies
25 Uniform titles
26 References

Appendices cover capitalization, abbreviations, numerals, glossary

1. Comments and concern about the cost of implementation of AACR2, especially for large libraries, and where the recommendations differ considerably from those of AACR1.

2. An underlying unease concerning the relevance of AACR2 to a largely and growing computerised cataloguing environment. Although a case can be argued to the contrary, many of the provisions of AACR2 which concern themselves with distinguishing between main and added entries, and entries and references, may be viewed as irrelevant in a data base in which online access is possible via a variety of search keys.

Proposals for revision are considered by the Joint Steering Committee which remains in being. Some revisions have already been announced. These include the extra category for works to be entered under the heading for a corporate body (see Chapter 10) and various other more minor amendments. Work continues on translations, and these will contribute to AACR's role as a truly international code. A French translation was published in 1980, and other translations are under way into Japanese, Spanish, Portuguese, Norwegian and Swedish.

AACR2 has been widely adopted and is extensively recognised as a model which shows many of the features of an international standard. However, to say that AACR2 is widely applied is not to say that libraries applying AACR2 generate identical catalogue records for any one document. Local interpretations of the rules, and modifications to suit local circumstances, certainly militate against standard records.

8.8 The Concise AACR2 (1980)

For some while there have been calls for an abbreviated version of AACR, for small libraries and for non-cataloguers. For some groups it is entirely unreasonable to expect them to grapple with the full 638 pages of AACR2. Plans were made to issue a concise version of AACR1, but these plans never came to fruition. The cataloguing code issued by the School Library Association: *Cataloguing rules for books and other media in primary and secondary schools,* Norman Furlong and Peter Platt, 1976, represents one attempt to provide a distillation of AACR for a specific group of libraries.

The Concise AACR2 by Michael Gorman is not a true abridged edition of the full edition, but rather a rewritten distillation of the essential rules and principles. Inevitably any abridgement poses the dilemma how to abridge, that is, what to leave out and what to include. This must to some extent be determined by the audience. *The Concise AACR2* is intended for cataloguers in small general libraries, especially one-person libraries, students who may want to learn about cataloguing without necessarily becoming cataloguers, and librarians who must use catalogues and need to understand the principles on which they are based. *The Concise AACR2* has 59 rules, arranged like AACR2 in two Parts, Part 1 Description, and Part 2 Entry and Heading.

Comment published so far is favourable, but the code still awaits widespread adoption. Its intended audience may mean that it will be a difficult and slow process to establish an awareness of the existence of the code, and allow the code to play a full role. As the result of a challenge, Michael Gorman has also produced a *Concise Concise AACR2* – a bookmarked-sized edition.

Chapter 8 Readings

1 *AACR2 decisions and rule interpretations: a consolidation of the decisions and rule interpretations for the Anglo-American cataloguing rules,* 2nd edition, made by the Library of Congress, the National Library of Canada, the British Library and the National Library of Australia/ compiled by C.D. Cook. Canadian Library Association: Ottawa, 1981.

2 'AACR2: a materiography', *Catalogue and Index* (54), 1979, 9–10.

3 American Library Association. *ALA Cataloguing Rules for Titles Entries,* 2nd edition, ALA: Chicago, 1949.

4 *Anglo-American Cataloguing Rules,* 2nd edition, prepared by the American Library Association, the British Library, the Canadian Committee on Cataloguing, the Library Association, the Library of Congress/ editors M. Gorman and P.W. Winkler. ALA: Chicago, 1978.

5 Brindley, L., 'The British Library's approach to AACR2', *Journal of Library Automation* 14(3), 1981, 150–60.

6 British Museum, *Rules for compiling the catalogues of printed books, maps and music in the British Museum,* rev. edition, British Museum: London, 1936.

7 Bulaong, G., 'Authorities and standards in a changing world. Part 2', *International Cataloguing,* 11(4), 1982, 41–4.

8 Cutter, C.A., *Rules for a dictionary catalog.* 4th edition, Government Printing Office: Washington, DC, 1904. Republished, Library Association; London, 1953.

9 Examples for applying the *Anglo-American Cataloguing Rules* 2nd edition/prepared under the auspices of the AACR2 Introductory Program Committee. American Library Association, Resources and Technical Services Division: Chicago, 1980.

10 Furlong, N. and Platt, P., *Cataloguing rules for books and other media in primary and secondary schools,* School Library Association: Oxford, 1976.

11 Gorman, M., 'The Anglo-American Cataloguing Rules, 2nd edition',

Library Resources and Technical Services, 22(3), 1978, 209–26.

12 Gorman, M., *The concise AACR2: being a rewritten and simplified version of Anglo-American Cataloguing Rules, 2nd edition*, American Library Association: Chicago, 1981.

13 Gredley, E.J., 'Authorship, corporate entry and mixed responsibility in AACR2', *Catalogue and Index* (57), 1980, 1–3.

14 Gredley, E.J., 'AACR2', *Catalogue and Index* (53), 1979, 7–8.

15 Gredley, E.J., 'Standardizing bibliographical data: AACR2 and international exchange', *Journal of Librarianship*, 12(2), 1980, 84–101.

16 Hagler, R. 'Where's that rule?' a cross-index of the two editions of the Anglo-American Cataloguing Rules incorporating a commentary on the second edition and on changes from previous cataloguing standards. Canadian Library Association: Ottawa, 1979.

17 Hinton, F., 'The concise AACR2', *Library Resources and Technical Services*, 25(2), 1981, 204–6.

18 Hinton, F. 'The concise AACR2', *Catalogue and Index*, (60), 1981, 6–7.

19 Hunter, E.J., 'AACR2: an introduction to the second edition of the Anglo-American Cataloguing Rules'. Bingley & Hamden: London, Linnet Books; Conn., 1979.

20 Hunter, E.J. and Fox, N.J., *Examples illustrating AACR2*, Library Association: London, 1980.

21 International Conference on Cataloguing Principles, Paris, 1961. *Statement of principles. Report of International Conference on Cataloguing Principles/* editors A.H. Chaplin and D. Anderson, Organizing Committee of the International Conference on Cataloguing Principles, National Central Library: London, 1963.

22 Kelm, C.R., 'The historical development of the second edition of Anglo-American Cataloguing Rules', *Library Resources and Technical Services* 22(1), 1976, 22–33.

23 *Library Association and American Library Association Cataloguing rules: author and title entries.* Library Association: London, 1908.

24 Lubetzky, S., *Cataloguing rules and principles: a critique of the ALA rules for entry and a proposed design for their revision*, Library of Congress: Washington, DC, 1953.

25 Richmond, P.A., 'AACR2: a review article', *Journal of Academic Librarianship* 6(1), 1980, 30–7.

26 Shinebourne, J.A., 'A critique of AACR', *Libri*, 29(3), 1979, 231–59.

27 Shinebourne, J.A., 'Fundamental considerations concerning author-title catalogues and cataloguing codes', *Catalogue and Index* 58, 1980, 3–5.

28 Simonton, W., 'An introduction to AACR2', *Library Resources and Technical Services* 23(3), 1979, 321–39.

9   The Anglo-American Cataloguing Rules and author headings

Chapters 7 and 8 have introduced the problems associated with author cataloguing and have surveyed the purpose of cataloguing codes. This chapter focuses more directly on the way in which one major code, AACR2, tackles the problems associated with author cataloguing. This not only serves as a fuller basis for the study of AACR2, but also provides an opportunity to study the range of problems and solutions associated with the formulation of author headings in more detail.

This chapter takes a condition approach to catalogue headings (see Chapter 7), and makes reference to principles, rules and practices as they are indicated in AACR2. In many respects, principles and practices outlined in this chapter apply equally to AACR1 and AACR2 and the Concise AACR2. However, the rules numbers which are cited here for ease of reference to AACR2 apply to AACR2 alone.

AACR2 deals with headings, uniform titles and references in Part II. Figure 8.2 in Chapter 8 shows the main chapters in this part of AACR2. The road to satisfactory author headings starts in Chapter 21 with the choice of access points.

9.1 Choice of access points

The first stage in the choice of access points must be the definition of an author. Most catalogue codes then proceed to recommend use of this author's name as heading in the author catalogue or index. For works written by one person or created by one person, this presents few problems. However, when more than one person is responsible for a work, particularly if these people perform different functions with respect to the work (such as illustrator and editor, or performer and composer) the situation is more complicated. First, it is normal for several access points to be necessary in order that access can be achieved via several of the names of the different authors. Then, since most catalogues currently function on a main and added entry system, it is necessary to select the author whose name will be used as the main entry heading. AACR2 assigns this main entry status to the person who is 'chiefly responsible for the creation of the intellectual or artistic content of a work'. The selection of a corporate body's name as heading is more complex, and problems and solutions are explicitly examined in Chapter 10. The remainder of any rules for choice of access points (such as in Chapter 21 of ACCR2) are really merely qualifications of this basic statement. In AACR2 the choice of main entry is described in relation to the conditions of authorship in each work.

9.2 Conditions of authorship

The main conditions of authorship can be categorised as follows. These conditions can be applied (usually) to both persons and corporate bodies, but in this section, examples will only be given in respect of personal authorship. For examples of corporate bodies as authors the reader is referred to Chapter 10.

Works for which a single person or corporate body is responsible (21.4)

For works of single personal authorship or emanating from one corporate body entry is made under the author. For example,

Project financing/by Christopher Emerson.

Entry under the heading for Emerson.

Collected writings/Francis Wormald

Entry under the heading for Wormald

Single personal authorship includes writers of books, composers of music, compilers of bibliographies, cartographers, artists, photographers, and, in certain cases, performers of sound recordings, films and videorecordings.

Note: All rules in Chapter 21 speak in terms of: 'entry under the heading for' – form and style of headings has yet to be established in later chapters.

Even in this apparently straightforward situation, complications can arise. Subrules of 21.4 deal, for instance, with works erroneously or fictitiously attributed to a person or corporate body, and official communications.

Works with unknown or uncertain personal authorship, or works emanating from a body that lacks a name are to be entered under title. This category includes anonymous works. For example,

The Birthday present.

No author given. Entry under title.

Works of shared responsibility (21.6)

A work of shared responsibility is one where the work has arisen from collaboration between two or more persons or corporate bodies performing the same kind of activity in the creation of the content of a work. In the interests of creating manageable numbers of entries, works of shared responsibility are divided into two main categories:

(a) Those works where a principal author is indicated, in which case entry is under the heading for that principal author (21.6B). For example,

The rough guide to Spain / written and researched by Mark Ellingham, John Fisher and Graham Kenyon with an additional account by Sarah Peel and enormous amounts of help from Pilar Vazquez and Esteban Pujals;

Entry under heading for Ellingham.

Animals by air / Neville Whittaker assisted by Jack Waterman.

Entry under heading for Whittaker.

(b) Those works where no principal author is indicated, in which case entry is under the heading for the author named first if responsibility is shared between two or three persons or corporate bodies. For example,

Instructor's manual to accompany Principles of accounting / John G. Helmkamp, Leroy F. Imdieke, Ralph E. Smith.

Entry under the heading for Helmkamp.

If responsibility is shared between more than three persons or corporate bodies (and no principal author is indicated), then entry is made under the title.

> Parental involvement in Anson House / S. Beveridge, R. Holmes, J. Houseman, J. Smith.

Entry under title

> Drawing for pleasure / Norman Battershill, R. Brown, S. Imdiehn, R. Look

Entry under title

These guidelines are reasonably satisfactory, but do involve establishing criteria, such as layout and type face, which can be applied in identifying whether or not an author should be regarded as having principal responsibility.

Collections and works produced under editorial direction (21.7)

Collections of independent works or extracts from independent works by different persons or bodies, and works produced under editorial direction are to be entered under title, if the work has a collective title. A collection without a collective title is to be entered under the heading appropriate to the first contribution named in the chief source of information. For example,

> The pleasures of murder / edited by Jonathan Goodman.

Entry under title.

> Focus on teaching: readings from The elementary school journal / edited by Walter Doyle and Thomas L. Good.

Entry under title.

> Inside classrooms: a collection of case studies by teachers / [edited by Mick Wilson].

Entry under title.

Note that AACR1 distinguished between collections and works produced under editorial direction, entering the first under title, and the second under editor. It was latterly agreed that this distinction, whilst it led to sensible entries in some instances, was difficult to maintain, and often led to works being arbitrarily allocated to one or other of the categories.

132

A work of mixed responsibility is one for which collaboration between two or more persons or corporate bodies performing different kinds of activities, such as the translator or reviser of a work written by another person, has occurred. The problem is to decide who to select as being mainly responsible. Rules in AACR2 give guidance on how to make this choice, or in other words how to identify who is chiefly responsible.

AACR2 divides works of mixed responsibility into two groups:

(a) Works that are modifications of other works, such as:

(i) adaptations of texts (21.10) Here entry is under adapter for a paraphrase, rewriting, adaptation for children or version in a different literary form (eg novelisation or dramatisation). For example,

> Naval wings/ Adrian Vicary; rewritten for children by Steven Zaloga.

Entry under heading for Zaloga.

(ii) illustrated texts (21.11) where an artist has provided illustrations for an already established text. Here entry is under the heading appropriate for the text (that is, normally the writer of the text). For example,

> Fanny and the monsters / Penelope Lively; illustrated by John Lawrence.

Entry under heading for Lively.

> George the tabby/ by Moomim "Mim" Mendelssohn, cat companion to Mollie Mendelssohn; illustrations by Andrea Reynolds.

Entry under heading for Mendelssohn.

(iii) revisions of texts (21.12). Here entry is made under the original author of an edition that has been revised, enlarged, updated, condensed, and so on by another person, if the original author is still considered to be responsible for the work. Otherwise entry is made under the reviser. For example,

> Zen doctrine of no-mind: the significance of the Sutra of Hui-neng (Wei-Lang) / Daisetz Teitaro Suzuki—2nd ed. / edited by Christmas Humphreys.

Entry under heading for Suzuki.

(iv) texts published with commentary (21.13) are entered under the commentator if the commentry is emphasised. If the edition of the work is emphasised, then the work is entered accordingly as an edition of the original work.

> Mother Courage and her children / Bertolt Brecht; translated from the German by John Willett; with commentary and notes by Hugh Rorrison.

Entry under heading for Brecht

> My truck / Margaret Wolff; illustrated by Val Hunt.

Entry under heading for Wolff.

> Colin and Maggie's odd little book—of ends / illustrated by Maggie Guillon; poems by Colin Stanley.

Entry under headings for Guillon.

(v) translations (21.14) are entered under the heading appropriate to the original. For example,

> Action and existence: anarchism for business administration / Pierre Guillet de Monthoux; translated by D.E. Weston.

Entry under heading for de Monthoux.

(vi) texts published with biographical/critical material (21.15) are entered under the biographer/critic if the work is presented as a biographical/critical work, and under the heading appropriate to the work(s) if the biographer/critic is represented as editor, compiler and so on.

Special rules also follow which deal with mixed responsibility in respect of adaptations of art works (21.16), reproduction of two or more art works (21.17), musical works (21.18), and musical works that include words (21.19) and other musical situations (21.20–21.22), sound recordings (21.23), but sufficient has been said to illustrate the nature of mixed responsibility in works that are modifications of other works.

(b) Mixed responsibility in new works

(i) collaboration between artist and writer (21.24). Works that involve collaboration between an artist and a writer are to be entered under the heading for the one who is named first in the chief source of information, unless the other's name is given greater prominence. For example,

> How to make and use your own visual delights / Richard Romo and Boone Brinson; edited by Nancy Stanley; illustrations by Boone Brinson.

Entry under heading for Romo.

(ii) reports of interviews of exchanges (21.25) are to be entered under the participant if the report is essentially confined to the words of the person(s) interviewed. If the report is to a considerable extent in the words of the reporter then entry will be made under the heading for the reporter.

(iii) Spirit communications (21.26) are to be entered under the heading for the spirit!

(iv) academic disputations (21.27) are generally entered under the heading for the faculty moderator.

Related works (21.28)

We now come to the sixth and last condition of authorship. Related works are separately catalogued works that have a relationship to another work. These include: continuations and sequels; supplements; indexes; concordances; incidental music to dramatic works; cadenzas; scenarios; screenplays, and so on; choreographies; librettos and other texts set to music.

A related work is entered under its own heading according to the earlier rules above. An added entry is made for the work to which it is related. For example,

Cumulative book index: a world list of books in the English language . . . supplementing the United States catalog.

Main entry under title of the work.
Added entry under the heading for the United States catalog.

9.3 Special rules

It is worth noting that AACR2 does not succeed in giving explicit instructions for the cataloguing of all categories of material within the framework of a conditions approach. Some categories of material defy helpful categorisation, and need to be treated as special cases. Thus Chapter 21 concludes with a number of special rules. These are:

21.31 Laws etc.
21.32 Administrative regulations etc.
21.33 Constitutions, charters and other fundamental laws
21.34 Court rules
21.35 Treaties, intergovernmental agreements, etc.
21.36 Court decisions, cases, etc.
21.37 Sacred scriptures
21.38 Theological creeds, confessions of faith etc.
21.39 Liturgical works.

9.4 Added entries

Added entries are made under any headings that 'some catalogue users might suppose that the description of an item would be found under . . . rather than under the heading or title chosen for the main entry.' In various of the rules concerning the choice of heading in AACR2 recommendations are made concerning appropriate added entries. In the interests of clarity an integrated account of the appropriate added entry headings is to be found in 21.29 and 21.30. In the interests of economy, and in order to avoid an over-complex catalogue these rules recommend selective use of added entries, that is added entries are only made under important subsidiary headings and not under every possible alternative heading. For example, in a work of shared authorship, if only two or three persons are involved, main entry will be made for the first named and added entries under the subsequent authors' names. If, however, four or more persons are involved, added entry is only made under the heading for the first named, with main entry under title.

Added entries appear in the form of personal name headings, corporate name headings, titles, series and name-title headings. These are discussed in more detail below.

Added entries under personal names are made in respect of:
1. Collaborators, if there are up to three. If there are four or more collaborators, entry is made under the first named.
2. Writers
3. Editors and compilers (for monographic works)
4. Translators (in certain cases)
5. Illustrators (in certain cases)
6. Persons with other relationships with the work, for example addressees of a collection of letters, a person honoured by a Festschrift.

Added entries under corporate names are made for a prominently named corporate body, unless it functions solely as distributor or manufacturer. For collaborating corporate bodies the same rules apply as for collaborating personal authors.

Added entries under title An added entry is made under the title proper of every work in which the title proper has not been used as the main entry heading, unless:

1. the title proper is essentially the same as a uniform title used as a main entry heading, or as a subject heading (in a dictionary catalogue).
2. the title has been composed by the cataloguer.

Added entries are also made for any other title, for example, cover title, caption title, which is significantly different from the title proper.

Added entries under series titles are made for each separately catalogued work in a series, if the heading provides a useful collocation. Instances in which series added entries are not made include:

1. Series where the items are only related to one another by common physical characteristics.
2. Series where the parts have been numbered primarily for the purposes of stock control.
3. Series where all items in the series have been entered under the heading for one person.

Added entries under name-title headings may be made in respect of related works. If both the heading and the title of the related work differ from those of the work to which it is related, then an added entry for the related work should include the heading and title of the related work, followed by the description of the work to which it is related. For example:

> Muirhead, L. Russell. Southern Italy with Sicily and Sardinia.
> Southern Italy.—4th ed. / Paul Blanchard.—Ernest Benn. £14.95.
> ISBN 0-85334-246-6

9.5 Forms of headings

Once the name of the person or corporate body to be used in the heading (either main or added entry) is known, the nature of the heading must be decided. There are three components in this decision:

1. Choice of name (if an author has or uses more than one name).
2. Choice of form of name (particularly if a name may be cited in various forms).
3. Choice of entry element (particularly where the name is in an unconventional form).

The problems pertaining to the form of headings are tackled in Chapters 22, 23, 24, and 25 of AACR2. Chapters 23 and 24 are concerned primarily with corporate bodies, and these will be considered in more detail in Chapter 10 of this work. Chapter 25 deals with uniform titles, and its implications are considered in Chapter 11. This section, then, will review the basic problems surrounding the choice of form of heading, and will illustrate these problems with reference to headings for persons. This involves consideration of the provisions of Chapter 22 of AACR2.

In Chapter 7 we have already discussed the relative merits of a uniform heading for all works of one author, and the alternative approach of using various headings according to the form of heading given in the work being catalogued. In respect of personal name headings, AACR2 in general seeks to achieve a uniform heading for any given author, irrespective of the number of names or forms of name that author has used.

All the rules in AACR2 on form of heading give guidance on the choice and form of the uniform heading. A number of different names or forms might be selected as the uniform heading. In order that the choice might be reasonably consistent, AACR2 recommends (22.1A):

> Choose as the basis of the heading for a person, the name by which he or she is commonly known.

Now, discovering the name by which an author is commonly known may well present problems, and certainly involves knowledge and judgement. This recommendation asks the cataloguer to ascertain the name by which an author is commonly known. This may be relatively easy for well-known authors, but can be difficult for more obscure authors. As an aid to selection the name by which a person is commonly known is determined from the chief source of information of works by that person in his or her language. If a library does not have all or most of the works of the person under consideration (and even establishing the extent of a library's collection of the works of any given author can take time), then the cataloguer will consult reference sources (such as biographical and bibliographical sources), in an attempt to identify the best-known name. If the person works in a nonverbal context (for example, a painter or sculptor), or is not known primarily as an author, again headings will be determined from the usage in reference sources. Apart from the fact that different librarians may consult different reference sources, there are other factors which may lead different cataloguers to different decisions. In addition, there is an element of perpetuation about the establishment of headings on the basis of reference sources. Compilers of reference sources may be consulting each other's sources in establishing their headings!

9.6 Headings for persons

Continuing from 9.5, this section picks up the three problems in respect of persons' names as headings enumerated at the beginning of 9.5.

9.6.1 Choice of name (22.2)

Many people use more than one name. An author may use a pseudonym (or assumed name) or even several different pseudonyms in his or her writings. Other authors may change their names, for instance, by marriage or elevation to the nobility. Generally, AACR2 recommends that the predominant name be used, even if that name is a pseudonym. In one instance, AACR2 deviates from the principle of uniform heading and in 22.2C3 permits works of authors writing under several pseudonyms, none of which can be identified as predominant, to be entered under the name appearing in the item, as the heading for that item. For example: all of the

138

following names may be used for one author, if none is predominant: Hamilton, Charles, Clifford, Martin, and Richards, Frank. But where there is a predominant pseudonym, entry would be made under that pseudonym e.g. under Lewis Carroll, and not Charles Lutridge Dodgson.

9.6.2 Choice of form of name (22.3)

For names which appear in more than one form it is necessary to determine the form to be used in the heading. This involves the consideration of:

(a) Fullness. Names commonly vary in fullness, especially in terms of the extent of abbreviations and initials used. The predominant form is recommended, for example:

Use Murray, Reginald N *Not* Murray R N

But Hall, J L *Not* Hall, James Logan.

(b) Language. Particularly for well-known persons, names are likely to appear in different language forms. The choice depends upon the languages involved, the types of names and the periods.

Some examples are:

Charles V, not Karl V or Carlos V

Homer, not Homeros or Homerus.

Omar Khayyam not 'Umar Khayyām

(c) Spelling. If variations in spelling of a person's name are encountered, then the form to be chosen is the official or predominant form. For example:

Nyanaponika, Thera not Nanaponika, Thera.

9.6.3 Choice of entry element (22.4)

Once the name to be used in a heading and its form have been settled, it is time to decide upon the entry element, or, in more general terms, to examine the preferred order of the components of a name as the name is to appear as a heading. The names of the majority of persons are entered with surname as the entry element. Thus we expect to find, James Brown entered as Brown, James. However certain special types of surnames present particular problems. Compound surnames, such as Henderson-Smythe, and surnames with separately written prefixes, such as Van Gogh present a dilemma as to which part of the surname should be represented as the entry element. For example, is Henderson-Smythe to be entered under Henderson or Smythe? And does the same practice apply is the name is originally written as Henderson Smythe (without the hyphen)?

Some people, particularly people of earlier times, and royalty, are not normally known by a surname. Headings for these people are normally in terms of the given name, for example, Anne Finch, Countess of Winchelsea;

John, the Baptist; Thomas Aquinas. The general principle for the choice of entry element of a personal name is the person's preference (if known), or if this cannot be determined, the way in which the name would normally be listed in authoritative lists in his or her language or country.

In some instances it may be necessary to make additions to names in order to clarify to whom the name pertains, or to distinguish the name from other similar names. AACR2 indicates how dates and other distinguishing terms may be used in this context. Two examples of such headings might be:

Smith, John, 1924–
Smith, John, ca 1837–1896
Smith, John, Captain
Smith, John, Rev.

AACR2 also contains some special rules which offer much-needed guidance on names in more unusual languages. The rules (22.21–22.28) cover personal names not written in the Roman alphabet, and names in a non-European language written in the Roman alphabet. Examples of language covered are: Burmese, Indic, Indonesian, Malay and Thai.

9.7 References

Once the uniform heading has been established for all main and added entries associated with a work, the cataloguer can proceed to consider the references, from alternative forms of heading. The different types of references have been introduced in Chapter 2. Although some guidance on appropriate references is given elsewhere in AACR2, Chapter 26 summarises the types of situations in which references might be appropriate in author cataloguing. One of the particularly helpful features of Chapter 26 is the extensive array of examples.

'See' references are made from: (26.2A)

(a) Different names (not used as headings in entries), such as pseudonyms, real names, secular names, earlier names and later names.

(b) Different forms of the name, such as different fullness, different language form and different spelling.

(c) Different entry elements, such as different elements of a compound name, part of a surname following a prefix or the family name of a saint.

A few examples of 'see' references covering all of these categories follow.

Moxham, Bernard *See* Moxham, B. J.
Nanaponika Thera *See* Nyanaponika Thera

Hammond-Innes, Ralph *See* Innes, Hammond
Hadithi, Nazar Al- *See* Al Hadithi, Nazar
Gunden, Heidi Von *See* Von Gunden, Heidi

'See also' references (26.2C) are made between different headings for the same person, if a person's works have been entered under more than one heading. For example:

Hall, Trevor see also Hancock, James

Explanatory references give a little more explanation as to why the link between two names is being made in the catalogue or index. The following examples serve to demonstrate how they might function.

Hammond, Ralph *For this author under other names see* Innes, Hammond
Hamilton, Charles, *1875–1961 For this author under other names see* Richards, Frank, *1875–1961*

Chapter 9 Readings

Various readings cited at the end of Chapter 8 are useful and appropriate.

10 Catalogue and index access points for the works of corporate bodies

10.1 Introduction

Increasing numbers of documents and information-carrying media are the product not of one individual, but of a group of individuals, which might be described as a corporate body. Early cataloguing codes had to concern themselves with works which were the responsibility of corporate bodies (see Chapter 8), but it was not until the Paris Principles and AACR1 that a systematic attempt was made to examine all facets of the creation of access points for the works of corporate bodies. The rationale, then, for a separate chapter of this work devoted to the cataloguing of the works of corporate bodies is threefold:

1. The number of documents which could potentially be treated as being the work of a corporate body is increasing, and the number and variety of bodies responsible for publishing and compiling information has expanded.
2. The principles which will be detailed in this chapter for the creation of catalogue headings for the works of corporate bodies are appropriate to a wide range of indexes, directories, data bases and other reference materials.
3. There is a good deal of scope for users and novice cataloguers to find difficulty in identifying the appropriate heading for many of the works which are the responsibility of corporate bodies.

This opportunity is taken to develop one important aspect of author cataloguing in some detail.

The problems that can arise without codes to guide the indexer in the compilation of headings for corporate bodies can be seen in too many circumstances where no codes have been acknowledged. A good example is British Telecom's telephone directories. Take the Birmingham Business section, Section 330. Now surprisingly, this includes government departments, local authorities, public services and doctors, none of which might be regarded as business. However, when we turn to tracing a local school, it is first necessary not only to know the name of the school, for example

Canterbury Cross Junior, but to realise that it will be listed under the heading for its appropriate local authority. Thus, for example, we need to decide whether to search under Birmingham City Council or Sandwell Metropolitan Borough Council. Once this selection has been made we then need to discover whether the school is listed under, for example Birmingham City Council, Education Department or Birmingham City Council, Schools. Now we might eventually find this elusive school and its address and telephone number. However, having learnt how to trace local authority institutions we might suppose that libraries would be similarly listed. No! All libraries are listed under the heading 'Libraries', which is then subdivided according to Birmingham City Council, Sandwell Metropolitan Borough Council, and so on. Truly this is a difficult tool to use.

In identifying the main stages in creating headings for the works of corporate bodies, the process is the same as that for personal authors. Here again reference is made to Chapter 21 of AACR2 in order to settle the choice of access points, with subsequent consultation of Chapter 23 for the form of geographic names, and Chapter 24 for the form of headings for corporate bodies. Although this chapter will consider primarily the recommendations of AACR2 it is important to recognise that there are other factors in the headings to be found in catalogues and indexes in respect of the works of corporate bodies. Perhaps the most important function of a study of AACR2 in this area is to alert the student to the problems of headings for corporate bodies, rather than to inculcate the solutions of one cataloguing code. In addition to AACR2, many existing catalogues will have used AACR1 for establishing some or all of the headings for works of corporate bodies. Smaller libraries may increasingly use the Concise AACR2, and here again the recommendations are not always precisely consistent with AACR2. Other indexes or directories may use in-house codes or no code at all. Equally important in maintaining consistency in the catalogues or indexes of one collection are in-house authority lists. These lists record the headings that have been established for a given body or person in the past by that cataloguing or indexing agency. Cataloguing codes give general guidance, which must be interpreted in specific instances. This authority list shows how the rules have been interpreted in the past by a given agency. Not all libraries maintain a separate authority list, but those that do not will often consult the catalogue in order to establish the heading that has been used for a corporate body in the past.

10.2 Choice of access points

The first decision in establishing headings for the works of corporate bodies is the one over which code makers have wavered. There would appear to be no inherently obvious point at which one work should be regarded as having been intellectually created by the co-operative thought of a corporate body, and another be regarded as the collection of separate contributions from a group of individuals. The pressure for the recognition of corporate authorship arises from the fact that the name of a corporate body will often be the sought heading for a particular work. This assignment of intellectual responsibility is important, as we have seen earlier, since it determines the heading for the main entry.

The first step in assigning intellectual responsibility to a corporate body must be a definition of a corporate body. AACR2 offers the following definition:

> A corporate body is an organisation or group of persons that is identified by a particular name and that acts, or may act, as an entity . . . Typical examples of corporate bodies are associations, institutions, business firms, nonprofit enterprises, governments, government agencies, projects and programmes, religious bodies, local churches, and conferences.

Note also that some corporate bodies are subordinate to other bodies . . . (21.1B1)

Note that this is a wide-ranging definition which permits a cataloguer to regard any group which works together and has a name (the name is the key) as a corporate body.

If a corporate body is deemed to have some intellectual responsibility for the content of a work, then the name of that body will usually feature as a heading on either a main or added entry. AACR2 identifies the following categories of works for which main entry may be under the name of a corporate body: (21.1B2)

> **21.1B2. General rule.** Enter a work emanating[2] from one or more corporate bodies under the heading for the appropriate corporate body if it falls into one or more of the following categories:
> a) those of an administrative nature dealing with the corporate body itself
>   *or* its internal policies, procedures, and/or operations
>   *or* its finances
>   *or* its officers and/or staff
>   *or* its resources (e.g., catalogues, inventories, membership directories)
> b) some legal and governmental works of the following types:[3]
>   laws (see 21.31)
>   decrees of the chief executive that have the force of law (see 21.31)
>   administrative regulations (see 21.32)
>   treaties, etc. (see 21.35)
>   court decisions (see 21.36)
>   legislative hearings
> c) those that record the collective thought of the body (e.g., reports of commissions, committees, etc.; official statements of position on external policies)

d) those that report the collective activity of a conference (proceedings, collected papers, etc.), of an expedition (results of exploration, investigation, etc.), or of an event (an exhibition, fair festival, etc.) falling within the definition of a corporate body (see 21.1B1), provided that the conference, expedition, or event is prominently named in the item being catalogued

e) sound recordings, films, and videorecordings resulting from the collective activity of a performing group as a whole where the responsibility of the group goes beyond that of mere performance, execution, etc. (For corporate bodies that function solely as performers on sound recordings, see 21.23.)

f) Cartographic materials emanating from a corporate body other than a body which is merely responsible for the publication or distribution of the materials.

(Note that the last of these categories (f) was not included in the published AACR2, but was issued as an amendment in 1982.)

The categories identified above are more limited than the categories of works for which corporate bodies may be used as main entry heading in AACR1.

Rule 21.1B2 identifies those cases in which corporate bodies may be used as the heading for the main entry. Other authorship conditions may also apply. For example, it is possible to encounter shared responsibility between two or more corporate bodies, or mixed responsibility where two or more corporate bodies share different functions in respect of the work.

Even in instances where the name of a corporate body is not required as the heading to the main entry, the corporate name may be used as a heading for an added entry. Chapter 9 considered the provisions for selecting headings for added entries. Firgure 10.1 shows some examples of brief catalogue records for corporate bodies.

10.3 Headings for corporate bodies

10.3.1 Choice of form of headings (24.1)

Once a decision has been made with regard to the number and choice of main and added entries for any work, attention must be focused on the form of the heading to be adopted for a body. Here Chapter 24 of AACR2, supplemented by Chapters 23 and 26, is important.

The basic rules of Chapter 24, 24.1 establish the principle for selecting names, on the basis of the name by which the body is predominantly identified:

Enter a corporate body directly under the name by which it is predominantly identified, except when the rules that follow provide for entering it under the name of a higher or related body or under the name of a government.

Determine the form of a corporate body from items issued by that body in its language or, when this condition does not apply, from reference sources.

Figure 10.1 Corporate bodies

Some examples of works entered under corporate body as main entry

British Waterways Board
  Annual report and accounts/ British Waterways Board.
  London: The Board: Distributed by HMSO, 1977.

British Standards Institution
  Method for test sieving/ British Standards Institution.—
  1st revision.— London: B.S.I., 1976.— (BS1796: 1976)
  £3.10

Eastbourne, Borough Council
  Policy statement for nursing & rest homes: adopted 28 February
  1983/ Eastbourne Borough Council.—Eastbourne: Technical
  Services Department, 1983.—

Anson House Preschool Project
  Anson House preschool project.—(Ilford): (Dr. Barnardo's)
I: Classroom provision/ written by Christine Gunstone; cartoons by
  Margaret Saul; photographs by Judy Sebba.— (1982).—

Some examples of works not entered under corporate body as main entry

Perraton, Hilary
  The cost of distance education/ Hilary Perraton.— Cambridge:
  International Extension College, 1982. (IEC broadsheets on
  distance learning; no. 17)

Weeks, John C.S.
  The professional development of secondary heads: a research
  paper and report to the Northern Sub-Region of the South
  West INSET Co-ordinating Committee/ by John C.S. Weeks.—
  Bristol: County of Avon Public Relations and Publicity Dept., 1983.

Provisions of mains and services by public utilities in residential
  estates/ National Joint Utilities Group.— London: (The Group),
  1979.— (NJUG publication; no. 2)

Great British potato recipes: 101 ways with Britain's favourite
  vegetable.— London: Potato Marketing Board, (1983).

146

Added entries under corporate bodies

University of Liverpool. Department of Geography
  Population mobility and multilocality in Ilorin. Kwara State, Nigeria/ Susan Watts and R. Mansell Prothero.— Department of Geography, University of Liverpool.
  307'.2'096695   B84-00673

Victoria and Albert Museum
  Felix H. Man.— The Museum
  779'.2'0924   B84-00112
  Unpriced

Thus an attempt is made to establish a uniform heading for all works issued by a corporate body. The exception to this general principle is when the name of a corporate body has changed. Each time a corporate body changes its name, a new heading is established, and appropriate references are made to link the two headings. In other words, a corporate body that has changed its name is treated as a separate entity.

10.3.2 Choice of form of heading (24.2–24.11)

Once a name has been selected, the form in which it is to be presented must be considered. Here an attempt is made to choose one form and supply references from the other forms. This involves consideration of:

  (a) fullness of name to be adopted
  (b) language of name to be adopted
  (c) spelling of name to be adopted.

In some cases modifications are made to the form chosen. These might involve additions (for example, the name of the place in which the corporate body is located, in order to distinguish two or more bodies having the same name), such as:

Trinity College (Hartford, Conn.)
Trinity College (Cambridge)

or omissions (for example, initial articles), such as Library Association and not The Library Association, or other special modifications for the names of certain types of corporate bodies. Special rules are included for specific types of corporate bodies, such as exhibitions, conferences, subordinate and related bodies, governments, government bodies and officials, and radio and television stations. The use of these rules is illustrated in two specific categories in the next two sections.

10.4 Conferences and conference proceedings

21.1B1 confirms that AACR2 regards a conference as a corporate body, and therefore conference proceedings may be regarded as the work of a corporate body. Note also from the definition of a corporate body in 21.1B1, that it is necessary that a corporate body has a name for it to be regarded as a corporate entity.

21.1B1 goes on to establish that conference proceedings may be entered under the 'heading for the appropriate corporate body', provided that the proceedings fit into category (d) of 21.1B2, and report the collective activity of a conference.

Where the conference cannot be seen to have a name, then the work will normally be treated as a collection (as it is a collection of individual contributions by a variety of persons). In this case, the application of 21.7 will normally lead to entry under title of the conference proceedings. Figure 10.2 gives examples of brief entries for conference proceedings.

Thus the name of a conference may be used either as a main or an added entry when cataloguing conference proceedings. In both cases it will be necessary to establish an acceptable form for the heading. 24.7A demonstrates that the components to be included in the heading for a conference, are: name, number, year and place. Further details are given as to the form of each of these components.

Added entries may also be necessary to cover other access points to the conference proceedings. It is normal to make added entries in respect of important editors, and significant organisations associated with the organisation or content of the conference. References will also be necessary, in respect of any variant forms of heading, for headings on both main and added entries.

10.5 Governments and government bodies

Figure 10.3 includes some examples of headings and entries for governments and government bodies. 21.1B1 defines governments and government agencies as corporate bodies. 21.1B2 goes on to identify various categories of work which may be generated by government bodies. Amongst these are numbered: some specific legal and governmental works, such as laws, decrees, treaties; works that record the collective thought of a body, for

Figure 10.2 Conference proceedings

Conference proceedings entered under title

Laser-solid interactions and transient thermal processing of materials: symposium held November 1982 in Boston,
Massachusetts, U.S.A./ editors J. Narayan, W.L. Brown and R.A. Lemons.— New York: Oxford: North Holland, c1983. (Materials Research Society symposia proceedings; v.13)

Medieval art and architecture at Winchester Cathedral.— (Leeds): British Archaeological Association, 1983. (Conference transactions; 6, 1980)

Conference proceedings entered under name of conference

International Gold Workshop (1982: Munich)
Modern aspects of gold therapy: International Gold Workshop, Munich, January 14-15, 1982/ volume editors M. Schattenkirchner, W. Müller.— Basel; London: Karger, c1983.— (Rheumatology; v.8)

International Brain Research Organization. Satellite Symposium (1982: Mannheim)
Monoamine oxidase and its selective inhibitors: satellite symposium of the International Brain Research Organization, Mannheim, March 29-30, 1982/ editors, H. Beckmann, P. Riederer.—Basel; London: Karger, 1983.— (Modern problems of pharmacopsychiatry; v.19)

Interamerican Congress of Clinical Pharmacology and Therapeutics (1st: 1982: Caracas)
Clinical pharmacology and therapeutics: proceedings of the first Interamerican Congress of Clinical Pharmacology and Therapeutics, Caracas, Venezuela, October 10-15, 1982/ editor, Manuel Velasco.— Amsterdam; Oxford: Excerpta Medica, 1983.— (International congress series; 604)

---

example, reports of commissions and committees; and various cartographic materials. Note that these provisions do not include research reports which have been prepared within a government agency but specifically authored by an individual. These would normally be entered under the heading appropriate to the personal author as main entry (the corporate body would probably merit an added entry).

Figure 10.3 Governments and government bodies

Local government

Lincolnshire. County Council
The County of Lincolnshire: the official guide to the county/ issued by authority of the Lincolnshire County Council.— Gloucester: British, (1983).

Hereford & Worcester. County Council
The County of Hereford and Worcester: the official guide to the county/ issued by authority of the Hereford and Worcester County Council.—Gloucester: British, (1983).

Central government: a column of entries sharing direct and indirect entry under government, entry not under government and forms of references

United Kingdom. Consultative Committee on the Curriculum
An Education for life and work/ Education for the Industrial Society Project, final report of the Project Planning Committee.— Consultative Committee on the Curriculum (pbk). £3.30
373.14'25'09411   B83-37581   ISBN 0-946584-00-1

United Kingdom. Consultative Committee on the Curriculum. Committee on Secondary Education See **Great Britain.** Committee on Secondary Education

United Kingdom. Corrosion Education and Training Working Party
Corrosion principles for engineering technicians/ by B. Perry.— Department of Industry (pbk). Unpriced
620.1'623   B83-36286

United Kingdom. Countryside Commission
Management agreements.— Countryside Commission (pbk). Unpriced
719'.0942   B83-36340   ISBN 0-86170-077-5

United Kingdom. Department of Education and Science
Study of HM Inspectors in England and Wales/ Department of Education and Science, Welsh Office.—H.M.S.O. (pbk). £4.50
354.410085'1   B83-36085   ISBN 0-11-270311-9

United Kingdom. Department of Health and Social Security
Health care and its costs/ Department of Health and Social Security.—H.M.S.O. (pbk). £5.95
338.4'73621'0941   B83-37662   ISBN 0-11-320828-6

The Supplementary Benefit (Resources) Amendment Regulations 1983.— H.M.S.O. (unbound). £1.65
344.104'2   B83-37750   ISBN 0-10-188240-8

United Kingdom. Department of Health and Social Security. Social Security Advisory Committee See **Great Britain**. Social Security Advisory Committee

United Kingdom. Department of Industry
Interim assessment of the small business loan guarantee scheme/ Department of Industry.— The Department (pbk). Unpriced
338.6'42   B83-36293
Local area networks/ by the Local Area Network Standardisation Project Team.— Department of Industry (pbk). Unpriced
651.7   B83-36299

United Kingdom. Department of Industry. Corrosion Education and Training Working Party **See Great Britain**. Corrosion Education and Training Working Party

United Kingdom. Department of Industry. Laboratory of the Government Chemist See **Laboratory of the Government Chemist**

United Kingdom. Department of Industry. Small Firms Service **See Small Firms Service**

United Kingdom. Department of Prices and Consumer Protection. Office of Fair Trading See **Great Britain**. Office of Fair Trading

United Kingdom. Department of the Environment
Conisbrough Castle/ Department of the Environment.— 2nd ed.— H.M.S.O. (unbound). £0.20
914.28'27   B83-36677   ISBN 0-11-671453-0
Mount Grace Priory/ Department of the Environment.— 2nd ed.— H.M.S.O. (unbound). '0.30
914.28'49   B83-36672   ISBN 0-11-671149-3

United Kingdom. Department of the Environment. Adult Inspectorate See **Great Britain**. Adult Inspectorate

United Kingdom. Department of the Environment London Housing Staff Commission See **Great Britain**. London Housing Staff Commission

United Kingdom. Department of the Environment. Sports Council See **Sports Council**

Continued

United Kingdom. Department of Trade
Hong Kong as a market for British textiles.— Department of Trade
(pbk). Unpriced
382'.45677   B83-36827
Ramor Investments Limited: Derritron Limited/ by Hugh Carlisle
and John Darby.— H.M.S.O. (pbk). £20.00
338.8'6'0941   B83-37661   ISBN 0-11-513673-8

United Kingdom. Department of Transport
Vehicle testing.— 2nd ed.— H.M.S.O. (pbk). £2.50
629.28'25'0941   B83-35423   ISBN 0-11-550587-3

United Kingdom. Departments of Industry and Trade Common
Services: Libraries. Ashdown House Library See **Ashdown House
Library**

United Kingdom. Equal Opportunities Commission
The job-splitting scheme.— The Commission (pbk). Unpriced
331.25'7   B83-37664

In considering the headings to be chosen for government agencies it is
as well to start by considering the headings for governments, since the
headings for some government agencies follow from the headings for their
governments. 24.3E instructs (for governments): 'Use the conventional
name of a government unless the official name is in common use. The
conventional name of a government is the geographic name of the area . . .
over which the government has jurisdiction.' Chapter 23, Geographic
Names helps in establishing the form of name of various areas. Application
of Chapter 23 and 24.3E will lead to headings for governments of the type:
Austria, Florence, Sweden, United Kingdom, Newcastle (N.S.W.). These
headings for governments will be used in respect of works produced
by governments. Some of these works are treated in the special rules at the
end of Chapter 21 and include laws, administrative regulations, and treaties.

Returning to government agencies, some agencies are treated as
subordinate to a government, whilst others are entered independently. 24.17
declares: 'Enter a body created or controlled by a government under its own
name unless it belongs to one or more of the types listed in 24.18.'

24.18 proceeds to identify and illustrate ten types of government
agencies to be entered subordinately. Once a body has been identified as
subordinate, in many cases it is necessary to decide whether to make a direct
or indirect subheading. For example should the heading be:

United Kingdom. Manpower Services Commission Training Division or United Kingdom Training Division?

24.19 directs:

> Enter an agency . . . as a direct subheading of the heading for the government unless the name of the agency has been or is likely to be used by another agency entered under the name of the same government.

Again, for the works of governments and government bodies it is necessary to consider added entries and references. These will be established in keeping with the principles established earlier.

Examples are given in order to illustrate the points made above.

References will also be necessary, and will fall into the same types as those identified for personal authors, that is, 'see', 'see also', and explanatory references.

Chapter 10 Readings

1 Hinton, F., 'AACR2 and IFLA recommendations on corporate headings', *International Cataloguing*, 12(1), 1983, 9–10.
2 Spalding, C.S., 'The life and death (?) of corporate authorship', *Library Resources and Technical Services*, 24(3), 1980, 195–208.
3 Verona, E., *Corporate headings: their use in library catalogues and national bibliographies: a comparative and critical study*, IFLA Committee on Cataloguing: London, 1975.

11.1 Types of title index

The title approach to documents and the information that they contain arises in a variety of different contexts. The title of a work is

> A word, phrase, character, or group of characters, normally appearing in an item, naming the item or the work contained in it.

Thus the title is a label associated with a work, which both identifies the document, and describes in broad terms its content. Title indexes are indexes in which the title is used as the heading or access point in entries. In a straightforward title index the first word of the title is likely to be the filing word, and thus the most important element of the access point. Other indexes based on titles, both printed and machine-held, may provide access to words other than the first in a title.

There are in fact two distinct types of title index:

(i) those indexes where entry is made under title so that a user can retrieve an item with a known title, according to its title.

(ii) those where the title is intended to function as a crude subject index.

Both of these types of index will be considered in this chapter.

11.2 Titles as indexes to titles

In any context where documents are listed, such as catalogues and bibliographies, indexers will sometimes provide some types of title index, or make some title entries in a sequence containing both title and author entries. A conventional title index is merely an index in which titles in direct order are used as the headings. Since titles are essentially alphabetical characters, the sequence will normally be arranged in alphabetical order. The titles will usually be accompanied by other bibliographic details, such as author's name(s), edition statement and imprint.

Title entries, whether part of an author/title index, or filed separately in a title index, are provided basically because the title of a work is one piece of information that a user may bring to a catalogue or index in a search for a specific document. Some evidence suggests that users are equally as likely to remember a title, as an author. Nevertheless current cataloguing practice tends to prefer the author's name as the heading for a main entry. In general title entries are regarded as secondary to author entries and may be used either as added entries, or as main entries when an author entry is not possible or suitable for some reason. Some cataloguers and bibliographers make added title entries under the title of most works in accordance with AACR2. Other catalogues and bibliographies only feature added entries under title where it is deemed that the author main entry heading is not likely to be obvious to the users.

Titles are viewed as subsidiary entries when compared with authors' names. There are various reasons why author entries are preferred:

(a) Entry under title has little collocative value in the sense that since titles are unique, two titles which file adjacent to one another are not particularly likely to be related to each other. Author entry gives direct access to particular documents whilst at the same time collocating documents with the same author. Thus it is possible in an author sequence to view easily the works of one author.

(b) Titles can be easily misquoted. In general the very uniqueness of titles makes it less likely that they will be remembered. For example, a user seeking a novel by Agatha Christie is much less likely to forget the author's name than the title of individual works. The fact that one author's name may be associated with several works means that the greater familiarity with the author's name increases the possibility of its being remembered.

(c) An author's name is usually shorter than a title, and thus is arguably easier to handle and remember.

(d) Titles present filing problems (particularly in the minds of users). Many titles begin with common phrases such as: an introduction to; proceedings of; a history of; simple; and the common occurrence of such words will lead to long sequences under such words or phrases. Further, titles like '101 ways to cook beans' and '1984' do not have an obvious place in an alphabetical sequence.

In addition to main or added entries under titles added entries are often also made in respect of distinctive series titles. AACR2 instructs: 'Make an added entry under the heading for a series for each separately catalogued work in the series if it provides a useful collocation.' (21.30L) In particular series entries are useful for series where the series title indicates a particular subject scope, style of approach, level or audience.

11.3 Title main entry

Title main entries are normally made in instances where there is difficulty in identifying a suitable author's name. If the recommendations of AACR2 are followed this includes the following conditions:

1. The personal authorship is unknown or uncertain, or a work emanates from a body that lacks a name (21.5) For example,

> Successful retailing through advertising
> Housing and supplementary benefits.

2. The personal authorship is diffuse (that is, shared between four or more persons without principal responsibility being indicated (21.6)). For example,

> Baedeker's AA Scandinavia: Denmark, Norway, Sweden, Finland/ [text Waltraud Andersen et al.].—

> Classroom provision and organisation for integrated preschool children / C. Gunstone [et al.].

3. The work is a collection or work produced under editorial direction (21.7) for example,

> Electrochemical, electrical, and magnetic storage of energy / edited by W.V. Hassenzahl.

> Steroids in asthma: a reappraisal in the light of inhalation therapy / guest editor T.J.H. Clark.—

4. The work emanates from a corporate body and has no identifiable personal authorship, yet does not fall into one of the categories for which main entry is to be made under a corporate body.

> Centrifugal pumps—hydraulic designs: sponsored by the Power Industries Division of the Institution of Mechanical Engineers: 16 November, 1982. The Institution of Mechanical Engineers, London—London: Mechanical Engineering Publications for the Institution of Mechanical Engineers, 1982.—

> Denial of parents' rights in maternity.—London (163 Liverpool Rd, N1 0RF): Association for Improvements in the Maternity Services, [1983].

> Divorce and your child: a guide for separated parents / edited by Jim and Pat Wheeler.—London (37 Carden Rd., SE15): Families Need Fathers, [1982].

5. The work is accepted as a sacred scripture by a religious group (21.37) for example

Bible, English. Authorized.

If a work has one clearly stated title on its chief source of information (for example, title page, label), then the instruction to make entry under the title presents few difficulties. If this is not the case then the title to be used as a heading for a work is less obvious.

11.4 Problems with title entries

There are a variety of problems that arise when a document is required to be entered under its title. Four situations may arise which will need careful consideration:

1. The title given in the chief source of information differs from one volume to another in a multi-volume or multi-part work.
2. The title of the document differs from one edition to another of the same work.
3. The document is known in different countries under different titles, and has titles in various languages.
4. The document has no title of its own.

These situations require some guidelines indicating which of the variant titles to choose in any particular circumstances, and what to choose as a substitute for a title if no title is available. Taking the second situation for the purpose of illustration, there are four options for choice of title:

1. Entry of each document under its respective title.
2. Entry of all works under a uniform title, chosen as the earliest title.
3. Entry of all works under a uniform title, chosen as the latest title.
4. Entry of all works under a uniform title, chosen as the predominant title.

In choosing the most appropriate title for use as heading the following two questions need to be considered:

1. Which title is the sought title?
2. Which title will collocate the various editions, translations, adaptations, and so on of this document?

If these two questions are considered in establishing the preferred title for use in headings, the choice of titles will be consistent with the choice of author headings, as outlined in Chapters 7, 9 and 19. As with author headings, sometimes one heading or title will be both sought and provide collocation, but on other occasions there will be a conflict between 'soughtness' and collocation.

Plainly the choice of an appropriate title for headings in main and added entries poses problems where there are a number of titles from which to choose. Titles are also an important secondary filing element in entries which are arranged primarily by author. In large catalogues covering extensive collections of work by major authors, for example, Shakespeare or Dickens, many works will be entered under the one author's name. Within the works of one author the entries will be arranged by title. The question arises as to whether to use the title page title of each work for the filing arrangement, or whether to seek to establish some uniform titles that can be applied to related works, for example, different editions, translations and adaptations of *Macbeth*, so that they file together, or whether to accept an arbitrary sequence under the author's name.

AACR2 generally recommends collocation although it is suggested that the extent of collocation and the need for uniform titles is a matter for local decisions. Works which are particularly likely to merit the establishment of uniform titles are those which are either well known, and/or available in a variety of adaptations, translations and editions. The local cataloguer must also take account of the purpose and nature of his collection and its catalogue.

11.5 Uniform titles

A uniform title is the title by which a work that has appeared under varying titles is to be identified for cataloguing purposes. 25.2A instructs:

When manifestations of a work appear under various titles, select one title as the uniform title . . . Use a uniform title for an entry if:
1. The item bears a title proper that differs from the uniform title or
2. The addition of another element (eg language) is necessary to organize the file.

Below a number of instances in which uniform titles are useful are considered:

1. Individual titles

(a) Works created after 1500. The uniform title is the title in the original language by which the work has become known through use in manifestations of the work or in reference sources, for example,

Dickens, Charles
[The Pickwick Papers]
The posthumous papers of the Pickwick Club.

(b) Works created before 1501. The title chosen as the uniform title is that which is used in modern reference sources. If these are inconclusive, the title most frequently found in (this order of preference)
1. modern editions; 2. early editions; 3. manuscript copies
is used.
The title in the original language is used except for a work originally written in, for instance, classical Greek, when a well-established English language title is preferred, for example,

Chaucer, Geoffrey
[Troilus and Criseyde]

Provision is also made for additions to uniform titles where this might clarify the title. Instructions are also included for parts of works, and two works issued together (25.6–25.7).

2. Collective titles

Various standard uniform titles can be use to cover collective titles including all of or part of the works of a given author. These are best demonstrated by example:

Maugham, W Somerset
[Selections]
The Somerset Maugham pocket book.

Shakespeare, William
[Poems]
The Complete poems of William Shakespeare

Tolkien, J R R
[Short stories. Selections]
Best short stories of J R R Tolkien

3. The Bible (25.17–25.18)

Sacred scriptures are entered under uniform title as main entry. Many of these works have many editions, translations, selections and so on, and it is necessary to control the components to be used in a uniform title. The general form of heading for the Bible is:

Bible. O.T. or N.T. Individual book or group of books. Language. Version. Year. For example:

Bible N.T. Corinthians. English. Authorized.
Bible. English. Revised Standard. 1959.

4. *Music* (25.25–25.36)

Music, especially classical works, often requires the establishment of a uniform title. The general form of uniform title for music is:

Title, medium of performance
for example, nocturne, piano, ballads, woodwind quartet, string orchestra

Some works require additional elements. In particular, a title that consists solely of the name(s) of type(s) of composition requires the following elements in addition to the statement of the medium of performance:

serial number, opus number or thematic index number, key for example:

trios, piano, strings, no. 1, op. 1, no. 1
scherzo, piano, op. 20, A major

5. *Laws, etc.* (25.15)

It is common to establish a uniform title for important laws. For single laws the title is chosen from (in this order of preference): (a) the official short title or citation title; (b) an unofficial short title or citation title as used in legal literature; (c) the official title of the enactment; (d) any other official designation. For example,

New Zealand
Copyright Act 1962

Collections of laws are entered under Laws, etc. for example,
United Kingdom
Laws, etc.
Halsbury's Statutes of England.

11.6 Title indexes as surrogate subject indexes

Printed title indexes which could be used as elementary subject indexes were one of the first products of computerised information retrieval systems. Such indexes are a simple example of natural language indexing. These indexes are based on the premise that titles, or more specifically the words in titles, convey the subject content of the document to which the title pertains.

Each title is arranged in an alphabetical sequence according to each of its keywords in turn. Thus a title such as: *Grow and freeze your own vegetables* might be entered in three places in the alphabetical sequence; under 'Grow', 'Vegetables' and 'Freeze'. The other words in the title for example, 'and, your, own' would clearly not merit index entries, and the compiler would have been instructed not to make entries for these words. The exact format of the index and its entries will vary from one method to another, as discussed below. Title indexes of this type could be generated manually, but they are particularly easy to produce with the aid of a computer.

Subject-type title indexes have two important attractions. These indexes are both cheap and quick to produce. The indexes are produced by computer, without necessarily any human intervention. Standard program packages are available which will create such indexes. Obviously if it were not for the fact that such indexes also have severe limitations there would be little need to produce any other type of subject index. These limitations are considered in the following sections. Title-based subject indexes have been used as indexes to local abstracting and indexing publications, published abstracting and indexing services, reports collections, bibliographies, and as subject indexes to classified catalogues.

11.7 KWIC and KWOC indexes

There are a number of variations on the basic subject-type title index. A KWIC or *Keyword In Context* index is the most readily produced type of index. A KWIC index is based upon the 'keywords' in the titles of the batch of documents to be indexed. All words in the titles of the documents to be indexed will be compared, by a computer, with a pre-selected stop list or stopword list. This stop list is input to the computer before indexing can commence, and is a list of the words which appear in text which have no value as access words in an index. Typically, connectives and qualifiers in text, such as 'than', 'a', 'where', 'he', 'she', 'it' will feature in the stop list. Any words which are present in the titles being indexed, but are not in the stop list will be treated as 'keywords'. An entry will be produced in respect of every keyword, with these entries arranged in alphabetical order according to the keywords. The keyword is printed 'in context', or in other words, together with the remainder of the title in which the keyword originally featured. Entry words may be aligned in a centre column or in a left hand column. The remainder of the space on the line is occupied by the remainder of the title, and some brief source reference which leads the user to the document, or to another listing perhaps including abstracts. Figure 11.1 shows the format of a typical KWIC index.

Figure 11.1 A KWIC index (extract) from chemical titles

1 ribo nucleic acid+ Genetic	mapping of a linked cluster of ribosoma	JOBAAY -0418-0621
DNA fragments: a physical	mapping of a EcoRf-fragment containing	JGAMA9 -0027-0419
icroscopic method for gene	mapping on polytene chromosomes by in	PNASA6 -0078-7059
of deformation mechanism	maps to the study of high-temperature	JMTSAS -0016-3171
vection at a plane interface	(Marangoni instability). = + driven con	JCISA5 -0034-0433
reaction veins in a dolomitic	marble roof pendants in the Bergell intr	AJSCAP -0281-1197
Petrology of chlorite-spinel	marbles from northwestern Spitsberge	LITHAN -0014-0203
Bunsen in	Marburg.=	BBPCAX -0085-0932
	Marine and estuarine pollution.=	JWPFA5 -0053-0925
e of alloy 1420 under	marine conditions.= Corrosion resistance	ZAMEA9 -0017-0827
ition, and + Petroleum and	marine fishes: a review of uptake, dispos	ESTHAG -0016-1372
tions: total synthesis of the	marine natural product (d,1)-Δ 9(12) capn	TELEAY -1981-4389
selenium in some	marine organisms.= Protein bound	CMSHAF -0010-2285
antimony in water, effluents,	marine plants and silicates.= +tion of	ACACAM -0131-0175
mate in Arctic and subarctic	marine sediments.= +glucose and gluta	AEMIDF -0012-0792
oxin from the venom of the	marine snail Conus geographus which ac	TOXIA 6-0019-0891
protein from the eggs of the	marine telcost. +erization of C-reactive	BBACAQ -0671-0044
lidia sphingosine, a bioactive	marine terpenoid.= +co-isemera of ap	TELEAY -1981-4429
Neutral maltase: enzymic	marker from human B lymphocytes.=	CRSEDA -0293-0019
tablets.= Evaluation of	marketed and formulated furosemide	PHARAT -0036-0628

Clearly a KWIC index format is very restrictive. Longer titles (since each title can occupy only one line) will be truncated and only brief source references are included. Some users find the format of KWIC indexes unacceptable; they find alphabetical arrangement by keywords down the centre of a page, and wrapped-round titles awkward.

KWOC or *Keyword Out of Context* indexes are intended to improve upon KWIC indexes, with regards to layout and presentation. A KWOC index is still a title index, and is constructed in exactly the same way as a KWIC index. However, the display of the index entries differs. The keywords are extracted from the titles and displayed as a heading. Under each keyword the complete title and source reference is given. There are no inherent limitations on the space available for each entry. There is a distinct superficial similarity between a KWOC index and an index arranged under assigned or controlled subject headings. A KWOC index can be spotted, since:

1. In a KWOC index all of the words that appear as headings have been extracted from titles.
2. In a KWOC index some of the headings are unqualified adjectives for example, circular, handicapped, young, and in an unmodified KWOC index all the headings will be one word terms.

11.8 Advantages of title-based subject indexes

These can be listed as:

1. A large number of documents can be indexed quickly and cheaply.

2. Absence of human interpretation of content leads to perfect predictability and consistency in the generation of index entries. If a word appears in the title of a document, then it is certain that, unless that word features in the stop list, an entry will be generated in association with that word.

3. The final index will mirror current terminology. The words provided as access points in the index have been drawn from those used by the authors of the documents being indexed. The language of the index automatically evolves with the language of the subject as used by authors in the titles of their works. Someone familiar with the terminology of the subject that the index covers will find the index easy to use.

4. The cumulation of separate index sequences into one integrated index is straightforward. The computer merely has to reprint the index to include all titles to be covered by the cumulated index.

11.9 Limitations of title indexes as subject indexes

The other part of the picture reveals title indexes to be only crude subject indexes, which for effective use demand imagination and searching skills on the part of the user.

1. Titles do not always constitute an accurate summary of the content of a document. The informativeness of the index depends upon the information contents of the titles that comprise the index. Even an informative title is by nature of a title, succinct, and therefore severely limited in the quantity of information that can be conveyed. Equally important is the fact that a title only reflects the main theme of a document; subsidiary themes are not represented. Some titles are designed with no intention of being informative, but rather are intended to attract the eye, for example, 'Piggy in the middle'.

2. Long sequences of entries under the keyword appear to be almost inevitable somewhere in the index merely because some words will be relatively common in the literature of any subject area. Several pages of entries under one keyword are discouraging to say the least. Subarrangement at entry terms can break up long sequences of entries listed under the same keyword. Double KWIC and Permuterm indexes arrange pairs of keywords, so that the entries under one keyword are organised according to the second keyword. Thus entries with any given pair of keywords will file next to one another. Unfortunately, Double KWIC and Permuterm indexes, in allowing for collocation by pairs of words require two entries for each pair of words, rather than the one entry per keyword in a normal KWIC index. Thus these indexes contain more entries than a straight KWIC index and are inclined to be relatively bulky.

3. Title indexes suffer from absence of tight terminology control. With machine indexing some irrelevant and redundant entries are inevitable. Entries are created merely according to the accident of the appearance of words in titles. Different words may be used to represent the same concept by different authors. What to one author is a 'strike' to another is an 'industrial dispute'. Similar and closely related subjects are likely to be scattered under different keywords. Further, no guidance can be expected on alternative terms that might prove fruitful, or that are related to the searcher's initial search term.

Some of the above limitations of title indexes can be overcome by exercising a measure of control over the index terminology, and by inputting and instructing the computer to print a number of pre-determined links or references between keywords. However, any refinement involves greater human intervention, and this in turn can easily overturn the arguments in favour of subject indexes based upon titles. Some of these issues are considered further in 16.8.

Chapter 11 Readings

1 Ayres, F.H. *et al.*, 'Author versus title: a comparative survey of the accuracy of the information which the user brings to the library cataloguer', *Journal of Documentation*, 24(4), 1968, 266–72.
2 Feinberg, H., *Title derivative indexing techniques: a compartive study*. Scarecrow Press: Los Angeles, 1975.
3 Matthews, F.W. and Shillingford, A.D., 'Variations on KWIC', *Aslib Proceedings*, 25(4), 1973, 140–52.

Note: Many of the texts cited at the end of Chapter 8 include comments on title cataloguing.

Part III   Subjects

12 The subject approach — introduction, processes, tools and simple evaluation

12.1 Subjects

Users often approach information sources not with names as has been considered in the preceding Part, but with a question that requires an answer, or a topic for study. Users seek documents or information concerned with a particular subject. In order to make some provision for this common approach to information sources it is necessary to arrange documents, and document surrogates, in catalogues, indexes, bibliographies, computer data bases and so on, in such a way that items on specific subjects can be retrieved. Thus, the subject approach is extremely important in the access to and the exploitation of information, documents and data.

Before we discuss the provision that libraries and information workers make for the subject approach, it will be profitable to pause for a moment and consider the preliminary question:

What is a subject?

In talking about a subject we generally refer to a given area of knowledge, or to the contens of an information source of a given scope. A subject might be considered to be defined by:

an area of interest
an area in which an individual researcher or professional works
an area in which an individual writes
an area of knowledge which is studied.

Consider a well-known subject area such as geography. Ask your friend what he thinks geography is. Examine the definition of geography in a few dictionaries and encyclopaedias. Examine a few syllabuses for basic courses in geography. Note the different definitions, and the different boundaries for this one subject area. It is easy to see that users and separate pieces of literature may hold different perspectives on one subject. The points of divergence in perspective can be broadly categorised as:

(a) different labels are used.
(b) different concepts of scope and associations with other subjects are evident.

These factors form the basis of the problems in identifying a satisfactory subject approach, and start to explain the vast array of different tools used in the subject approach to knowledge.

It is possible and convenient to select a viewpoint on the scope, associations and labels for subjects which coincides with the way in which subjects are handled in the literature. In libraries, most devices for the organisation of knowledge concern themselves primarily with organising literature. This policy of reflecting the subject labels and relationships present in the literature of a subject is known as being consistent with *literary warrant*. On the basis of literary warrant, any classification scheme or indexing language will reflect the subjects, and the relationships between subjects present in the literature that the scheme or language has been designed to organise. This could be regarded as a pragmatic approach to the design of devices for the organisation of knowledge by the subject approach. The main limitation of this pragmatic approach lies in the time and collection dependency of the resulting tool. Even the same collection some years on will have altered, and the device, in order to remain effective, must evolve in keeping with the development of the collection. There is an alternative method for the design of subject retrieval devices, and that is to build languages or schemes which depend upon some theoretical views about the nature and structure of knowledge. As will become apparent later this theoretical approach is also important in determining the nature of subject devices for the organisation of knowledge.

12.2 Indexing languages

The term indexing language can seem rather daunting, and has certainly had different meanings in its different incarnations. Here an indexing language is simply defined as:

a list of terms or notation that might be used as access points in an index.

This definition does not exclude the names of persons, bodies, chemicals, trade names and so on, but since in this chapter we are concerned primarily with the subject approach, this list as discussed in the next few sections will concentrate on terms which describe subjects.

An alternative definition of an indexing language is:

the set of terms (the vocabulary) and the devices for handling the relationship between them in a system for providing index descriptions.

An indexing language may also be referred to as a retrieval language.

Indexing languages may be of three distinct types:

1. Controlled indexing languages are indexing languages in which both the terms that are used to represent subjects, and the process whereby terms are assigned to a particular document are controlled or executed by a person. Normally there is a list of terms which acts as the authority list in identifying the terms that may be assigned to documents, and indexing involves a person assigning terms from this list to specific documents. There are two types of controlled indexing languages: alphabetical indexing languages and classification schemes. In alphabetical indexing languages, such as are embodied in thesauri and subject headings lists, subject terms are the alphabetical names of the subjects. Control is exercised over which terms are used, but otherwise the terms are ordinary words. In classification schemes each subject is assigned a piece of notation. The usual objective of assigning notation is to place a subject within a context with respect to other subjects. Both classification schemes and alphabetical indexing languages are used in a variety of contexts, and most of the remainder of this part will concentrate on controlled language indexing. Both types of device can be found applied in catalogues, indexes to books and periodicals, bibliographies, current awareness bulletins, selective dissemination of information, computerised data bases and data banks, abstracting and indexing services, encyclopedias, dictionaries and directories. Classification is also prominent in the physical arrangement of documents.

2. Natural indexing languages are not really a separate language at all, but the 'natural language' or ordinary language of the document being indexed. Any terms that appear in the document are candidates for index terms. In practice, natural language indexing tends to rely upon the terms present in an abstract or a title of a document. Only occasionally although increasingly is the full text of a document used. Natural language indexing based upon the full text of a document, depending on how it is achieved, may lead to very extensive indexing of each document, or will involve establishing some mechanism for deciding which terms are the most important in relation to a particular document. In computer indexing this will involve statistical analysis of the relative frequency of occurrence of terms. In human indexing some judgement would be required in selecting terms. Many of these problems can be minimised by restricting indexing to titles and abstracts. Either a computer or a person can execute natural language indexing. In computer indexing the computer may well use a list of terms deemed to be useful in indexing (that is, a type of thesaurus) to identify appropriate terms.

3. Free indexing languages again, is not a listed language of terms which is distinct from the terms used to describe concepts in a subject area. Indexing is 'free' in the sense that there are no constraints on the terms that can be used in the indexing process. Free language indexing is distinct from natural language indexing in that natural language indexing is constrained by the language of the document being indexed; free language indexing does not even recognise these constraints. Free language indexing may be conducted by humans or computer. When executed by humans with a sound knowledge of a subject and its terminology, free language indexing can result in an index which is both consistent in the assignment of index terms, and which matches the perspective of index users. However successful, human free language indexing is very dependent upon the skills of the individual indexer. Computerised free language indexing is, for all practical purposes, the same as natural language indexing. The computer must have some basis for the assignment of indexing terms, and if a pre-assigned list of terms is not supplied, the computer must assign terms on the basis of the terms present in the document being indexed.

Both natural language indexing, and to a lesser extent free language indexing are used extensively in producing both printed indexes, and in access to computerised data bases and data banks. Some applications of natural language indexing based upon titles of documents have already been considered in Chapter 11. Natural language indexing will be used throughout this Part for purposes of comparison with controlled language indexing, and is considered in some detail in parts of the chapters on alphabetical indexing languages and alphabetical indexing systems.

12.3 Functions of a subject device

A subject device normally seeks to fulfil both the following functions:

1. To show what a library or information source includes on a particular subject.
2. To show what a library or information source includes on related subjects.

Different devices for the organisation of knowledge place differing emphasis on the relative importance of these two objectives, but it is difficult to neglect either entirely, without impairing the effectiveness in fulfilling the other objective. The two objectives are interdependent, and this can be demonstrated first by examining the first objective:

Specific subject

A book for instance on 'vegetable gardening' may contain equally valuable information on 'growing tomatoes' as a book devoted entirely to 'growing tomatoes'. Thus a book on a related subject can, to varying extents, be accepted as a book on the specific subject being sought. Even a user who starts a search with a specific subject in mind, may be seeking a specific subject which does not quite match his requirements. A user might start by looking for a map of London, when he really wants a map of Camden, because he believes that the more specific subject, Camden, will not be covered independently. Later, after examining maps of the area he may discover that the area that he is really interested in is Parliament Hill. The inclusion of related subjects can help even the user with a specific search, particularly where the user is not adequately familiar with the subject that is sought or the way in which the subject is likely to be handled or packaged in the literature.

Relationships

Figure 12.1 shows a small hierarchy of subjects, or a group of ranked subjects which incorporates some statement of the relationships between those subjects. This hierarchy shows a general subject area, buildings, and its *subordinate* subject areas: building materials, auxiliary construction practices, construction in specific materials, wood construction, roofing and so on. Subordinate to each of these subject areas are other topics. For example, plumbing and pipe fitting are subordinate to utilities. The converse of a subordinate subject is a *superordinate* subject. Again, then, buildings is superordinate to building materials, auxiliary construction practices, construction in specific materials, wood construction, roofing and so on. Two subjects at the same level in the hierarchy (for example, both subdivisions of the same parent or superordinate subject) are said to be *co-ordinate*. Thus, utilities and heating are co-ordinate to one another, and so also are wood and slate.

Relationships such as those shown in the hierarchy in Figure 12.1 are known as *semantic* relationships. These represent connections between subjects, which are associated with the nature of the subject. Although we may disagree about the fine detail, semantic relationships are the relationships between subjects, which are reasonably stable, and reflect the consensus of opinion concerning the connections between subjects. Thus, we all agree that one component of a building is a roof (and not vice versa!), and that chemistry is a branch of science, or that an Alsatian is a dog. There is some agreement as to the presence of these relationships, and they are expected to alter only as knowledge advances.

There are other relationships between subjects. These are known as *syntactic* relationships. Syntactic relationships arise from the context of subjects in specific documents, or the syntax. Thus a document such as

A farm spelling pictures teaching jigsaw

brings the concepts farming and spelling into a context in which they are

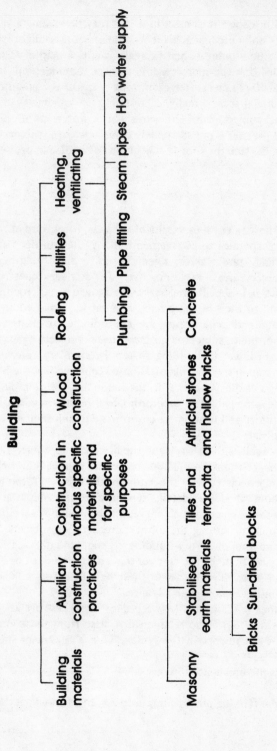

Figure 12.1 The subdivisions of building in the Dewey Decimal Classification Scheme

related. Plainly, it is not always the case that there is a connection between farming and spelling, and many other documents can be identified where these subjects are not connected. So, syntactic relationships do arise in documents, but are less permanent than semantic relationships. In any subject device it is necessary to distinguish between syntactic and semantic relationships and to make a different kind of provision for the two types of relationship.

Both classification schemes and alphabetical indexing languages fulfil both of the basic objectives of a subject device. The distinction arises from the different emphases. Classification schemes specialise in showing networks of subjects and displaying the relationships between subjects, and thus are particularly suited to achieving the first objective. Alphabetical indexing languages specialise in establishing specific labels for subjects, and providing direct access to individual subjects. Nevertheless, as will be amply demonstrated throughout the remaining chapters in this Part, all subject devices must attempt to fulfil both objectives.

12.4 The subject indexing process

Indexing is the process whereby indexes and associated tools for the organisation of knowledge are created. Indexing may be conducted entirely without the aid of a computer, or may rely to varying extents upon the facilities for the manipulation and ordering of data offered by the computer.

The assignment of notation from a classification scheme or the application of subject headings from a list of subject headings involves skill and judgement, if the resulting index is to be effective and efficient. Clearly, the only totally adequate indication of the content of a document is the text of the document in its entirety. Any other indication of document content, such as classification notation or alphabetical subject headings are partial representations of content. Three stages are necessary in assigning terms from indexing languages:

Familiarisation → Analysis → Translation

The objective in executing these three stages is to construct a document profile which reflects its subject. Most documents have many characteristics that might be identified by a searcher as the criterion by which the document would be selected as relevant. Any set of search keys for a document can be described as a document profile. Different types of indexes and different user groups may require different sets of search keys, or different document profiles to be developed in respect of one document. Some of the available search keys have already been considered in Part II, that is, personal and corporate names. The other important class of search keys are the subject labels which will be discussed in this Part of the work. Now to consider the various stages in framing a document profile:

Step 1 Familiarisation This first step involves the indexer in becoming conversant with the subject content of the document to be indexed. Documents are comprised of words, and searchers and indexers use words to represent or convey concepts, but at this stage it is important for the indexer to attempt to identify the concepts that are represented by the words. In order to achieve good consistent indexing the indexer must have a thorough appreciation of the structure of the subject and the nature of the contribution that the document makes to the advancement of knowledge. From time to time it may be necessary to consult external reference sources in order for the indexer to achieve a sufficient understanding of the document content for effective indexing. Certainly it will always be necessary to examine the document content, concentrating particularly on the clues offered by the title, the contents page, chapter headings, and any abstracts, introduction, prefaces or other preliminary matter.

Step 2 Analysis The second step towards an index involves the identification of the concepts within a document which are worthy of indexing. Any one document covers a number of different topics. Take for example a book entitled *Wills and Probate*. This book contains sections on making a will, executors, administration of an estate, pensions, tax, house ownership, grants and intestacy, to name but a few of the sections. Usually it is possible to identify a central theme in a document, and to produce a summary of document content based upon this central theme. Frequently, but not always, this same process will have been attempted by the author when inventing the title, and this explains why the title is often a useful aid to indexing. Clearly an index must permit access to a document by its central theme, but, to what extent should access be provided to secondary or subsidiary topics considered within a document? This question can only be answered with reference to specific indexing environments. In catalogues, for instance, it is common to index no more than three separate subjects for any one document. Indexers for Chemical Abstracts are instructed:

> index every measurement, observation, method, apparatus, suggestion and theory that is presented as new and of value in itself; all new chemical compounds and all elements, compounds and other substances for which new data are given.*

It is helpful to have such guidelines concerning the types and range and number of concepts to be indexed, in any indexing situation, although

*American Chemical Society, *Chemical Abstracts Service Directions for Abstractors;* Columbus, Ohio: ACS, 1971.

precise guidelines are not always drafted, and choice of concepts to be indexed may be left to the discretion of the indexer. More consideration will be given to this topic in section 12.5.

Many of the traditional indexing approaches have sought to find a label or indexing term which is *co-extensive* with the content of the document being indexed, that is, the scope of the indexing term and the document are similar. For example, for the book, on *Wills and Probate*, it would not be sufficient to index this book under the term 'Wills' alone, since this heading would not reveal the section of the book on 'Probate'.

Note: The term 'analysis' has been used here in its restrictive meaning. Some authors use 'analysis' to apply to all processes associated with the construction of a document profile of any kind. In this definition 'analysis' subsumes cataloguing, indexing classification and abstracting.

Step 3 Translation Having identified the central theme of a document this theme must be described in terms which are present in the indexing language. In controlled language indexing, this will involve describing the concepts in terms of the classification scheme, thesaurus or list of subject headings which is being used. For example, a free interpretation of the subject of a document might be:

Social conflict and educational change in England and France between 1789 and 1848.

The concepts represented in this summary might be translated into an alphabetical description of the form

Education— History— England—Social Conflict—France

or into a classification notation such as:

942.073.

To take another example

Radioactivity in the surface and coastal waters of the British Isles, 1977

which might be converted to an alphabetical description such as:

Water–Pollutants—Radioactive materials—Great Britain—
or into a classification notation, such as:

628.16850941

This translation will involve not only labelling the subject, but possibly also indicating related subjects, as has been discussed earlier. The guiding principle in translating concepts into the indexing language of any given system must be that the terms selected and the relationships that are indicated must be consistent with the 'normal' user's perspective on the subject. This coincidence between indexing and user approach is known as *user warrant*. In other words the indexing system must be tailored to the needs of the users of the index. Given that different users may have different perspectives on the same subject, it is clear that different indexing languages and systems may be appropriate for different subjects and environments, and even for the same subject in a different environment. Consider, for example, medicine. The approach which is suitable in specialised indexing tools for medical research will need to be very specific in order to differentiate between two closely related subjects. A collection of medical books for the general public in a public library may deal with the same range of topics, but the indexing can probably be more broad than in a specialist index, and the terms used for the same thing may be different. What a doctor might refer to as 'rubella', will probably be called 'German measles' by the mother of the child with the complaint. Apart from differing needs of users, indexing approaches may differ on policy grounds. Some types of indexing are appropriate where it is desired to concentrate effort on generating good indexes. Others lend themselves less to perfect indexing, but rather rely upon the searcher to exercise skill in searching, and offer the facilities for the searcher to exercise this skill. It is important to recognise, then, that a variety of different indexing approaches are inevitable, not only for reaons of history and indexer preference, but because different situations demand different approaches.

12.5 The searching process

Information retrieval follows from the generation of an index. Although this work concerns itself primarily with the organisation of knowledge and the production of indexes and catalogues, it is imperative that the indexer should have an appreciation of how the index is to be used. Indeed the selection of an indexing approach is crucially dependent upon the way in which the index is to be used. Equally, it is important that a searcher should have a clear understanding of indexing methods. Indexing and searching, then, are integral one to another, and so a few comments on searching are in order here. These comments are also intended to demonstrate the similarity between indexing and searching and to show how indexing tools feature in the searching process. These comments are as true for author searching (Part II) as subject searching, and they are introduced here only for convenience.

Searching an index, a catalogue or a data base can be viewed as involving the same three stages as indexing:

Step 1 Familiarisation A searcher must be adequately familiar with that which he wishes to retrieve. Although this may seem an obvious statement, there are many instances when the searcher is not fully aware of what can or might be retrieved. Two common circumstances may arise:

(a) the searcher is an information worker trying to extract documents or information on behalf of someone else. Here familiarisation can be partially achieved by conducting a reference interview with the end user. The reference interview should ascertain both a clear subject profile, and also other characteristics of the required documents or information, such as any constraints on date, language, source, level. The intermediary (information worker) also needs to be conversant with the sources to be searched.
(b) the searcher may be the end user, but the end user is approaching the search in some ignorance of his real requirements, or of the literature that might be available to meet those requirements. Some degree of ignorance of this kind is not unusual since the usual objective in consulting an information source is to become better informed. If the search is to be successful, the user will learn about the subject and its literature during the searching process.

(Of course, there is an even more catastrophic situation than either of the two outlined above, and this is where the end user exhibits a good deal of ignorance about the information or documents required, and the information worker is charged to conduct the search on the basis of incomplete or inaccurate information from the end user. This situation requires a very skilled information worker if total disaster is to be avoided.)

Step 2 Analysis With a clear objective, the next step is to analyse the concepts that are present in a search. Sometimes, particularly for a straightforward search in a printed index, it will be sufficient to establish these concepts in the searcher's mind. On other occasions, where the search must be specified with a number of interacting concepts and other parameters, it will be necessary to write the concepts down. For example, if information is required on 'primary education' and this is a heading in the appropriate printed index then the search profile merely involves the term 'primary education'. If, however, the searcher seeks information on

Recovering hydrogen from coal tar in a continuous electrofluid reactor

and is interested only in reports, books or periodical articles which review the subject after 1980, then there is clearly scope for a more complex search profile. Aspects of this will be considered in Chapter 17. Building a search profile has much in common with building a document profile during indexing. The *search profile* will comprise a series of search keys representing subjects and other characteristics of the search requirements which together indicate the scope and nature of the search.

Step 3 Translation of the concepts in a search profile will involve consultation of the thesaurus, classification scheme (or its index), or list of subject headings that has been used in constructing the index to be searched. Often the quality of the translation may be tested by examining the items indexed under a number of possible terms that might have been used to described a subject in an index. Thus a searcher might consider perusing entries under sweets, chocolates and confectionery. Once a satisfactory entry point has been identified in an index, the instructions or guidelines in the index may help the searcher in improving retrieval.

Although there are parallels between searching and indexing, it is important to remember that successful information retrieval does not depend only upon effective exploitation of indexing. It is no good searching an information source, printed, or computer-held, efficiently and with a sound understanding of its construction, if that source does not provide access to the information or documents that are being sought. Many searches involve the use of more than one index, and all searches require that the most appropriate index be chosen. There is more to effective information retrieval than indexing, but this is certainly an essential component in the process.

12.6 Measures of index effectiveness

Some simple measures of index effectiveness are introduced here so that it is possible to consider different indexing methods critically. There is an extensive theory of the evaluation of indexes and indexing, but regrettably there is not space to treat this topic at any length in this work. Some authoritative texts on the subject are listed at the end of this chapter.

For any user who approaches an index or a computerised information retrieval system there are a number of records in the system that are relevant to the topic of this search and the remainder are of no interest on that occasion. Even for those items that are designated relevant some may be judged to be highly relevant, whilst others may be regarded as partially relevant or only marginally relevant. Various scales of relevance ratings may be established. For example, if a user desires information on asbestos roofing there may be records for documents in the index that deal specifically with this topic which would be selected as being highly relevant. However, although the subject may be the primary consideration in the assessment of relevance, subject is not the only factor that determines whether a user wishes to be alerted to the existence of a document. A user may reject a document because it is in a language that he cannot read or because it was written too long ago. Relevance is a subjective measure. Documents rarely exactly match a user's requirements because information can be packaged in almost as many different ways as there are participants in a subject area. Inevitably an author writes from his understanding and perspective; a user probably has a different background, level of understanding and experience of the same subject.

Consider again those documents indexed by the system that may be partially relevant to a given user's search. Suppose that, although our reader is primarily interest in asbestos roofing there is only a limited quantity of material directly concerned with this topic represented in a collection. It is, however, possible to broaden the search and find additional information on asbestos roofing by retrieving documents on roofing, and extracting sections from these documents that are pertinent to asbestos roofing. The end result will be that more information on asbestos roofing has been traced, but in order to collect this additional information it has been necessary to consider all of the documents in the index in a much broader category—roofing. Thus many non-relevant documents have been retrieved and examined in the process of sifting relevant and non-relevant documents. These non-relevant documents are frequently referred to as *'noise'*. Notice that it would be possible to improve recall indefinitely by scanning the entire document collection but that this perfect recall (that is, every relevant document retrieved), can only be achieved by a drop in the proportion of relevant documents considered.

We have begun to identity, then, two conflicting objectives which are present in any search. Ideally we would like both to maximise recall, or the number of relevant documents retrieved, at the same time ensuring that the documents retrieved all remain relevant. These twin objectives are, in practice, not possible to achieve simultaneously.

The concepts which have been introduced in the preceding paragraphs have been more precisely defined so that there can be a consensus as to their meaning, and so that experimental measurements can be made. The following definitions are important in the evaluation of indexes:

$$\text{Recall ratio} = \frac{\text{Number of relevant documents retrieved}}{\text{Total number of relevant documents in the system}} \times 100 \ \%$$

$$\text{Precision ratio} = \frac{\text{Number of relevant documents retrieved}}{\text{Total number of documents retrieved}} \times 100 \ \%$$

One easy observation from these definitions is that indexes are measured in terms of their effectiveness in retrieval. This serves to support some of the statements made in Section 12.5, and again emphasises that a good index is one which permits effective retrieval.

As discussed above, precision, or the proportion of relevant documents retrieved, is related to recall, the extent of retrieval of relevant documents. More specifically, it is the case that recall is inversely proportional to precision, and vice versa, or in other words, as one increases, the other must decrease. In practice the application of recall and precision in the evaluation of indexes is hindered by the difficulty of evaluating some of the components in the definition. For example, without scanning the entire index it is impossible to estimate the total number of relevant documents in the system, a figure that is required in the calculation of recall. Thus it is apparent that it is easier to measure precision than recall. A useful application of recall in practice is not to seek a measure of absolute recall (as defined above), but rather to use recall to compare two different indexing systems, by defining what is known as *relative recall*.

$$\text{Relative recall} = \frac{\text{Number of documents retrieved in system 1}}{\text{Number of documents retrieved in system 2}} \times 100\ \%$$

Clearly this definition can be generalised in order to compare a number of different systems, and provides a useful comparative measure.

Since recall goes up as precision goes down, it is clearly not possible to achieve in general a system which gives full recall at the same time as full precision. Thus in index or catalogue or data base design the indexer must choose an appropriate blend of recall and precision for each individual application. Quite frequently a user will be satisfied with a few items on a topic, as long as they are relevant, and meet other criteria such as language, date and level. Here, high precision, but low recall is satisfactory. On other occasions a user wants every document or piece of information on a topic traced, and then high recall must be sought, to the detriment of precision.

12.7 Other features of indexes

Recall and precision interact with other characteristics of indexes. Some of these are briefly introduced here.

Specificity, or the degree of specificity of indexing in any index must be set during planning for the index, and reviewed from time to time thereafter. Specificity of a system is the extent to which the system permits the indexer to be precise about the subject of a document. A completely specific statement of document content would have to be the text of the document itself. Obviously a more formal, and a more summarised profile is required in most indexing systems. In any index the level of specificity is normally settled by the extent and type of subjects listed in the system. For instance, it is desirable that a scannable number of documents be listed under each heading in a catalogue. With a given size of collection, say, 20,000 documents, the appropriate number of headings can be identified on the basis of seeking to create scannable categories. With a set number of categories the specificity of the headings to be included in the index must be determined to a large extent. A fundamental theoretical rule of subject indexing is that each heading should be *co-extensive* with the subject of the document, that is, the label and the information or documents found under that label should match. In practice this can only be achieved within the constraints of any given indexing language and system.

The relationship between precision and recall and specificity is interesting. The higher the specificity of indexing the more likely it is that search outputs will show high precision. Lower specificity will be associated with lower precision but high recall. In our search for asbestos roofing, if the term 'asbestos roofing' does not exist in the system then we must search under the broad term 'roofing'. Documents can only be identified as relevant by scanning the rather larger number of documents listed under the broader heading.

Exhaustivity of indexing has some impact on recall and precision. As has already been discussed, most documents have more than one theme. The indexer is required to consider which topics within a document will be represented in an index. In many traditional catalogues access will only be provided to two or three main themes. A more specialised collection or indexing service may be indexed in greater depth, or with greater exhaustivity; up to twenty or thirty separate themes may be identified and indexed in one document. The indexer can be constrained as to the number of themes per document to be indexed, or given the option of indexing as many themes as possible. The exhaustivity of the indexing of a document is the number of themes that are indexed in a document. This is approximately measured by the number of index terms assigned to a document (although it is possible that more than one index term may be necessary to represent some themes).

In contrast to higher specificity, higher exhaustivity increases precision at the cost of impaired recall. The more secondary themes that are indexed in a document, the more documents that will be retrieved, but in many instances those documents which are retrieved will treat the topic being sought only as a subsidary subject, and thus these documents may be judged to be only marginally relevant. A high exhaustivity of indexing, then, is beneficial where a thorough search is required, but may be a handicap when only a few highly relevant documents are sought.

Error will be present in any system which involves human intervention. Computers are reliable, and less prone to error provided they are instructed or programmed appropriately and correctly. Errors such as indexers assigning unsuitable terms to concepts, or relationships being omitted, will affect precision by producing unsuitable documents in response to a search, and on the other hand, will not produce the same documents when a search is conducted under the terms which should have been assigned to the document, thus reducing recall. Documents and information can be lost forever by faults in inputting. Thus care in indexing is essential, and systems should be designed in such a way as to minimise the possibility of error. Clear instructions are essential in indexing tools, such as thesauri, subject headings lists and classification schemes.

Chapter 12 Readings

A. General texts on subjects

1 Bakewell, K.G.B., *Classification and indexing practice,* Bingley: London 1978.
2 Buchanan, B., *Theory of library classification,* Bingley: London, 1979.
3 Foskett, A.C., *The subject approach to information,* 4th edition, Bingley: London, 1982.
4 Foskett, D.J., *Classification and indexing in the social sciences.* 2nd edition. Butterworths: London, 1974.
5 *Indexers on indexing,* ed. L. Harrod, Bowker: New York, 1978.
6 Langridge, D.W., *Approach to classification,* Bingley: London, 1973.
7 Langridge, D.W., *Classification and indexing in the humanities,* Butterworth: London, 1976.
8 Maltby, A., *Classification in the 70's: a second look,* Bingley: London, 1976.
9 Maltby, A., *Sayer's manual of classification for libraries,* 5th edition, Deutsch: London, 1975.
10 Palmer, B.I., *Itself an education,* 2nd edition, Library Association: London, 1971.
11 Rowley, J.E., *Abstracting and indexing,* Bingley: London 1982.
12 Vickery, B.C., *Classification and indexing in science and technology,* 3rd edition, Butterworths: London, 1975.

Note: Some general works, which also include topics other than the subject approach, have been listed in the introduction.

B. Evaluation

14 Cleverdon, C.W., 'The Cranfield tests on index language devices', *Aslib Proceedings,* 19(6), 1967, 173–94.
15 Cleverdon, C.W., 'User evaluation of information retrieval system,, *Journal of Documentation,* 30(2), 1974, 170–80.

16 Keen, E.M., 'The Aberystwyth index languages test', *Journal of Documentation*, 29(1), 1973, 1–35.

17 Keen, E.M. and Digger, J., *Report of an information science index languages test*, College of Librarianship: Aberystwyth, 1972.

18 Lancaster, F.W., 'Aftermath of an evaluation'. *Journal of Documentation*, 27(1), 1971, 1–10.

19 Salton, G., 'The evaluation of automatic retrieval procedures—selected test results using the SMART system', *American Documentation* 16(3), 1965, 209–22.

20 Salton, G., 'A new comparison between conventional indexing (MEDLARS) and automatic text processing (SMART)', *Journal of the American Society of Information Science*, 23(2), 1972, 75–84.

13 The theory of bibliographic classification

13.1 Why theory?

A study of bibliographic classification could concentrate solely upon the major, and some of the more minor bibliographic classification schemes used today. However, although such a study may permit some comparison of different schemes, this pragmatic approach would not provide the parameters for comparison, nor, indeed, identify any criteria that classification schemes should meet. A study then of the underlying features of the classification process and the components of a classification scheme is a preparation for the more critical and informed application of classification schemes. Further, classification and the network of relationships between subjects can be a fascinating study in itself, even devoid of any applications.

This chapter is relatively succinct and goes little further than identifying the major ideas concerning classification theory that have emerged during the twentieth century and before, and indicating their applications. There are in summary two important applications for classification theory:

1. New theories can be applied in the development and revision of existing schemes. These are often large general schemes.
2. New theories can be used as the basis for new schemes. Mostly such new schemes will not be general schemes, but rather special classification schemes, designed for a particular application or subject.

Before proceeding it may be wise to offer some definitions. The *Shorter Oxford English Dictionary* defines a class as

a number of individuals (persons or things) possessing a common attribute and grouped together under a general or 'class' name; a kind, sort, division.

To continue, a classification scheme is defined as:

an orderly arrangement of terms or classes.

The application of such a scheme to a set of documents should result in the ordering or arranging of that set of documents into groups or classes according to their subject content. In so doing the classifier should group documents on the same subject together into one class, and, arrange classes of documents in a useful order with respect to one another.

Classification, then, is the grouping of like objects. This grouping is not self-evident. If a small child is asked to group a set of objects he may gather together items according to their colour, for example, all brown objects, or according to their normal use, for example, all cutlery. Similarly with classification the grouping is not self-evident. The classification scheme is intended to act as an authority in the selection of the relationships to be shown.

A classification scheme comprises three components:

the *schedules*, in which subjects are listed systematically showing their relationships;
the *notation* which is the code for use in the index or catalogue, and has a self-evident order which helps in signalling the arrangement;
and the alphabetical *index* which provides an entry vocabulary, or a list of terms for first consultation, and identification of the place of a subject within the scheme.

In order to support these three elements, and to ensure that schemes are updated it is important to have some organisation which takes responsibility for revision and publication.

This chapter considers each of these components of a classification scheme in turn. The ideas introduced in this chapter form the basis for the comparison and evaluation of some of the major schemes in Chapter 14.

13.2 Schedules

The schedules, or the list of subjects in a classification scheme are the heart of the scheme. The schedules determine which subjects can be effectively represented by the scheme, and which relationships are most effectively reflected by the scheme. It is most important to recognise that different collections, different periods in time and different users place different requirements on a scheme, both in terms of the subjects that should be included and also in terms of the relationships that need to be shown. Any scheme which attempts to remain stable over an extended time period, for a variety of different groups of users approaching many different collections is in some sense a compromise.

13.2.1 *The requirements of an effective schedule*

Before examining the two main means of constructing classification schedules it is as well to consider what the objective of the designer of a classification scheme should be. Although some of the criteria listed below may appear obvious it is necessary to state them partly because, sadly, some of the major schemes do not meet these criteria. It is easiest to discuss the criteria for effective schedules on two levels: first, in the terms of the main classes or groups in the scheme, and second, in relation to the treatment of specific subjects.

A main class, in a general classification scheme, is one of the broad classes into which knowledge is divided before further analysis begins, and for which there is no broader containing class. In respect of the main classes the following requirements can be specified:

1. All major disciplines should be represented. Any major omission will lead to a group of documents which cannot be classified under the scheme. In a general scheme, obviously all disciplines in human knowledge must be represented. In a special scheme it is sufficient to identify the main subjects for the subject or application to be covered.

2. The space in the scheme for a discipline should be approximately proportional to the size of the literature of that discipline. If this is not the case, subjects with limited literature may be subdivided extensively, producing unused or little used subdivisions, whereas 'large' subjects, if they are subdivided with only the same number of subdivisions, will have subdivisions in which unmanageable quantities of literature accumulate. If main classes are unbalanced in size and more subdivisions are made in some classes than others (to cater for the extensive literature of a larger subject), then long notation may result in the 'larger' areas. Measuring the size of the literature of a discipline may present problems, however.

3. The order of classes should bring related subjects into proximity. The object of classification is to group related subjects, and at the same time, to separate them from other subjects in other groups. With a large stock the order of main classes may not be particularly important, although most users would appreciate disciplines placed adjacent to related disciplines. Thus, language and literature, medicine and physiology, and botany and agriculture could conveniently be placed close to each other. Although recognising some such affinities between subjects, it is more difficult to find an overall order of main classes which suits everybody.

4. 1, 2 and 3 have assumed a stable body of knowledge. This is not the case, so the fourth criterion must require that there is provision for major change in the main classes, in order to reflect:

(a) the extension of developing disciplines, as measured by the relative size of the literature, and as has been evident recently in various areas of the social sciences and in computer science.

(b) the reduction of contracting disciplines, as measured by the relative size of the literature, and as has been evident for some time in religion and philosophy.

(c) the changing relationships between disciplines, and the growth of interdisciplinary topics, such as energy, industrial safety.

Within main classes, the schedules must meet requirements in respect of their ability to cover all subjects and their relationships, that might be encountered in the literature to which the scheme will be applied. It is important that:

1. There be a clear place for each simple subject, which is regarded as falling within one of the disciplines in the scheme. So there must be a clear place for poetry, probably in the discipline of literature, and a clear place for lasers, probably in the discipline of physics.

2. There must be a clear place for every complex subject likely to be encountered in the literature. So, within the discipline of literature, there must be a place for, not only poetry, but also nineteenth-century German poetry, and a place somewhere for the use of fibre optics in cable television.

3. The order of subjects must be systematic and generally acceptable to the anticipated users of the index or collection, and should facilitate effective browsing between related subjects. Thus, for example, various books on growing different flowers such as roses, chrysanthemums, dahlias and sweet peas should be close to one another when arranged on shelves in accordance with the classification scheme.

4. There must be provision for changes necessary to keep the coverage of subjects adequate for new literature. In other words, there must be scope for:

(a) new simple and complex subjects. Although provision must be made for new simple subjects, new complex subjects are much more likely to occur. Knowledge generally evolves from an identifiable base, and often new subjects arise from the coming together of two previously separate subjects.

(b) topics which have ceased to be the subject of new literature to be deleted from the scheme at an appropriate moment.

(c) a recognition in the changes in the relationships between subjects.

5. Schedules must be published (either internally or externally), so that the scheme can be applied by those to whom it might be useful.

In the attempt to match the above criteria, there are two fundamentally distinct avenues to the construction of the schedules of a classification scheme. These two methods, faceted classification and enumerative classification, are introduced in the next two sections. Faceted classification is now accepted as the more systematic way of constructing a classification scheme in today's environment of rapid development of knowledge, and the literature in which that knowledge is recorded. However, many of the major bibliographic classification schemes in use in libraries today were constructed according to the principles of enumerative classification, and so an appreciation of both methods is necessary to an understanding of classification schemes.

13.2.2 Enumerative classification

Enumerative classification schemes aim to enumerate or list all subjects present in the literature which the scheme is intended to classify. Thus all simple and all compound or complex subjects are listed. Inevitably all subjects present in the literature cannot be listed for this would generate very lengthy schedules, and therefore the listing of subjects must be selective. The enumeration is normally achieved by starting by identifying the main disciplines to be covered by the scheme, either on a philosophical or pragmatic basis. These main disciplines are each allocated a main class status, and enumeration proceeds by dividing each discipline into subclasses. This process of subdivision of classes is continued until an appropriate level of specificity has been achieved, and all subjects that are required to be represented have been listed in their appropriate place in the scheme. The object is to provide one place, and only one place for each subject. Figure 13.1 shows how this process can be executed.

The Library of Congress Classification Scheme is very evidently an enumerative classification scheme, but all the major classification schemes are basically enumerative. The enumeration in such schemes reflects an analytical approach to knowledge, that is subjects are subdivided into their component subfields. The subdivision of a subject defines the categories in that area of the scheme. Such schemes are essentially analytical in nature, but do not permit any synthesis or joining together of concepts that have been divided from one another.

Enumerative classification can be reasonably effective if subjects are divided by applying a consistent 'characteristic of subdivision'. In other words, it is important that all subclasses of a more general class are types of the same thing. One major criticism of many of the major schemes is that they do not subdivide subjects according to consistent characteristics of subdivision. A quick examination, for instance of the subclasses of the architecture schedules in Dewey, shows that the subdivisions of architecture are not all of the same type. The subclasses of architecture include classes covering architectural styles (for example, ancient and Oriental architecture, medieval architecture), the purpose of buildings (eg public structures, buildings for religious purposes) and method (architectural construction). (See Figure 13.1.)

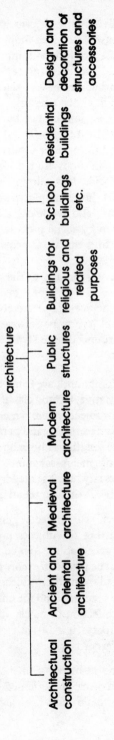

Figure 13.1 The subdivisions of architecture in the Dewey Decimal Classification Scheme

architecture

- Architectural construction
- Ancient and Oriental architecture
- Medieval architecture
- Modern architecture
- Public structures
- Buildings for religious and related purposes
- School buildings etc.
- Residential buildings
- Design and decoration of structures and accessories

To consider effective division by a 'principle' or 'characteristic' of division, consider the garments in a clothes shop. They can first be divided by the principle or characteristic of function, into, for example, overcoats, underwear, stockings, dresses, and then further subdivided, within these functional groups by other principles or characteristics of division. Some possible principles of division might be size, price range, material, colour. It is important to recognise that division must be by one principle at a time. In other words, all the classes for function of the clothes must be first enumerated before we proceed to consider subdivision by other principles, such as price. This consistency in subdivision is important in improving the predictability of the classification and minimising the opportunities for cross-classification (see below). For example, if we seek a document on the economic history of Germany, and we know that works on history are arranged first by country, then by social process, and then by period, this will make it easier for us to find this document, than it would be if the subdivision was less systematic.

Although the enumerative approach to the design of a classification scheme can be traced to the Greeks, long experience has shown that enumerative classification schemes are relatively inflexible, and, whilst providing a working subject order, do not always adequately allow for all subjects. The problems that are encountered with enumerative classification schemes can be identified as:

1. If all subjects, simple or compound, are listed in schedules, then the list becomes very long. The alternative, faceted classification, requires only the listing of simple one concept subjects (from which notation for compound subjects can be constructed as necessary), and permits much more succinct schedules. Excessive schedule length has been one reason for the use of the faceted approach in updating major schemes. For instance, in a fully enumerative scheme it is necessary to list a category for: 'flavourings used in the cooking of foods in hotels', if this degree of specificity is required.

2. Since the enumeration of all subjects generates excessively long schedules, in practice the listing of subjects must be selective (even if relatively long schedules are acceptable). Any complex subjects which are not present in the scheme must be placed in a more general category, and this subject cannot be distinguished from other subjects in that general category. The selection of subjects to be specified, and the omission of other subjects is rather dependent upon the collection to be classified, and thus, especially with regard to this selection process, it is difficult to design a scheme which is suitable for a number of different libraries.

3. Cross-classification, or the availability of more than one place for a subject, is quite common in a discipline-oriented scheme, that is a scheme which starts by producing main classes which coincide with major

disciplines. Pottery, for example, may be treated as art, science or technology, and within a discipline-oriented scheme there is likely to be the opportunity to classify pottery in at least any one of these three disciplines. In general, schemes with disciplines as main classes present problems in classifying 'concretes'. In such schemes it is often difficult to identify all literature on a given concrete at one location. For example, railways, children, substances (for example, gold), ethnic groups, computers, rabbits, may all have more than one place in an enumerative discipline-based classification scheme.

4. Enumerative schemes can be difficult to revise to take account of new developments. Every new subject which emerges in the literature and has a reasonable number of documents associated with it must be added to the list in the enumerative scheme. Further, because it is difficult to overhaul the basic structure of an enumerative scheme without complete revision of sections of the scheme, it is necessary to add new subjects into the existing framework of relationships. Especially if the new subject is one which upsets the previous structure of relationships, it will be difficult to fit into the existing order. Even when drastic revision is seen to be necessary and accepted, the point in time at which to conduct this extensive review can be difficult to select. The emergence of new subjects which are complex subjects presents no cause for revision in a faceted scheme, provided that the simple subjects from which the complex subject can be constructed are already present. Of course, in both enumerative and faceted schemes, it is necessary to take cognition of new simple subjects.

This list of problems with enumerative schemes is not intended to demonstrate that enumerative schemes are not effective in the organisation of knowledge. Most major libraries use enumerative classification schemes in order to organise their stock on shelves, and many use these schemes in the catalogues that provide access to their stock. However, it is necessary to recognise these limitations of enumeration so that they can be overcome in the application of the schemes. Further, these less than satisfactory aspects of enumerative classification help to explain the rationale for the search for more effective methods of designing classification schemes.

13.2.3 Menu-based information retrieval systems

Over the past few years a number of information retrieval systems which use the menu approach to information retrieval have been designed. A menu-based information retrieval system displays, on a television or other terminal connected to a computer, a list of categories from which the user must select one by keying the code which represents the chosen category. Typically, many systems will then need to display a further screen of possible options, from which a further selection will be made. Further menu screens will be necessary until the user has specified the task that he wishes executed or the information that he wishes to retrieve sufficiently for execution or retrieval to be effected. These menu-based information retrieval systems have been adopted for a number of information retrieval systems intended for the general public. (Most specialist information retrieval systems for more expert users concentrate on access via a command language with which the user must be familiar, and classification codes or alphabetical index terms as search keys.) Menu-based information retrieval systems have found favour because of their apparent simplicity. The user only has to select one of the given options – little imagination is needed (except in guessing what might be available under the various category headings). Additionally, menu-based information retrieval systems permit the selected option to be indicated on a simple numeric keypad if so designed. This has two advantages. This simple keypad, with no alphabetical characters, can be manufactured cheaply. Further, the user is not required to have any of the typing skills that are useful when faced with an alphanumeric keyboard, and the need to key in complete search terms.

Two figures, Figure 13.2 and Figure 13.3, demonstrate how the menu-based approach is used in one viewdata system, PRESTEL. Further discussion of the use of menu-based information retrieval in online public access catalogues is to be found in Chapter 23.

Now why has menu-based information retrieval been introduced in the middle of a chapter on the theory of classification? Menu-based information retrieval could be the area in which the extensive experience with enumerative classification may come to fruition. The author contends that it is possible to view the search conducted with the aid of a series of menus as having strong similarities with the search through the hierarchy of an enumerative classification scheme. (It is also possible to view searching through a menu-based information retrieval system as involving not hierarchies, but networks. This does not devalue the comparison between enumerative classification and menu-based information retrieval systems.)

Having just demolished enumerative classification to some extent in the previous section, it is reasonable to ask how effective menu-based information retrieval systems might be. It may well be that the computer-based environment of such systems may overcome many of the limitations of enumerative classification schemes in their traditional applications. For example, the scope of many menu-based information retrieval systems is much more restricted than that of a general bibliographic classification scheme. Also, the linear order of subjects which is a feature of the traditional applications of classification schemes may be less important. Nevertheless, it is worth drawing a comparison between menu-based information retrieval and enumerative classification so that menu-based information retrieval systems might avoid some of the pitfalls of traditional classification.

Figure 13.2 Main index to PRESTEL

1 Special feature - air services
2 Information - news and weather, amusements . . . .
3 Business, stocks and shares etc . . . .
4 Local information by town and region
5 Alphabetic indexes to subjects and IP's
6 What's new
7 Talking back to PRESTEL
8 Information for PRESTEL users
9 Micronet 800

Figure 13.3 A hierarchical tree diagram of a search for information on 'Apple' microcomputers

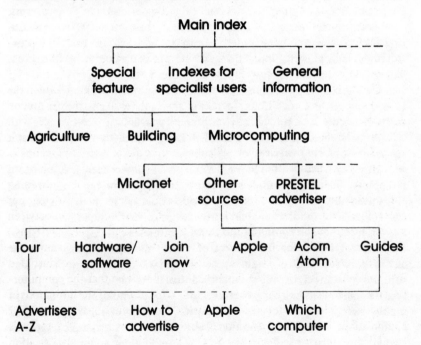

13.2.4 Faceted classification

Faceted classification is accepted as providing a sound theoretical basis for the construction of classification schemes. In various guises, the basic concepts have found application in the design of a number of special classification schemes, and have influenced the revision of major bibliographic schemes. Some years ago it seemed that a new general classification scheme based upon the theory of faceted classification might emerge and be widely adopted. Organisational factors would have appeared to have militated against the emergence of this scheme, although the Bliss Bibliographic Classification Second Edition makes a contribution in this direction (see 14.6).

Faceted classification rests upon the definition of the concept of a facet. First, however, some preliminary ideas. Faceted classification arises particularly from the need for classification schemes to accommodate complex, or multi-concept subjects. Any area of knowledge embraces a number of complex subjects, and some single concept subjects. Complex subjects must, for systematic treatment, be divided into their component, single concept subjects. Thus, the list in Figure 13.4 (page 198) shows some title-like statements of complex subjects, and within each of these statements, in general, more than one simple concept can be identified. These single concept subjects are referred to as *isolates*. Faceted classification starts by examining the literature of an area of knowledge, and identifying its isolates. Thus, in taking the isolates from the literature, faceted classification rests firmly on literary warrant.

A *facet*, then, is the sum total of isolates formed by the division of a subject by one characteristic of division.

In other words, in the literature of a given subject area, it is normally possible to identify a number of facets, and by applying a number of characteristics of subdivision to divide isolates into the facets. A characteristic of subdivision is an attribute or property which all concepts in a given facet have in common, and by which isolates can be grouped. Some examples of facets for the subject of office management are: kinds of office, services and procedures, accommodation and equipment and supplies, personnel, organisation and control and finance. In music literature the main facets are: composer, executant (for example, instrument playing the piece, or voice), form of composition, elements of music, character of composition, technique, common subdivisions (for example, such as periodicals, encyclopaedias).

This process of analysis into facets is called *facet analysis*, and the resultant classification is termed a faceted classification. Using this type of analysis as a basis it is possible to produce a schedule of standard terms to be used in the subject classification of documents. It should be plain that the making of a classification scheme by this process involves *analysis*, as single concepts must be identified, and distinguished one from another. The application of the classification schemes, once constructed, involves *synthesis*, or the drawing together of the single concepts which are listed in the scheme from their different facets, in order to specify compound subjects. Thus, these schemes are sometimes known as *analytico-synthetic*.

Making a faceted classification scheme

In order to demonstrate further how a faceted classification scheme is constructed it is necessary to identify the various stages in the construction of such a scheme, and then to illustrate these points by applying them to a specific subject area. This we will now procede to do. The making of a faceted classification scheme is a six-stage process:

1. *Identify facets and group isolates into them.* It is important that the characteristics of division used in this process should be mutually exclusive, in order to avoid cross-classification (documents on one and the same subject being classified at different places in the scheme). The enumeration of isolates should be exhaustive or complete for the subject area. This can only be achieved by examining the literature of the subject area thoroughly for any isolates that might possibly have been overlooked. Once organised into facets, the single concepts that have previously been referred to as isolates, become known as 'foci' (singular – focus).

Ranganathan proposed five basic types of facets which may occur in many subject fields, and these five form a useful checklist for the possible facets to be expected in many subjects. These types of facet are:

Personality, for example, types of libraries, crops, languages
Matter – constituent materials, for exmaple, metals, plastics, components
Energy – problem, method, process, operation, technique
Space – place, location
Time – period

Vickery has postulated that the following series of facets may be expected (or a sub-set of them):

Thing – part,   constituent – property – measure – patient – process/action
operation – agent – (space – time).

2. *Order foci within facets* A helpful order of foci within facets is to be sought. Standard reference works and experts may be consulted, and the appropriate order will depend upon the nature of the subject and the perspectives of its users. First, a facet may be divided into subfacets or

subclasses by the application of an additional single characteristic of subdivision. For example a health and safety engineering facet has subfacets: fire protection, explosive prevention, radiation and electrical protection, and others. The process of identification of subfacets within facets will depend very much upon the nature of the facet. One facet within a subject area may have several subfacets, whilst, other facets may have none. Once subclasses or subfacets have been identified and the foci grouped into these, then foci can be arranged in an order within the facet or subfacets, as appropriate. Many potential orders are possible for foci, but some common ones are:

simple to complex (that is, simplest aspects of a subject first, followed by more complex aspects, methods or equipment)

spatial or geographical or geometric (for example, the arrangement of geographical areas according to their spatial location)

chronological, historical or evolutionary

cannonical, that is according to the established order

alphabetical (a useful choice when there is a list of similar types of properties or objects, and no other obvious order is preferred).

3. *Decide combination order of facets* The combination order of facets, or their citation order when the scheme is to be applied in classifying documents has to be settled next. The scheme lists simple or single concepts which will have to be combined in order to accommodate complex subjects as they are encountered in documents. This citation order must be selected in accordance with the user's requirements and perspective; it may follow the educational and scientific consensus of opinion as to which are the more important groupings. It is important to recognise that citation order determines the main categories for shelf arrangement, and determines the nature of collocation. Classification scatters as it collocates, since it can only group primarily by the features listed in one of the facets applied in classifying a document. For example, a document on mathematics in primary schools could be classified first by the grade facet or first by the subject facet. Although the classification notation will subsequently be subdivided by the notation from the other facet, the document will be placed physically according to the first facet, that is, this document will either be placed with other documents on mathematics, or with other documents on primary schools. It is necessary to decide upon a citation order so that such documents are classified in a consistent manner.

Various standard citation orders have been proposed. Ranganathan's fundamental facets have been important in this area. The five facets identified above have been used as the basis for a standard citation order which follows the order in which the facets are cited above, that is PMEST. A variety of variations on this basic order was also proposed by Ranganathan.

4. *Decide schedule order of facets* Before the schedules can be finalised, the order of the facets in the schedules must be determined. In the interests of ease of application, the schedule order of facets is usually the combination order of the facets defined in stage 3 above, or in some cases the reverse of the combination order. Deviations from this basic order may be useful, particularly with regard to what are known as differential facets and common facets. *Differential facets* are subfacets which are placed adjacent to specific facets to which they are applicable; they are not generally used with all of the facets in the scheme.

Common facets may be listed anywhere in the schedule order, because they are facets that, although only listed once can be applied anywhere in the citation order, as required to qualify the concept to which they apply.

5. *Append notation* Naturally a classification scheme is not complete until the notation has been added. However, it is important to note that notation is not added to the schedules until the basic order of subjects has been determined. Notation for classification schemes will be considered at greater length in section 13.3.

6. *Compile and index* The compiler of the classification scheme will no doubt be all too familiar with the order of subjects within the scheme, but in the interests of other users, an index will be a necessary guide to the concepts present in the scheme and their location within the scheme. More about indexes is available in section 13.4.

The scheme may well now be complete, but revision is recommended from time to time, and thought must be given as to how this might be achieved. Revision is considered in section 13.5.

An example of a simple faceted classification for literature

This section examines the application of the principles of facet analysis to the design of a simple classification scheme for documents on literature. This scheme can also be used to classify the literature to which these labels apply, but if it is so applied, this ceases to be a purely subject classification, and becomes to some extent a classification by the form in which the literature is written, for example its language and literary form. We follow through the six steps enumerated above.

1. The titles shown in Figure 13.4 can be used as a basis for the types of subjects available in the literature to be classified. From these subject statements, it is possible to gather isolates, and to note that isolates can be divided into the following facets:

period, for example medieval period, twentieth century

Figure 13.4 Some titles in literature for the identification of isolates

Note: These title-like statements are used to show statements of compound subjects, in literature

1. A Collection of nineteenth century French literature
2. Golden age Spanish poetry
3. Italian fiction
4. A Collection of eighteenth century literature
5. A Collection of essays on nature
6. English medieval fiction
7. Russian drama
8. Tibetan epic poetry
9. Early Hebrew literature
10. Twentieth century Bulgarian literature
11. A Collection of poetry
12. A Collection of English poetry
13. American satire
14. German speeches of the 1600s
15. A Collection of humour about cricket
16. Dutch Renaissance literature
17. Afrikaans literature
18. Danish letters about politics
19. Scottish literature.

---

form, for example, essays, poetry
theme, for example, about cricket, about politics
language, for example, English, Italian

Obviously once these facets have been identified it is a relatively simple matter to group the isolates into the appropriate facet.

2. Once foci have been grouped into facets, they must be ordered. For this scheme it would seem sensible to order the foci within each facet differently according to the nature of the facet. Thus we might propose the following broad arrangements within facets:

period facet, ordered chronologically
form facet, ordered by grouping related forms
theme facet, ordered by grouping related themes
language facet, ordered by giving precedence to major languages and their literatures.

At this stage it becomes possible to start to draft the types of lists that are shown in Figure 13.5. Obviously Figure 13.5 does not show an exhaustive

Figure 13.5 A draft of a faceted classification scheme for literature

Notation for Facet	A	C	E	G
Notation for Foci	Language	Form	Period	Theme
1	American	Poetry	Pre-Medieval	Nature
2	English	Epic poetry	Medieval	Cricket
3	German	Drama	15th C*	Politics
4	Dutch	Fiction	16th C	
5	Afrikaans	Essays	17th C	
6	Danish	Speeches	18th C	
7	French	Letters	19th C	
8	Spanish	Humour	20th C	
9	Italian	Satire		
10	Russian			
11	Tibetan			
12	Hebrew			
13	Bulgarian			

Notes:

1. C=Century
2. Much more enumeration would be necessary to complete this first draft.
3. To classify 'A collection of nineteenth century French literature', this would be given as A7E7
* 'English medieval fiction' would attract the notation A2C4E2.

---

listing of all foci, but merely identifies and organises those that can be derived from Figure 13.4 and its subject statements.

3. Next the combination order of facets must be settled. We could accept: language, form, period, theme. Thus materials are classified and grouped first by language and conversely, for example, poetry is scattered according to language.

4. The schedule order of facets must next be decided. Here, in Figure 13.5 we have adopted a schedules order which follows the citation order.

5. Once all other preliminary decisions have been made, the notation can be assigned to the scheme. Figure 13.5 shows a simple but effective notation.

6. No index is shown here, but this would be the last stage in the compilation of the scheme, besides attempting to classify some items by the scheme, in order to check that the scheme seems likely to be effective.

13.2.5 Developments in classification theory and the Classification Research Group

The concepts associated with the application of facets in the theory of library classification, and the associated citation orders were first tested extensively by Ranganathan in the Colon Classification (see 14.5). Other ideas on the theory of classification were enumerated by Bliss, and embodied in the Bliss Bibliographic Classification Scheme, First Edition. The work on the theory of classification has extended beyond that which is evident from a study of classification schemes and the practice of library classification.

The Classification Research Group (CRG) has been a major force in the development of classification theory, and has made a major contribution towards work on a new general bibliographic classification scheme. The CRG was formed in 1948 after the Royal Society Scientific Information Conference. Early work led to the production of over twenty special schemes in various areas of knowledge. The experience gained with these special schemes provided a grounding for work on the development of a new general scheme. The first step towards this new general scheme was to identify the main classes of such a scheme. It was felt to be important that these main classes should be selected on the basis of a theory or set of principles, which would guide in the selection of main classes. This theory would ensure that the need for new main classes was minimised and that the basic framework of the scheme would appropriately admit every subject. The search for main classes was first concentrated upon 'entities' or things. The theory of *integrative levels* emerged. The essence of the idea is that the world of entities evolves from the simple towards the complex by an accumulation of properties or influences from the environment. Thus an early draft of some of the major integrative levels was of this form:

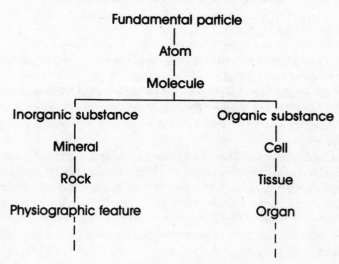

The CRG set about trying to define a series of integrative levels upon which it would be possible to base the main classes and their order for a new general classification scheme. Work was centred upon the tabulation of entities. Simultaneously with the work on integrative levels work was in progress on citation order. Five fundamental relationships were noted between concepts, and these relationships were expressed in terms of a series of relational operators. Eventually this work on citation orders came to fruition in the rather unlikely context of a new indexing system, PRECIS.

Although the work of the CRG makes fascinating reading, and magnificent contributions were made towards the clarification of the principles of classification, much work remains to be done. The original impetus has been diverted into specific applications. Later work of members of the CRG has tended to concentrate on specific applications. Significant contributions include the development of the PRECIS indexing system (see 17.2.4), and the preparation of the second edition of the Bliss Bibliographic Classification Scheme (see 14.6).

In parallel with the work of the classification theorists, general systems theory was evolved to consider similar problems. General systems theory is the product of various philosophers of science, such as Bertalanffy and Laszlo, and is an important area of study for the intending classification theorist.

Other work relating to the development of classification has been conducted under the auspices of UNISIST. In 1971 plans were established to provide an international switching language which could be applied to all publications to indicate the subject fields that they cover. Although the original intention was that this would be an intermediate language between two established languages, for example, German natural language – switching language – French natural language – the product of the work has been a new general classification scheme known as the Standard Reference Code or the Broad System of Ordering (BSO). The final draft of the BSO was published in 1978. More details are given in section 14.8.

Work on automatic classification should not be overlooked, although a brief mention only is permitted. Various studies have been conducted in order to assess the extent to which computer analysis of text can contribute to the generation of a classification scheme, and the subsequent classification of documents. This is a fresh avenue of approach to classification, and shows some promise.

13.3 Notation

Notation has an important impact on the effectiveness of a classification scheme. A poor notation can impair the ability of a scheme to accommodate new subjects and can hinder effective retrieval. Nevertheless, it is worth reiterating that notation is added to the list of subjects that comprise the schedules of a classification scheme after the subjects to be included and their order have been settled. A unique notational symbol should be provided for each individual subject, whether it be simple or complex. The purpose of notation is to impose a self-evident ordering on the subjects listed in the scheme. As we have already seen, the systematic ordering of subjects, whilst it might adhere to some consensus, is not an obvious order to all users of a scheme; it is the purpose of notation to permit ease of filing or ordering.

13.3.1 Types of notation

If notation is to offer a self-evident ordering then it is important that the symbols that are used for the notation have a self-evident order in themselves. There are only two sets of symbols whose orders are reasonably universally recognised: the letters of the Roman alphabet (either small or capitals), and Arabic numerals. Other symbols are encountered in the notation for classification schemes, and although on occasions it may be an advantage to include symbols whose filing position is not predefined, these symbols always detract from the automatic ordering. Any symbols other than letters and numbers need to have their filing value defined. Consider, does a ':' file before or after a '?'? Some schemes use punctuation marks in their notation, others use letters from the Greek alphabet.

Apart from the different character sets that can be used for notation, there are two different types of notation: pure notation and mixed notation. A *pure notation* is a notation that uses only one kind of symbol, for example, letters or numbers. The notation in the Dewey Decimal Classification Scheme is one such pure notation. Numbers only are used (in most instances) eg 714.67, 456.7. A *mixed notation* uses more than one kind of symbol such as, for example, a mixture of letters and numbers, or a mixture of lower case and upper case letters in specifying subjects. Mixed notations are relatively common; the Library of Congress Classification Scheme uses a mixed notation consisting of letters (upper case) and numbers, for example, DA783.

Notation is used in two contexts: in catalogues and indexes, and in shelf arrangement of stock. In this respect, not only is notation important in providing an ordering in both of these contexts, but it also frequently acts as the vital link between any of: the schedules in a classification scheme, the printed and published index to the schedules of the classification scheme, the classified sequence in a catalogue or index, and the classified order adopted for shelf arrangement. Since notation has this function of linking various sequences there are certain basic requirements that an acceptable notational system must offer. It is easiest to discuss these requirements in terms of the human requirements upon notation, and indeed, even with computer based catalogues and indexes, people will be required to use and write or remember notation (at least until the day when shelf arrangement is no longer relevant, or when machines are widely available that will re-shelve books and other materials, regardless of their size and form). Obviously, computers and the use of notation in computerised systems may place additional constraints upon the nature of the notation, or may eliminate the need to consider some of the characteristics below. For instance, whilst a person may be concerned about the length of notation, this is not usually important to a computer, and a computer has little use for mnemonics (it does not forget!). Expressiveness, on the other hand, can be extremely useful in building search strategies in computer-based systems.

13.3.2 Ease of use

The notation must be easy for users to remember, write, type and match. Factors which influence the ease of use of notation include:

(a) *Simplicity*, or the ease with which notation can be remembered. It is, for example, generally easier to remember 681.945.6 than 6819456, and yet easier to remember a mixed notation such as 532CRM721.

(b) *Brevity* has an obvious contribution to make to ease of use. The shorter the notation, the easier it is to remember. A number of factors determine the length of the notation in a classification scheme. These include:

The *base* of the notation, or the number of characters in the character set. Obviously, using A to Z as the basic character set, twenty-six subjects can be represented by single character notation. Using 1 to 9 as the base, to cover twenty-six subjects requires that some subjects be allocated notation that uses two characters.

The *allocation* of the notation will also affect its length. Uneven allocation of notation to subjects with the same size of literature, and approximately the same number of subdivisions being allocated different notational space will cause some notation for some subjects to be exceptionally long. For example, suppose French literature is denoted by 56 and Bulgarian literature by 768, then all the subdivisions of Bulgarian literature will have notation which is one character longer than their equivalents in French literature. Uneven allocation will lead to some subjects having relatively short notation at the expense of others with relatively long notation. Uneven allocation often arises in practice with the development of subjects, and the original allocation of the scheme becoming less balanced with time and the emergence of new subdivisions of some subjects. Provision for *synthesis* often also leads to long notation, for two reasons. First, synthetic schemes tend to facilitate detailed specification, and thus specification of a larger number of subjects. In order to distinguish between all these subjects it is inevitable that longer notations are used. In addition, synthesis often requires the use of a facet indicator, which marks the beginning of a new facet for example, ',',':'.

Expressiveness can be another feature which contributes to a lengthier notation. Each step of subdivision involves an extra character (see below). (c) Deliberate *mnemonics* are devices which help the user to remember and recall the notation for given subjects. In addition to ease of use and brevity, either systematic and/or literal mnemonics may be exploited. *Systematic mnemonics* is the use of the same notation for a given topic wherever that topic occurs. Synthetic devices often lead to this type of mnemonics. For example, in the Tables in the Dewey Decimal Classification Scheme, 42 is always used for England and Wales, and 03 for Dictionaries and Encyclopaedias.

Further, '9' is used to represent history and geography in a number of different contexts. *Literal mnemonics* are abbreviations or letters which are easily associated with the name of a subject. Thus we might use 'C' for Chemistry or 'M' for Music. Unfortunately, literal mnemonics can only be applied to a very limited number of the subjects in a scheme, unless the order of subjects in the scheme can be distorted. Thus 'M' for Music, will mean that an adjacent class must be denoted 'N', and so, Fine Arts may be denoted by 'N'.

13.3.3 Hospitality

It is necessary that any notation be hospitable to the insertion of new subjects. It is fruitless trying to revise the subjects represented in a scheme, unless a notation can be appended to any new or modified subjects. Generally, updating calls for the insertion of new topics within existing classes, but it should be possible to insert a new main class if the need arises. There are two means whereby notation can accommodate, or be hospitable to new subjects:

(a) unassigned notation within the sequence, or gaps into which subjects can be inserted. For example, examine Figure 13.6. Plainly, any new subjects can be offered the notation which has not previously been used. This approach is not always satisfactory because gaps may not be left in the notation at the place in the order of subjects where it is desired to place a new subject. Further, it is necessary to predict in advance the areas in which new subjects are likely to arise and to leave gaps accordingly; this forecasting is obviously difficult.

(b) decimal notation. Decimal notation facilitates the insertion of new subjects. A new subject can be inserted almost anywhere in a sequence by the use of decimal subdivision. Thus, if 51, 52, 53 are all allocated, and a new subject needs to be inserted between the subject at 51 and that at 52, the notation for this subject can be provided by decimal subdivision, and will be given the notation 515 (or any notation from 511 to 519). Note that decimal notation is also possible with letters. Thus, ABN can be inserted between AB and AC.

Figure 13.6 Allocation of notation to leave gaps for insertion of new subjects

(An extract from Library of Congress Classification Scheme)

	Invention
1517	General (II)
1519	Special products and processes, A-Z (III)
	.A8 Atomic power
	.C45 Chemicals
1521	Employees' inventions
1525	Designs and models (II)
	Licenses
	Including compulsory licenses
1528	General (II)
1530	Foreign licensing agreements (II)
1532	Assignments (II)
1536	Infringement. Patent litigation and procedure (II)
1544	Patent attorneys. Patent practice (II, modified)

13.3.4 Expressiveness

An expressive notation expresses or displays the relationship structure of subjects within the scheme. In this it helps the user to recognise the structure of the scheme and to identify general subjects and their associated subdivisions. Expressiveness can be difficult to maintain as new subjects are added. Expressiveness often relies upon decimal subdivision, and this may become less systematic with the addition of new subjects.

Thus, in the Dewey Decimal Classification we find:

620 Applied Physics
621 Mechanical Engineering
621.3 Electrical Engineering
621.48 Nuclear Engineering
624 Civil Engineering.

The need to insert Electrical Engineering and Nuclear Engineering at a later time, subsequent to the original drafting of the scheme, has detracted from the original attempt to build an expressive notation. An expressive notation, might for instance have shown:

620 Applied Physics
621 Mechanical Engineering
623 Electrical Engineering

625 Nuclear Engineering
627 Civil Engineering.

with all the different branches of Engineering shown as equivalent. In order to achieve the above expressive notation for branches of Engineering major reallocation of notation would have been required, and this would be deemed undesirable.

Some schemes deliberately opt for a non-expressive notation. A good example is the British Catalogue of Music Classification which abandons expressiveness in favour of allocating brief notation to the most common concepts. Figure 13.7 shows a small extract. The column which shows a hypothetical expressive notation demonstrates that the expressive notation is longer in most instances than the actual notation allocated in this particular scheme. A compromise between expressive and non-expressive notation is to be found in the Second Edition of the Bliss Bibliographic Classification Scheme.

13.3.5 Synthesis

There must be the possibility within the notation of achieving synthesis if any synthetic elements are present in the scheme. In major enumerative schemes synthesis is often controlled by careful instructions regarding citation order and the way in which the notation for complex subjects is to be built up from its components. In faceted schemes synthesis is often achieved with the intercession of a facet indicator. A facet indicator makes it possible to identify which parts of the notation have been drawn from a distinct facet. Capital letters, and various punctuation symbols eg :, (), ', may be enlisted as facet indicators. Thus in the notation FcdEdm, it is possible to observe that the notation Fcd comes from one facet, and the notation Edm comes from a second facet. Without the use of the capital and small letters in combination it would not have been possible to identify how a piece of notation has been synthesised.

Figure 13.7 Extract from the British Catalogue of Music Classification Scheme

Actual notation	Subject	Hypothetical expressive notation
RW	String instruments	RW
RX	Bowed string instruments	RWA
S	Violin	RWAA
SQ	Viola	RWAB
SQQ	Viola d'amore	RWABA
SR	Cello	RWAC

Some schemes use *retroactive notation* in order to signal new facets. Retroactive notation makes it possible to indicate distinct facets without recourse to mixed notation. Thus, the self-evident order of a single character set is maintained. Retroactive notation is achieved when allocating notation, by only subdividing a letter by letters which follow it in the alphabet (retroactive notation based upon numbers would be rather restrictive in the number of classes or facets that could be indicated so letters are normally used). Take, for example: BMNFRSMXZWY, as a synthesised piece of notation. In the synthesised notation, an earlier letter than the letters prior to it in the notation signals a new facet, for example above B, F, M and W signal a new facet.

13.3.6 Flexibility

Some users and classifiers find it beneficial to have a notation which is sufficiently flexible to permit a variety of citation orders to be adopted as appropriate to the document and the user's perspective. Thus, for instance, the Universal Decimal Classification would permit notation to be combined in different orders. 766 for commercial graphic art and 659.3 for mass communication may be combined as 766:659.3 or as 659.3:766.

13.3.7 Shelf notation

Notation which is to be inscribed on the spine of books may be required to be shorter than the notation which is used in catalogues, indexes, databases and bibliographies. It is helpful if an abbreviated notation (which merely shows the broad subject categories into which documents can be grouped) can be readily derived from the full notation. Expressive notation is generally easier to truncate, that is, delete final characters to create the notation for a more general subject. For example, in Figure 14.3, the notation 641.493 could be assigned for the Preservation of Poultry and used in the catalogue, but the truncated notation 641.4 could be used for shelf arrangement.

13.4 Index

The index to the classification scheme, that is, the index which is published as part of the classification scheme serves two purposes:

1. The location of topics within the systematically arranged classification.
2. The display of related aspects of a subject which have been scattered by the order of subjects chosen for the sequence of subjects in the main classified order.

The index should complement the classification scheme, and the relationships shown in the index should supplement those in the main classified sequence. There are two types of index to be found in classification schemes: a relative index and a specific index. The relative index is the more common.

A *relative index*, as originally proposed by Melville Dewey, contains at least one entry for each subject in the scheme, and, by use of the alphabetical sequence, gathers together all aspects of a concrete subject, which are likely to have been scattered by a discipline-orientated approach in the basic order of the scheme. Figure 14.4 shows a number of entries concerned with Landscape and Landscapes and located at a variety of places in the main sequence.

A *specific index* can be devised if the classification scheme is such that there is only one location for each subject. Thus one specific entry can be made for each subject in the index. This will be appropriate for simple subjects in a faceted classification scheme.

Many of the points which are made concerning alphabetical indexes in Chapters 15, 16 and 17 may also be applied to the construction of indexes to classification schemes.

13.5 Organisation and revision

For a scheme to be successful in the long term it is vital that there should be an organisational structure to support the scheme. Initially, it is necessary that the scheme be published and available for purchase, and that its use is generally promoted. But the most important function of the organisation is to provide a mechanism for the revision of the scheme. The use of a scheme in centrally or co-operatively produced catalogue records can also be important in establishing its future.

Revision is necessary to make provision for emerging subjects. In order that the scheme remain popular it is vital that revision is conducted with regard to users' needs. To this end some consultative procedure is to be recommended. However, lengthy and complex consultative committees can hinder revision, and make for a slowly changing scheme. A number of publication strategies are possible for announcing the modifications to classification schemes. These are:

1. Publish a new edition at appropriate intervals, for example every few years.
2. Publish new editions of parts of the schedules at intervals, for example, new editions of specific subject areas.
3. Publish changes as they are accepted, in a periodical publication, cumulating these in a new edition of all or parts of the schedules, as suitable.

These new schedules will reflect the following means of revision of the new subject structure and listing:

expansion, to permit the additions of new subjects or more specific subdivision of existing subjects;

reduction, to take out subjects and their subdivisions which are no longer used;

relocation, in order to rectify an inappropriate placement, to eliminate dual provision (more than one place for one subject) to make room for new subjects;

changes in terminology, to allow for new subject descriptions to be incorporated into the scheme as subjects change their names.

Although revision is necessary so that the schedules remain suitable for classifying new literature, it must be remembered that there is a gulf between publishing the schedules in an updated form, and applying the schedules. When new schedules are made available to a library using a classification scheme they have three options:

1. Ignore the new schedules.
2. Use the new schedules to classify new stock, but leave the old stock classified according to earlier editions of the schedules.
3. Use the new schedules to classify new stock, and also reclassify the old stock, which has usually been classified previously according to an earlier edition of the scheme.

Option 3 clearly requires the most work, but equally clearly is the most satisfactory. However, as Figure 13.8 demonstrates, reclassification can be a major exercise involving much relocation of stock, and this is clearly a disincentive to the complete revision of the classified stock.

Particularly in a large library, reclassification can be a major exercise, although it can be facilitated by the support given by computer based

Figure 13.8 The elements of a reclassification exercise

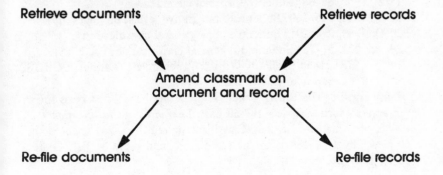

catalogue records. Thus Dewey's policy of *integrity of numbers* has found great favour. An undertaking has been made that a piece of notation will not be revised and given another meaning, and thus any change of the meaning of a piece of notation is avoided. This limits the need for libraries to re-classify, but also restricts the revision process of the Dewey Decimal Classification Scheme.

Chapter 13 Readings

1 Austin, D., 'The CRG research into a freely faceted scheme', In: Maltby, A. *Classification in the 1970's: a second look*, Bingley: London, 1976, 158–194.
2 Austin, D., 'Prospects for a new general classification', *Journal of Librarianship*, 1(3), 1969, 149–169.
3 'The Broad system of ordering'. *International Forum on Information and Documentation* 4(3), 1979, 3–27.
4 *BSO: Broad System of Ordering. Schedule and index.* 3rd revision/ prepared by the FID/BSO Panel. FID: The Hague. Unesco: Paris, 1978. (FID Publication no. 564).
5 *The BSO manual: the development, rationale and use of the Broad System of Ordering*, prepared by the FID/BSO Panel. FID: The Hague, 1979. (FID Publication no. 580).
6 *Classification Research Group Classification and information control.* Library Association: London, 1970. (LA Research pamphlet no. 1)
The work of the CRG is reported in its bulletins. The first three of these were published as separates and are now out of print; since no. 4, the bulletins have appeared in the *Journal of Documentation*, in the following issues:
12(4), 1956, 227–230 (Bibliography of publications by members)
14(3), 1958, 136–143 (Bulletin 4: BCM classification)
15(1), 1959, 39–57 (Bulletin 5: Cranfield)
17(3), 1961, 156–168 (Bulletin 6: new general classification)
17(3), 1961, 169–172 (Bibliography of publications)
18(2), 1962, 65–88 (Bulletin 7: special classifications)
20(3), 1964, 146–169 (Bulletin 8: integrative levels; bibliography)
24(4), 1968, 273–291 (Bulletin 9: new general classification)
29(1), 1973, 51–71 (Bulletin 10: general classification; PRECIS)
34(1), 1978, 21–50 (Bulletin 11: new general classification; PRECIS; BSO; bibliography of publications)
7 Dahlberg, I., 'The Broad System of Ordering (BSO) as a basis for an integrated social sciences thesaurus?', *International Classification* 7(2), 1980, 66–72. Also editorial: 'Classification and the social sciences and review', by I.L. Travis in the same issue, and reply by E.J. Coates, 8(1), 1981, 46.

8 Ferradane, J.E.L. 'Fundamental fallacies and new needs in library classification', In: *Sayers memorial volume*, chapter 9. Library Association: London, 1961.

9 Farradane, J.E.L., 'Analysis and organization of knowledge for retrieval', *Aslib Proceedings*, 22(12), 1970, 607–616.

10 Foskett, A.C., 'The Broad System of Ordering: old wine into new bottles?' *International Forum on Information and Documentation*, 4(3), 1979, 1–12.

11 Foskett, D.J., *Classification for a general index language*, Library Association: London, 1970 (L.A. Research Publication No. 2).

12 Jeffreys, A., 'Classification in British university library practice', *Catalogue and Index*, 57, 1980, 6–8.

13 Leo Jolley memorial seminar, Aslib June 20 1977. 'The theory of integrative levels and its application to classification and indexing systems', *Aslib Proceedings*, 30(6), 1978, 192–237.

14 Soergel, D., 'The Broad System of Ordering – a critique', *International Forum on Information and Documentation*, 4(3), 1979, 21–24.

14 Bibliographic classification schemes

14.1 Introduction

There are a number of important general classification schemes. Each of these is sufficiently significant that they repay study in their own right, and some of these are an essential preliminary to understanding catalogues, indexes and shelf arrangement of stock in libraries. In addition, an appreciation of the distinction between such general schemes and special classification schemes is a component of the complete appreciation of classification practice.

A study of the major general schemes reveals a wide gulf between theory, as outlined in the previous chapter, and practice, as reflected in the major schemes. The existing major general classification schemes observe few of the theoretical bases for sound classification. In particular, most were constructed before the ideas of facet analysis were developed. Thus these major schemes are essentially enumerative, and suffer from the limitations of enumerative classification outlined in the last chapter. Clearly, the originators of the major schemes cannot be criticised for being ignorant of principles which were not recognised when their schemes were initiated. Indeed, knowledge was more limited and collections generally smaller when the schemes were devised, and so an analytic approach to classification was less appropriate than it is today.

Nevertheless, whatever the basis for the major enumerative schemes they must be judged for their suitability for application in current libraries and information centres, and it is therefore reasonable to apply the principles of facet analysis in order to evaluate the schemes, and to identify any limitations. Also, the revisers of the major schemes do attempt, within the constraints imposed by the basically enumerative framework, to take account of a more systematic approach to classification in any proposed revisions of these schemes.

The three major schemes, the Library of Congress Classification Scheme, the Universal Decimal Classification Scheme and the Dewey Decimal Classification Scheme are treated in most detail, since they account for a good proportion of classification practice. The Bliss Bibliographic Classification Scheme and the Colon Classification Scheme are also considered, mainly because they are important in demonstrating specific features of classification theory or practice. Unfortunately, in the interests of space, no treatment is given of other major schemes, such as J D Brown's Subject Classification. Readers are referred to Chapter 12 Reference 9 if they wish to pursue a study of such schemes.

It should be noted that the space devoted to a scheme in this chapter is not necessarily a reflection of its significance. Some schemes have features which necessitate lengthy explanation. Also, some aspects of some of the schemes have already been considered in the last chapter, and these will obviously not be directly repeated.

14.2 The Dewey Decimal Classification (DC)

The Dewey Decimal Classification (abbreviated to either DC or DDC) is arguably the most important bibliographic classification scheme. It boasts a strong organisational basis, being published and revised regularly by the Forest Press, and edited by part of the Processing Department of the Library of Congress on the advice of the Decimal Classification Editorial Policy Committee. It features elements of many of the trends in classification theory and practice over the past one hundred years. And, perhaps most important of all, it is used in libraries of all types throughout the English-speaking world. It has found particular favour in public libraries in the United Kingdom and the United States of America and is also used extensively in school and college libraries. It has been translated into many languages. It is difficult to ascribe the popularity of the DC to any particular feature, and its continuing use is probably related to the combination of desirable or acceptable features. DC has also been used in the British National Bibliography (BNB) and is used in both BNB MARC and LC MARC records.

Despite its pre-eminence, or possibly because of it, DC has its critics. DC is certainly not regarded as the perfect classification scheme even in sectors where there is no serious alternative. DC is regarded rather as a pragmatic solution to the classification of library and information materials, and its contribution in this context should not be under-rated.

The scheme has passed through nineteen editions. The nineteenth edition is published in three volumes: volume 1, introduction and tables; volume 2, schedules; and volume 3, index. The scheme has been praised for its clear and well-presented schedules, and this is definitely one of its strengths, even if the schedules may seem a little daunting on first acquaintance.

Figure 14.1 Dewey Decimal Classification main classes

000 Generalities
100 Philosophy and related disciplines
200 Religion
300 Social sciences
400 Language
500 Pure sciences
600 Technology (Applied sciences)
700 The arts
800 Literature (Belles-lettres)
900 General geography and history and their auxiliaries

14.2.1 Main classes

The scheme is divided into ten main discipline oriented classes as shown in Figure 14.1. The scheme is basically enumerative with simple and composite or compound subjects listed within each class. Each main class can be subdivided into ten major subclasses, and then each of these subclasses can be subdivided into ten more specific classes, and so on, until all subjects that need to be specified have been enumerated. There are ten subclasses available at each step of division. This restriction to ten classes at each stage has sometimes hindered the systematic development of division (where, for instance, a subject needs to be subdivided into twelve main subclasses or branches). Obviously sometimes not all ten of the possible subclasses are necessary, and subdivision of a subject may be into less than ten subclasses. This limit of ten has been a particular handicap in respect of the main classes.

The limited notational base provided by numbers (instead of, say, letters) has required that all subjects be fitted into ten main classes. This has led to some unlikely liaisons. For instance, Music and Sports both find themselves in the Arts. Agriculture and Medicine are both treated in the Applied Sciences, and the Social Sciences class, 300, subsumes Economics, Politics, Law and Education. Some would argue that many of these areas are disciplines in their own right and merit their own main class.

Other critics have turned their attention to the order of the main classes in DC. This order is consistent with the established relationships between subjects at the time that the scheme was first published (1876), but produces some strange collocations for today's literature. In particular:

Language 400 is divided from Literature 800
Technologies are separated from their underlying class, for example Chemistry 540: but Chemical technology 660.
Buildings at 690 is separated from Architecture at 720.

Also within main classes there are occasional unlikely collocations. One of the most obvious of these is Psychology at 150, within the Philosophy class, 100.

Another problem with the main classes is that they are unbalanced. Today, the quantity of literature in the class 100 Philosophy, is small compared with that in, say, the 500 Science, or 600 Technology classes. The apportionment of subjects to main classes reflects the state of knowledge when the scheme was designed.

14.2.2 Synthesis

Elementary synthesis was introduced to the scheme as early as the second edition. By the nineteenth edition synthesis is a well established feature of the scheme, as a mechanism for allowing detailed specification without resorting to exceedingly lengthy schedules. Synthesis operates in two ways: through the tables, and through the 'add to' instructions.

The nineteenth edition (like the eighteenth) has seven tables, as listed in Figure 14.2. These tables may be applied, in carefully selected subject areas, and under the guidance of explicit instructions, in order to subdivide a subject found in the main schedules. Thus whilst the main schedules may give a number for 'Cats', by the application of Table 1 it is possible to distinguish between a document which is an encyclopaedia concerned with cats, and a document on societies concerned with cats. The Tables remove the need to list 'common subdivisions' in each of the many places where they might be applied, and permit one list to suffice for applications with respect to many different subjects.

The content of the Tables is reminiscent of the Tables in the Universal Decimal Classification, and, indeed, they were to some extent inspired by the Tables in UDC. However, the use of the Tables in DC is much more closely monitored than the use of the equivalent Tables in UDC. Table 1 may be used anywhere in the schedules, entirely at the discretion of the classifier. Tables 2, 5, 6 and 7 however, may only be applied where instructions lead the classifer to use them. Sometimes such instructions are

Figure 14.2 Dewey Decimal Classification Tables

Table 1 Standard Subdivisions
Table 2 Areas
Table 3 Subdivisions of Individual Literatures
Table 4 Subdivisions of Individual Languages
Table 5 Racial, Ethnic, National Groups
Table 6 Languages
Table 7 Persons

in the main schedules, but on other occasions the instructions may be found in one of the other Tables, for example Table 1 or Table 4. Table 3 is intended solely for use in the 800 literature main class, and Table 4 for use in the 400 language main class.

Generally, notation from the Tables is added to notation in the schedules to make a more specific number. A few examples are useful. In the first examples below 743 for Drawing is taken from the main schedules, and 03 for Dictionaries is added from Table 1 to make the notation 743.03 for a dictionary of drawing.

	Main schedule	Table		Final notation
1.	Drawing	Dictionaries		A Dictionary of Drawing
	743	03		743.03
		Table 1		
2.	Farmhouses	Delaware		Farmhouses in Delaware
	631.21	09	751	631.2109751
		Table 1	Table 2	
3.	Psychology	Eskimos		Psychology of Eskimos
	155.82	97		155.8297
		Table 5		
4.	French language	Dictionary/English language		English/French bilingual dictionary
	44	3	21	443.21
		Table 4	Table 6	

Instructions for the use of Tables is always given either in the Tables, or in the main schedules where the Tables are to be applied. These instructions determine the citation order of the various concepts represented by the Schedules and the Tables, and remove the need for facet indicators such as would be required where more flexibility of citation order was permitted.

The other synthetic device in DC is the 'add to' instructions. This permits subdivisions which are enumerated under one subject in the schedules to be used in other specified parts of the schedules, as instructed. For example, the extract in Figure 14.3 instructs the user to apply various preservation techniques (in 641.41–641.47) to various meats and allied foods (in 641.49). Thus 'freezing poultry' is 641.49353, taking '53' from 641.453.

Like tables the 'add to' instructions removes the need to repeat subdivisions under several different subjects.

Figure 14.3 Dewey Decimal Classification extract showing 'add to' instructions

▶ **641.4-641.8 Preservation, storage, cookery**
Class comprehensive works in 641.3
.4 **Preservation and storage**

641.41-641.47 Preservation techniques
▶ Fruits and vegetables, food as a whole
Class comprehensive works in 641.4, preservation techniques for meats and allied foods in 641.49

.41 Preliminary treatment
.42 Canning

.44 Drying and dehydrating

.45 Low-temperature techniques

.452 Cold storage
.453 Deep freezing

.46 Brining, pickling, smoking

.47 Use of additives

.48 Storage

.49 Meats and allied foods
Class storage of meats and allied foods in 641.48

.492 Red meats
Add to base number 641.492 the numbers following 641.4 in 641.41-641.47, e.g., canning red meat 641.4922

.493 Poultry
Add to base number 641.493 the numbers following 641.4 in 641.41-641.47, e.g., freezing poultry 641.49353

.494 Seafood
Add to base number 641.494 the numbers following 641.4 in 641.41-641.47, e.g., brining seafood 641.4946

.495 Other
Frogs, turtles, snails, insects

14.2.3 Notation

The notation used in DC is pure, and numbers. The numbers are used decimally. The simplicity and flexibility of the notation of DC is recognised to be one of its strengths.

A particularly attractive feature of the notation is the expressiveness of the notation. Expressiveness is maintained as far as possible, but has to be sacrificed on occasions in order to insert new subjects. So, for example, we find:

551.577 Precipitation
551.578 Specific forms of precipitation
551.579 Snow surveys

where the latter two numbers are strictly subdivisions of the first. Generally, the notation is hospitable to new subjects, since they can be inserted by decimal subdivision. For example 611.5 can be used to represent a new subject which has links with the subjects at both 611 and 612, although, unless the next subject is a subdivision of 611, to place it at 611.5 will impair the expressiveness of the notation.

The notation is reasonably simple. It is made easier to remember by inserting a decimal point after the first three numbers, and by grouping subsequent digits into threes for example 641.738 423. The notation from the Tables provides systematic mnemonics to a limited extent, since the same notation is used for a concept whichever main class number it qualifies. Thus 03 (from Table 1) becomes identified with a dictionary or encyclopaedia and recurs in the notation for the Generalia class 030 for general dictionaries and encyclopaedias. Similarly 09 from Table 1 represents geographical and historical treatment and 900 is the main class for Geography and History.

The concept of a three-figure minimum for all notation was introduced in the second edition. Thus main classes are denoted by 300, 600, 800 and so on, and not just 3 or 6.

The expressive notation facilitates abridgement of notation in order to specify broader categories. Thus long notation with exact specification may be used in catalogues, or national bibliographies, and the class number appropriate to shelf arrangement for a small collection may be derived from the full notation merely be deleting final digit(s).

14.2.4 Index

An important feature of the scheme in its creator's eyes was the relative index. The rather more detailed enumeration (1000 classes listed) than previous schemes necessitated an alphabetical index to the classes. Note how related subjects are drawn together in the extract from the index in Figure 14.4. The relative index has been influential in indexing practice, and many

Figure 14.4 Dewey Decimal Classification extract from relative index

Landing-gear
  aircraft eng.
    soc. & econ. aspects **see**
      Secondary industries
    tech. & mf.   629.134 381
Landing-lights
  aircraft eng.   629.135 1
Landing-maneuvers
  mil. sci.   355. 422
    s.a. spec. mil. branches
Landing-systems
  spacecraft **see** Flight
      operations systems
      spacecraft
Landkreise
  local govt. admin.   352.007 3
Landlocked seas
  internat. law   341.444
  other aspects see Special
      salt-water forms
Landlords' liability insurance   368.56
  misc. aspects see Insurance
Landlord-tenant relations
  land econ.   333.54
  law   346.043 4
    spec. jur.   346.3-.9
Landowners
  biog. & work.   333.009 2
  s.a.   **pers. - 333**
Land's End Cornwall Eng.   **area-423 75**
Landscape
  architects
    biog. & work   712.092
    occupational ethics   174.971
    s.a.   **pers. - 71**
  architecture   712
  art   712
  design   712
Landscapes
  art representation   704.943 6
  painting   758.1
  s.a. other spec. art forms

of its principles are incorporated into indexing methods, such as chain indexing.

14.2.5 History and organisation

In 1876, Melville Dewey published *A Classification and subject index for cataloguing and arranging the books and pamphlets of a library*. This first edition consisted of twelve pages of introduction, twelve pages of tables and eighteen pages of index. It had three novel features:

1. relative location, instead of the more usual fixed location. In fixed location notation was physically attached to certain places on the shelves and books were always filed in the same place. Fixed location is difficult to maintain with a fast-growing collection.
2. relatively detailed specification, which was made possible because of the change from fixed to relative location.
3. the relative index, which became necessary once a reasonable number of subjects had been enumerated.

With the second edition a further important principle was established. This was the concept of 'integrity of numbers'. Dewey recognised that extensive reclassification was unpopular, and that a classification scheme needed to remain relatively stable from one edition to the next. In the second edition Dewey announced that the structure of the scheme would not be fundamentally changed.

Up to and including the fourteenth edition progress led to ever-increasing detail. However, much of the detail in the fourteenth edition was a product of haphazard revision. For example, medicine ran to eighty pages, whilst the schedule for chemical technology had hardly been modified since the second edition. The fifteenth edition, published in 1951, represented a determined effort to update and unify the schedules. More balanced schedules were achieved by pruning the 31 000 subjects enumerated in the fourteenth edition to 4700. Also many subjects were relocated and the index was drastically pruned. Although the fifteenth edition met with some success, it was not generally popular.

A period of seven years was set as the publication cycle for the new editions, and the sixteenth edition appeared in 1958. In extent of enumeration and location of some topics, the sixteenth edition went back to the fourteenth edition. A detailed index was published in a separate volume. The sixteenth edition contained the first of the Pheonix schedules. Thus completely new, or Pheonix schedules were included for Inorganic and Organic Chemistry. The sixteenth edition was probably the first of the more recent editions to be widely accepted.

The seventeenth edition met with mixed reactions. It introduced greater facilities for synthesis, and the Areas Table appeared for the first time. The distinction between common and subject subdivisions was made more carefully. Pheonix schedules for General and Special Psychology were included. Examples of Western bias were less evident. For example, non-Christian religions were developed in more detail, and it is possible in many places for a user to treat his own country or religion as the preferred category.

The eighteenth edition was published in 1971 and is most important for its adoption by the Library of Congress and BNB for their MARC records. This move has probably affirmed the future of DC. The eighteenth edition continued changes made in the sixteenth and seventeenth editions. In the interests of clarity the 'divide like' instructions of earlier editions were modified to 'add to' instructions. The last five tables listed in Figure 14.2 were first introduced in the eighteenth edition. Pheonix schedules for Law and Mathematics were included.

The nineteenth and, to date the last edition, has already been the subject of much of the earlier discussions of DC. This edition included Pheonix schedules which merge 329 and 324 to give a new schedule for the Political process, and provides a completely new schedule for Sociology. There are also a range of expansions, in, for example, the schedule for energy and energy resources. Transfer of Civilization from 910–919 to 930–990, and new area divisions for 41–42 are also incorporated. This edition was published in 1979.

Although libraries may classify new stock by the latest edition of DC, earlier editions remain important because many libraries are reluctant to reclassify stock, and thus leave stock classified according to earlier editions long after the earlier edition has been superseded.

The main method of revision has been by the publication of new editions. However, 'DC&: Decimal classification: additions, notes, and decisions', is a useful means by which modifications can be announced in advance of a new edition so that reactions can be assessed, before a revision is finally settled. In 1983 Forest Press decided on a policy of continuous revision.

Abridged editions of DC which gave less detail than the full edition have been available since 1894. The latest abridged edition, the eleventh, was published in 1979, shortly after DC19 on which it is based. The abridged edition is widely used in smaller general libraries, specifically school libraries and small public libraries. There is also an *Introduction to Dewey Decimal Classification for British schools*, third edition, compiled by B A J Winslade and published in 1977. This is a further abridged version. An expansion of this edition which will serve school librarians throughout the English-speaking world is planned.

Dewey established the Lake Placid Club Education Foundation which has provided funds for the continuation of the scheme. In 1923 the Editorial

Office was moved to the Library of Congress.

Thus the scheme has a sound organisational backing. Consultation with users is achieved via the Decimal Classification Editorial Policy Committee, the British Liaison Committee, and the Australian Liaison Committee.

The use of DC in BNB has also been important in establishing DC in British libraries. When BNB began publication in 1950 it relied upon the fourteenth edition of DC. This edition was found to be inadequate in several respects, and the same could be said of all editions until the eighteenth. By 1971, BNB was using a mixture of DC15, 16 and 17 grafted on to a DC14 base, and modified according to BNB's own scheme. The emergence of the MARC Project led BNB to opt for standard DC18, and confirmed the inclusion of DC numbers in both LC and BNB MARC records.

14.2.6 The future

The future of DC is assured. The scheme is extensively used in many libraries, and in national bibliographies such as the British National Bibliography. Co-operation between the British Library Bibliographic Services Divsion, publishers of BNB and the Decimal Classification Division has become more fruitful in recent years, and this is likely to further confirm the future of DC. Many changes in cataloguing and classification can be expected in the next ten years and these must impinge upon DC. They are likely to influence the future function of DC, and the way in which the scheme will evolve, but since there will be a continuing need for shelf arrangement, DC will remain necessary.

Planning for DC 20 is well under way. Regular updating and revision must continue, in order to provide for: better balance of detail throughout the scheme, new topics and complex subjects, and to make the scheme more attractive to users outside the English-speaking world.

Appropriate revision should ensure that the scheme remains up to date, but large scale reclassifying remains unpopular, and an uneasy balance between updating and stability must be maintained; this balance is becoming increasingly difficult to achieve as knowledge changes rapidly. One proposal is that of 'Alternative Dewey'. Alternative Dewey will be based upon DC19, which will be modified by any library that wished to adopt Pheonix schedules which are published from time to time in DC&. Thus libraries would be able to reclassify gradually, and as little or as much as they wished.

However, in 1983, Forest Press decided to opt for the concept of continuous revision. Continuous revision means that Pheonixes and major revisions will be released as separates between editions. The changes will be included on MARC copy as soon as they are published. This method should make it easier for libraries to absorb the changes. The ramifications of this policy are:

1. New editions will be essentially cumulations and therefore a longer gap will exist between editions. A gap of ten to twelve years is to be expected.
2. More than the normal two Pheonixes will be published between editions. This policy has, for instance, allowed the preparation of the Pheonix on data processing and computer science, which can be published in a year of two without waiting for the twentieth edition.

The following areas are expected to be published before edition 20:

004, 003–006, 621.39 Computer science
301–307 Sociology (already published)
312, 210 Statistics
Table 2 revisions for Japan, Sudan, South Africa, New Zealand and Papua New Guinea.

The following revisions are expected to appear in edition 20:

570–590 Life sciences
Table 2 – expanded and improved and with atlas
Revised index
780 Music

Other areas which are under consideration, but which have not been scheduled for specific publication include: 351/354, 350–354 Public administration, 370 Education, 624/690/711 Buildings, Tables 1, 3 and 4, 340 Law and 800 Literature.
(Thanks are due to J A Humphry, Executive Director of Forest Press for his most helpful comments.)

14.3 Library of Congress Classication Scheme

The detailed classification scheme of the Library of Congress was evolved between 1899 and 1920, and was largely the responsibility of Herbert Putnam, Librarian of Congress, 1899–1939. The scheme consists of twenty-one classes published in thirty-one separately published schedules. Some schedules for some subject areas have now gone through several editions. Science, for instance, is in its sixth edition. Other schedules, notably those for Law, have yet to be published in a complete form and indeed parts for some countries have not yet been created. There is no classification at present for Africa, Asia and the Soviet Union. Law of Europe is in progress. The scheme was designed for the Library of Congress and many of the features of the scheme derived from this fact. Nevertheless, other libraries do use the scheme. In particular LCC has been regarded as suitable for the classification of large general libraries, and specifically those large libraries that have been established for research purposes. Included amongst those libraries are university and large research libraries in the United States and the United Kingdom.

Although LCC is used by other libraries, in order to understand the format of the scheme it is necessary to recognise that the scheme was intended to fit the LC collections and services as closely as posible, without reference to outside needs and influences. In this sense, LCC although general in scope is a special scheme in its purpose.

14.3.1 Principles

The following five principles underlying the construction of LCC are important in determining its character:

1. LC is based on literary warrant, as is evident in the collections of the Library of Congress, that is, on library collection, not theory.
2. The emphasis in the scheme is to some extent on the social sciences, as this reflects the interest of the Congress. Political science and Education are well represented.
3. The minutely detailed classification is of the type appropriate to an extensive collection.
4. The scheme is intended to provide a systematic approach to the arrangement of books on shelves.
5. The scheme covers all knowledge, despite being special in purpose.

14.3.2 Main classes

The basic outline of main classes is based upon Charles Ammi Cutter's Expansive Classification, and classification is essentially by discipline. The alphabetical notation used to designate main classes permits many of these to be included, as shown in Figure 14.5.

Main classes are divided into subclasses which are further subdivided into form, place, time and subject aspects. The scheme is largely enumerative. Like all enumerative schedules, the LC schedules are bulky, extending to some 8000 pages. Since the scheme is essentially intended for one library the scheme's compiler and classifier are within one library, and this is given as one reason why the need for synthesis is limited. Individual classes were originally developed by different specialists, and are now kept up to date by individual cataloguers as new topics are added to the collections. There is not necessarily any overall plan for the development and maintenance of the schedules. Parts of the schedules differ in various respects from other parts of the schedules. It thus becomes difficult to talk in general terms about the scheme, although there are a number of features which appear reasonably consistently between different parts of the schedules.

Figure 14.5 Library of Congress Classification main classes

A	General Works
B— BJ	Philosophy, Psychology
BL— BX	Religion
C	Auxiliary Sciences of History
D	History: General and Old World (Eastern Hemisphere)
E— F	History: America (Western Hemisphere)
G	Geography: Maps. Anthropology. Recreation
H	Social Sciences
J	Political Science
K	Law (General)
KD	Law of the United Kingdom and Ireland
KE	Law of Canada
KF	Law of the United States
L	Education
M	Music
N	Fine Arts
P— PA	General Philology and Linguistics. Classical Languages and Literatures
PA Supplement	Byzantine and Modern Greek Literature. Medieval and Modern Latin Literature
PB— PH	Modern European Languages
PG	Russian Literature
PJ— PM	Languages and Literatures of Asia, Africa, Oceania. American Indian Languages. Artifical Languages
P— PM Supplement	Index to Languages and Dialects
PN, PR, PS, PZ	General Literature. English and American Literature Fiction in English. Juvenile Literature
PQ, Part 1	French Literature
PQ, Part 2	Italian, Spanish, and Portuguese Literatures
PT, Part 1	German Literature
PT, Part 2	Dutch and Scandinavian Literatures
Q	Science
R	Medicine
S	Agriculture
T	Technology
U	Military Science
V	Naval Science
Z	Bibliography. Library Science

14.3.3 Synthesis

The scheme boasts very little synthesis. Nevertheless, some classes contain tables which may be used to extend the classes shown in the main schedules. Types of tables can be divided into three groups:

1. Form divisions exist in some classes, sometimes listed as a separate table. For instance the History schedules show period divisions as part of the schedules.
2. Subject subdivisions are gathered together into tables in some schedules, such as Language and Literature. See Figure 14.6(a).
3. Geographical divisions are sometimes given in full in the main schedule, and sometimes elsewhere as tables in classes. The notation for any given geographical division varies between classes and between different parts of the same classes. See Figure 14.6(b).

14.3.4 Notation

The notation of LCC is mixed, including both letter and numbers. Main classes are denoted by a capital letter, and in most classes a second capital letter is used to signal major sections or subclasses. For example, Q stands for Science, and QA stands for Mathematics, a subclass of Science. Arabic numerals are used to denote further divisions, in an integral manner, running from 1 to 9999, as necessary. Gaps are left in the apportionment of notation in order to permit new subjects to be inserted. Alternatively new subjects can be inserted by decimal subdivision. Figure 14.6(b) shows extracts

Figure 14.6(a) Subject subdivisions—an extract from the literature schedules

Tables of subdivisions under individual authors

I (98 nos.)	II (49 nos.)		Authors with ninety-eight or forty-nine numbers—Continued
	23	73	Doubtful, spurious works Cf. 70 (Table 1); 36, 86 (Table II)
42	.A2+	.A2+	Collections
43	.A5-Z	.A5-Z	Special, A—Z
44			Works edited by the author under consideration
45	24	74	Imitations. Adaptations
46			Parodies
47	25	75	Relation to the drama and the stage. Dramatization.

I (98 nos.)	II (49 nos.)		Authors with ninety-eight or forty-nine numbers— Continued
48	26	76	Translations (Comparative studies, etc.)
			Illustrations (Portfolios, etc. without text, illustrations with quotations)
			Prefer N8215, or the special artists in NC—NE as the case may be
			Classification of illustrations in P may be preferred in the case of a few authors of the first rank whose works have inspired many artists
			Illustrated editions with other editions
			Portraits, etc., of the author with his biography
			Biography, criticism, etc.
			Bibliography, see Z8001+
51	29	79	Periodicals. Societies. Collections
52	30	80	Dictionaries, indexes, etc.
			Class here general encyclopaedic dictionaries only
			For special dictionaries, see the subject, e.g. characters, see 78 (Table I); 39, 89 (Table II); concordances and dictionaries, see 91-92 (Table 1); 45, 95 (Table II)
.5	.5	.5	Historical sources and documents of the biography of authors
			For sources of literary works, see 71 (Table I); 36, 86 (Table II)
			Autobiographical works
53	31.A2	81.A2	Autobiography
54	A3-39	A3.-39	Journals. Memoirs
.3	.A4	.A4	Letters (Collections). By imprint date
.4	A41-49	A41-49	Letters to and from particular individuals. By correspondent (alphabetically)
55	.A5-Z	.A5-Z	General works
56	⎫	⎫	Early life. Education
57	32 ⎬	82 ⎬	Love and marriage. Relation to women
58	⎭	⎭	Later life
59	33	83	Relations to contemporaries. Times, etc.
			Cf. 73 (Table I); 36, 86 (Table II)
60	34	84	Homes and haunts. Local associations. Landmarks
			Cf. DA

Figure 14.6(b) Geographical subdivisions—an extract from the Fine Arts schedules

Tables of subdivisions

I		II	III	III-A
	South America-Continued			
35	Colombia	69	104	104
36	Ecuador	71	107	107
37	Guyana (British Guiana)	73	110	110
.2	Surinam (Dutch Guiana)	.2	.2	.2
.4	French Guiana	.4	.4	.4
38	Paraguay	75	113	113
39	Peru	77	116	116
40	Uruguay	79	119	119
41	Venezuela	81	122	122
42	Europe	83	125	125
43	Great Britain. England	85	128	128
44	England— local	87	131	131
45	Scotland	89	134	134
46	Ireland	91	137	137
47	Wales	93	140	140
	Special artists, A— Z		142	142
48	Austria	95	143	143
49	France	97	146	147
50	Germany	99	149	151
.6	Germany (Democratic Republic, 1949-)	100.6	151.6	154.6
51	Greece	101	152	155
52	Italy	103	155	159
53	Netherlands	105	158	163
54	Holland	107	161	167
55	Belgium. Flanders	109	164	171
56	Russia in Europe	111	167	175
	For Caucasian republics, see Russia in Asia			
57	Scandinavia	113	170	179
58	Denmark	115	173	183
59	Iceland	117	176	187
60	Norway	119	179	191
61	Sweden	121	182	195
62	Spain. Spain and Portugal	123	185	199
63	Portugal	125	188	203
64	Switzerland	127	191	207
65	Turkey	129	194	211
66	Other Balkan states	131	197	215
67	Bulgaria	133	200	219
(68)	Montenegro, see 71, 141, 212, 235 (.Y8)	(135)	(203)	(223)
69	Rumania	137	206	227

from the tables, where decimal subdivision has been necessary. Cutter numbers are used to further subdivide subjects. These consist of a capital letter followed by numbers. For example at HD 8039 for Labour, .B3 may be added (that is, HD8039.B3) to represent bakers, or .E5 (ie HD8039.E5) added to represent Engineers. There is little mnemonic value to the notation, but some literal mnemonics have been attempted, for example, G for Geography, T for Technology.

14.3.5 Index

Each class has its own index. There is no official index to the whole scheme, although an index has been published. In the absence of a full index, users must be sure of selecting the appropriate main class before consulting the index of a specific class. The Library of Congress List of Subject Headings can be exploited as a general index, since it shows LCC numbers for many of the headings listed.

14.3.6 Organisation and revision

Each main class is revised individually without any reference to other classes. Occasionally cross-references are included between classes. Revision, which is done by subject cataloguers at the LC, is continuous. As new books are received, new places are found to accommodate them. When it seems necessary to record a number of such changes a new edition of the specific class is published. Often revision is achieved by reprinting the previous edition with a supplementary table and index listing additions and changes. All changes are published as soon as they occur in *LC Classification – Additions and Changes*, a quarterly publication. The publication of revised editions of main classes is noted in the *LC Information Bulletin*. Another useful publication is the *Library of Congress Classification Schedules – A Cumulation of Additions and Changes*, which is issued periodically by Gale Research Company.

Both LC and BNB MARC records contain LCC class numbers. These reflect revisions in practices concerning the application of LCC class numbers as they occur. Equally the class numbers used on LC cards perform the same function.

14.3.7 The future

It is difficult to predict what the future holds for LCC. The scheme is primarily used by LC itself, and by other large research collections such as large academic libraries. In such contexts, computerisation of cataloguing and diversification of media will undoubtedly affect the application of LCC, but changes are likely to be slow because the libraries involved are large and computerisation of large numbers of cataloguing records is a huge task. The size of the collections in which the LCC is currently employed is likely to be a significant factor in its perpetuation.

The improvement and refinement of classification at the Library of Congress is done with the recognition that any change will affect the location of previously classified books.

14.4 The Universal Decimal Classification Scheme (UDC)

The Universal Decimal Classification Scheme (UDC) emerged from an attempt by two Belgians, Paul Otlet and Henri LaFontaine who, in 1894, sought to commence the compilation of the 'universal index to recorded knowledge'. Contributors to the scheme would be drawn from all over the world, and the index would be international in its scope. Had this venture succeeded, the complete face of bibliographical control today would have been different. However, the most valuable long-term effect of the plans for this index was the classification scheme which was devised in order to arrange the index. A classified approach was necessary in the index, rather than an alphabetical approach because an internationally acceptable notation was important. DC was already in existence, and indeed had a notation which, in being numbers was reasonably universal. With Dewey's permission, UDC was developed from the fifth edition of DC. A conference in 1895 established the Institut International de la Bibliographie (IIB) to be responsible for the index. The first edition of UDC was published in 1905. We return to the history of the scheme later.

UDC is designed, as its origins suggest, for detailed indexing of documents, and not for shelf arrangement. Thus, over the years it has been used to index reports, trade literature, periodical articles and other similar documents. The features which contribute to UDC's suitability for detailed indexing are particularly valued in special libraries. Thus, UDC has been extensively employed in special libraries and information centres in locations all over the world since the early 1900s. It is also the most widely used general classification scheme in the Continent of Europe, and this against an environment where libraries have not generally seen the virtue of published classification schemes, and prefer to use their own private schemes. Since there is a preponderance of special libraries and information units in the science and technology subject areas, and, in the light of UDC's consultative revision policies, UDC has been developed most fully in the areas of science and technology.

Prior to the 1970s UDC was frequently to be found in large card indexes in special libraries and sometimes to be encountered in abstracting and indexing tools. Since the introduction of computer-based indexing systems alphabetical indexing languages have become more prevalent, and UDC has suffered a reduction in use. Ironically, this has left as one of the main domains of application of UDC, shelf arrangement of stock in special libraries.

The features which characterise UDC, and which make it appropriate for the applications discussed above are:

(a) its extensive synthetic devices
(b) its co-operative revision procedures
(c) its detailed specification.

14.4.1 Main classes

The overall outline of the schedules follows DC, but there are some differences in notation, and the two schemes have diverged at various points since the original adoption of the structure of DC5 for UDC. The main classes are shown in Figure 14.7. This outline shows no class 4. Linguistics has been moved from 4 to 8 (after the publication of the 1961 Abridged English Edition). Otherwise the general structure can be readily seen to be reminiscent of DC. With this structure, UDC adopted various of the weaknesses of DC. UDC, like DC, is essentially enumerative (although extensive provision for synthesis is made). The main class order can, like DC, be criticised on the grounds of the separation of Sciences from their respective Technology, and the division of some topics between Economics

Figure 14.7 Colon Classification

Main classes

a/z	Generalia
1/9	Preliminaries eg. Library Science
A/M	Science, Technology, Useful Arts including Mathematics, Physics, Geology, Mining
N	Fine Arts
O	Literature
P	Language
Q	Religion
R	Philosophy
S	Psychology
T	Education
U	Geography
V	History
W	Politics
X	Economics
Y	Sociology
Z	Law

and Commerce. Some of the problems in main class order and allocation are alleviated by careful definition of any classes that overlap with each other in order to make it more plain where any given document should be classified.

14.4.2 Synthesis and common auxiliaries

The auxiliaries are a central feature of UDC. They permit much more scope for flexible synthesis than can be achieved with DC or LCC. The auxiliaries may be divided into two groups according to whether they can be used anywhere in the scheme, namely, are common auxiliaries, or whether they are only appropriate to specific parts of the scheme, namely, special auxiliaries. The auxiliaries offer a series of facets and facet indicators which permit flexible synthesis. These auxiliaries may be used at the discretion of the individual cataloguer, and when required (unlike DC where specific instructions are given for most applications of the Tables or the 'add to' device). Also, any number of auxiliaries may be included in one class number, if they are all required in order to label the document adequately.

The first three auxiliaries are essentially devices which permit the combination of two or more numbers from the main schedules. These auxiliaries are:

+ for example, 539.1+621.039 Nuclear science and technology

+ is used to join the notation for two subjects which are commonly associated with one another, but which are separated by the normal sequence in UDC. In essence the use of the '+' is defining a new broader discipline by creating a piece of notation which represents the new discipline formed by merging two other subjects.

/ for example, 22/28 Christianity

/ is used to indicate a broader heading in the same way as +, the only difference being that the component subjects are normally found adjacent to one another in the basic sequence. Thus 22/28 represents the amalgamation of all of the subjects with notation between 22 and 28 into a new broader subject. Thus 22/28 is equivalent to 22+23+24+25+26+27+28, provided that all of these notations have been assigned to subjects. Both + and / are extending devices and compounds formed with them file before the simple number.

: or relation sign for example, 331.2:687.9 Wages in the brush industry.

: is used to combine two or more numbers from the main schedules in order to represent the separate concepts present in a multi-concept subject. The relation sign, :, is the most commonly used of these three devices, and is characteristic of UDC numbers. It should be noted that the relation sign does not indicate anything about the nature of the relationship between two subjects, but merely states that two or more concepts are treated in relation to one another in a document. Some theorists feel that the : is too imprecise, and that there is a need to state the nature of a relationship, and not just to signal its existence.

It is evident that when two or more pieces of notation are combined with, for instance, the colon, the order in which they are combined, or their citation order, needs to be considered. For example should the final class number be: 331.2:687.9 or 687.9:331.2? Criteria must be established for the citation order to be preferred in any given library. Further comments on citation order are included later. In addition, a mechanism for generating added entries under second and subsequent numbers in a combined number must be invented and adopted. A process known as 'cycling' where each number is in turn brought into the first position in the combined number can be employed in order to generate the headings for added entries. Plainly if only two numbers have been put together for the main number, added entry headings can be generated merely by reversing the component number eg main entry under 331.2:687.9, and added entry under 687.9:331.2. The alternative to extensive added entries in the classified sequence, which can lead to extremely complex sequences, is to rely upon thorough subject indexing.

The other common auxiliaries have more in common with the Tables in DC:

(i) Language,=symbolises the language in which a document is written. for example, 657=395 a work on accountancy written in Scandinavian.

(ii) form of presentation, (0 . . .) lists bibliographical forms for example 623.821 (042) Lectures on battleships

(iii) Place, (1/9) lists places both in the usual specific geographical divisions and also other aspects of place, for example, 656.1(85) transport in Peru

(iv) Race and nationality, (= . . .) are based on the common auxiliaries of language and may be developed from the main linguistics schedule. For example, 394.25(=951) Chinese carnivals.

(v) Time, '. . .' permits date to be specified in detail, or other features of time to be reflected. For example, 551.509 '405' Long term weather forecasting

(vi) alphabetical and non-decimal numerical division is merely an indication of how to list individuals or items, which can be symbolised by a number or alphabetical abbreviation. For example,

92 Schil Biography of Schiller
820 (Shak) The Works of Shakespeare

(vii) Point of view, .00. . . may either be added to the main number or used in conjunction with the colon to give an extended facet indicator. In either application the device is intended to provide a means of ordering systematically the subdivisions of a given number.

Other auxiliary devices are indicated in Figure 14.8.

Special auxiliaries are signalled by –0/.9.0 . . ., or '. Special auxiliaries are listed in the area of the schedule to which they may be applied. An auxiliary listed under a given number may be applied to any subdivision of that number. For example in 534 –6, the –6 may be applied to subdivisions of 534, such as 534.63. So,

534–6 Subsonic vibrations provides –6 which can be applied with 534.63 Measurement of frequency to give 534.63–6 Measurement of the frequency of subsonic vibrations.

Given this array of auxiliaries and the possibility of applying them, or at least a number of them simultaneously, it is plain that a citation order for the inclusion of auxiliaries in a number must be settled. The recommended citation order is the reverse of filing order.

Not only is a citation order necessary for individual numbers, but a filing order for arranging numbers for different subjects with respect to one another must be settled. None of the notational devices used in synthesis have any inherent filing order with respect to one another, so any proposed order will be artifical and must be learnt by classifiers and users. The recommended order is shown in Figure 14.8, except that the simple number is inserted after '+' and '/', and direct divisions added after special auxiliaries.

Libraries may settle their own filing and citation orders. The extent of application of the synthetic devices will vary from one library to another. There are no particular benefits to be gained from identical application of UDC in different libraries, even though standard schedules from which local variations may depart have some value.

14.4.3 Notation

The notation is similar to that of DC. The three figure minimum is not required for main classes and their sub-classes. Consequently notation such as:

6   **Technology. Applied Sciences**
63   **Agriculture. Forestry. Stock breeding. Animal produce. Hunting.**
     Fisheries
633 **Field crops. Industrial crops**

is to be found. Note also the notation for each of the main classes as shown in Figure 14.7. The decimal point is introduced after *every* three digits, for example, 631.589.2 Hydroponics. Each of the auxiliaries has a unique piece of notation as shown in the previous section. The main criticism of the notation that has been voiced is that the notation for more specific subjects can be extremely long. Imagine trying to remember, mark on the spine of a book or file under: 633.888(729.1/.5):677.6 '19' (058)=50

14.4.4 Index

The indexes are generated for the identification of numbers in specific parts or subject areas of the schedules. The index to the abridged edition is relative, and, in general, satisfactory.

14.4.5 History and organisation

After the publication of the first edition of UDC in 1905, the 1914–1918 War and the unfavourable climate after that war led to the demise of the index, but UDC continued. The second edition of UDC was published between 1927 and 1933. The third edition was published spanning the years 1934–52. The IIB became the Fédération International de Documentation (FID) in 1937, and continued to support UDC. Eventually the British Standards Institution became the official British editorial body, and the publication of the full English edition, which was long overdue, began with the fourth edition in 1943. This edition (the full English edition) is still incomplete. Work has now commenced on the second and third full English editions. The full edition is published in a number of separate volumes each pertaining to a specific subject area. There is no real distinction between successive English full editions.

In addition to the full edition, there exist abridged and medium editions of the scheme. The first British abridged edition was published in 1948, the second in 1957, and the third, and last to date in 1961. Unfortunately resources have been concentrated on the completion of the full English edition, and more recently upon a planned medium edition, and the abridged edition still awaits revision. The medium edition which is available in various languages (but not English) contains about 30 per cent of the full tables. In actual application special libraries will often use the abridged edition as a general scheme which is bound to cover all subjects in their collection, together with the full edition for their particular subject speciality.

Figure 14.8 Universal Decimal Classification—auxiliary tables and filing order for devices

Common auxiliary tables

+ (plus) Addition, e.g. 59+636 Zoology and animal breeding

/ (stroke) Extension, e.g. 592/599 Systematic zoology (everything from 592 to 599 inclusive)

: (colon) Relation, e.g. 17:7 Relation of ethics to art

( ) (square brackets) Algebraic subgrouping, e.g. 31:(622+669) (485) Statistics of mining and metallurgy in Sweden (the auxiliary qualifies 622+669 considered as a unit)

:: (double colon) Order-fixing or irreversible relation, especially in computerized systems, e.g. 061.2 (100) :: 002FID International Federation for Documentation (if no entry is required under 002)

= (equals) Language, e.g. =20 in English; 59=20 Zoology, in English

(0 ...) (brackets-nought) Form, e.g. (051) Periodicals; 59 (051) Zoology periodicals

(1/9) (brackets-one-to-nine) Place, e.g. (4) Europe; 59 (4) Zoology of Europe

(= ...) (brackets-equals) Race and nationality, e.g. (=3) Germanic races; 17 (=3) Ethics in Germanic races

" ..." (quotation marks) Time, e.g. "19" the 1900s (loosely, 20th century); 17"19" Ethics in 20th century

* (asterisk) Codes and notations (non-UDC), e.g. atomic mass number; 546-42*90 Strontium 90

A/Z (alphabetic extension) Names etc., e.g. REM (or Rembrandt); 75REM Paintings of Rembrandt

.00 (point-nought-nought) Point of view, e.g. .002.5 Tools, machinery, equipment aspect; 622.002.5 Mining: tools, machinery, equipment

-0 (hyphen-nought) To be developed. So far, there are two sections: -03 Materials, e.g. -033.5 Glass etc.; 683.512-003.5 Glass bottles

-05 Persons, e.g. -053.2 Children (in general); 17-053.2 Ethics in children

Special auxiliary tables

The meaning of these varies according to where in the main table they are listed; the notation used is:

-0/-9 (hyphen-nought-to-nine), e.g. 62-1 General characteristics of machines etc. (in engineering)

.0 (point-nought), e.g. 624.01 Structures according to material and material method of construction (in civil engineering)

' (apostrophe), e.g. 547.1'13 Organometallic compounds (in organic chemistry)

Main classes of UDC

0	Generalities. Documentation. Bibliography. Librarianship etc.
00	Prolegomena. Fundamentals of knowledge and culture
01	Bibliography and bibliographies. Catalogues
02	Librarianship
03	Encyclopaedias. General reference works
04	Collections of miscellaneous essays
05	Periodicals and other serials
06	Organizations. Congresses. Museums
07	Newspapers. Journalism
08	Polygraphies. Collective works
09	Manuscripts. Rare and remarkable works

From: UDC: A brief introduction. by Geoffrey Robinson. FID; The Hague, 1979 (FID574).

Figure 14.9 Agencies involved in revision of UDC

Users
  ↕
National Subject Committee
  ↕
International Subject Committee
  ↕
FID Central Classification Committee
  ↓
FID/UDC Assembly

Revision is a consultative process. Users make suggestions for modifications and these are then channelled through a series of committees. This structure of committees for proposals for revision can be summarised as in Figure 14.9. When revisions have been accepted by the Central Classification Committee, they are first issued as P-notes for discussion. Provided that no substantive objections are received revisions will then be cumulated into Extensions and Corrections to the UDC. International consultation is bulky and time-consuming, and this makes revision a slow process. For example, it took ten years to produce a schedule for Space science and Astronautics. Many committees do not meet more than once a year, and all work on the committees is voluntary. The revision process is very sensitive to the expressed requirements of users, but is correspondingly slow.

14.4.6 The future

UDC is widely used despite the difficulties in keeping the schedules up to date. For some time there have been insufficient funds to support the central management of the scheme. Some believe that an organisation other than FID would be better equipped to manage the scheme, and that the management of the scheme should be transferred to a large library. The potential for the scheme is good, but already opportunities to act as a switching language have not been exploited. The future of the scheme is questionable, unless more positive central management can be achieved. The medium edition of UDC in English is nearing completion and publication is imminent.

14.5 Colon Classification (CC)

The Colon Classification, devised by S R Ranganathan, and first published in 1933 is chiefly of interest for its development of facet analysis.

Each edition since the fifth in 1957 has been published in, theoretically, two parts: Stage 1, the 'basic classification', which gives sufficient detail for most books; and, Stage 2, 'microthought' to cover periodical articles, patents, and so on.

However, Stage 2 has never actually been published. The latest edition, the sixth, was reprinted in 1963 with some significant amendments, and all subsequent comments in this chapter relate to this 1963 reprint.

The first edition comprised basic classes analysed into facets, using the colon as the notational device for synthesis. Thus the colon was so much an integral feature of the scheme, that it gave its name to the scheme.

The Colon Classification (CC) is widely used in India, but the style of enumeration of the foci (subjects) is not regarded as appropriate for Western libraries. This is the only scheme described in this work which could be accused of an Eastern bias!

14.5.1 Principles of the scheme

Initially, Ranganathan used an *ad hoc* approach to analysis and citation order, but by the fourth edition he had started to establish the different kinds of facet to be found in each class. Facets, he observed, could be accommodated in the five groups, identified by Personality, Matter, Energy, Space, Time, as introduced in 13.2.4. The citation order PMEST and various other facet formulae can be ascribed to Ranganathan.

Ranganathan also sought to achieve 'autonomy for the classifier'. By establishing a set of devices and rules of universal applicability, Rangathan attempted to make it possible for the individual classifier to construct class numbers for new foci. This reduces the need for central control over the scheme.

Existing basic classes may be modified in two ways. New subjects (or changes in approach to a subject) may be recognised, or sometimes, part of a basic class may be considered in a special context. CC gives five ways in which new foci may be enumerated. These are:

1. The chronological device where a new focus is specified by its date of origin.
2. The geographical device where the place facet is used.
3. The subject device, or the use of a schedule from elsewhere in the overall order.
4. The mnemonic device, which is an attempt to establish notation in relation to dimension.
5. The superimposition device is used to specify compound topics arising from the combination of foci which fall into the same facet.

14.5.2 Main classes

The outline of the main classes in Figure 14.7 shows that the overall pattern is Science and Technology, then Humanities, and lastly the Social Sciences. The sixth edition consists of three parts: Part 1, the rules; Part 2, the schedules; and Part 3, schedules of classics and sacred books with special names. Rules for any given class must be used in conjunction with the schedules for that class. Because all classes comprise simple isolates, grouped as foci within facets and sub-facets, the schedules themselves are relatively succinct. Specialised subjects are catered for by combination of foci. Thus notation such as that given can be constructed for the following subjects by combination of foci:

D885.594.3Z.p8 stands for Street cleaning in Zurich during the snow period.
X:5.440j56 stands for Commercial relations between India and Great Britain.

In each class the most significant facet is placed first, the next most significant next, and so on. The final order on the shelves is the reverse of this, so that an order of increasing speciality is achieved. The combination order is given for each class in terms of the fundamental categories.

14.5.3 Notation

As amply demonstrated in the examples above, the notation in CC is mixed. Capital letters are used to designate main classes. Within the classes, Roman numerals are used for subfacets and foci. For example, the main class for Medicine is designated by L. Facets such as Abdomen and Eye are allocated 14 and 185 respectively. Occasionally letters are introduced to extend the base. Numbers, although they do not feature decimal points, are used decimally. Within one main class the same piece of notation may be used to signify different concepts. For example, 4 can signify Respiratory system in the P facet and Disease in the E facet. Thus in combining concepts in order to classify a book it is necessary to signal which facet is being applied. This is achieved by reserving a specific symbol to introduce various facets. These symbols are:

:E ,P ;M .S 'T

There are also common facets for Forms where lower case letters are used. Thus a represents Bibliography, c represents Concordance, and v represents History. Numerals are used for the place facet and capital letters for time.

Clearly, with such a complex range of symbols a filing order for the symbols must be defined, as there is no obvious order. The recommended order: lower case letters, inverted comma, semi-colon, colon and lastly commas or direct foci, aims to achieve an order of increasingly speciality (the inverse of PMEST). The notation is hospitable to new foci and new compounds.

In practice, the notation has been criticised for its length when applied to classify given subjects. The length of the notation is related to the extensive synthesis and the high level of specificity that can be achieved with the scheme. Also, the mixed notation leads to complicated-looking class numbers containing a variety of symbols.

14.5.4 Index

The general index of CC lists isolates and indicates where they may be found as in a relative index. There is a geographical index, and indexes to natural groups are provided in connection with Botany I and Zoology K.

14.5.5 History and organisation

The early editions of the CC were the work of Ranganathan. More recently, the Documentation Research and Training Centre, an organisation endowed by Ranganathan, has taken charge of the maintenance of the CC. New editions of the CC are published at intervals. Work on the seventh edition is in progress. An extensive preview was published in an article in *Library science with a slant to documentation*. This preview shows that the seventh edition, like its predecessors, reflects further theoretical ideas, which have necessitated considerable revision of the scheme. For example, it is anticipated that with the seventh edition the number of main classes may be extended from 46 to 105. This is a reflection of the rapidity with which disciplines emerge. Other impending modifications include work on the nature of many foci in energy facets which has led to them being reconstituted as Matter Property isolates. Notational provision for the increase in the arrays of classes within the main subject is made by using the lower case alphabet as well as numerals. Also considerable attention is paid to the redefinition of terms.

After Ranganathan's death, the DTRC published in 1973 a further outline differing in several important respects from Ranganathan's. A review article written in 1976 suggests that the seventh edition may emerge in more than one volume. There is some doubt as to the publication date of the seventh edition which has now been promised for some time.

14.6 The Bibliographic Classification (BC)

The Bibliographic Classification was the work of Henry Evelyn Bliss.

Besides BC, he also published two other major works on classification: *The organization of knowledge and the system of the sciences*, in 1929, and *The organization of knowledge in libraries and the subject approach to books*, first edition in 1933, second edition in 1939. These works, together with BC represent a significant contribution to classification theory, but the scheme, despite some very sound features, has been unable to rival the three major bibliographic schemes, LCC, UDC and DC in application in libraries. The first edition of BC was adopted by about eighty major libraries, but with no new edition on the horizon several changed to other schemes. The full schedules of the first edition appeared between 1940 and 1953, and the second edition started to emerge in 1976. Since there are major differences between the two editions, this section now considers each edition in turn.

14.6.1 The first edition of BC – main classes

Bliss believed that the most important part of a classification scheme was its order of basic or main classes. Although Bliss identified principles for establishing the order of main classes, in practice BC sometimes has subjects arranged in an undesirable order. For example, the separation of science from the useful arts, by the intrusion of the social sciences could not be regarded as helpful collocation. All main classes can be grouped into four main areas: Philosophy, Science, History and Technologies and Arts.

Despite criticisms of the main class order, collocation of related subjects is relatively successful and is achieved by making special groupings in places, such as grouping fundamental sciences and their applications. For example, Electricity and Electrical Engineering are to be found at BJ/BO, and Language and Literature are grouped with Bibliography in W/Z.

In addition to the main classes there are Anterior numerical classes (notation 1/9) which fulfil the function of a Generalia class. Thus Class 1 (Reading room collections) provides for general encyclopaedias and dictionaries, atlases, gazetteers, yearbooks, bibliographies and special collection. Class 2 provides an alternative special scheme for bibliography and librarianship. Class 5 is for Archives, and Class 6, Periodicals special collections.

Bliss was generally hostile to complete analysis, preferring to opt for a more complete, or enumerative listing of subjects. Many alternative locations are offered. For example, many of the applied sciences and technologies can be classified with their related science, or together with other useful arts. Thus, Applied Botany may be classified in Class F, Botany or with WA, Agriculture Aviation and Aeronautics can be treated as branches of science in Physics or as useful arts in Engineering and Shipbuilding. Alternatives are also offered within classes. For example, in Class HM/HZ Medicine, the surgery of particular organs can be classified with the Diseases of the organ or with general Surgery. The schedules are variable in their acceptability and the amount of detail given. Many of the schedules are somewhat out of date.

14.6.2 First edition – synthesis

In many classes (main classes) the facets are carefully identified and kept separate. Within each facet foci are listed without enumeration of compounds. For example in J Education the following facets are given:

JA/JI Problem facet (for example, JF Tests, measurements, standards, JI Teaching methods
JK Subject taught facet (for example, JKM Teaching of mathematics)
JL/JV Person and grade of education facet (for example, JL Elementary education)

However, the analysis is not sustained throughout, and, in places, compounds are enumerated. Other problems are evident in the absence of some simple elements, non-exhaustive division, uninspired facet (schedule) order, and occasional absence of recommendations for combination order of concepts.

Specification of compounds is largely achieved through use of the 'Systematic schedules'. These schedules are an extension of the 'common subdivisions' of other schemes. Those schedules which are of general application correspond to the common subdivisions in other schemes. These are:

Schedule 1 (1/9) comprising basically form divisions (for example, 2 Bibliography, 6 Periodicals)
Schedule 2 (a/z) comprising geographical divisions (for example, e England)
Schedule 3 (,A/,Z) comprising Language and nationalities divisions (for example, ,M English)
Schedule 4 (A/Z) comprising period divisions (for example, R Twentieth century)

In total there are more than forty systematic schedules, the remainder being for use only in specified classes.

14.6.3 First edition – notation

The notation is mixed. The base consists of the anterior numeral classes (1/) and the main classes (A/Z). Lower case letters are used for country divisions, and numerals are used for form divisions. Commas are used frequently as facet indicators, and the dash (–) is used to synthesis elements from different main classes.

The long base and non-expressive notation and careful apportionment of notation results generally in brief notation. For example a subject such as 'Water-based paints in interior house decoration' can be symbolised by UTHJ. With the mixed notation, the filing order can be difficult to ascertain. Hospitality is permitted by the alphabetical notation, and with the support of synthesis by applying the 'Systematic Schedules'. The notation uses some literal mnemonics, such as AM for Mathematics, and UE for Engineering. The numeral (form) subdivisions and the lower case letter (geographical) divisions also have mnemonic value.

14.6.4 First edition – index

The index is a relative index. It has been criticised on various grounds. Not all appropriate key words are present, and the index has more entries than are necessary since the divisions of a subject which are collocated in the classified sequence tend to be listed.

14.6.5 First edition – history and organisation

BC had a long gestation period. The first outline was published in 1910, with a more detailed outline being published in 1935 under the title 'A System of bibliographic classification'. Full schedules appeared in three separate volumes between 1940 and 1953. Although others aided in the compilation of the schedules they were essentially the work of one man. The scheme was published by the H W Wilson Company. In 1967 this company handed over responsibility for the scheme to the British Committee representing users of the scheme. From 1954 the Bliss Classification Bulletin was published. From 1963 this was issued annually and contained new schedules for a number of subjects, for example, nuclear reactor engineering, electronics, astronautics, and painting.

14.6.6 The abridged edition

Since BC adheres closely to the educational and scientific consensus, BC found most favour with libraries in educational establishments. The School Library Association, therefore, deemed it worthwhile to draft and publish an abridged version of BC in 1967.

14.6.7 Second edition

In 1967, the British, Bliss Classification Association (BCA) was formed and took over the responsibility for BC. Work began on the revision of BC under the editorial direction of Jack Mills in 1969, with some support from the Polytechnic of North London where Jack Mills held a lecturing post.

In 1975 the BCA decided to publish the second edition of the scheme in parts, commencing in 1977 with the Introductory Volume and classes J Education, P Religion and Q Social Welfare. This mode of publication permits special libraries to purchase relevant parts and facilitates revision at a later date.

14.6.8 Second edition – main classes

The scheme remains discipline oriented, but each class is developed in accordance with strict application of analytico-synthetic principles. Each main class will have its own index. The overall order of main classes remains the same as in the first edition. Changes have been made to accommodate modern approaches or new groupings of subjects. For example, Recreation, previously dispersed over several main classes, is now brought together as a new main class, and Space Science has been added between Astronomy and the Earth Sciences. The Systematic Schedules have not survived in their original form, and have been mostly supplanted by a systematic analysis into facets in each class. Again, like the first edition, there are many alternative locations provided for individual subjects. For example, Geography may be placed entirely within the Earth Sciences; International Law, normally in Political Science, may be placed with Law; and Social psychology, normally included in Psychology, may be placed in Sociology.

14.6.9 Second edition – synthesis

Volume 1, the introductory volume, contains not only a lengthy introduction, which is a very authoritative account of various aspects of classification theory, but also the common facets. The common facets or auxiliary schedules are comprehensive, and include:

Schedule 1: Common subdivisions, including common form subdivisions, common subject divisions, and auxiliary schedule 1A Persons.
Schedule 2: Place
Schedule 3: Language
Schedule 3A: Ethnic groups
Schedule 4: Periods of time

The schedules contain concepts occurring in the literature of all or most fields of knowledge, and are to be applied in qualifying the classes enumerated in 2/9 and A/Z. The concepts are organised into facets, and the facets are arranged and applied in such a way that the general to special order is preserved. It must however be emphasised that the entire scheme is synthetic, such that notation for very specific subjects can be constructed, for example,

HPK PEY FGK The nurse as a caregiver for the terminal patient and his
family
KVO POT YCF Adjustment to Israeli life of American immigrants

14.6.10 Second edition – notation

In keeping with the synthetic nature of the scheme, the notation is
almost entirely synthetic; any given compound class will nearly always be
constructed by adding components from different facets or different arrays.

The notation uses upper case letters and Arabic numerals 1 to 9; and on
occasion the hyphen (–). The filing order is 1/9 – A/Z, so the auxiliary
schedules are introduced by numerals, and within any class qualifications by
auxiliaries file before qualifications by the facets peculiar to that class.

Within classes the notation is retroactive. This does present some
problems for facets with notation later in the alphabet; various modifications
to the basically retroactive notation are introduced in order to achieve an
adequate notational base for all facets. The notation is non-expressive, and is
split into groups of three digits as in DC.

14.6.11 Second edition – indexes

Each part has its own index, constructed using the principles of chain
indexing (see 17.2.3). Such indexes should be reasonably easy to generate,
since the structure of subjects within the schedules has been carefully
analysed. However, the fact that the index contains no entries for composite
subjects can be inconvenient, and makes the need for a subject index to any
classified catalogue or shelf arrangement organised according to BC even
more pressing than usual. The absence of an index to the complete scheme
cannot be regarded as too serious a problem in the use of the scheme until all
the schedules are available. Nevertheless, an index to the complete scheme
will be an important feature of the complete second edition, and it is not clear
when the publication of such an index can be expected. However, since
physical production of BC2 is now computerised, production of a
consolidated A/Z index should not be difficult.

14.6.12 Second edition – organisation and future

Plainly much of the schedules of the second edition remain to be
published. Figure 14.10 shows anticipated publication dates. Certainly the
scheme contributes much in demonstrating the essential features of a good
general classification scheme, but as ever with classification there would
appear to be a gulf between theory and practice. The future of BC as a
practical classification scheme used to classify documents in libraries and
information centres is unsure.

246

Figure 14.10 Outline of BC2

2	Generalia
4	(Phenomenon classes)
	°For multidisciplinary treatments of anything
	(Discipline classes)
A	Philosophy, logic
AM	Mathematics, statistics
	Physical sciences
B	Physics (and alternative for Physics-based technologies)
C	Chemistry (and alternative for Chemistry-based technologies)
D	Space science, astronomy; Earth sciences, geography
E/G	Biological sciences
	Microorganisms/Plants/Animals
GS	Applied biology (alternative to technology)
H/Z	Human sciences & human studies
H/I	Human biology, health sciences, psychology, psychiatry
J/Z	Social sciences & humanities
J	Education
K	Society: sociology, social anthropology, customs & folklore
L/O	Area studies, history & description
P/Z	(Special social sciences & humanities)
P	Religion, The Occult, Ethics
Q	Social welfare, applied social ethics
R/S	Political science, law
T	Economics, Management
U/V	Technology, industry
W	Recreative arts, fine arts
X/Z	Language & literature

BC2 published so far:

Introduction and Auxiliary Schedules. 1977.

CLASS H Anthropology, Human biology, Health Sciences. 1980.
CLASS I Psychology & Psychiatry, 1978.
CLASS J Education. 1977.
CLASS P Religion, The Occult, Morals & Ethics. 1977.
CLASS Q Social welfare. 1977.

Forthcoming:

CLASS K Society. 1984
CLASSES A, E/G, R/S, T, 2/9, B, C, D, L/O and U/V

The BCA hopes that the sales of the schedules will go most of the way towards making the scheme self-sufficient. Revision should certainly be eased because BC2 starts with full and up-to-date schedules, and the fully faceted structure facilitates revision (see 13.2.4). An important factor in the survival of BC as a practical classification scheme could be its acceptance by a centralised cataloguing agency for inclusion on computer data bases. The British Library is prepared to consider this option for BNB MARC, but the Library of Congress has expressed reluctance to consider BC for inclusion on LC MARC records. One factor which could possibly redeem the situation is that BC class numbers can be generated relatively easily from PRECIS strings (see 17.2.4). Another possible application of BS2 is as a series of special schemes. It may be easier for BC to become established in special collections than it will be for it to be accepted in general libraries and data bases of library records. A large-scale appeal for funds was made in 1984 and raised sufficient funds to support the completion of BC2. (Thanks are due to Jack Mills for his helpful suggestions.)

14.7 Special classification schemes

The classification schemes that have been considered so far are general bibliographic classification schemes in that they attempt to encompass all of knowledge. Not all classification schemes need to aim for this comprehensive treatment. Special classification schemes are schemes which cover just one main subject area, or are compiled in accordance with the interests of one user group. Apart from the separately published special classification schemes, there are also many local variations of general classification schemes in use for special applications. In some senses these could also be regarded as special classification schemes.

Special classification schemes are generally devised for a particular purpose, and environments in which such schemes are to be found include:

1. Catalogues, indexes and abstracting services that are published, for example, Library and Information Science Abstracts, the British Catalogue of Music.
2. Catalogues and shelf arrangements of special collections, especially industrial and research establishment libraries, for example, London School of Business Classification.
3. Catalogue and shelf arrangements of special collections, especially those of public libraries, such as children's collections and local studies collections, and map collections.

14.7.1 Different types of special classification scheme

A list of the different types of special classification scheme may help to indicate that these schemes may be designed for a variety of different purposes:

1. Schemes restricted to a conventional subject area or discipline, for example, music, insurance, chemistry.
2. Schemes restricted to an association of topics, such as are encountered in local collections such as a collection of an industrial library.
3. Schemes restricted to a certain type of reader, for example, children; university students, general browsers.
4. Schemes restricted to a certain physical form, for example, pictures, records.
5. Schemes restricted to a certain form of publication, for example, patents, trade catalogues, unpublished archives.
6. Schemes restricted to bibliographies and indexing and abstracting services, and associated data bases.
7. Schemes restricted to a certain form of presentation of ideas, for example, fiction, plays.

14.7.2 Rationale for special classification schemes

Special classification schemes are generally devised for an application in which no major general scheme is suitable. Typical problems which arise with major schemes are that:

1. they often do not give sufficient detail for accurate specification of highly complex subjects;
2. they do not cater for the specialist viewpoints of any given application, since alternative approaches are not normally provided;
3. they do not provide for flexible combination as is demanded by highly specific subjects;
4. any flexibility or detailed specification which is possible is too often achieved by unnecessarily lengthy notation;
5. the filing order is not always helpful.

Many of the more recent special classification schemes have been devised with the aid of facet analysis, and are thus faceted classification schemes.

Whilst it may seem attractive to design a classification scheme for each different set of circumstances, it is important to remember the drawbacks of special classification schemes, and to thoroughly assess whether a published general scheme will not, after all, be acceptable. Amongst the disincentives to compiling and maintaining a special classification scheme can be numbered:

1. The work involved in the compilation of the scheme.
2. The work involved in revision, especially if it seems a good idea to publish the scheme, or if the scheme needs drastic revision to adapt to changing remits of a special library or information service.
3. Limited opportunity is usually available for co-operation in application of classification or in its compilation and revision.
4. Users need to learn a scheme which they will probably only encounter in one application, and with which they might then find difficulty.

Despite the problems of special classification schemes, they do represent an opportunity to match users' perspectives and the organisation of literature to an extent not often possible in a general classification scheme, and such schemes will always have a place in the organisation of knowledge.

Perhaps the major problem in devising a special classification scheme is the definition of the subject area to be covered. First, it will be necessary to define 'core' topics which form a homogeneous subject field, and then the needs of users must be assessed in order to discover whether they can be matched by one field, or whether two are necessary. Having identified core topics, marginal or fringe topics must be listed, and the type of treatment that they are to receive settled. It is important to note that the scope of even a scheme which focuses on a relatively narrow area may be quite wide, by the time all fringe topics which are relevant to or have some impact upon the core area have been noted.

14.7.3 Some examples of special classification schemes

The easiest means of illustrating some of the foregoing points is to introduce in outline some special classification schemes.

1. Cheltenham Classification The Cheltenham Classification is a scheme for a specific user group. Although it covers all knowledge it has been designed to be specifically applicable to the collections in school libraries. It aims for a more helpful order than the major schemes, by following the groupings of subjects as they are taught in schools. For example, each language is followed by its literature, and material on jobs and careers is given a significant place.

2. Bogg's and Lewis Map Classification This is an example of a classification which is restricted to a specific physical form, as it is used to classify maps and atlases. Main classes are based upon a division of localities into continents. One particular strength is that it is possible both to specify

Figure 14.11 Some fiction classification schemes

A. Corbett

A	Adventure
C	Collections of short stories
HL	Historical
HR	Humour
L	Love
M	Mysteries, thrillers, etc.
S	Sea stories
W	Western stories

B. McClellan

0	Thrillers, Adventure, Crime, Spies
1	Detectives
2	Westerns
3	Sea stories
4	Science fiction
5	Romantic novels
6	Family chronicles
7	Country life, rural backgrounds
8	Historical and Period
9	Humour and Satire
10	Biographical and Occupational
11	Contemporary Literary Novels
12	English Classics and International Classics in English

Subdivisions

a	Easy
b	Average
c	Difficult
d	Very difficult

the area and the subject of the map. Detailed specification is achieved with a relatively limited length of notation.

3. Fiction Classifications Fiction Classifications are used extensively in public libraries. It is widely recognised that it is difficult and unhelpful to categorise fiction according to a subject classification. Many public libraries follow a scheme similar to Corbett. In 1978, McClellan proposed the scheme based on the categories listed in Figure 14.11. Subdivision is by readability ratings. Thus, the symbol for easy reading historical and period novels would be F8a.

4. The London Classification of Business Studies The London Classification of Business Studies is a classification and a thesaurus for business libraries, the second edition being published in 1979. The first edition of the scheme met a growing need for a special classification scheme in this area, since it was published in 1970, during a period of rapid growth for business schools and business libraries. By the publication of the second edition the scheme had been adopted by seventy-five libraries, many of which were outside the United Kingdom. The schedules are divided into three main areas, as reflected in Figure 14.12. The notation is primarily letters, but also uses numbers to denote concepts in the auxiliary schedules. Thus

China's industrial revolution: politics, planning and management, 1949 to the present, is classified at JKD 552/61T

and

Interview skills training: role play exercises, is classified at FBGD/NFJ.

5. Classification of Library and Information Science This scheme was developed by the Classification Research Group. The final version of the scheme was published in 1975, but possibly the earlier version which is used in Library and Information Science abstracts is better known. The citation order was at first unsatisfactory and modifications were made in order to better reflect the needs of users. The citation order now gives precedence to processes, such as circulation control and cataloguing rather than to types of libraries.

6. British Catalogue of Music Classification The British Catalogue of Music Classification was developed by Coates for the British Catalogue of Music in 1960. It is also used in various music libraries, and has influenced the development of music schedules in BC2 and DC. The schedules are divided into two parts, one covering music scores and parts and the other concerned with music literature. The facets for music scores and parts are: Executant

Figure 14.12 The London Classification of Business Studies

A brief synopsis of the schedules

Management Responsibility in the Enterprise

A   Management
AY   Administrative Management
AZ   The Enterprise
B   Marketing
BZ   Physical Distributions Management
C   Production
D   Research and Development
E   Finance and Accounting
F   Personnel
G   Industrial Relations

Environmental Studies

J   Economics
JZ   Transport and Transport Planning
K   Industries
L   Behavioural Sciences
M   Communication
N   Education
P   Law
Q   Political Science
R   Philosophy, Science and Technology

Analytical Techniques

S   Management Science
T   Operational Research
U   Statistics
V   Mathematics
W   Computers and Computer Science
X   O and M and Work Study

Library and Information Science
Y   Library and Information Science

Auxiliary Schedules

1   People and Occupational Roles
2   Industrial products and services
3/4 Standard subject subdivisions
5   Geographical divisions
6   Time
7   Form divisions.

(for example, trumpet), Form of Composition (for example, March), and Character of Composition (for example, Military). The facets for music literature need to be more numerous, and include: Composer, Executant, Form, Elements of music, Character, Technique and Common subdivision. It is necessary to identify several subjects in the Executant facet. For instrumental music, for example, this includes: Type of executant, size or complexity of executant body, accompanying executant, original executant (for arrangements). The notation is also interesting, being entirely comprised of letters. More details of this notation are given in 13.3.

14.8 The Broad System of Ordering

The Broad System of Ordering (BSO) is a general classification scheme which was designed primarily for information exchange and switching. Together with BC2 it represents one of the major new general classification schemes of recent years. BSO was prepared by the International Federation for Documentation with the support of Unesco, and was published in 1978/9. The scheme was initiated under the auspices of UNISIST with the intention of providing a switching language. However, it is not in the true sense a switching language, which might permit the translation of natural language concepts expressed in, say, German, into a classification notation, and then from that notation to provide a natural language expression of those same concepts in, say, French. One essential feature of a switching language is that it is at least as specific as the languages to and from which it supports switching. The BSO is not likely to support this function very successfully because it is a relatively broad and inspecific classification scheme, with only sufficient specification for the classification of organisations concerned with the control of information, for example, libraries, clearing houses, abstracting and indexing agencies, and not sufficient specification to support the indexing of, say, individual periodical articles.

The scheme was essentially devised by a team of three: Coates, Lloyd and Simandl, and has a number of interesting features. The system has fairly low specificity, and topics are not included on the usual basis of literary warrant, but rather on the basis of organisational warrant. In other words, a topic is included if there is an information centre, source or service covering it. Not surprisingly this can lead to gaps in coverage, and uneven coverage of subjects. The BSO includes 3500 concepts. Within each class the concepts are analysed, using gradation by speciality and facet techniques. Facet analysis underlies the structure, but is not emphasised by facet indicators as in a more conventional faceted classification scheme. Extensive provision for synthesis is made including auxiliary schedules, expand like instructions, and synthetic features in the notation. However, the rules for synthesis are fairly complex, and may be difficult to operate. The basic order of main class resembles fairly closely that of BC, identifying the following main areas (into which main classes can be categorised):

Knowledge generally
Science and technology
Education
Human needs
Humanities, cultural and social sciences
Technology
Language, linguistics and literature
Arts
Religion and atheism

There is an index to the schedules, but this has been criticised in connection with the size of the entry vocabulary. The number of entries in the index only exceeds those subjects listed in the schedules by about 25 per cent and this leads to a rather poor index. Further work on the index would make the scheme more effective. The notation is basically numerical and non-expressive. Some feel that the non-expressive nature of the notation limits the scheme's usefulness in computerised data bases. Probably the major factor which must be addressed before the scheme can be moved from the realm of interesting exemplification of developments of classification theory into a practical classification scheme, is its organisational backing. As already noted, development and revision of classification schemes is essential to their continued usefulness. BSO was designed by a team of three. Financial and organisational support needs to be forthcoming from Unesco if BSO is to have an assured future.

Chapter 14 Readings

A. Dewey Decimal Classification Scheme

1 Batty, C.D., *An Introduction to the nineteenth edition of the Dewey Decimal Classification*, Bingley: London 1981.
2 Berman, S., 'DDC 19: an indictment', *Library Journal*, 105(5), 1980, 585-9.
3 Bull, G. and Roberts, N., 'Dewey Decimal Classification, 19th edition (Review)', *Journal of Librarianship*, 12(2), 1980, 139-42.
4 Butcher, P., 'Dewey? We sure do! A review of DDC 19', *Catalogue and Index*, (55), 1979, 1, 7-8
5 Comaromi, J.P., *The eighteen editions of the Dewey Decimal Classification*. Forest Press: Albany, New York, 1976.

6 Comaromi, J.P., 'Conception and development of the Dewey Decimal Classification', *International Classification*, 3(1), 1976, 11–15.

7 Comaromi, J.P., 'Use of the Dewey Decimal Classification in the United States and Canada' *Library Resources and Technical Services*, 22(4), 1978, 402–8.

8 Custer, B.A., 'Dewey 19', *Catalogue and Index*, (53), 1979, 1–2.

9 Custer, B.A., 'The responsiveness of recent editions of the Dewey Decimal Classification to the needs of its users' In *General classification systems in a changing world*, Federation Internationale de Documentation: The Hague, 1978, 81–4.

10 Dewey, M., *Dewey Decimal Classification and relative index. 19th edition*, edited under the direction of B.A. Custer, Forest Press: Albany, New York, 1979.

11 Dewey, M., *DDC, Dewey Decimal Classification: proposed revision of 780, music*, prepared under the direction of R. Sweeney and J. Clews, Forest Press: Albany, New York, 1980.

12 Dewey, M., *Abridged Dewey Decimal Classification and relative index, 11th edition*, edited under the direction of B.A. Custer, Forest Press: Albany, New York, 1979.

13 *European Centenary Seminar on the Dewey Decimal Classification, Banbury, 1976: Dewey International/ papers* edited by J.C. Downing and M. Yelland. Library Association: London, 1977.

14 Hobart, A., 'The work of the Dewey Decimal Classifaction Sub-committee 1968–1979', *Catalogue and Index*, (58), 1980, 5–6.

15 Jelinek, M., 'Twentieth Dewey: an exercise in prophecy', *Catalogue and Index* (58), 1980, 1–2.

16 Koster, C., 'Dewey in the UK: a British viewpoint', *Catalogue and Index*, (62), 1981, 5–7.

17 Sealock, R.B., 'International commitments of the Dewey Decimal Classification', In: *General classification systems in a changing world*. Federation Internationale de Documentation: The Hague, 1978, 31–5.

18 Sweeney, R., 'Music in the Dewey Decimal Classification', *Catalogue and Index*, (42), 1976, 4–6.

19 Trotter, R., 'Dewey 19 – a subjective assessment', *Catalogue and Index*, (59), 1980, 1–5.

20. Vann, S.K., 'Dewey Decimal Classification', In: Maltby, A., *Classification in the 1970s: a second look*, Bingley: London 1976, 226–55.

21 Winslade, B.A.J., *Introduction to the Dewey Decimal Classification for British schools*, 3rd edition, Forest Press for the Library Association: Albany, New York, 1977.

B. Library of Congress Classification Scheme

22 Canadian Libary Association, *An Index to the Library of Congress*

Classification by J. McRee Elrod *et al.*, preliminary edition, Canadian Library Association: Ottawa, 1974.

23 Immroth, J.P., 'Library of Congress Classification', in: Maltby, A. *Classification in the 1970s: a second look*, Bingley: London, 1976, 81-98.

24 Library of Congress, *Annual report* – lists changes in classification each year.

25 *Library of Congress Classification schedules: a cumulation of additions and changes*, Gale Research Company: Detroit, 1974.

26 *Library of Congress, Subject Cataloguing Division. Classification*. 34 vols., Library of Congress: Washington, DC, 1901-.

27 *Library of Congress, Subject Cataloguing Division, LC Classification – additions and changes*. Library of Congress, Washington, DC: List 1-March/May 1928-.

28 Olsen, N.B., *Combined indexes to the Library of Congress Classification schedules*, US Historical Documents Institute: Washington, DC, 1974.

C. *Colon Classification Scheme*

29 Batty, C.D., *Introduction to the Colon Classification*, Bingley: London, 1966.

30 Gopinath, M.A., 'Colon Classification', in: Maltby, A., *Classification in the 1970s: a second look*, Bingley: London, 1976, 51-80.

31 Neelameghan, A. *et al.*, 'Colon Classification. Edition 7. Schedules of basic subjects'. *Library Science with a Slant to Documentation*, 10(2), 1973, 222-60.

32 Ranganathan, S.R., *The Colon Classification*, The State University, Graduate School of Library Science: Rutgers 1965. (Rutgers series on systems for the intellectual organization of information, vol. 4)

33 Ranganathan, S.R., 'Colon Classification, Edition 7 (1971): a preview', *Library Science with a Slant to Documentation*, 6(3), 1965, 123-42.

D. *Universal Decimal Classification Scheme*

34 British Standards Institution, *British Standard full English Edition of the Universal Decimal Classification*, BSI: London, 1943.

35 British Standards Institution, *British Standards 1000A: 1961 Abridged English Edition of the Universal Decimal Classification*. 3rd edition. BSI: London, 1961 (FID no. 289).

36 Foskett, A.C., *The Universal Decimal Classification: the history, present status and future prospects of a large general classification scheme*, Bingley: London, 1973.

37 Hindson and Partners, UDC survey 1979/80: Report no. 1. The use of the Universal Decimal Classification in Scotland. Report no. 2. The use

of the Universal Decimal Classification in South West England and the Channel Islands. Hindson & Partners: Bridport, Dorset: 1980.

see also:

Hindson, R., 'UDC in the UK: a report on the 1979/80 survey', *Aslib Proceedings*, 33(3), 1981, 93–101.

38 Lloyd, G.A. 'Universal Decimal Classification', in: Maltby, A., *Classification in the 1970s: a second look*, Bingley: London, 1976, 99–118.

39 Perreault, J.M., *Towards a theory for UDC*, Bingley: London, 1969.

40 Robinson, G. *UDC: a brief introduction*, International Federation for Documentation: The Hague, 1979 (FID no. 574).

E. Bliss Bibliographic Classification Scheme

41 *Abridged Bliss Classification*, School Library Association: London, 1967.

42 Bliss, H.E. *A Bibliographic classification*, H.W. Wilson: New York, 1940–1953, vol. 1, 1940, vol. 2, 1947, vols. 3 and 4, 1953.

43 Bliss, H.E., *The organization of knowledge in libraries*, 2nd edition, H.W. Wilson: New York, 1939.

44 Maltby, A. and Gill, L., *The case for Bliss*, Bingley: London, 1979.

45 Mills, J., 'Bibliographic classification', in: Maltby, A., *Classification in the 1970s: a second look*, Bingley: London, 1976, 25–50.

46 Mills, J. and Broughton, V., *Bliss Bibliographic Classification*, Vol. 1 Introduction and auxiliary schedules; Class H. Human biology and medical sciences; Class I. Psychology and Psychiatry; Class J. Education; Class P. Religion; Class Q. Social Welfare, Butterworth: London, 1977.

47 Stoddard, H., 'Reclassification by Bliss' *Catalogue and Index*, (55), 1979, 41–5.

Note: The Introduction in (46) is an important and readable introduction to many ideas in classification theory.

F. Special classification schemes

48 Barnard, C.C., *A classification for medical and veterinary libraries*, 2nd edition. H.K. Lewis: London, 1955.

49 Carpenter, A.M. *et al*, 'Retrieval tests on five classification schemes: studies on patent classification schemes', *International Classification*, 5(2), 1978, 73–80.

50 Coates, E.J., *The British Catalogue of music classification*, Council of the British National Bibliography: London, 1960.

51 Foskett, D.J. and Foskett, J., *The London educational classification: a thesaurus/classification of British educational terms*, 2nd edition. University of London Institute of Education Library: London, 1974.

52 Moys, E., *A classification scheme for law books*, Butterworth: London, 1968.

53 National Library of Medicine, *The National Library of Medicine Classification: a scheme for the arrangement of books in the field of medicine and its related sciences* 3rd edition. NLM: Bethesda, Maryland, 1969.

54 Vernon, K.D.C. and Lang, V., *The London classification of business studies: a classification and thesaurus for business libraries*, 2nd edition, revised by K.G.B. Bakewell and D.A. Cotton, Aslib: London, 1979.

55 Vickery, B.C., *Faceted classification: a guide to construction and use of special schemes*, Aslib: London, 1960.

15 The alphabetical subject approach

15.1 Introduction

Although there are a number of different means of providing for the alphabetical subject approach to documents and information, the problems to be solved by these different approaches are common. Some aspects of the creation of a good alphabetical subject index, whether it be printed or machine-held, are common to any subject approach to information. The underlying problems of the subject approach, the components of the indexing process, and some concepts which facilitate discussion of the subject approach have already been introduced in Chapter 12. It is important that Chapter 12 should be familiar to the reader before any attempt is made to consider the alphabetical subject approach further. This brief chapter merely serves to draw together some common problems in alphabetical indexing (which feature in a different way in classification schemes). Perhaps predictably many of these problems are concerned with the label that is given to a subject in an alphabetical index.

15.2 Naming a subject

On first inspection it may appear that the words used in indexes to represent concepts can merely be determined by considering normal usage, but unfortunately the labels that must be applied to concepts even in an alphabetical index for effective indexing need more careful consideration. Many different words may be used to represent the same concept. In order to achieve some helpful grouping of concepts and clear labels for those concepts it is necessary to recognise closely related variants. Natural language indexing has its own solutions for the problems identified below, but even in this context these problems are encountered; this aspect is discussed further in Chapter 16. It is simpler to think about the problems outlined below in the context of controlled language indexing.

Labelling of subjects presents problems mainly because, in order to achieve a user-orientated approach, the various approaches of different users must be catered for. If a subject has more than one name a library catalogue or index must bring all material on that subject together (within the limitations of the scope of the collection or index) under one of those names, and also cater for users who use different names. Specific problems are:

1. *Synonyms*, that is, terms with the same or similar meanings, are present in every subject area. Near synonyms are most common, with true synonyms which mean exactly the same thing, and which are used in precisely the same context being more unusual. However, even near synonyms may be regarded as equivalent for some purposes, but not others. For example, in a general index it might be adequate to regard Prisons and Dungeons as one and the same, but in a specialist index devoted to Criminology this would probably not be acceptable. Some of the situations in which synonyms arise are listed:

(a) Some subjects have one stem, for example, sterilizer, sterilizing, sterilized, or computing, computers, microcomputers, computed, computation. Sometimes it is acceptable to treat such words or concepts as equivalent to one another, and on other occasions it is important to differentiate between such terms.

(b) Some subjects have both common and technical names, and the different names must be recognised, and reflected in the index in accordance with the audience for whom the index is intended. Examples of such terms are: salt and sodium chloride, radish and raphanus sativus.

(c) Changes in usage of terms over time can also present problems. The Library of Congress, for instance, started with the term 'Electronic calculating machines', and had to modify this in keeping with later normal usage to 'Computers'.

(d) Some concepts are described differently in different versions of one language. American and English English are two good examples of differences in usage. For example, the following terms may all be used for the same object: Eyeglasses, Spectacles, Glasses.

The merging of synonyms carries implications for the effectiveness of the index in terms of precision and recall. If two terms are merged precision is impaired but recall may be improved.

All unused terms must be included in the entry vocabulary of an index, that is, they must be present as access points in some form, if it is likely that a user might seek information under the unused term. These unused terms will normally be present in an index only in order to direct the user to the used or preferred terms.

2. *Homographs*, or words which have the same spelling as each other, but very diverse meanings, must be identified. In normal usage (as opposed to index usage) the meaning of a homograph is established by its context. If one word is used out of context as an index heading, plainly it will be difficult to

establish the interpretation to be placed on the homograph. Examples of homographs are: Duty (obligation), Duty (taxation) Ring (to ring, as in telephone, or to draw a circle around), or Ring (as in a mathematical concept, a finger ring, a ring of toadstools). In a special index the meaning of a homograph may be obvious by its having been placed in an index on the given subject. Thus the term Ring in an index to mathematics is well defined. In a general index it may only be possible to distinguish between different meanings of the one homograph by using scope notes or qualifying terms wherever the term arises, and thus in some way replace the context that is normally removed in using a term as an index term.

3. *Plurals and singulars* All nouns have a plural and a singular form. It may seem petty to distinguish between the plural and singular form, and therefore unnecessary to include both forms in the index. If both are nouns is there any difference between Farms and Farm? Generally the plural and singular of the same noun are regarded as equivalent, but there are a number of instances when it is necessary to treat the plural and the singular form as distinct. Consider the different meanings, for example of: Exercise and Exercises, Church and Churches. If one form only is permitted it is common practice to adopt the plural form.

4. *Multi-word concepts* Some subjects cannot be described satisfactorily with one word, and require two or more words for their specification. Some examples might be: Origin of Species, Information retrieval, Country walks, Extra-terrestrial beings. Whichever word in the term is used as the main entry point in an index, the user might choose to seek the subject under the other word in the term first. Once an entry has been identified, the user will expect to find the complete term, in order to distinguish this term from others containing the same words. Access must be provided via all significant words in the multi-word term. Thus, for Exceptional children, if this is the preferred term, when the user looks under Children he must also be able to trace a route to the document. Usually references can serve to direct users from words not used as the primary entry word to the word that does have this status. Sometimes terms are presented in direct order, for example, Military Hospitals, but on other occasions the terms may be inverted for example, Hospitals, Military. Inversion may offer the advantage of grouping like subjects. For example, inversion to Hospitals, Military will cause this heading to file alongside other headings commencing with the word Hospitals. The disadvantage of inversion of words is that inversion or indirect word order reduces predictability. How is a user to know which multi-word terms in a system have been inverted and which have not, and, with three word terms or more, which option for rearrangement of the words has been chosen?

5. *Complex subjects* like multi-word terms may require labels which contain

many words. The distinction between complex subjects and multi-word terms is that complex subjects contain more than one unit concept. However, each of these concepts may be potential search keys, and each of these concepts may be described by terms which exhibit any of the problems listed in 1 to 4 above. With complex subjects citation order becomes even more vital. For example, it is evident that 'a bibliography of history' is not the same thing as 'a history of bibliography'. The same two terms, 'bibliography' and 'history' serve to describe both subjects, and it is only the order in which they are cited and, in natural language, the connecting words that distinguish the statements of the two subjects. The presence of a variety of concepts in the statement of one subject area has been referred to in Chapter 12 as defining syntactic relationships. It is these syntactic relationships, and the ways in which they can be handled which are primarily responsible for the distinction between pre-co-ordinate and post-co-ordinate indexing systems. These approaches to indexing systems will be considered in Chapter 17.

15.3 Indicating relationships

Although the predominant problem of the alphabetical subject approach concerns the naming of subjects, as has already been demonstrated in Chapter 12, any tool for the organisation of knowledge must take into account the relationships between subjects. To reiterate, there are two main categories of relationship: the syntactic relationships referred to in the last paragraph and plain, for example in a topic such as:

Sugar and health

where the concepts

Sugar, and, Health

are drawn together in this particular context. Obviously any of these concepts may also be present in other circumstances, where the existence of the relationships defined in this document is largely irrelevant.

Semantic relationships show aspects of the genus–species relationships and are expected to reflect assumed and widely accepted subject relationships. For example 'Terrier' will always be a type of 'Dog'. Provision must be made for linking related subjects. This is normally effected by references and other devices indicating relationships in thesauri and subject heading lists, and alternative entries.

This then is a brief résumé of the problems which must be recognised by any indexer, and which the index must take into account.

Chapter 15 Readings

The following work is a useful compilation of topics in the general area of indexing. Although its scope goes much beyond that of this chapter, it does deal primarily with alphabetical indexing languages and systems: *Indexing specialized formats and subjects*, editor H. Feinberg, Scarecrow Press: Metuchen, N.J. and London 1983.

16

Alphabetical indexing languages: thesauri and subject headings lists

16.1 Introduction

Control is exercised in respect of the terms used in an index because of the variety of natural language. Such control may involve the barring of certain terms from use as index headings or access points. The terms which are to be used are likely to be specified, and synonyms recognised and probably eliminated (for example, Packaging may be indicated as preferable to Wrapping). Preferred word forms will also be noted; for instance, Heat may be preferred to Hot. The easiest way to exercise this type of control over index terms is to list or store the acceptable terms in a vocabulary. Such lists will embody both specific decisions concerning the preferred words, and also, by example, decisions relating to the form of words to be used, for example, singular or plural, nouns or adjectives. There are two types of controlled indexing language: thesauri and subject headings lists. These two tools have the same two basic functions, that is,

to control terminology used in indexes
to control the display of relationships between concepts in indexes,

but they differ in their area of application, and to some extent in the way in which they seek to fulfil the two basic functions.

16.2 Subject headings lists

Subject headings lists are lists of index terms, normally arranged in alphabetical order, which can be used to determine the terms to be used in an index, catalogue or data base for describing subjects. Such a list seeks to negotiate the problems of the alphabetical subject approach as outlined in the previous chapter, Chapter 15. A later section, section 16.6, makes a more direct comparison between subject headings lists and thesauri. Section 16.7 considers the compilation of such lists.

The basic functions of a subject headings list as identified in section 16.1 above may be focused more precisely in the following terms:

1. the list records terms which shall be used in a catalogue, index, or data

base, and indicates the form in which they shall be shown, and thus acts as an authority list for index terms and their form.

2. the list makes recommendations about the use of references for the display of relationships in a catalogue, index or data base, in order to guide users between connected or associated terms.

Thus, a subject headings list is primarily a guide to the indexer or cataloguer in the creation of index records. Most information about terms and their relationships that could be of assistance to the user of the index will be transferred from the list to the index or catalogue.

Subject headings lists are normally generated for a particular purpose. Since, like any alphabetical indexing language, it is important that the language reflect the requirements of the user and the literature, it is fairly common to have to modify a standard list, or compile a fresh list when a new application is envisaged. It is therefore more important to understand the principles on which such lists are based, than to be able to negotiate all the niceties of any particular list. There are some published lists of subject headings which are plainly intended for a special purpose. Amongst these might be numbered the School Library Association's *List of Subject Headings, Medical Subject Headings* (or MeSH) from the National Library of Medicine (US), and *Subject Headings for Engineering* (or SHE) used in Engineering Index. It would be impossible to consider all such lists, but the School Library Association's list is considered as an example in section 16.4. Nevertheless, the most effective means of reviewing the structure of subject headings lists is to consider one of the traditional subject headings lists which cover all subjects: *Sears' List of Subject Headings*, or the *Library of Congress List of Subject Headings*. These two lists have formed the basis of indexing practice, theory, and discussion in respect of alphabetical subject catalogues for some years.

16.3 Sears' List of Subject Headings

Now in its twelfth edition, (1982) *Sears' List of Subject Headings* was first written by Minnie Sears and published in 1923. It was designed as a list of subject headings for use in the dictionary catalogues of medium-sized libraries and is still widely used by school and small public libraries, particularly in the United States. Its overall structure and principles are similar to those of the *Library of Congress List of Subject Headings*, except in respect of the differences that arise from Sears' being designed for smaller libraries.

The headings, for instance, are less complex (Sears' would include city planning, rather than LC's Cities and towns – planning); less numerous (e.g. Sears' includes only Art, French instead of LC's Art-France and Art, French); and less specific.

Apart from its undoubted value in its own right, Sears' provides a valuable model or point of departure for others wishing to devise alphabetical subject headings lists for applications in which Sears' itself would not be appropriate.

Both functions of subject headings lists are fulfilled by Sears'. Terminology is controlled by establishing the terms that are to be used in an index or catalogue. These are indicated in bold type, and other terms which are useful access points, but which will not be used as index terms, are listed in light type. The form of terms is also controlled, by indicating for each term, the extent of abbreviation or the order of the words. In general, the following word forms are included, with, where it is possible to describe a subject with a single noun, preference being given to these:

1. single nouns, for example, Diseases.
2. compound headings, for example, Disinfection and disinfectants.
3. adjective with noun, for example, Cultural relations, Art, French.
4. phrases, for example, Discrimination in housing.

Some headings may be subdivided. In each instance guidance is given on how subdivision is to be made, and on the form of headings.

Types of subdivisions include:

1. subdivisions by physical form of the document, for example, Diseases – Dictionaries.
2. subdivisions that show non-comprehensive treatment, for example, Chemistry – Societies.
3. subdivisions that show special aspects, for example, Education – History.
4. subdivisions that show chronology, for example, US – History – 1783– 1809.

Some headings may also be subdivided by place, or alternatively, some places may be subdivided by subject, for example, Agriculture – France, or Paris – Population. Sometimes geographical subdivision is in terms of the adjectival form, for example, Music, German.

The display of these subdivisions in the list varies. Some are listed adjacent to the term to which they are to be applied and in the form in which they are to be applied in the main list. Other, generally applicable subdivisions, are shown in a separate list for easy reference. Subdivisions that might be applied to certain types of headings, such as places, literatures, and so on, are shown under key headings in the main list. Key headings exist for: persons, for example, Presidents – United States; places, for example, United States, Ohio, Chicago; languages and literatures, for example, English language, English literature; and wars, for example, World War, 1939–1945.

Three principles are employed in Sears' in the selection and assignment of subject headings, namely,

1. Specific entry is generally recommended. The level of specificity that is desirable in any index is a function of the collection being indexed, its use and its patrons. The principle of specific entry as applied in Sears' recommends that as specific a heading as is available in the list should be assigned. For example, a book on Bridges should be entered under Bridges and not under a broader heading such as Engineering, nor doubly under both headings.

2. Headings are selected for inclusion in Sears' on the basis of common usage. Thus popular or common names of subjects are included in preference to technical or specialist jargon. Unfortunately for the non-American user, the headings consequently correspond to current American usage in both use of terms and spelling and often need amendment to make them consistent with local usage.

3. Uniformity and consistency in application of subject headings is important. An attempt is made to offer one heading for each concept, and the indexer should try to adhere to this consistently.

In acknowledging these principles, Sears' is consistent with traditional ideas on the construction of alphabetical subject catalogues which are also followed in the Library of Congress List of Subject Headings.

Some categories of headings are deliberately omitted from Sears'. These include:

proper names, for example, names of persons, names of families, names of places;

corporate names, for example, names of associations, names of institutions, names of government bodies;

common names, for example, names of animals, tools, diseases, and chemicals.

Plainly, to list a reasonable number of terms in each of these categories would expand the list considerably. The indexer is expected to insert headings into the index or catalogue in these categories as they are required. Such headings should be constructed in accordance with the principles underlying Sears'.

Relationships between subjects are shown by the references in Sears, and the instructions in Sears' for creating references for insertion in an index or catalogue. Any terms in light type which are not to be used as headings in the catalogue lead the cataloguer to a used heading covering the same or a similar concept. See, for example, Country churches in Figure 16.1.

Most used headings, such as Country life in Figure 16.1 will be accompanied by some indication of their relationship to other terms. A fairly full entry is displayed as an example in Figure 16.1. This extract from Sears' includes two types of guidance to the cataloguer:

1. assistance in considering alternative headings, (for example, see also Agriculture – Societies; Farm Life; and so on);
2. suggested headings from which references might be constructed and inserted in the catalogue (for example, Rural life).

References to be inserted in the catalogue may be either 'see' or 'see also'. Figure 16.1 shows how the instructions in the extract from Sears' can be converted into the entries and references in a catalogue. The references

Figure 16.1 A small extract from Sears' List of Subject Headings

Country churches. **See** Rural churches
Country houses. **See** Architecture, Domestic
Country life (May subdiv. geog.)
Use for descriptive, popular and literary works on living in the country. Works dealing with social organization and conditions in rural communities are entered under Sociology, Rural

See also Agriculture—Societies; Farm life; Farmers; Outdoor life; Sociology, Rural
x Rural life
xx Farm life; Outdoor life; Sociology, Rural

Entries generated by the instructions under Country life

Main subject entry

Country life
Cottage life today/ M N Rimmer.—London: Granada Publishing, 1983.—286p.— (Lifestyles).

References

Rural life see Country Life
Farm life see also Country Life
Outdoor life see also Country Life
Sociology, Rural see also Country life

which are suggested are not obligatory, and references should be made as appropriate with regards to the item being indexed.

'See' references are generally used to link two terms which represent similar concepts, but which are presented in a different form. These might include references from:

1. synonyms, for example, Gaels see Celts.
2. the second part of a compound heading, for example, Dusting and spraying see Spraying and dusting.
3. the second part of an adjectival heading, for example, Furniture, Built-in see Built-in Furniture.
4. an inverted heading to the normal order, for example Natural Gas see Gas, Natural.
5. variant spellings, for example, Color see Colour.
6. opposites, for example, Intemperance see Temperance.
7. singular to plural forms, for example, Mouse see Mice.

'See also' references link two headings, both of which will be accepted for indexing. Such references permit the users to extend their search to related subjects. 'See also' references link connected subjects which may be co-ordinate, for example, Vases see also Glassware. Alternatively, the subjects linked by 'see also' references may be a general subject and its more specific subdivision. For example:

Crime see also Crimes without victims.

General references, in the form of either 'see' or 'see also' references, may also be employed on occasions. Such references will be used where the entry term is a relatively common term, and where the use of specific entries instead of the one general reference would probably lead to extensive lists of specific references. Typically general references may be used in respect of a common subdivision. Although traditional subject headings lists are important, they do have limitations. Both Sears' and the Library of Congress List of Subject Headings have been criticised on the following counts:

1. Headings tend to be broad and cannot represent complex or specific subjects accurately.
2. Headings are not constructed and selected systematically. Scan, for example, the headings listed under 'Libraries'. It is far from obvious whether a term will be inverted or in direct order, when we find terms such as Libraries, Children's alongside Business libraries. Such variations not only make it difficult for users to be confident about the form of a heading, but also make it difficult for a cataloguer inserting a new heading for local use

to discern the principles which should be heeded in the construction of such a heading.

3. References are not always constructed systematically. References may not be recommended where they might be appropriate, or in other places, too many references could make for a very tedious search.

4. Subarrangement at headings is not purely alphabetical. For instance 'Sculpture – Technique' precedes 'Sculpture in motion'.

These limitations of traditional lists of subject headings should not necessarily be taken as faults in their construction. Some of the criticisms arise from conflicting opinions as to the purpose of a list of subject headings. Nevertheless, the fact that these general lists cannot serve for every application has triggered a search for more consistent approaches to constructing headings, and the development of special lists of subject headings and thesauri.

16.4 School Library Association List of Subject Headings

Published in 1981, this recent list is designed to meet the need for a list of subject headings which is suitable for use in secondary school libraries and resource centres in the United Kingdom. It is mentioned here as an example of a specialised list of subject headings, special in the sense that it is intended for a particular type of application. The list is intended for use in subject catalogues, including both dictionary catalogues and subject indexes to classified catalogues. It could also form the basis of a controlled indexing language for use in a computerised information retrieval system, in a school. Like any subject headings list it is unlikely to be exploited precisely as published, but is a useful model based on sound principles.

In general principles and approach the SLA List has much in common with Sears'. For instance, the SLA List recommends the choice of specific headings in the same way as Sears'. Also simple, rather than technical terms, are preferred. 'See' and 'See also' references are indicated in the list, and like Sears', only a limited range of headings is listed, and it is expected that the user will add further headings.

Headings can be subdivided with the aid of lists of standard subheadings. There are thirty lists of standard subheadings. Adjacent to those headings which might be subdivided are numbers indicating which list of standard subheadings may be applied to that particular heading.

Recommendations for the references that should appear in a catalogue are made under headings in the list. The examples show how the instructions might be executed (see Figure 16.2). The style of recording instructions for references differs from that in Sears', and can at first seem strange, but instructions are clear.

Figure 16.2 A small extract from the lists of subject headings published by the School Library Association

CABINET GOVERNMENT sGovernment-
   Cabinet System
CABLE RAILWAYS sRailways-Cable
CABLES sElectricity-Cables;
   Telecommunications; Tele-
   graphy/Telephone-Cables
CACTI (22)
   sa Deserts-Plants; House
   Plants
CAGEBIRDS s Birds (as) Pets
CAKES (28)
   sa Baking
CALCIUM
   sa Bones, Elements-Metallic;
   Food - Chemistry; Limestone;
   Nutrition; Teeth

CALCULATING MACHINES (27)
   sa Computers; Office Equipment; Slide-Rule
   (xr Abacus; Adding
   Machines)
CALCULUS
   sa Geometry - Analytical;
   Mathematics
CALENDAR
   sa Astronomy - History; Time
   (xr Year)
CALIFORNIA (4)
   sa America - West; Gold Rush
   - California

Entries and references resulting from instructions above under Calculating Machines

Main subject entry

Calculating Machines

A student's primer to the basic calculator functions/ R T Yale. 2nd edition.—Leeds: Makie, 1983.—96p.

References

Calculating Machines see also Computers; Office Equipment; Slide-Rule

Abacus see Calculating Machines
Adding Machines see Calculating Machines.

16.5 Thesauri

A thesaurus could be defined as: 'a compilation of words and phrases showing synonyms, hierarchical, and other relationships and dependencies, the function of which is to provide a standardized vocabulary for information storage and retrieval systems'. The thesaurus is an authority list showing terms which may, and sometimes may not be used in an index to describe concepts. Each term is usually given together with terms which are related to it in one of a number of ways. The object of the thesaurus is to exert terminology control in indexing, and to aid in searching by alerting the searcher to the index terms that have been applied.

Although there are standards which provide guidance on the construction of thesauri, until recently there has not been a 'standard' thesaurus, or even a thesaurus like Sears or Library of Congress Lists of Subject Headings, which is widely used as a norm. In 1981, the British Standards Institution published its *Root Thesaurus*, which is intended to be a model thesaurus from which terms may be drawn. This is discussed in more detail later in this section. Thus there are many different thesauri, some published and others strictly in-house. A thesaurus is normally tailored to meet the specification of a particular application. Very often thesauri will be limited in subject scope, for example, music, education, agriculture. Thesauri have been used extensively since around the 1950s to index special collections of documents, abstracts bulletins, current awareness tools, Selective Dissemination of Information Systems, online data bases, encyclopaedias, and a variety of other bibliographical tools. Since there is no typical thesaurus, an examination of some of the more common features of existing published thesauri is the most fruitful way to proceed.

16.5.1 Key features of thesauri

The main list of index terms is the core of the thesaurus and defines the index language. This listing must be present in any thesaurus, and normally features, in a single alphabetical sequence:

1. Descriptors, or terms which are acceptable for use in indexes to describe concepts, and
2. Non-descriptors, or terms which are not to be used in the index but which appear in the thesaurus in order to expand the entry vocabulary (terms through which the user can enter the thesaurus, and be directed to the appropriate term) of the indexing language.

Descriptors are normally accompanied by some display of relationships between them and other words in the indexing language.

Most indexing terms in a thesaurus are 'uniterms' or single concept terms, although in some instances a deliberate decision may be made to include some multi-concept terms. The form of terms, whether they be descriptors or non-descriptors, may be one of:

1. single words, for example, Horror, Hosiery, Journalism, Counting.

2. phrases of two or three words, often comprising a noun and an adjective, for example, Country life, Electric meters, Electric power plants.

3. two words linked by 'and' or '&', for example, Joy and sorrow, Boats & boating.

4. compound phrases, for example, Employees' representation in management, Victim offender relationships.

5. names of persons, bodies, places, for example, Smith, John, BLCMP, Paris (Note: names of persons, bodies and places may be included in the main thesaurus, or they may be the subject of a distinct authority list).

Concepts are represented by these words or terms. Concepts should, in general, be described as simply as possible, whilst retaining sought and well-known terminology. Thus, single word terms, or failing an appropriate single word term, two word terms are preferred to longer terms in describing the concepts. Shorter terms are more likely to be present in the same form in both the indexer's and the searcher's normal vocabulary for the subject.

Index terms do not always stand alone, but are sometimes defined more precisely by the use of both qualifiers and scope notes. Qualifiers function as an integral part of the index term, so that terms of the form:

Moving (House)
Mergers (Industrial)

are created and used. Scope notes, on the other hand, may be present in a thesaurus but are unlikely to be transferred to an index. Scope notes define the scope of the index term by indicating its meaning, and clarifying the use of the term in the thesaurus. Scope notes are sometimes designated by the abbreviation SN (for Scope Note). So we might have:

Remedial education
(Instructing individuals to overcome educational deficiencies or handicaps in content previously taught but not learnt).
Industrial management
SN – Application of the principles of management to industries.

Relationships between the terms in an indexing language are also indicated in most published thesauri. These relationships can be viewed as belonging to one of three main categories: preferential, affinitive or hierarchical:

Preferential relationships generally indicate preferred terms or descriptors and distinguish such terms from non-descriptors or non-preferred terms. These relationships thus perform the vital function of identifying index terms. Statements conveying preferential relationships between terms indicate which terms are to be treated as equivalent to one another, or which concepts are to be grouped together under one index term. Preferential relationships are indicated by statements of the form:

A is not authorised, see B instead

where A and B are taken to be two index terms, with A a non-descriptor, and B a descriptor. Examples might be:

Temperance see Intemperance
Disabilities USE Handicaps
Urban Life USE Urban culture

There are variations on the basic statement of a preferential relationship. The following statement, for instance, suggests that in indexing or searching for Folk drama, both of the terms Drama and Folk Culture should be used:

Folk Drama
USE Drama and Folk Culture

The following statement represents another variation on the basic preferential relationship:

Programming languages USE Fortran, Algol, Cobol, Basic

This statement directs the user to adopt a number of more specific terms in preference to the general term.

All statements indicating preferential relationships will usually appear in both direct and inverted forms. Thus the thesaurus user may approach a term from 'either direction'. It would be normal, for instance, for the statement:

Games USE Sports

to be complemented, at the appropriate point in the alphabetical sequence, by

Sports UF Games

were 'UF' is a common abbreviation for 'use for'.

Hierarchical relationships are represented in the thesaurus by statements of the form:

275

A is permitted, but consider using B or C or, . . ., N instead.

where, as above, A, B, C, . . ., N are index terms (that is, descriptors) and B and C and so on are related to A via some hierarchy of relationships. Hierarchical relationships must be indicated in order that users may transfer from a first access term to related terms, and to broaden or narrow the search parameters. The indication of such relationships helps the searcher and the indexer to select the most specific term available as a label for any given concept in the thesaurus. The searcher is kept better informed as to related terms under which additional information or documents have been indexed. Hierarchical relationships take one of two forms, depending upon whether A is subordinate to B, C, . . ., N or B, C, . . ., N are subordinate to A. Broader terms are generally indicted by the abbreviation 'BT' For example:

Remedial reading
BT Reading

suggests that Remedial reading is a subordinate topic to Reading. Narrower terms are signalled by the abbreviation 'NT'. So:

Libraries
NT Public libraries

notes that Public libraries are a type of Library. In most instances it is to be expected that 'NT' and 'BT' statements should be accompanied by their inverse. Thus the above example would normally be complemented by:

Public libraries
BT Libraries

Hierarchical relationships may also take the form of co-ordinate relationships, in which case they may be represented by 'RT' or related term, in a similar manner to affinitive relationships below.

affinitive relationships are a further type of connection between index terms, and thus may be codified by a similar statement to the statement that has been encountered in respect of hierarchical relationships:

A is permitted, but consider using B or C or, . . ., N as well or instead

Although the statements of affinitive and hierarchical relationships are similar they differ in the nature of the relationships that they signal. Affinitive relationships that exist between terms are not necessarily connected to one another in any fixed hierarchical manner. Affinitive relationships are often indicated by the code 'RT'. An example might be:

Food
RT Vegetarianism
Dinners
Cookery

It is usual for 'RT' to be reflexitive and the above example concerning Food would be accompanied by a series of inversions of the statement of the form:

Vegetarianism
RT Food
Cookery
RT Food

It is important to remember that such relationships as are displayed in the thesaurus may not be transferred to the index, and this is an important reason why the searcher should consult the thesaurus prior to the start of a search.

Other abbreviations are encountered in some thesauri. Amongst them can be listed: 'GT' Generic to; 'SA' See also: 'TT' Top term in a hierarchy; 'XT' Overlapping term; 'AT' Associated term; 'CT' Co-ordinate term; 'ST' Synonymous term; and 'SU' See Under.

Figure 16.3 shows some extracts from thesauri.

In addition to the relationship display which is incorporated into the alphabetical list of subject terms, thesauri often incorporate other lists which help to show the relationships between terms. Published thesauri, in particular, are likely to include one or more of the following types of lists:

1. Hierarchical displays. Various of the key terms in the thesaurus may be drawn in an alphabetical sequence, with a more complete hierarchical display of the connected terms with more specific meanings.

2. Categorised displays. Thesaurus terms are grouped under a series of category headings, which correspond to the main subfields within the area covered by the thesaurus.

3. Permuted lists of terms. These lists arrange terms under each of the words in a term, thus Industrial management would appear in two places in the alphabetical sequence: under industrial and under management. Such lists aid the access to second and subsequent words in terms.

4. Graphic displays. Various imaginative graphic displays have been proposed. Numbered amongst these are: Euler circles, arrowgraphs, and the circular thesaurus. The attraction of such displays is that the multi-dimensional relationships between subjects may be shown since any one subject can be displayed in juxtaposition with several others.

5. A classification scheme. ThesauroFacet, compiled by English Electric, is a notable example of a thesaurus supported by a full faceted classification scheme. This format is becoming common in new thesauri, partly because of

Figure 16.3 Thesauri - some extracts

INSPEC Thesaurus

Main alphabetical list

climatology
UF	synoptic climatology
BT	meteorology
TT	natural sciences
RT	atmospheric humidity
	atmospheric precipitation
	sunlight
	wind
CC	A9260S B7710B C3380D C7320
FC	a9260Sy b7710By c3380Dv
	c7320+f
DI	January 1973

climb, dislocation
    USE   dislocation climb

clinical equipment
    USE   biomedical equipment

clinical measurement
    USE   biomedical measurement

clipping circuits
    USE   limiters

clock paradox
    USE   special relativity

clocks
NT	atomic clocks
	chronometers
BT	instruments
TT	instruments
RT	time measurement
CC	B1265Z B7320K C5150
FC	b1265Zw b7320Kc c5150+b
DI	January 1973

closed circuit television
UF	CCTV
BT	television systems
TT	telecommunication systems
RT	teleconferencing
	television equipment
	video signals
CC	B6430F C3370J
FC	b6430Fx c3370Ja
DI	January 1977
PT	television systems

closed loop control systems
    USE   closed loop systems

Hierarchy list

crystal growth
. crystal growth from melt
. crystal growth from solution
.. crystal growth from gel
. crystal growth from vapour
.. vapour phase epitaxial growth
... molecular beam epitaxial growth
. epitaxial growth
.. liquid phase epitaxial growth
.. vapour phase epitaxial growth
... molecular beam epitaxial growth

crystal properties
. crystal chemistry

crystallography
. electron diffraction crystallography
. isomorphism
. lattice constants
. neutron diffraction crystallography
. space groups
. X-ray crystallography

crystals
. bicrystals
. dendrites
. epitaxial layers
.. magnetic epitaxial layers
.. metallic epitaxial layers
.. semiconductor epitaxial layers
. plastic crystals
. whiskers (crystal)

Main alphabetical list

DOGMATISM 040
BT   Philosophy
RT   Authoritarianism
     Opinions

DOMESTICS 380
SN   Any female household
     employee working in a private
     home
NT   Maids
BT   Service Workers
RT   Attendants
     Service Occupations

DOORS 210
BT   Architectural Elements
     Equipment
RT   Building Design
     Building Materials

DORMITORIES 210
UF   Residence Halls
BT   College Housing
RT   House Plan
     Resident Assistants

Double Employment
USE   MULTIPLE EMPLOYMENT

DOUBLE SESSIONS 020
     School Schedules
RT   Flexible Schedules
     Scheduling
     School Administration
     School Organization
     Student Enrollment

Downs anomaly
USE   MONGOLISM

Rotated descriptor display

         BUSINESS RESPONSIBILITY
         BUSINESS SKILLS
         BUSINESS SUBJECTS
NEGRO BUSINESSES
         CABINET TYPE PROJECTORS
         CABINET MAKING
         CABLE TELEVISION
SCHOOL CADRES
         CAKCHIQUEL
         CALCULATION
         CALCULUS
SCHOOL CALENDARS

         CALISTHENICS
         CALORIMETERS
         CAMBODIAN
LABOR CAMP COMMISSARIES
         CAMP COUNSELORS
DAY CAMP PROGRAMS
RESIDENT CAMP PROGRAMS
         CAMPING
LABOR CAMPS
OFF CAMPUS FACILITIES
         CAMPUS PLANNING
         CAMPUSES

Subject categories

040 **Attitudes**
Attitudes of individuals or groups toward a given object or condition, e.g., Student Attitudes, Class Attitudes, Personal Interests, Values, etc.

050 **Audiovisual Materials and Methods**
Audiovisual materials and methods used for instructional purposes, e.g., Closed Circuit Television, Mass Media. **See also** COMMUNICATION, EQUIPMENT.

060 **Behavior**
Kinds and types of human behavior and factors related to the study of behavior, e.g., Violence, Socially Deviant Behavior, Conditioned Response, Overt Response, etc. **See also** LEARNING AND COGNITION, PSYCHOLOGY, SOCIOLOGY.

070 **Biology**
Study of life including Zoology and Botany, e.g., Ecology, Heredity, Plant Science, Animal Science, Physiology, Neurology, etc. **See also** HEALTH AND SAFETY.

Figure 16.3 Continued

INIS Thesaurus

Main alphabetical list

MAGNETIC CIRCUITS (20; 20)
   UF   -circuits (magnetic)
   RT   electric coils

-magnetic coils
   USE magnet coils

MAGNETIC COMPRESSION (95; 95)
   BT1 compression
   RT   magnetic fields
   RT   pinch effect

MAGNETIC CORES (21; 21)
   (For the storage of information in
   machine-readable form only.)
   UF   -cores (magnetic)

   BT1 magnetic storage devices
   BT2 memory devices
   RT   computers

MAGNETIC DIPOLE MOMENTS (189; 189)
   BT1 dipole moments
   BT1 magnetic moments
   RT   nuclear magnetic moments

MAGNETIC DIPOLES (114; 114)
   BT1 dipoles
   BT2 multipoles
   RT   magnetic fields

Thesaurus of psychological terms

Main alphabetical list

Children's Personality Questionnaire[73]
   B   Nonprojective Personality
        Measures
        Personality Measures

Childrens Recreational Games[73]
   B   Games
        Recreation
   R   Childhood Play Behavior
        Childhood Play Development
        Toys

Chile[82]
   B   South America

Chimpanzees[73]
   B   Mammals
        Primates (Nonhuman)
        Vertebrates

Chinese Americans
   Use Asians

Rotated descriptor display

Cross Cultural Differences
Human Sex Differences
Individual Differences
Racial and
   Ethnic Differences
Sex Linked
Develop-
   mental Differences
   Species Differences
        Differential Aptitude
        Tests
        Differential Diagnosis
        Differential Personality
        inventory
        Differential
        Reinforcement
  Semantic Differential
        Difficulty Level (Test)
        Digestion
        Digestive System

the recognition of the importance of viewing both relationships and subject terms in one tool. With such an arrangement, the thesaurus provides direct alphabetical access to a subject and class notation. The classification scheme shows relationships, and facilitates browsing between the subjects. The Root thesaurus described in the next section also incorporates this arrangement.

16.5.2 The Root Thesaurus

The British Standards Institution *Root Thesaurus* is an important attempt to provide a standard list of terms from which terms for thesauri and indexing languages can be selected, and more application-oriented lists derived. It is potentially important both with regard to making the compilation of thesauri for specific applications easier, and also with regard to enhancing the similarities between lists for different applications. Since the Root Thesaurus did not emerge until 1981, it has not had a great impact on existing thesauri so far, but it could well be important in the future.

The thesaurus is available in a printed version or on magnetic tape. Not all topics are covered, but a broad group of industrial topics are represented, including measurement, environmental and safety engineering, energy technology and communication. Figure 16.4 shows that there are two lists, a classified list, and an alphabetical list, and demonstrates the relationships between these two lists. Note that the alphabetical list shows synonyms, broader terms, narrower terms and related terms, but these are signalled by different notation to that traditional in thesauri, introduced earlier in this chapter. The Root thesaurus designations are independent of specific language (that is, French, German, Italian). So

$=$ is equivalent to UF
$-$ is equivalent to Use
$<$ is equivalent to BT
$>$ is equivalent to NT
$—$ is equivalent to RT

Other refinements are also available which permit the part of the hierarchy from which a term is drawn to be specified.

16.5.3 Multilingual thesauri

A multilingual thesaurus is a thesaurus which can be used to support indexing and searching in several languages. There is growing interest in multilingual thesauri for application in international information retrieval networks. Multilingual thesauri present a special set of problems. Several parallel editions in the different languages are to be recommended. Difficulties may arise where equivalent terms do not exist in all of the languages of the thesaurus. A switching language, in the form of a notation,

Figure 16.4 Extract from The BSI Root Thesaurus showing subject display schedule and alphabetical list

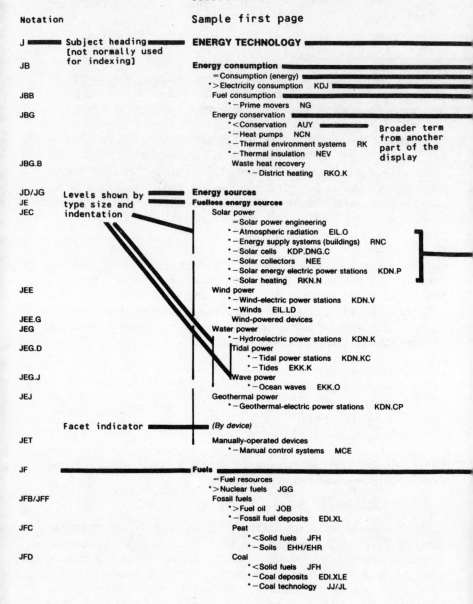

SUBJECT DISPLAY SCHEDULE

Notation

Sample first page

J ▬▬ Subject heading ▬▬ [not normally used for indexing]	**ENERGY TECHNOLOGY** ▬▬
JB	**Energy consumption** ▬▬
	= Consumption (energy)
	* > Electricity consumption KDJ ▬▬
JBB	Fuel consumption ▬▬
	* – Prime movers NG
JBG	Energy conservation
	* < Conservation AUY ▬▬
	* – Heat pumps NCN
	* – Thermal environment systems RK
	* – Thermal insulation NEV
JBG.B	Waste heat recovery
	* – District heating RKO.K

Broader term from another part of the display

JD/JG Levels shown by	**Energy sources**
JE type size and	**Fuelless energy sources**
JEC indentation	Solar power
	= Solar power engineering
	* – Atmospheric radiation EIL.O
	* – Energy supply systems (buildings) RNC
	* – Solar cells KDP.DNG.C
	* – Solar collectors NEE
	* – Solar energy electric power stations KDN.P
	* – Solar heating RKN.N
JEE	Wind power
	* – Wind-electric power stations KDN.V
	* – Winds EIL.LD
JEE.G	Wind-powered devices
JEG	Water power
	* – Hydroelectric power stations KDN.K
JEG.D	Tidal power
	* – Tidal power stations KDN.KC
	* – Tides EKK.K
JEG.J	Wave power
	* – Ocean waves EKK.O
JEJ	Geothermal power
	* – Geothermal-electric power stations KDN.CP
Facet indicator ▬▬	(By device)
JET	Manually-operated devices
	* – Manual control systems MCE
JF ▬▬▬▬▬▬▬	▬ **Fuels**
	= Fuel resources
	* > Nuclear fuels JGG
JFB/JFF	Fossil fuels
	* > Fuel oil JOB
	* – Fossil fuel deposits EDI.XL
JFC	Peat
	* < Solid fuels JFH
	* – Soils EHH/EHR
JFD	Coal
	* < Solid fuels JFH
	* – Coal deposits EDI.XLE
	* – Coal technology JJ/JL

282

CORRESPONDING ENTRIES FROM ALPHABETICAL LIST

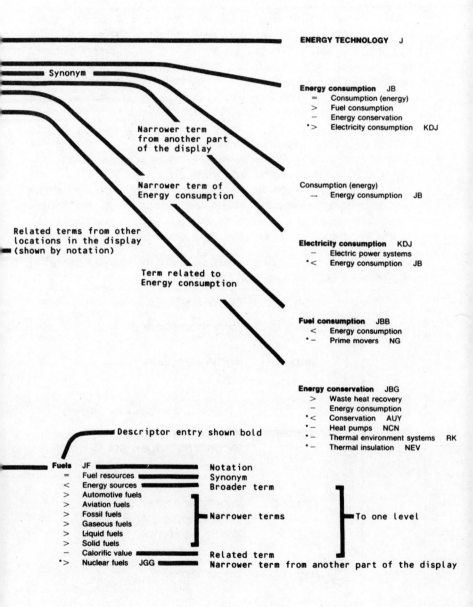

ENERGY TECHNOLOGY J

Synonym

Energy consumption JB
- = Consumption (energy)
- \> Fuel consumption
- \- Energy conservation
- *\> Electricity consumption KDJ

Narrower term from another part of the display

Narrower term of Energy consumption

Consumption (energy)
- \- Energy consumption JB

Related terms from other locations in the display (shown by notation)

Electricity consumption KDJ
- \- Electric power systems
- *< Energy consumption JB

Term related to Energy consumption

Fuel consumption JBB
- < Energy consumption
- *\- Prime movers NG

Energy conservation JBG
- \> Waste heat recovery
- \- Energy consumption
- *< Conservation AUY
- *\- Heat pumps NCN
- *\- Thermal environment systems RK
- *\- Thermal insulation NEV

Descriptor entry shown bold

Fuels JF — Notation
- = Fuel resources — Synonym
- < Energy sources — Broader term
- \> Automotive fuels
- \> Aviation fuels
- \> Fossil fuels — Narrower terms — To one level
- \> Gaseous fuels
- \> Liquid fuels
- \> Solid fuels
- \- Calorific value — Related term
- *\> Nuclear fuels JGG — Narrower term from another part of the display

283

may be used to translate terms from all natural languages, and as an intermediate language between the various languages.

16.5.4 Computers and thesauri

Thesauri may exist in either online display of machine-held thesaurus records, or in hard copy. Figure 16.5 shows a thesaurus display in ADLIB, from LMR Information Systems. There may be some differences between thesauri intended for these different formats. With printed thesauri there are limits on space, if the publication is to be economically viable, and easy to handle. No such constraints exist where online display is anticipated, since only one segment at a time is displayed. Also, with online display, the user should be able to request displays indicating different levels of specificity. With online display, the alphabetical arrangement can become less significant, since all look-ups can be achieved with the computer, and there is less need for the scanning of alphabetical lists.

In addition to the application of computers in the display of thesauri during the indexing or searching process, computer processing can facilitate the compilation and maintenance of thesauri. During the construction of a thesaurus, the computer can be enlisted to sort, merge, edit and compare

Figure 16.5 An extract from a machine - held thesaurus supported by ADLIB, from LMR Information Systems

THESAURUS BROWSE SCREEN		
Current Term (Library and information science)		
Use		
( ) Broader	communication	
( )		
( )		
( )		
( ) Narrower	information retrieval	
( )	records management	
( )		
( )		
( ) Related	information services	
( )	information systems	
( )	library equipment	
( )		
( ) Use For	documentation	
( )		
( )		

terms. Programs are available which generate alphabetical listings, including lead-in terms, reciprocal entries, hierarchical displays and other special sections of the thesaurus. The computer cannot replace the intellectual work of selecting and providing relationships between terms, but in other respects the computer can greatly assist in thesaurus compilation and updating.

16.6 Thesauri and subject headings lists – a quick comparison

The previous two sections have introduced thesauri and subject headings lists. Clearly both tools record controlled indexing languages, but they are utilised in different environments. A clearer demarcation might be drawn between the traditional subject headings lists and thesauri by the following summary of differences:

1. Thesauri are likely to contain terms that are more specific than those found in subject headings lists.
2. Thesauri tend to avoid inverted terms (such as Sculpture, German).
3. Headings in thesauri are not subdivided. For instance Education-Bibliographies would not normally be featured in a thesaurus, but headings of this type are common in traditional subject headings lists. Situations where subdivisions might have had some utility are served by the co-ordination of index terms at the search stage (see 17.3).
4. The relationship display in a thesaurus is often more extensive than the relationship display in a subject headings list.
5. Different types of relationships are noted in a thesaurus by the use of 'RT', 'NT' and 'BT', instead of 'see also' which is frequently used to indicate all relationships, whatever their nature, in a subject headings list.
6. The relationships between the terms listed in a thesaurus will often not be transferred to the index. Dictionary catalogues usually contain 'see' and 'see also' instructions linking related headings.
7. Thesauri often boast an additional explicit statement of the structure of the relationships between terms in the form of categorised lists or displays.

16.7 Compiling a thesaurus or list of subject headings

All alphabetical indexing languages must be tailored to the application for which they are intended. Whilst standard published lists of terms provide useful models and certainly aid the searcher of a large publicly available data base, any information worker needing to establish an in-house data base, catalogue or index, will need to consider devising a local list of indexing terms. Even in situations where there is a published list covering the requirements of the type of library, or the subject area to be indexed, this list is likely to require adjustment in order to make it compatible with local requirements. A good thesaurus or list of subject headings is not necessarily one that has been carefully presented, printed and published, with a plethora of effective relationship displays, but rather a list that has been compiled to serve in the retrieval environment in which it is called upon to operate. This section, then, identifies a three-step process for the compilation of a thesaurus or a subject headings list.

Step 1 Decide the purpose of the indexing language

Preliminary decisions concerning the anticipated use of the thesaurus must be made before any further work is undertaken. This planning phase involves moving from a vague impression that a thesaurus might be useful to a fairly precise profile for the thesaurus, in terms of the following parameters:

1. *Subject field* to be covered must be determined by making explicit statements concerning the limits of topic coverage, and the depth in which various aspects of the subject are to be treated. Subject field definition arises from the scope of the information service or system that the indexing language is expected to serve. This, in turn, depends upon users and user interests, and it may be necessary to conduct a survey to discover or update the profile of user interests.

2. *Type of literature* to be covered may determine, amongst other features, the amount of detail required. Books, for example, are normally indexed in less detail than periodical articles.

3. *Quantity of literature.* The sophistication of a thesaurus and the specificity of its index terms is usually related to the number of documents to be covered by the indexing system for which the indexing language has been planned. In simple terms, the essence of subject organisation is the division of literature (or references to literature) into manageable, or scannable categories, with each category being associated with an index term. Thus, the more documents that an indexing system is likely to embrace, the greater the number of index terms that are likely to be necessary for convenient retrieval (given that the number of documents which constitute a scannable category does not vary).

4. *Type of information storage system* in which the list is to be used may carry implications for the nature of the terms to be listed. The system may be essentially pre- or post-co-ordinate, or neither, and may be either manual or computerised.

5. *Resources of the information system* will impose constraints upon the nature of the indexing language. There are two types of resources: those available and necessary for initial design, and those resources for the

development and application of the indexing language. Probably one of the most essential resources is sufficient time for initial thesaurus construction to permit the compilation of a high-quality thesaurus or list. A good list will save time in later indexing and searching.

6. *Users* of the information system may influence the explicitness of the detail in a list. The nature of the users, their background, their work, the frequency with which they use the system, and their mode of access to the system (that is, through an intermediary information officer, or directly) are all factors to be considered.

7. *Use* to which the information system will be put impinges upon most of the earlier issues, but there are elements of the nature of use which can be considered in their own right. The number and type of questions posed to the system has implications for the effort that it is worthwhile to divert into thesaurus construction.

Full consideration of the above factors should form a firm basis for the design of an effective thesaurus or list of subject headings.

Step 2: Decide the characteristics of the indexing language and the way in which it is to be embodied in the thesaurus or list of subject headings

The purpose of the list will colour the decisions concerning the indexing language. Again decisions have to be made. A number of the factors to be considered in this stage include:

1. *The nature of the language* – the relative merits of free, natural and controlled language need to be evaluated. It is easiest to see the comments in this section as pertaining to controlled indexing languages, but the imaginative student will be able to see that some of them are equally relevant to natural or free indexing languages.

2. *Specificity* of the language must be settled at a suitable level for the application.

3. *Exhaustivity*.

4. *Level of pre-co-ordination* (see Chapter 17)
In planning the nature of the indexing language, the basic language evaluation devices must be taken into account (see Chapter 12).

5. *Thesaurus or list of subject headings and its structure*. Once the characteristics of the retrieval language have been agreed, the way in which

the language will be recorded or printed must be determined. A straightforward alphabetical list must form the core of the language list. Some type of graphic or other relationship display may also be helpful, as may separate lists of subheadings, instructions for use, and so on. The thesaurus may be kept in machine-readable form and only sections printed as required.

Step 3: Start to compile the language

Now, the compilation of index terms can begin. This involves:

1. *Identification of the main subject areas* in a more explicit manner than might be required in the planning stage. A description of the main subject areas forms the skeleton of the main list of terms. Such deliberations on subject scope will normally lead to a preliminary list of significant terms especially the more general terms, with these terms collected into groups that reflect the relationships between terms.

2. *Selection of* terms to be included in the thesaurus. Once terms have been accepted for inclusion they must obviously be recorded, so that this stage and the next one must proceed simultaneously. The preliminary list which was compiled in the last sub-stage must be developed. Synonyms, related terms and other variants must now be collected, either by human selection, or with the aid of the machine. Humanly selected terms may be derived from a number of sources. In particular, other lists of words used in the subject area such as:

(a) other thesauri, classification schemes and information retrieval tools.
(b) documents in the subject area, such as periodical articles, data bases, indexing and abstracting journals, encyclopaedias, dictionaries.
(c) previous knowledge and experience of indexers, index language compilers and users.

The more structured the source of words, the more likely it is that the terms in the source will already be in a standard form ready for lifting wholesale and little modified into a thesaurus. These sources which form the basis of the intellectual selection of terms may be augmented by or ousted by the machine selection of terms. Some or all of the terms in an index language may be derived automatically from the text of the documents to be indexed. Here again the documents of the subject area, such as periodical articles and research reports, will provide the terms to be included in the language.

3. *Recording of terms.* In a totally machine-selected thesaurus, the listing of terms will be printed or displayed by the computer, and often no further effort is necessary. If the thesaurus includes humanly selected terms,

it is necessary to record the chosen terms. The most convenient manual format for recording terms is to write each term on a card, and to note on the card any comments about the term that are to feature in the thesaurus or list of subject headings. Each card will show a term and any necessary scope notes, related terms and synonyms. For ease of consultation, cards should be kept in alphabetical order in accordance with the main term on the card.

4. *Checking of relationships* which are to be indicated under each of the terms. Most relationships should be shown in both their direct and inverse forms. Checks on relationships that must be represented can be executed by examining each card in turn and seeking cards which show related terms. A more systematic approach involves assessing terms and their relationships in subject-related groups. These subject groups may be refined by constructing facets and hierarchies relevant to the subject being investigated. Any new concepts or terms that emerge during this examination of relationships must also be inserted in the deck of cards.

5. *Finalisation of the thesaurus.* Now is the time to conduct the final check on each of the features of the list. Terms should be reviewed for consistency and appropriate level of pre-co-ordination, word form and level of specificity. Classificatory or other indicators of relationships should be checked and recorded in their final form. If any links are necessary between displays and listings, some notation must be introduced. All listings for the final thesaurus must be converted to the format appropriate for typing, printing or input to a computer data base, and each feature checked, edited and tested on some examples. An introduction explaining the nature and scope of the indexing language will enhance its value.

6. *Revision of the list.* The list or thesaurus cannot be static. It must be updated. New terms and relationships may be added as they arise, or in batches at pre-determined intervals. Updating an in-house thesaurus is relatively easy. A published thesaurus or a thesaurus or list which is involved in an international indexing effort may need a more clearly established revision programme. Each amendment may need to be agreed by users and equivalent terms in various languages may need to be added to a multi-lingual list. Lists of amendments or new editions are possible mechanisms for announcing changes.

16.8 Natural indexing languages

In a text such as this which focuses primarily upon controlled indexing languages and systems it is difficult to place natural language indexing in an appropriate context. This is partly because with natural language indexing, the indexing language is the language of the documents to be indexed, and thus in its pure form it is not possible to list all of the terms in such a language, and expect that list to remain current for any longer than the time period before the indexing for the next batch of documents is added to the system. Furthermore, since each system indexes a separate set of documents, each system will have a different natural indexing language. Thus, the language is derived from the documents input to the system, whether they be abstracts, full text, citations (including titles, periodical titles and so on) or lists of controlled or uncontrolled index terms. Obviously one of the unique features of natural language indexing is the lack of control of vocabulary. This permits the entire variety of natural language to be reflected in the indexing, and the strengths and weaknesses of natural language indexing derive from this basic characteristic.

This work tackles two other areas which are relevant to natural language indexing: Chapter 11 discusses the generation of printed indexes based upon the words in titles, and reviews some of the basic strengths and limitations of natural language indexing in the context of printed indexes based entirely upon titles alone; Chapter 17 considers the search devices used in post-co-ordinate indexing, and online searching of data bases. These devices are important in searching of data bases with natural language indexing. It should be noted that printed indexes are not the only context in which natural language indexing is important. It is also used in association with data bases, such as full text legal data bases, online catalogue data bases, and other online bibliographic data bases.

16.8.1 *Stop-lists and go-lists*

In its pure form natural language indexing has some obvious limitations. Plainly, indexing on the text of a document involved indexing every word, and some words in, say, an abstract do not convey any subject concepts. Thus we can easily start to compile a list of prepositions, conjunctions and articles, for example, an, a, the, and, for, to, his, these, which can be ignored in indexing. Most natural language indexing operates with the aid of a stop-list which lists all such redundant terms (redundant as far as indexing is concerned), and no index entries will be stored in connection with such terms. Of course some terms may be difficult to categorise as stop or non-stop. Think, for instance of: machine, lines, plunge. In some systems these might be useful in indexing, in others they might not. Thus although it is possible to establish a stop-list covering a number of standard terms not suitable for indexing, this normally needs to be modified to reflect the circumstances of each system. The use of a stop-list in title indexing is shown in Chapter 11.

In natural language indexing which uses a stop-list only, the indexing language is open, and there is no record other than the index itself of the indexing terms that have been assigned. The indexing changes gradually with time, as the natural language of the documents covered by the index evolves.

The other approach to natural language indexing is to index on both a stop-list and a go-list. A go-list includes all of those terms that would create useful index entries in the subject area being indexed. Thus the go-list must be machine-stored and is used by the computer in the assignment of index terms. Like the stop-list, the go-list can also be displayed or printed out for consideration prior to updating or other modification. The go-list is sometimes known as a thesaurus, and indeed is a form of natural language thesaurus. In the process of indexing each new batch of documents, new words will from time to time appear in the text. Since these words are new they will not appear in the go-list and the computer will not know whether or not to treat them as indexing terms. In this case, the human indexer will be provided with the terms not recognised by the computer, and must decide whether to list them in the go-list or the stop-list, or perhaps to leave them unlisted in either list, so that they will be output for human indexer consideration on each occurrence. Obviously this last option permits the human indexer some control over the allocation of index terms. Perhaps it is useful to observe that the human indexer selects the terms for inclusion in the go-list, and in that sense the indexing language is controlled. However, the allocation of index terms, and the variety of forms in which concepts or names might appear is not controlled.

16.8.2 *Attractions of natural language indexing*

The attractions of natural language indexing may be divided into two categories:

1. *Economic factors.* The intellectual input at the indexing stage is minimal, even in systems where in the interests of enhanced consistency there is some intervention at the indexing stage. Indexing can thus be achieved at a detailed level, with often many terms per document, with almost no indexing effort. The effort must be input in another way. Effective retrieval from natural language indexed data bases requires sophisticated search software. The user must become familiar with the facilities of this search software, and therefore may need more training than that which might be necessary for the retrieval of information in a data base which has been indexed with a controlled indexing language. For example, search software offers the type of facilities discussed in Chapter 17, including the ability to search on words in pre-determined fields, the ability to search on word stems and to search on words with variant spellings, and then the ability to rank the retrieved material according to its relative significance.

2. *Language factors.* In some circumstances natural language indexing may reflect more closely the terms used by the searcher. For instance, if the searcher seeks documents on 'Greenhouses' and this is not an index term in the appropriate controlled indexing language, then documents on this topic will be difficult to retrieve directly. Also, in controlled indexing language data bases, there is often an assumption that a user will be prepared to chase strings of references, or to consult a sometimes complex thesaurus. This may not always be the case. The other problems that sometimes occur in controlled language indexing which are avoided by natural language indexing arise from the limitations of the human mind. Human indexers sometimes make inappropriate judgements, misinterpret ideas, have lapses of memory or concentration, and generate omissions and inconsistencies in their indexing.

Although printed indexes tend to be either controlled or natural language, many large data bases now can be searched in both ways. Often, controlled index terms are used in identifying a relatively large set of potentially relevant references, and then string searching (or natural language searching) will be used to identify specific documents from within that set. For example, to pursue our simple example above, if Greenhouses is not a term in our controlled language, then we might search under Glasshouses instead, and retrieve a set of documents which had the controlled index language term Glasshouses assigned, and then perform a string search on the term 'Greenhouses' to discover whether this term appeared in the text of any of the documents retrieved by the original search. Thus we might identify the documents concerned with Greenhouses. This mixture of approaches is designed to yield maximum retrieval for as many users as possible by combining the different strengths of controlled and natural language indexing.

16.8.3 *Circumstances in which natural language indexing is particularly appropriate*

1. Searches that predominantly involve specific words or phrases known to have been used in the source material. Obvious examples are the unique proper nouns such as brand names and company names, although there can be problems with:

company names that may be in full or abbreviated, for example DEC, Digital Equipment
company names that may appear with or without a hyphen, for example Perkin Elmer, Perkin-Elmer
brand names that consist of common words, for example Crest, Tube Investments and, companies known by two or more names, for example GPO, British Telecom

Most of these problems can be overcome with the use of Boolean and contextual logic.

2. Slogans, quotations and catch phrases, which may or may not be indexed under a controlled indexing language, for example inter-racial adoption.

3. Geographic names can be very direct labels, but there are a number of well-known problems with geographic names. These include:

place names which recur in different states and countries, for example Berlin in New Hampshire and Germany
vague place names, for example Tyneside, the Peak District
different levels of specificity, for example West Midlands, Birmingham, Midlands.

To overcome these problems users must think of all the various names that might have been applied, and must understand something of the geography and administration of the locality concerned. A further problem is the fact that place names may appear in a trivial context. For example, a headline announcing 'Mrs Thatcher at Oxford hears of Second Falkland Crisis', does not merit retrieval under Oxford, but does require to be retrieved under Falkland.

16.8.4 *Circumstances in which natural language indexing meets with many problems*

Indexers have used controlled language indexing and authority lists of standard forms of terms and names for many years. These practices have emerged from the fact that natural language indexing is often not adequate, as discussed in Chapter 12. However, it seems worth rehearsing some of the arguments again here in this particular context and identifying specifically how these problems are negotiated in a data base using natural language indexing.

1. Semantics, including synonyms, variant word forms, autonyms and so on. The user must consider all the possibilities. In this he may be assisted by the opportunity to use truncation, alphabetical lists of terms showing word variants, and so on.

2. Homographs, and words where the meaning is context-dependent. Terms with more than one meaning, for example, intelligence, which means either an individual's analytical and reasoning abilities or information on an adversary, must be recognised by the searcher to have possible dual meaning. Contextual logic may help in the elimination of unwanted uses of the homograph.

3. Hierarchical and other relations. No cross-references can be

expected. Retrieval of documents on a search topic, but using the terms for a broader or narrower concept, relies heavily upon the searcher's ingenuity, and any additional relationships that the data base indexer might have added to link the natural language index terms.

To cite a small example, of thirty randomly chosen *New York Times* articles dealing with price increases, price indexes, increases in wages and salaries, or the (US) Federal Government's budget and spending policies, only seven items included the term 'inflation', yet all would have been pertinent to a search on the topic of inflation.

Chapter 16 Readings

1 Aitchison, J. and Gilchrist, A., *Thesaurus construction: a practical manual*, Aslib: London, 1972.
2 Aitchison, J. *et al.*, *Thesaurofacet: a thesaurus and faceted classification for engineering and related subjects*, English Electric Company: Whetstone, Leicester, 1979.
3 American National Standards Institute, *American national standard guidelines for thesaurus structure, construction and use*. ANSI Z 39.19, 1974.
4 Askew, C., *Thesaurus of consumer terms*, Consumers' Association: London, International Organization of Consumer Unions: The Hague, 1979.
5 British Standards Institution, British Standard 5723: 1979. *Guidelines for the establishment and development of monolingual thesauri*, BSI: London, 1979.
6 British Standards Institution, *BSI Root thesaurus*, 2 vols. BSI: Hemel Hempstead, 1981.
7 *Construction Industry Thesaurus*, 2nd edition, compiled by the CIT Agency at the Polytechnic of the South Bank under the direction of M.J. Roberts, Department of the Environment, Property Services Agency: London, 1976.
8 English Electric Co. Ltd., *Thesaurofacet*, English Electric Company: Whetstone, Leics, 1969.
9 Engineers' Joint Council, *Thesaurus of engineering and scientific terms*, Engineers' Joint Council: New York, 1967.
10 Foskett, D.J., 'Thesaurus' in: *Encyclopaedia of Library and Information Science*, vol 30, Marcel Dekker: New York, 1981.
11 Gilbert, V., 'A list of thesauri and subject headings held in the Aslib library', *Aslib Proceedings*, 31(6), 1979, 264–274.
12 Gilchrist, A., *The thesaurus in retrieval*, Aslib: London, 1971.
13 Haykin, D.J., *Subject headings: a practical guide*, Government Printing Office: Washington, DC, 1951.

14 *INSPEC thesaurus 1983*, Institution of Electricial Engineers: London, 1983.

15 *International Road Research Documentation Thesaurus* (IRRD). OECD: Paris, 1972.

16 International Standards Organisation, International Standard 2788. *Guidelines for the establishment and development of monolingual thesauri, ISO:* Geneva, 1974.

17 Lancaster, F.W., *Vocabulary control for information retrieval*, Information Resources Press: Washington, DC, 1972.

18 Library of Congress, Subject Cataloguing Division, *Library of Congress subject headings*, 9th edition, Library of Congress: Washington, DC, 1980. (With quarterly supplements accumulated annually. Also available in microform with the entire list cumulated quarterly.)

19 MacCafferty, M., *Thesauri and thesaurus construction*, Aslib: London, 1977. (Aslib bibliography no 7)

20 *Medical Subject Headings (MeSH)*, National Library of Medicine: Bethesda, MD, Annual update.

21 *Sears' List of Subject Headings*, 12th edition, editor B.M. Westby, H.W. Wilson: New York, 1982.

22 Soergel, D, *Indexing language and thesaurus construction and maintenance*, Melville Publishing Co.: Los Angeles, 1974.

23 *Subject headings for engineering*, Engineering Index Inc.: New York, 1972.

24 Swatridge, C., *A list of subject headings for school and other libraries*, School Library Association: London, 1981.

25 *Thesaurus of ERIC descriptors*, 7th edition, Macmillan Information: New York, 1977.

26 *Thesaurus of metallurgical terms*, 5th edition, American Society for Metals: Ohio Metals Society, London, 1981.

27 Townley, H.M. and Gee, R.D., *Thesaurus-making: grow your own wordstock*, Deutsch: London, 1980.

28 Viet, J., *Macrothesaurus for information processing in the field of economic and social development*, OECD: Paris, 1978.

17.1 Introduction

The following two definitions of an indexing system are offered:

1. An indexing system is the means whereby an indexing language can be applied to make an index.
2. An indexing system is a set of prescribed procedures for organising the contents of records of knowledge or documents for the purposes of retrieval and dissemination.

Both definitions have common roots, but their perspectives differ somewhat, the second definition being slightly broader in scope.

The creation of a series of entries for inclusion in a catalogue or printed index is an indexing process which must involve some system, which we might call an indexing system. Nevertheless, this situation does not appropriately demonstrate what is normally conceived to be the realm of indexing systems. Most of the work on indexing systems stems from the need to devise index headings or search keys in such a way that it is possible to retrieve compound or multi-concept subjects. Although elementary one-concept subjects are also represented in indexes constructed according to these methods, the problems that such subjects present are limited, and so much of this chapter is concerned with the specification or retrieval of multi-concept subjects.

Although compound subjects have been introduced in Chapters 12 and 15, it is useful to review the nature of such subjects with the aid of an example. Take the subject:

Torsion in the reinforced concrete in service cores in tall buildings.

If we were to seek to index or retrieve documents on this subject, we could start by recognising that this subject contains four separate elementary or unit concepts:

torsion, reinforced concrete, service cores, tall buildings.

In indexing or retrieving such a subject it is not only necessary to recognise the presence of the various unit concepts, but it is also necessary to cater for each concept. One user might look under torsion, another under reinforced concrete, and yet another under tall buildings, each user possibly seeking the document for different purposes. It is in order to tackle this type of problem that indexing systems have been evolved.

In the interests of some polarisation for effective analysis, indexing systems can be divided into two basic groups: pre-co-ordinate and post-co-ordinate. Not every index necessarily exhibits all the features of either of these types of indexing systems, and indeed, some will possess elements of both types of systems. Nevertheless, this basic divide remains a useful distinction between two major categories of indexing systems. A brief introduction to the specific kinds of indexing systems will be given here, and more details will be developed in subsequent sections.

Pre-co-ordinate indexing systems

Pre-co-ordinate indexing is conventional indexing of the type commonly found in printed indexes, where a document is represented in the index by a heading or headings consisting of a chain of terms. The leading term determines the position of the entry, and the qualifying terms are subordinate to it. Thus for the previously cited example a heading of the form:

Buildings, Tall: Service cores; Concrete, Reinforced: Torsion

might be established. A second example: The use of computers in the cutting of shoes might be shown by a heading such as:

Shoes: Manufactures: Computers: Cutting

Because the co-ordination of index terms in the index description is decided before any particular request is made, the index is termed a pre-co-ordinate index. Note that the headings in such an index are relatively specific compared, for example, with one-concept headings such as Shoes or Cutting.

Pre-co-ordinate indexes are particularly prevalent as printed indexes. Often, the computer is used to aid in the processing of such indexes, and sometimes computer processing is responsible for the creation of multiple entries from one string of index terms. Printed indexes which incorporate the principles of pre-co-ordinate indexing to varying extents are to be found in abstracting and indexing journals, national bibliographies, indexes to journals, and to some extent, in subject indexes to library catalogues. Pre-co-ordinate headings do occasionally emerge in the assigned index terms in computer data bases.

Two issues recur in all pre-co-ordinate indexes. The first issue concerns the consistent description of subjects. With many concept headings consistency must be instilled both into the terms used to describe the individual concepts that comprise the multiple concept heading and also into the order in which those individual concept terms are cited or listed. Before a consistent citation order can be achieved, some principles must be established and agreed concerning the acceptable citation order. At the two extremes, the order may simply be decided for each topic as and when it arises, and followed thereafter, or, some theoretical basis or rules for the ordering of terms or concepts may be derived. A theoretical basis to citation order should produce a more highly structured system whose objective is to achieve consistent citation orders between similar, yet distinct subjects. The description of one subject by two different headings with different terms and citation orders is less likely to be overlooked if some rationale determines the order that should be adopted. However, many indexing systems have evolved over the last century, and have their roots in a time when detailed specification of subjects was unnecessary. Indexes based on traditional subject headings lists tend to use very little structuring of citation order. Citation orders need not be comparable between subjects, nor is there any comprehensive set of principles that determines the citation order that is selected. Yet even these indexes recognise some rules concerning the structure of headings.

The second issue that all indexers must consider is the need to provide access for those users who approach the subject under consideration for indexing from one of the 'secondary' concepts. Only one term can appear in the primary position in the prescribed citation order. The preferred citation order should be that order which is believed to match the approach of many users who can be expected to retrieve information on the topic. No citation order, no matter how well founded, will prove suitable for every searcher. References or added entries must supplement the first or main entry and cater for access from other angles. At least one reference or added entry is usually deemed to be necessary from each of the 'secondary' concepts in the preferred order. In the same way that citation orders may have more or less theoretical foundations, equally reference generation may follow a pre-determined pattern or the reference or added entries to be included may be designed on an *ad hoc* basis. Usually there is some pattern to the generation of additional references in order to keep the number of auxiliary references to an acceptable level. Also, if a simple algorithm for the generation of index entries can be stated then additional entries and references can be printed by computer, using the primary index string as input data.

Both the above issues arise because pre-co-ordinate systems are fundamentally one-place systems. One-place systems are convenient under circumstances where it is desirable to have only one main entry for each document, as in many bibliographies and catalogues. Such systems may also have advantages for the searcher. A number of searches can be conducted simultaneously, by tracing entries under similar headings. Also search strategy can be modified relatively easily, where only refinements or slight modifications in index terms are appropriate.

Post-co-ordinate indexing systems

Post-co-ordinate indexing systems (sometimes known as co-ordinate indexing systems) start from the same identification of multi-concept subjects and their component unit concepts as pre-co-ordinate indexing systems. However, once the multi-concept subject has been analysed into its component concepts the two systems diverge. The entries made in a post-co-ordinate index are made under terms which represent the unit or elementary concepts. No attempt is made to establish index headings or search keys which reflect all the component elementary concepts at any one time. Thus a post-co-ordinate index for the examples considered previously might have entries under the following headings:

Buildings, Tall and	Shoes
Service cores	Manufacturers
Concrete, Reinforced	Computers
Torsion	Cutting.

Thus for each of these two examples there will be four entries under relatively broad headings. This approach eliminates, at one blow, both the problems which exercise the designer of a pre-co-ordinate index, that is citation order and reference structure. However, new problems are introduced. If the collection being indexed is the same collection as that for which a pre-co-ordinate index might be considered as the other alternative, then it is likely that, with time, some of these relatively broad headings which avoid co-ordination will have a large number of entries associated with them. Thus, in order to search the index, the searcher will seek some type of assistance in sorting through these large numbers of entries which are likely to be found under various headings. Therefore, co-ordination, in order to specify the search topic more closely, will be sought at the search stage. Co-ordination is effected after a request for a search has been initiated, and hence, these systems are referred to as post-co-ordinate. Search aids are available in the form of logical statements which combine terms in order to be able to trace subjects according to a more specific document profile.

In general, then, a post-co-ordinate index is simpler to produce than a pre-co-ordinate index, because it shifts the responsibility for co-ordination of index terms to the searcher. Post-co-ordinate systems, which rely upon either controlled indexing languages (particularly those which comprise mainly one-concept terms) and/or natural language indexing are common in online searching of computer data bases, and are evident in SDI profiles and other applications which involve retrieving a set of documents from a more comprehensive computer data base.

The indexing language used in either a post-co-ordinate or a pre-co-ordinate indexing system might be very similar. There is no reason why, for example, the terms representing unit concepts in each system should not be the same, and might not be drawn from the same thesaurus listing.

17.2 Pre-co-ordinate indexing systems

17.2.1 *Citation orders*

Very early in the history of alphabetical subject headings it was recognised that headings should be formulated in accordance with some principles. The forerunner of many recent ideas, and the force behind some of the remaining traditional systems was Charles Ammi Cutter.

1. *Cutter's Rules for a Dictionary Catalogue* were published in 1876, and form one of the earlier codifications of the problems and some solutions concerning the alphabetical subject approach. The issue of citation orders for composite subjects is not considered systematically and Cutter's recommendations serve more to illustrate problems than to demonstrate solutions. Cutter selected headings on the basis that headings in a catalogue should be those terms that are in general usage, and are accepted by educated people. In addition to problems with new subjects which lacked 'accepted' or established names, this guiding principle engendered inconsistency in the form of headings. Equally, Cutter's devotion to natural language posed problems with multi-word terms. Sometimes the natural language ordering of words in a term would cause filing of the term under the first and possibly less significant term. To avoid unhelpful sequences, Cutter argued that when it could be established that the second term was definitely more significant then inversion of headings was acceptable. This was all very tidy, but who was to judge significance?

Despite the inconsistencies inherent in Cutter's fundamental premises, he did give some guidance on citation order under certain specialised conditions. For example, he believed that where subject and place are both elements of a topic, subject should precede place in scientific and related areas, but that place should take precedence in areas such as history, government and commerce. For the humanities, for example literature and art, the adjectival form of the country or language is recommended, for example, German Poetry.

Cutter's practices and policies were a starting point and remain important today because they are embodied in the *Library of Congress List of Subject Headings* and Sears' *List of Subject Headings*. Both of these lists are widely used in dictionary catalogues in the United States. These lists have evolved through several editions, with no radical modification to meet modern problems. Composite subjects were less prevalent in Cutter's day and principles in subject heading formulation were less vital. The information that most modern indexes must organise emerges in greater quantities and concerns much more complex subjects than Cutter could have anticipated. The sheer bulk of the headings and the complexity of reference structures in a dictionary catalogue based on the Library of Congress Subject Headings is sufficient to confirm that a more systematic approach might prove fruitful.

2. *Kaiser's Systematic Indexing* embodied the first consistent approach to the problems of significance order. The treatise arose from Kaiser's work in indexing information relating to business and industry. Kaiser's stepping-off point was the observation that many composite subjects can be analysed into a combination of a concrete and a process. He suggested that if subjects with these two components were cited in the order Concrete, then Process, that the headings thus produced would usually coincide with natural language usage to some extent. Thus a document on the 'Servicing of ships' may be indexed under: 'Ships; Servicing'. Where place is one of the concepts present in a subject Kaiser makes double entry, once under the Concrete and once under Place. Thus a document on 'Shipbuilding in Japan' would be entered under each of the two headings: Shipbuilding – Japan and Japan – Shipbuilding. One problem on which Kaiser alighted was that many processes can be further analysed into a concrete and a process for example, 'Steelmaking' can become 'Steel-Production'. This feature hinders consistency because some subjects have potential for being analysed in different ways. Kaiser also investigated the effect of grouping subheadings of a subject. Instead of straight alphabetical arrangement, subheadings are grouped according to their subject. For example, all subheadings representing processes may be grouped and precede those referring to places. This may help in subject organisation, but one of the main advantages of an alphabetical sequence, its self-evident order, is sacrificed in the process.

3. *Coates and British Technology Index* E J Coates made one of the most significant contributions to the formulation of subject headings. His ideas are embodied in the then *British Technology Index* and now *Current Technology Index*, of which he was the editor for many years. Coates started his study of citation order by noting Kaiser's theories of Concrete-Process and reaffirmed this aspect of Kaiser's work. Coates went on to evolve rules to cater for the citation orders appropriate to a wide range of composite subjects. Kaiser's Concrete-Process was relabelled Thing – Action. Coates believed that in order to conceptualise an action it is necessary to visualise the thing on which the action is being performed. This principle was used to establish an extended citation order:

According to Coates, this results in headings whose first component is the most likely to come into the mind of the searcher. The following headings show the citation order advanced by Coates:

1. Steel, Low alloy: Welding, Electron beam
2. Steel: Production: Coking: Coal: Blending: Plant
3. Sugar Cane: Harvesters
4. Technical Colleges: Piles; Concrete, Bored: Testing: Ultrasonics
5. Television: Transmission: Computers

Note that headings when read backwards with appropriate prepositions inserted make a title-like phrase describing the subject. Thus, often index headings derive easily from natural language order by straight inversion and the omission of prepositions.

4. *Articulated subject indexes* are based on title-like phrases that have some conventions concerning citation order, but these conventions do not require any theoretical structure which recognises concept categories.

The title-like phrase combines concepts in the order in which they would be listed in a sentence or phrase. For example, an indexing string for an articulated subject index might take the form:

<Soil-resistant <Finishing>> of <Carpets> and <Wall-Coverings>

where the brackets are used to designate terms that are to appear as index headings. The indexer then expresses the subject using a stylised English sentence and the computer generates a series of entries with a complete subject statement at every entry point. The computer is programmed to recognise cues such as prepositions and punctuation, and thus generates a series of entries each comprising an entry term and a qualifying phrase.

17.2.2 *Reference structure*

In order to permit the index user to approach a composite heading via one of the concepts that does not take the first position in the citation order it is necessary to consider how access may be provided to secondary concepts. Remember that it is also possible that a user may approach the index with a synonym or related term to one of those used to describe concepts in the headings. Links between related terms and synonymous terms must also be a feature of the index. But, for now, we will concentrate on access to the secondary concepts in the primary citation order. Each type of pre-co-ordinate indexing system must incorporate some rules for the generation of references or added entries. Many systems rely upon moving the index terms in the heading through the various positions in the heading. Particularly if the computer is to be responsible for creating a series of headings from one index string, it is desirable that there be some algorithm for the generation of references and added entries. Also, economy dictates that every possible entry cannot be printed. Consider a complex heading with six individual concepts. Obviously, for each term to appear in the lead position, at least six entries are necessary. If it is intended that each term should occupy each position in a heading, the largest number of possible distinct headings or arrangements of the index terms is 720. Obviously this is far too many references or added entries. Some means must be found of selecting from the 720 possible entries those entries which are the most helpful. Several different solutions to this problem have been tried.

Cutter recommended a network of references and recognised that a systematic approach to reference structure was necessary in order to produce an effective index. However, in the interests of economy, Cutter restricted links to downward references leading from broader to narrower subject, and largely ignored upwards and sideways links. This practice is continued in dictionary catalogues but is of limited success and makes little contribution to the structure of references that are necessary to cater for a composite subject.

Chain indexing creates a number of index entries, as shown in the next section. The second and subsequent entries cater for the hidden terms in the first entry. Each heading becomes at the same time simpler and less specific. *British Technology Index* also bases its reference structure on chain procedure. The first reference comprises all the components in the heading, but in inverted order. The second reference retains the order of the first (that is, inverted), but the first element of the preferred citation order is removed. Other references follow, with the progressive removal of terms. If A, B, C and D are index terms chain procedure creates the following four entries:

A B C D
B C D
C D
D

or the following entries for a document on 'the law concerning Sunday performances in the theatre in France':

Law: Sunday performances: Theatre: France
Sunday performances: Theatre: France
Theatre: France
France

The reference structure used in PRECIS indexing will be developed in 17.2.4. Known as shunting, this procedure would create the following entries with A, B, C and D as index terms:

1. A
     B C D
2. B A
     C D
3. C B A
     D
4. D C B A

which, using the same example as above, would cause entries such as:

1. Law
     Sunday performances   Theatre   France
2. Sunday performances   Law
     Theatre   France
3. Theatre   Sunday performances   Law
     France
4. France   Theatre   Sunday performances   Law

Other approaches to the movement of the components of index headings in order to generate additional entries are also possible. Three techniques are: cycled or cyclic indexing, rotated indexing and SLIC indexing. Cycled indexing involves the movement of the first lead term to the last position in the subsequent entry. This process is repeated until each concept has occupied the lead position. Rotated indexing involves each element in turn becoming the heading under which an entry is filed, but no change in citation order takes place. SLIC indexing, or Selective Listing in Combination involves the combination of elements, but in one direction only. These techniques are demonstrated below:

Cyclic indexing

A	B	C	D	Law: Sunday performances: Theatre: France
B	C	D	A	Sunday performances: Theatre: France: Law
C	D	A	B	Theatre: France: Law: Sunday performances
D	A	B	C	France: Law: Sunday Performances: Theatre

Rotated indexing

A	B	C	D	Law: Sunday performances: Theatre: France
A	*B*	C	D	Law: Sunday performances: Theatre: France
A	B	*C*	D	Law: Sunday performances: Theatre: France
A	B	C	*D*	Law: Sunday performances: Theatre: France

SLIC indexing

A	B	C	D	Law: Sunday performances: Theatre: France
A	C	D		Law: Theatre: France
A	D			Law: France
B	C	D		Sunday performances: Theatre: France
C	D			Theatre: France
D				France

17.2.3 *Chain Indexing*

Chain indexing is an indexing system which was devised in order to generate subject indexes to a classified sequence in a catalogue or on shelves, or to a classification scheme. Thus chain indexing has been widely used in generating subject indexes to classified catalogues, and similar systems are used to produce the relative indexes which form part of the published editions of many classification schemes. In principle, chain indexing is a manual means of generating index entries although some aspects of the system may be seen in computer-generated printed indexes, such as *Current Technology Index*, and it is possible to use a computer to produce a subject index to a classified sequence using the basic structure of chain indexing.

A subject index to a classified sequence in a catalogue, index or bibliography has essentially the same functions as the subject index to the published schedules of a classification scheme. These are to:

translate a natural language term into a class number
collocate distributed relatives

These functions have already been considered in 13.4 when discussing relative indexes to classification schemes. Chain indexing is closely connected with relative indexes. Index entries of the form, for example:

Nervous system:Surgery 617.48

are generated. Plainly such an entry permits the location of an appropriate classification number. 'Nervous system' is the entry term under which the user would search. 'Surgery' helps to distinguish between the type of documents that have been classified at 617.48 from those classified at other numbers related to the Nervous system. In this sense it provides a context for the entry term.

17.2.3.1 *Chain indexing procedure*.

Chain indexing is a procedure which is supposed to lead to the inclusion of entries in an alphabetical index for every helpful entry point, without uneconomical use of index entries. In that it suggests a method for establishing the citation order of subjects within a heading for an index entry chain indexing is an indexing system. As a system in application, chain indexing relies upon the existence of and the structure of subjects in a classification scheme. With a fully faceted classification scheme (see 13.2.4) chain indexing is purely mechanical, and straight-forward. In less well structure schemes, the application of chain indexing is more of an art.

The steps in producing index entries according to chain indexing are:

1. Assign the appropriate class number from the schedules of the classification scheme in use to the document to be indexed. Indexing is dependent upon the specific classification scheme in use.

2. Examine the hierarchical or other subject structure of the area of the schedules from which a class number has been drawn. Specifically, locate the appropriate class number and note the more general topics under which it has been placed.

3. Construct the first index entry by taking a natural language description of the most specific concept in 'the chain', as revealed in step 2 above, and qualify this term with terms which represent other concepts in the chain. These qualifying terms should be included in the order that they appear in the chain, moving from the specific to the more general subjects. Only such qualifying terms as are necessary to give the context of the entry term within the classification scheme need be included.

4. Make the second entry by choosing a term to represent the second most specific concept in the 'chain' and then qualify this term with more general concept terms, in the same way as in the first index entry.

5. Construct the remainder of the index entries in a manner consistent with the previous index entries, as above.

Example: Suppose that we have a document to index which is an item of Classical Period German Poetry.

1. First the class number is assigned. In DC19 this would be 831.6
2. The hierarchical chain may be recorded, thus:

8   Literature
  3   German
    1   Poetry
    .6   Classical Period.

In this case, since DC has largely expressive notation each notational digit stands for an additional step in the relationship structure.

3. The first index entry is under the most specific concept 'Classical Period', thus:

Classical Period: Poetry: German: Literature   831.6

4. The second index entry, under the next more general subject is:

Poetry: German: Literature   831

5. The remaining index entries are:

German: Literature	830
Literature	800.

17.2.3.2 *Some points to note.*

1. Chain indexing is a simple mechanical routine for generating a limited number of index entries for a subject.

2. Chain indexing is closely tied to the structure (but not necessarily the terminology) of the classification scheme. A poorly structured scheme requires the exercise of a good deal of initiative on the part of the indexer in order to overcome or avoid the poor structure.

3. The procedure generates a number of index entries for each subject, but only one of these entries is specific. The other index entries are more general. This means:

(a) a searcher finding a more general entry is expected to scan the subdivisions of the number to which he has been directed. This may be an unrealistic expectation.

(b) economies are made in the total number of index entries required for a collection of documents because frequently many of the more general index entries will apply to more than one specific subject. Literature 800, for example, will be included in the entries for every class number in the Literature schedules or 800s. Once this entry has been included in the index it will not be necessary to add it again.

4. The effect of the procedure is to invert the structure of the classification scheme. Thus, subjects which are divided by the classification scheme will be drawn together by the index. For example, under Poetry one might find:

Poetry: German Literature	831
Poetry: Latin Literature	871
Poetry: Russian Literature	891.71

Thus various types of poetry are shown in juxtaposition in the index despite having widely differing class numbers.

17.2.3.3 *Some problems in using chain indexing with the DC.* Chain indexing is intended for use with a fully faceted classification with a sound basic structure. Expressive notation also makes indexing more straight-forward. Despite the example just employed to demonstrate the procedure, it is plain that DC does not boast a fully faceted structure nor a completely expressive notation. In order to overcome some of the inherent weaknesses of the structure of DC it is important to chain index with reference to the essential relationships between subjects, and not to rely too heavily upon the schedules for guidance. The problems that might be encountered in using chain indexing with DC can be grouped into three categories:

1. Problems arising from the fact that chain indexing gives guidelines as to index entry structures only, and of itself gives no help with vocabulary control (that is, the words to use in the index entries are not controlled unless a separate list of index terms is used in conjunction with chain indexing).

2. Problems arising from weak or outmoded structuring of subjects in the schedules of DC.

3. Problems arising from the breakdown of the expressiveness of the notation of DC, or the introduction of some special notational device which impairs expressiveness. Not all digits in the notation have a subject concept associated with them, and some concepts do not have their own specific digit.

17.2.4 PRECIS indexing

The PRECIS indexing system (Preserved Context Indexing System) is a set of procedures for producing index entries which is important for both its practical and theoretical contributions to the field of indexing. PRECIS indexing takes a very systematic approach to citation order, and demonstrates the effective application of computers in the production of printed indexes. PRECIS indexing is also important in that it is the method used to produce the subject indexes to the British National Bibliography and the British Education Index, and various other indexes to catalogues and library materials.

In keeping with its acronym, PRECIS is an alphabetical subject indexing system that both present a 'precis' of the subject content of a document at each entry point in the printed index, and also displays index terms in context. The index user can enter the index via any of the concepts present in the complex subject, and locate at that entry point the full description of the subject. Each index entry has both a lead term and terms conveying the context, which are displayed in such a way that the entry is as explicit as possible. However, in any given application, there must also be a controlled vocabulary to which the PRECIS routines can be applied. Thus PRECIS is an indexing system, which like any such system must be supported by an indexing language. The small extract from the index to BNB in Figure 2.1 demonstrates some of the features of index entries generated according to PRECIS indexing, namely

1. All entries contain all of the index terms used in the description of the topic.

2. Access is possible via each and any of the index terms.

3. All terms in the line following the lead term appear in an order that ensures that specific terms are listed first, followed by more general terms.

4. The subject description is clearly stated in each entry.

5. Index entries usually occupy two lines.

Figure 17.1 PRECIS role operators

Role operators

[handwritten: most important]

Main line operators

Environment of observed system	0	Location
Observed system (Core operators) *[handwritten: must have one]*	1	Key system: object of transitive action; agent of intransitive action
	2	Action/Effect
	3	Agent of transitive action; Aspects; Factors

A _____

Data relating to observer	4	Viewpoint-as-form *[handwritten: perspective eg physiological]*
Selected instance	5	Sample population/Study region
Presentation of data	6	Target/Form *[handwritten: eg students/eg dictionary Research/Periodical]*

Interposed operators *[handwritten: p Hand figures / p Table / p tall Characteristic of the figures]*

Dependent elements *[handwritten: skilled workers / say women]*	p	Part/Property
	q	Member of quasi-generic group
	r	Aggregate *[handwritten: r Trade Union]*
Concept interlinks *[handwritten: 2 ideas compared]*	s	Role definer *[handwritten: Role of group of people in context]*
	t	Author attributed association *[handwritten: Islam + Jewism]*
Co-ordinate concepts	g	Co-ordinate concept *[handwritten: Animals (dogs) → (cats)]*

B _____

[handwritten: Phrases]

Differencing operators (prefixed by $) *[handwritten: ✳]*	h	Non-lead direct difference
	i	Lead direct difference
	j	Salient difference
	k	Non-lead indirect difference
	m	Lead indirect difference
	n	Non-lead parenthetical difference
	o	Lead parenthetical difference
	d	Date as a difference

[handwritten: Students add acl Evaluation $v (b) $w (a) Teacher]

[handwritten: Help situate terms]

Connectives

(Components of linking phrases; prefixed by $)	v	Downward reading component
	w	Upward reading component

C _____

Theme interlink *[handwritten: two different themes]*	x	First element in co-ordinate theme
	y	Subsequent element in co-ordinate theme
	z	Element of common theme

From: Austin, D. **PRECIS: a manual of concept analysis and subject indexing.** London: Council of the British National Bibliography, 1974.

All index entries and references in a PRECIS index derive from index strings, one string for each multi-concept subject indexed. This string codifies syntactic relationships, establishes a citation order, and triggers the generation of references for semantic relationships. The role of the string in establishing a citation order for the component parts of each index entry is probably the most important feature of PRECIS indexing. Citation order must be related to the syntactic relationships that are inherent in the subject to be indexed. Syntactic relations, that is, those relationships that arise from the syntax, are document-dependent, and need not be constant. For example, both the following two topics are composed of the same component concepts, but the relationships between the concepts are different:

'The indexing of computer software'
'The use of computer software in indexing'

It is the distinct syntactical relationships in these subjects which are responsible for their separate identity as subjects. PRECIS relies upon citation order (with some support from prepositions and so on) to record syntactical relationships, and the role operators which are a central feature of the system are assigned to concepts in such a way that this is achieved. Role operators are listed in Figure 17.1.

17.2.4.1 *Steps in PRECIS indexing*

1. Identify the elements or concepts of the compound subject that are to be reflected in the index entries. A concept is defined to be a topic matching a PRECIS operator (see below) and may on occasions be a composite subject.
2. Express the concepts to be indexed in terms acceptable in the vocabulary to be used in the index. The vocabulary used in conjunction with PRECIS by the British National Bibliography is split into two sections, one part for Entities (or things) and the other for Attributes (properties of things, for example colour, weight; activities of things, for example flow, machining; and properties of activities, for example, slow, turbulent). The terms present in these vocabularies are hierarchically arranged in order to indicate any fundamental generic relationships, and to suggest references that might be made as links between terms.
3. Assign a role operator to each term identified in 2 above. Role operators reflect the role that each concept plays in the context of this particular subject. A role operator may designate a term, for example as a location, or as a statement of viewpoint. Each operator has a filing value which has been designated in order to ensure that terms appear in the index string in an order that will produce a meaningful set of index entries. The order thus determined embodies 'context dependency'; each term in the string sets each successive term in context.

4. Arrange the index terms in an order, in accordance with the filing values of the role operators that the terms have been allowed. The end product of this stage will be an index string which encompasses both terms and operators.

5. Speculate as to the index entries that the index string will cause to be generated, and make any necessary adjustments to indexing. In particular note, for example by ticking them, those terms that merit a turn in the lead position, and those that do not.

6. Insert computer instruction codes in the positions of the operators in the string. These instruction codes convert the role operators into machine-readable manipulation codes, and show which terms are to be used as entry terms. The order of terms in the string is retained. This stage marks the end of the indexer's task. The computer has now been provided with the wherewithal to complete the generation of index entries.

7. The computer takes the index string with its machine-readable manipulation codes and creates a series of entries by rotating the component terms with which it has been provided. Each entry has three fundamental positions:

LEAD   Qualifier
Display

This layout gives the lead term, in the context of wider terms on the same line (the Qualifier) and narrower terms (the Display) on the second line. The first entry takes the first component of the string as the index term, and leaves the remainder of the string in the Display position. In successive index entries the previous lead term is shunted into the Qualifier position, and the first term in the Display moves into the lead position. This procedure will generate entries according to the standard pattern. Sometimes, in the interests of comprehension or helpfulness, modifications to the standard pattern are desirable.

The computer will also examine individual terms in the string in order to assess whether any references are necessary in order to show semantic relationships between terms and other related terms. These relationships will be indicated automatically by the printing of 'see' and 'see also' references for terms which the computer has encountered previously, and for which instructions for the generation of 'see' and 'see also' references already exist in its store. Obviously for new terms instructions must be given to the computer concerning the generation of 'see' and 'see also' references.

17.2.4.2 *An example.* Each of the above steps will now be applied to a specific example. The topic for which index entries are to be generated is:

'The Measurement of the diameter of bearings in a dynamo'.

The first two steps require the recognition of the individual concepts present in the topic, and their expression in the terms available in the controlled vocabulary. These terms might be:

Dynamos
Bearings
Diameter
Measurement

The third step involves the assignment of role operators. First, an action term is located. Here 'Measurement' is an action term, and so, the operator for an action term is assigned to 'Measurement', namely

(2) Measurement

The object of the action is next identified, and coded (1). Hence

(1) Dynamos

'Bearings' are part of the Key system 'Dynamos', and thus may be denoted by (p), thus

(p) Bearings

and likewise

(p) Diameter

Next, the organisation of terms according to the filing value of their operators gives an indexing string:

(1) Dynamos
(p) Bearings
(p) Diameter
(2) Measurement

Step 5 involves the designation of lead terms. If all terms merit a lead term, except 'Measurement', then

(1) Dynamos ✓

(p) Bearings ✓

(p) Diameter ✓
(2) Measurement

Once the computer instruction codes have been inserted in step 6, the computer will generate the following index entries:

1. Dynamos
   Bearings. Diameter. Measurement
2. Bearings. Dynamos
   Diameter. Measurement
3. Diameter. Bearings. Dynamos
   Measurement

and other references, such as:

Size see Diameter
Dimensions see also Diameter
Ball bearings see Bearings
Lubrication see also Bearings

17.3 Post-co-ordinate indexing systems

17.3.1 *Principles*

Post-co-ordinate indexes are most common as indexes to computer data bases today, but earlier indexes were card-based. Many of the principles are common whether the index is stored on cards or in a computer. In a post-co-ordinate index each document is first assigned some type of accession or serial number, and is then analysed, and its subject represented by a number of index terms, perhaps as many as ten or twenty. The accession number or an address pertaining to a given document is then entered under each of these index terms. The searcher compares entries under several index terms in order to retrieve document numbers for documents that cover the specific subjects represented by a combination of index terms. As already indicated, the essential feature of a post-co-ordinate index is that index terms which represent concepts are co-ordinated at the search stage, that is, a number of headings are searched in such a way that document numbers assigned to more than one term in the combination can be selected. A post-co-ordinate index depends upon specialised equipment and storage devices.

All post-co-ordinate indexing systems have the following three features which may make their use without any degree of co-ordination very tedious:

1. None of the entries in the system are specific. There are a relatively large number of documents under each heading, and if the searcher approaches the index as a conventional index he is liable to become involved in extensive scanning of the many entries under each heading in order to discriminate between relevant and less relevant documents.

2. There is usually a larger number of entries in a post-co-ordinate indexing system than in an index based upon pre-co-ordinate indexing principles, although the number of entries in a pre-co-ordinate system will depend upon the incidence of references and multiple entries.

3. The number of different headings in the index is relatively small, because, as in classification, a synthetic scheme needs fewer categories or headings than an equivalent enumerative scheme.

Post-co-ordinate indexing systems, whether manual or computerised, can be grouped into two main categories: those systems or indexes based on 'item records' and those using 'term records' as their fundamental unit. An *'item record file'* is a file in which records are serially ordered by document identifier or number; each entry or record stores the total information relating to the document that is available in the system, including reference and index terms. A *'term record file'*, conversely, is a file that is ordered by index terms, with each entry an index term and the document representations 'listed' in association with that term.

Item record indexes, whatever their physical format, share certain advantages and disadvantages. The advantages can be summarised as follows:

1. Storage medium and associated equipment (for example, sorting and punching devices, cards, magnetic tape) tends to be cheaper than the term record index equivalent.

2. A fair amount of detail can be stored as part of each record. Computer magnetic tapes may store, if desired, full documents, and even marginal storage cards normally have capacity for storing citations and abstracts.

3. Several index approaches can be stored as part of one record. For example, subject, trade name, corporate body and patent number indexes may all feature upon one magnetic tape or deck of cards.

4. Items can be added almost *ad infinitum*. The only limitation on capacity stems from the excessive search time associated with very large databases.

The main inconveniences of item record indexes arise from the necessity of searching the entire file. Obviously the larger the file, in general, the longer the search time. Searching can be unacceptably slow if the file is large. Thus, computer-held item record files are most suitable for applications like Selective Dissemination of Information (SDI) systems, where files are relatively compact as they include only references to the current literature, or where interactive retrieval is not regarded as essential.

In the same way, files of item record cards can be difficult to manage if the file size exceeds, say, 2000 cards. In situations where item record indexes are not appropriate, such as online access to computer data bases, inverted files must be established.

17.3.2 Card-based systems

Marginal storage cards or edge notch cards are probably the commonest form of non-computerised item record index. As used in an index each card acts as a surrogate for one document, and the index terms for that document are encoded around the edge of the card. Edge notch cards have a series of holes around their perimeter, and the piece of card between the hole and the edge of the card may be removed, using a punch, to form a notch. The pattern of notches and holes along the edge of a card stores the index terms assigned to the document for which the card is acting as surrogate. Searching is performed by inserting a needle through the whole pack of cards at the position of the hole(s) which represent the terms to be searched. The notched cards, representing relevant documents, will drop off the needle and fall from the bulk of the pack. The term 'false drops' which is encountered in other aspects of information retrieval can trace its pedigree to edge notch cards. False drops are cards which drop from the needle when the documents that the cards represent are not truly relevant to the topic of a search. To take an example of needling the pack, suppose that in an index covering 'Education' it is necessary to identify all of the documents indexed under the term 'Curricula'. If 'Curricula' is a term in the indexing language used in the index this might be coded and represented by a hole numbered '7' as in Figure 17.2. When a needle is inserted through the '7' position all cards in the pack with the hole '7' notched out will drop from the needle. Thus, all cards corresponding to documents covering 'Curricula' are withdrawn from the pack. The sequential sorting of the pack and subpacks permits searching to proceed on combinations of terms.

The coding used in the example discussed above is known as single row direct coding. Edge notch cards are often ordered in a size tailored to the demands of the index, and can be purchased with any coding that the index designer specifies. Hence there is a vast range of different sizes and codings of marginal storage cards. Single row direct coding restricts the numbering of coding positions and thus the number of admissible index terms to the number of holes that can be fitted around the edge of a card. So, even with relatively large and expensive cards, only two or three hundred coding positions are possible, and with smaller cards, many fewer holes are possible. Hence, it is often thought desirable to extend the capacity of the index beyond that available with direct single row coding, by resorting to double row coding, and combination coding, in a variety of different patterns. Some of these coding patterns appear extremely complex, but their purpose is merely to expand the capacity of an edge notch card. Edge notch cards can be used in term record indexes, with one card per term, and coding representing document numbers.

Figure 17.2 An edge on an edge notch card showing single row direct coding

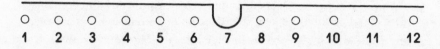

Aperture cards are a special form of marginal storage card which permits the entire document to be stored in the centre of the card. A microform insert which contains the full text of the document being indexed is attached to the centre of the card. An index using aperture cards is more than an index, it is a complete document collection, and cards must be withdrawn in order to read documents. The reader is left to debate the relative merits of such a format – obviously its applications are limited. Aperture cards are a useful form for storing technical drawings and have been used in connection with patents. Documents may be retrieved by means of the coding around the edge of the card, and apart from the microfiche insert are similar to other marginal storage cards.

Dual dictionaries are not card-based, but are printed computer produced post-co-ordinate indexes. Usually two identical lists are printed on continuous computer stationery. In each list index terms are arranged alphabetically, and document numbers are listed under each index term. Numbers may be grouped in columns according to their terminal digit. Searches are executed by comparing the numbers entered under two or more index terms. A dual dictionary, as distinct from card-based indexes, can be produced in multiple copies. The format, however, shares many of the limitations of cards. Searching can be tedious and prone to error, and relevance judgements can only be made by reference to a second list or index. This particular problem can at least be partially remedied by giving titles in addition to document numbers.

Optical coincidence cards are one of the more popular physical formats for a post-co-ordinate index. Such cards, alternatively known as Peek-a-boo or Batten cards are available in various sizes and styles. They all have space at the top for a keyword and the index is arranged in alphabetical order by keyword. Each card has a grid covering most of the body of the card which provides for the coding of document numbers. When a document number is to be stored on the card pertaining to a given index term a hole is punched in the position that serves to represent that number. Searching involves reading the coding corresponding to the position of the holes, and comparing the holes that recur on more than one card, by 'optical coincidence'. Cards are superimposed, one on top of another, and carefully aligned. Examination reveals positions on the cards where the light passes through all the cards in a stack. These positions correspond to documents that have been indexed under each of the index terms whose cards have been selected from the index and compared.

Optical coincidence cards are usually stored in a tray which displays the index terms at the top of each card in such a way that the alphabetical sequence can be readily followed and interesting cards can be withdrawn easily. Other necessary equipment is a punch and a light box. Special light boxes are manufactured which incorporate the punching facility. Optical coincidence cards have been one of the more common formats for post-co-ordinate indexes, and they have achieved this status because they have the potential to store a relatively large number of documents; larger cards have 9999 coding positions, and can thus store 9999 document numbers, or represent the indexing of 9999 documents. Smaller cards exist which have more limited capacity. Further post-co-ordinate indexes covering in excess of 9999 documents can be compiled by starting a second and possibly a third or fourth set of cards as the earlier sets become fully occupied. Limits on total index size are set by the practicalities of searching several sets of index cards in order to complete a search. Various refinements feature on optical coincidence cards, such as notches on the bottom of the card to facilitate storage, space for scope notes, and holes along one or more edge for edge punch coding. Most of the less satisfactory aspects of optical coincidence cards are associated with the punching. Punching equipment is not always as accurate as it might be; holes may not be well centred upon their coding position, and holes are sometimes not completely cut away. Also it is difficult to correct any errors in punching, and to make any modifications to the index, corresponding, for instance, to withdrawals.

17.3.3 *Retrieval in a post-co-ordinate index*

The output from a post-co-ordinate index depends both on the input to the system, and the physical nature of the store. Different stores offer access to distinct types of information or data and permit the information to be manipulated to varying extents. Some possible levels of access are:

1. Store provides a reference or document number.
2. Store allows direct retrieval of data or information (as in legal and statistical computer-held data banks and some other item record indexes).
3. Store permits the manipulation of data after it has been selected and

retrieved, but both the outcome of the manipulations and the original data are available from the store.

4. Store permits the processing of the information that it contains, but, after processing, the data in the store differs from the initial content (for example, in the editing and amending of catalogue records).

Each of these levels of access is evident in some system. Many such applications are discussed in Chapter 19 in respect of externally available data bases and their hosts, and in Chapter 20 in respect of local information retrieval systems.

Boolean search logic and search profiles

Search logic is the means of specifying combinations of terms which must be matched in retrieval. Boolean logic is the logic system employed in searching most post-co-ordinate indexes, and which is employed to link terms from both natural and controlled indexing languages. The logic is used to link the terms which describe the concepts present in the statement of the search. As many as twenty, thirty or more index terms may be linked together with search logic in order to frame the search statement. Search logic permits the inclusion of all synonyms and related terms, and also specifies acceptable and unacceptable term combinations. The Boolean logic operators are AND, OR and NOT. Figure 17.3 uses Venn diagrams to help explain how each of these operators may be used. The sets of documents indexed under the two index terms A and B, are each represented by a circle.

Boolean logic may be applied in both card-based and computer-based information retrieval systems. Boolean logic is important in computerised index systems whether the store is searched in batch or online mode. Batch mode can be used to conduct retrospective searches but has generally been superseded by online searching in this application. Batch mode computer searching remains important in the production of current awareness services, especially in selective dissemination of information systems. In such applications the search statement, usually referred to as a user interest profile is a linked set of index terms, which remains relatively stable over several computer runs. The search statement is matched against the indexing assigned to the latest batch of document records that have been input to the system. Figure 17.4 shows a very simple search profile that might be suitable for generating SDI notifications. The terms linked by the search logic may be drawn from free or controlled index languages. Profiles will usually need to be more complex with free language searching as greater provision for the entry of documents under synonyms and related terms is necessary. The search profile is fixed for the duration of any given search,

318

Figure 17.3 Boolean logic operators

Operator	Search type	Venn diagrams	Meaning
AND	Conjunctive		Logical product, symbolised by A AND B, A,B, AxB or (A) (B). Both index terms A and B must be assigned to a document for a match for example, Optic × Fibre × Cable × Television implies that all of the above four terms must have been assigned to a document for a match.
OR	Additive		Logical sum, symbolised by A or B, or A + B Only one of the two index terms A, or B need be associated with a document for a match. This operator is usually introduced when A and B can be regarded as equivalent for the purposes of the search. for example, TV + Television would serve to retrieve all documents with either the term TV or the term Television assigned.
NOT	Subtractive		Logical difference, symbolised by A NOT B, or A - B. The index term must be assigned, and assigned in the absence of the term B for a match. for example, Fibre Optics - British Telecom requires all documents on Fibre Optics except those indexed also under British Telecom.

319

Figure 17.4 An SDI profile on the INSPEC data base

```
     BROADCAST 16. MARCH 1984
— BD-UPDATES: CIND,CMPT (16.3) DKFL, FNTL (15.3) BIOL, CANC, CHEM, PTAR,
PTIN (14.3) EMED, PTSP (13.3) CNAM, INSP, PREM (10.3).
—SWISS CUSTOMERS CAN NOW ENTER TELEPAC WITH 049041111 (300: 300BDS)
048042111 (1200: 75 BDS) 048043111 (1200: 1200 BDS).
048021220 AND 048021221 (1200: 1200 BDS) VALID UPTO 30.6.84.
—NEW TRAINING DATES NOW AVAILABLE. CONSULT 'NEWS' (SEARCH AS NEWS—
USERMEETINGS) FOR DETAILS.
ENTER DATA BASE NAME   : INSP
  SIGN-ON  17.47.42          16.03.84
D-S/INSP/1980-V84,I07/1984
COPYRIGHT BY INSTITUTION OF ELECTRICAL ENGINEERS, LONDON, GB.

D-S—SEARCH MODE      —ENTER QUERY
    1—:  FIB$3 ADJ OPTIC$1 OR OPTICAL ADJ FIB$3
    RESULT  7897

    2—: CABLE AND (TV OR TELEVISION)
    RESULT  668

    3—: 1 AND 2
    RESULT  161

    4—: .. SDI
RA616   SPECIFY STATEMENT NUMBER—: 3
RA613   SPECIFY PARAGRAPHS—: ALL
RA615   SPECIFY ID FIELD IN FORMAT 'ID= '—: ID=CABLE TV
YOUR OFFLINE QUERY HAS BEEN SAVED UNDER THE NAME OF Q0001

D—S—SEARCH MODE   —ENTER QUERY
    4—: .. P 3/ALL/DOC=1

           1
AN    B84011384.
AU    MULLER-ROMER-F.
TI    THE FUTURE IS ALREADY WITH US. NEW TECHNOLOGIES CHANGE THE WORLD OF
      MEDIA.
SD    ELEKTRON INT. (AUSTRIA), NO.11, P: 299-302, 0 REFS.
CD    EKITA.
LG    GE.
RN    ISSN: 0374-3098.
YR    83.
PT    JOURNAL PAPER.
TC    GENERAL OR REVIEW.
DE    CABLE-TELEVISION, OPTICAL-FIBRES, SATELLITE-RELAY-SYSTEMS, TELEVISION-
      BROADCASTING, VIDEO-RECORDING.
ID    GERMANY, CABLE-TV, INTEGRATED-OPTICAL-FIBRE-LOCAL-NETWORKS, TARIFFS,
      DIRECT-SATELLITE-BROADCASTING, VIDEO-RECORDERS, LARGE-SCREEN-TV,
AB    A GENERAL DISCUSSION OF THE CABLE TV, GERMAN INTEGRATED OPTICAL FIBRE
      LOCAL NETWORKS, THE TARIFFS, DIRECT SATELLITE BROADCASTING, VIDEO
      RECORDERS AND LARGE SCREEN TV.
CC    B6430D, B6260, B6420, B6250G, B6430H.

                    END OF DOCUMENT
```

```
—:.. PURGE Q0001
QUERY 0001: SDI      ID=CABLE TV
HIT "ENTER" TO CONFIRM DELETE OR ENTER NEW COMMAND TO ABORT

I4610  SAVED QUERIES HAVE BEEN PURGED.
R0531  SPECIFY DOCUMENTS
```

and will only be modified periodically as the quality of the set of notifications output from the search drops to unacceptable levels.

In an online retrospective search, the profile is evolved or modified as the search progresses. The statements are framed one at a time, and feedback is available at each stage, hence the term 'interactive searching'. For instance, a request posed to the computer to search for the occurrence of an individual term usually results in a statement which gives the number of documents whose records are stored in association with that term, such as

1   616   CARNATIONS

At any stage in the search the result of linking terms by the search logic of the system can be viewed. A request to the computer such as

COMBINE 1 AND 2

where 1 and 2 are sets of documents that have previously been noted, leads to something of the form:

4   8   COMBINE 1 AND 2

Here the number of documents satisfying the previous logic statement (that is, 8 documents) is indicated. With this type of facility search strategy can be refined to give the most profitable output. Further complex search strategies are possible with the intercession of other kinds of logic (see below) and the use of brackets. Figure 17.5 shows how the statements in an online search make use of Boolean logic operators.

Weighted term search logic

In most search statements or document profiles it is possible to designate certain concepts as being more significant than their neighbours. Weights are a quantitative measure of the prominence of various index terms in the description of a subject and may form the basis of an alternative search logic. This section discusses the use of weights in search profiles, but it should be noted that it is also possible to assign weights to the concepts in document profiles, that is to indicate the primary concepts in a document and discriminate between these and subsidary concepts.

Figure 17.5 An online search on the INSPEC data base

```
? B13
                    13MAR84 12:36:57 USER6466
         $10.44      0.116 HRS FILE13
          $1.16      DIALNET
          $0.32      11 TYPES
         $11.92      ESTIMATED TOTAL COST


FILE13: INSPEC—77-84/ISS06
(COPR. IEE)
SEE FILE 12(1969 THRU 1976)
         SET ITEMS DESCRIPTION
         --- ----- ----------
? S FIB?(W)OPTIC? OR OPTICAL(W)FIB?
          4224 FIB?(W)OPTIC?
          9210 OPTICAL(W)FIB?
     1   10752 FIB?(W)OPTIC? OR OPTICAL(W)FIB?
? S CABLE?(S)TV? OR CABLE?(S)TELEVISION?
           497 CABLE?(S)TV?
           769 CABLE?(S)TELEVISION?
     2     960 CABLE?(S)TV? OR CABLE?(S) TELEVISION?
? C 1 AND 2
         3 211 1 AND 2
? PR3/7/1-30
PRINTED3/7/1-30 ESTIMATED COST: $12.90 (TO CANCEL, ENTER PR-)
? END/SDI
SERIAL£BL9Q
                    13MAR84 12:41:11 USER6466
          $6.48      0.072 HRS FILE13 8 DESCRIPTORS
          $0.72      DIALNET
          $7.20      ESTIMATED TOTAL COST


? L3/ENG
     4 142 ?/ENG
? T4/6/1-10
4/6/1

1200569  B84011335
   DBS PROGRAMMES ON CABLE


4/6/2
   1185867  B84006921
      CABLE TELEVISION


4/6/3
   11855753  B84006804
      BIT-RATE REDUCTION FOR 140 MBIT/S LINKS


4/6/4
   1185459  B84006506, C84005468
      A FIBER-OPTIC BROADBAND LAN/OCS USING A PBX
```

4/6/5
  1174208 A84005733, B84002695
  FIBRE OPTICS IN A MULTI-STAR WIDEBAND LOCAL NETWORK

4/6/6
  1171393 B84002720
  WHAT IS BIGFON?

4/6/7
  1171376 B84002698
  ECONOMICS OF OPTICAL FIBRE TRANSMISSION SYSTEMS

4/6/8
  1156395 B83062899
  A WIDEBAND INTERCITY NETWORK USING OPTICAL FIBRES

4/6/9
  1156239 B83062738
  COST BENEFITS OF FIBRE-OPTIC SYSTEMS

4/6/10
  1155702 B83062158
  COMPANIES AND THEIR CAPABILITIES (WEST GERMANY)

? T4/5/5
4/5/5

  1174208 A84005733, B84002695
  FIBRE OPTICS IN A MULTI-STAR WIDEBAND LOCAL NETWORK
  FOX, J.R.
  BRITISH TELECOM RES. LAB., IPSWICH, ENGLAND
  SPONSOR: INST. MEASUREMENT AND CONTROL; IERE
  PROC. SPIE INT. SDC. OPT. ENG. (USA) VOL.374 84 §90 1983 CODEN:
PSISDG ISSN: 0277-786X
  FIBRE OPTICS 1983 19-21 APRIL 1983 LONDON, ENGLAND
  TREATMENT: GENERAL, REVIEW
  DOCUMENT TYPES: CONFERENCE PAPER
  LANGUAGES: ENGLISH
  (7 REFS)
  EARLY EXPERIENCE HAS BEEN GAINED WITH THE SWITCHED-STAR TYPE OF NETWORK
IN THE FIBRE-VISION CABLE TV TRIAL AT MILTON KEYNES, AND BRITISH TELECOM
ARE PROGRESSING TOWARDS A FULL-SCALE MULTI-STAR WIDEBAND LOCAL NETWORK.
THE AUTHOR DISCUSSES BOTH THE PRESENT AND FUTURE USE OF FIBRE OPTICS IN THIS
TYPE OF NETWORK
  DESCRIPTORS: OPTICAL LINKS; OPTICAL FIBRES; OPTICAL COMMUNICATION
EQUIPMENT
  IDENTIFIERS: FIBRE OPTICS; SWITCHED STAR NETWORK; MULTI-STAR WIDEBAND
LOCAL NETWORK; FIBRE-VISION CABLE TV TRIAL
  CLASS STUDIES: A4280S; A4280M; B6260; B4130

In its role in formulating search profiles, weighted term logic may be introduced either as a search logic in its own right, or as a means of reducing the search output from a search whose basic logic is Boolean. Whichever application is encountered, weighted term search logic is most commonly associated with computer-based systems.

In an application where weighted term logic is the primary search logic, search profiles are framed by combining index terms in a simple logical sum. Each term is assigned a weight which reflects its significance in determining the relevance of a document to the search question, and document references worthy of printing are selected on the basis of a threshold weight. A simple SDI-type profile using weighted term search logic is displayed below:

Search description: The effect of alcohol on the performance of drivers of motor vehicles.

A simple search profile (which does not explore all possible synonyms, but does serve to illustrate weighted term logic), might be:

Search profile

7 Motor vehicles
7 Cars
7 Vehicles
7 Motor cars
7 Motor vehicles
7 Buses
6 Alcohol
5 Blood alcohol
4 Drivers
3 Performance
2 Drowsiness
1 Ergonomics

A threshold weight appropriate to the specificity of the searcher's enquiry must be established. For instance, a threshold weight of 13 would retrieve all documents with the following combinations of terms assigned:

Motor vehicles and Alcohol
Cars and Alcohol
Cars, Drivers and Performances
Motor vehicles, Blood alcohol and Drowsiness

But documents with the following terms assigned would be rejected on the grounds that their combined weights did not exceed the pre-selected threshold:

Alcohol and Drivers
Performance and Drowsiness
Ergonomics and Motor vehicles

A different threshold weight would cause either a larger or smaller set of documents to be selected as being relevant. By modifying the threshold weight the search specification can be broadened or narrowed.

Weighted term search logic may also be used to supplement Boolean logic. Here weighted term logic is a means of limiting or ranking the output from a search that has been conducted in response to a search profile which was framed in terms of Boolean logic operators. In the process of the search, prior to display or printing, the computer ranks references according to their weighting, and those documents with sufficiently high rankings will be deemed relevant and eventually retrieved.

Other search devices

Each system has its own unique features, and whilst Boolean search logic is common to many information retrieval systems, ranging from online public access catalogues, through selective dissemination of information and to the search facilities available on external data bases, other features of systems may vary from one application to another. Some of the more common devices are briefly introduced in this section.

Contextual logic or promixity operators. These are a useful means of searching for more than the mere occurrence of a term; they also permit the searcher to specify the context in which the term should appear in some sense or other. The term may, for instance, only be regarded as significant if it appears alongside other terms. Contextual logic may be of particular benefit in natural or free language information retrieval situations, where these devices are the only means of specifying concepts which require more than one word for their description, for example, in the IBM STAIRS package the following contextual logic devices are available. Similar devices appear in other systems, but their form or the terminology used to represent the facility will vary between systems:

SAME, for example MANAGEMENT SAME HOUSING, which causes a search for only those documents which contain the words MANAGEMENT and HOUSING within the same paragraph.

WITH, for example MANAGEMENT WITH HOUSING, which causes a search for only those documents which contain the words MANAGEMENT and HOUSING in that sequence in the same sentence.

ADJ, for example MANAGEMENT ADJ HOUSING, which causes a search for the documents which have MANAGEMENT and HOUSING in the same sentence immediately adjacent to one another, in the same sequence as in the query. Contextual logic frequently specifies the number of words that may be permitted to occur between the two terms specified. For example, in STAIRS, MANAGEMENT (2) HOUSING requires that MANAGEMENT and HOUSING occur within two words of each other.

Truncation. Truncation is another search device which is to be found to be particularly useful in natural language information retrieval systems, although it can be applied with controlled languages. In any given system certain characters will be selected to designate truncation. When the computer recognises one of these characters, it will search on word stems. The computer will search for the specified stem, regardless of whether it is found in the text as a full and complete word, or whether other characters are necessary at the beginning or end of the stem in order to construct a true word. The effect of truncation is that, in searching, all words with common stems are treated as equivalent, and thus the need to make an exhaustive list of word variants is eliminated. This is likely to lead to shorter and less complex profiles for searches, and the gains will be most obvious in a natural language system. Here, for example, it is possible that all the following words might be relevant to a search on the applications of computing in a specific sector (say, accountancy): Computer, Computers, Computing.

If the computer was instructed to search on the stem 'Comput*' all of these words would be acceptable, and documents indexed under any of them would be retrieved as relevant. It should however be noted that truncation can be the cause of 'False Drops'. For example, the stem 'Comput*' might retrieve documents indexed under Computation and Computed, in addition to those documents indexed previously under other words with this same stem. Over severe truncation must be carefully avoided. For example, Cat* could retrieve documents on both Catalogues and Cats!

Truncation may be more restrictive. The number of characters required to appear either before or after the stem may be specified. For example, Comput $2 could select all words with the stem Comput followed by precisely two characters, and would thus retrieve documents indexed under Computed but not those under Computers, and so on.

The examples cited to date have used right hand truncation, which results in the amalgamation of words with different suffixes. Left hand truncation which involves the neglect of prefixes, or the elimination of characters from the beginning of a word is also possible in many systems. Left hand truncation is especially useful in chemical data bases, where, for example, *phosphate can be used to match diphosphate, dipolyphosphate, orthophosphate, trimetaphosphate and so on. Sometimes truncation may be operative on both ends of a stem. So, for example, *Comput* might retrieve documents indexed under any of Microcomputers, Microcomputer, Minicomputer, Computing, Computers, and so on. Truncation can also be used internally, usually in order to mark alternative spellings, for example:

SUL*UR   to cover sulphur or sulfur
PROT*N*   to cover protein, proteins, proton

Some systems permit the use of both contextual logic and truncated terms simultaneously, but others only permit their application one at a time. Figure 17.6 shows truncation and full text operators (that is, contextual logic) in Dialog.

String searching. String searching is a technique for locating a string of characters, even if it is embedded within a larger term. String searching is relatively slow, since the computer searches the sequential file of bibliographic records. Thus string searching is not usually performed on complete bibliographic data bases, but tends to be used to search a subset, as perhaps in a previously retrieved set of records. String searching can be used to retrieve records with character strings where these character strings have not been listed in the inverted file. String searching can be particularly useful for refining search profiles, once a fairly large number of documents have been retrieved in response to a fairly broad search profile. Thus terms can be located which might not have been anticipated as future search terms during indexing, by first selecting records from the data bases according to some broad criteria. Also string searching can be useful in identifying chemicals.

Example

SDI and retrospective searches online (as in Figures 17.4 and 17.5)

Search Question: I am interested in articles on fibre optics applications to cable television.

The INSPEC data base covers this subject. INSPEC covers all aspects of physics, electronics and electrical engineering, computers and control, and information technology. Papers from 1969 to the present can be retrieved. INSPEC is available on most of the online host computer systems.

Figure 17.6 Truncation and contextual logic facilities in DIALOG Information Retrieval Service

TRUNCATION
? (question mark)

- Unlimited number of characters after the stem:
  SELECT EMPLOY?
  SELECT AU=JONES, R?
  SELECT PY=197?

- Specified maximum number of characters after the stem:
  SELECT HORSE? ?
  SELECT THEAT?? ?

- Embedded variable character:
  SELECT WOM?N
  SELECT ADVERTI?E

- Combinations of the above:
  SELECT WORKM?N?

- Use with SuperSELECT:
  SELECT EAGLE? AND EXTINCT?

- Use with full-text searching:
  SELECT LIBRAR?(F)BUILD?

- Use with field limiters:
  SELECT HYPERACTIV?/TI, DE
  SELECT CHILD(W)PSYCH?/TI, DE, ID

FULL-TEXT OPERATORS (Contextual Logic)
Used only with the SELECT or SELECT STEPS commands.

Symbol	Function	Example
(W)	To request Word A immediately adjacent to Word B, and in this sequence.	S SOLAR(W)ENERGY
(nW)	To request Word A within n words of Word B, and in this sequence.	S SOLAR(3W)ENERGY
(F)	To request Word A in the same field as Word B in any order and in any field.	S SOLAR(F)ENERGY
(C)	To request Word A in the same citation as Word B, in any order, and in any field. Equivalent to: S SOLAR; S ENERGY; C1 AND 2 or S SOLAR AND ENERGY.	S SOLAR(C)ENERGY
(L)	To link parts of multilevel Descriptors. Capability varies per database.	S SOLAR(L)ENERGY
(S)	To link sub-field parts within the same field and in any order. Capability varies per database.	S SOLAR(S)ENERGY

1. *Lockheed Dialog*

The host computer is situated in Palo Alto, California and can be accessed through various networks, for example, PSS, Dialnet, TELENET, TYMNET.

Question marks on the extreme left of the printout are prompts from the host computer. Question marks within SELECT commands specify truncation, for example, PROGRAM? in a command will match the words PROGRAM, PROGRAMS, PROGRAMME, PROGRAMMES, PRO-GRAMMING, and so on in a document record.

After the first prompt, the user has typed B13, short for BEGIN13. The search will be carried out in Dialog's file 13, INSPEC 1977–84 (issue 6) at the time of searching. Previous articles will be found in file 12 (1969–76).

Immediately after the second prompt, S is short for SELECT. The first half of the command looks for words hit by FIB? immediately followed by a word hit by OPTIC? The (W) operator could have been written (OW), that is specifying no words in between the two. (1W), (2W), and other operators can also be used, specifying maxima of 1, 2, and so on interposing words. FIB? will cope with both English and American spellings, FIBRE and FIBER, as well as plurals. The second half of the command looks for OPTICAL FIBRES, and so on. The 2 halves are joined by an OR. The computer replies by listing the numbers of documents in each sub-command, and places 10752 hits in set 1.

Immediately after the third prompt, a similar SELECT command looks for articles on cable TV. To show the various features of the system, we have used the (S) operator. CABLE(S)TV? specifies that the two hit words can be in the same title, abstract or indexing field, and in either order. It is therefore a more general operator than (nW). The computer finds 960 appropriate hits. An alternative strategy would have been to search for the thesaurus (descriptor) term CABLE TELEVISION. The search statement would have been SELECT CABLE TELEVISION/DE.

Immediately after the next prompt, the COMBINE command finds 211 document records relevant to the search question.

The searcher now decides to set up an SDI profile. This must follow a PRINT command (PR for short). This example requests that a search is carried out every month on new items as specified by the search logic 3, that relevant items should be printed in format 7 and sent to the searcher by mail, and that no more than 30 should be printed each time. Format 7 is the complete record less indexing terms. The computer replies to the END/SDI command with the 4-character profile identifier. An SDI profile can be terminated at any future time by the commands .RECALLXXXX and .RELEASEXXXX, where XXXX is the identifier (BL9Q in this example).

After setting up the SDI profile, the searcher now considers the full retrospective search, going back to 1977. He may feel that 211 hits is too many, and try to reduce this number. One way is to use the LIMIT command. Here set 3 is limited to English language articles. Other LIMIT options are available. Set 4 results with a reduced number of documents records.

In this example the searcher has chosen to look at the titles of the most recent 10 articles from set 4. T is short for TYPE. This command types the information immediately at the user's terminal, as opposed to the PRINT command generating offline prints which are subsequently mailed to the user. The PRINT command is cheaper. Format 6 specifies accession number, abstract number(s) plus title.

After a glance at the 10 titles, the searcher decides to look closer at item 5. Here T4/5/5 takes set 4, specifies format 5 and the fifth record. Format 5 is the full record.

After the computer has obeyed this command, the searcher is prompted again. He may wish to print set 4 offline or to refine the search logic further before a final PRINT or TYPE command.

Finally, the searcher will LOGOFF.

2. *Datastar*

The host computer is situated in Berne, Switzerland. The service is run by Radio-Suisse and can be accessed via the PSS.

The first prompt requests the data base name. INSP is entered by the searcher. As shown, this covers (at the time of searching) the INSPEC data base from 1980 to the seventh issue of 1984. This search was carried out at a later date to the previous Dialog example. New data base items are sent to customers on magnetic tape. There are 24 issues each year.

The computer is the search mode automatically, so search terms are entered. ADJ is the adjacent operator. FIB$3 will hit words where the stem 'FIB' is followed by not more than three characters.

Yet another possible strategy for finding papers on cable TV is shown.

The ..SDI command originates an SDI profile. The searcher requests a profile with strategy as in set number 3, ALL paragraphs (that is, whole records), and calls the profile CABLE TV. The query number Q0001 is needed for deletion at a later date.

The command ..P 3/ALL/DOC=1 prints the whole record for the first (that is, most recent) document in set 3.

(This section was kindly prepared by E.G. Jones, of INSPEC.)

17.4 Citation indexing

Almost all papers, notes reviews, corrections and correspondence published in many scientific and other journals contain citations to associated works, listed usually in reading lists or bibliographies at the end of the work. Such citations are intended to place the document in the context of the other literature which makes a contribution in a similar subject area. The documents cited may support and provide precedent for, illustrate or elaborate on what the author has to say. Citations, then, are explicit author-designated links between various items in the literature. For each document that is cited a reference will be given which serves to identify its original; each reference normally includes title, author, and when and where the cited document was published. A citation index seeks to exploit these in-built links between documents and facilitate the identification of networks of cited, and thus associated documents.

What is a citation index?

Undoubtedly the most important citation indexes are the products of the Institute of Scientific Information: Science Citation Index, Social Sciences Citation Index and Arts and Humanities Citation Index, together with their machine-readable and searchable data bases, SCISEARCH and SOCIAL SCISEARCH. Other citation indexes have been produced, such as a Citation Index for Statistics and Probability in 1973. Citation indexes have always been important in Law literature, and Shephard's Law Review Citations has been published since 1968 as a continuing index to more than a hundred law reviews and journals.

ISI's Citation indexes comprise two central components: the Citation index and the Source index. Although, as Figure 17.7 shows, other indexes are available, these are the indexes which are essential to a citation index; they can be held in printed or machine-readable form. The Source index lists all documents included in the journals covered by the index, and issues published in the time span of the particular cumulation. The Citation index lists, in alphabetical order by author's name, the citations made in any of the source documents, and indicates for each cited document, the source document which cites it. Thus, under a cited document, all source documents that cite the document are represented. More complete details of source documents are to be located in the Source index. Figure 17.7 demonstrates these points for Social Sciences Citation index.

Advantages of citation indexes

Citation indexes represent a very different approach to the indexing, organisation and retrieval of documents than that offered by the

Figure 17.7 Social Sciences Citation Index

PERMUTERM® SUBJECT INDEX

SPENDING
PSYCHOLOGY . . . KOJIMA S

Uses:
Locate items on new topics.

Locate items on very specific topics.

Locate items involving more than one concept.

KOJIMA S

CITATION INDEX

TAMAKA M
74 PSYCHOL SPENDING
KOJIMA S   JPN PSY RES   24 29 82

Uses:
Locate newer works on the same subject.

Develop a bibliography.

Locate book reviews.

KOJIMA S

CORPORATE INDEX
(Geographic Section)

JAPAN

KYOTO
● DOSHISHA UNIV
  • FAC LETTERS
  • DEPT PSYCHOL
KOJIMA S   JPN PSY RES   24 29 82

Uses:
Find out what type of research is going on at an institution.

Find out who is publishing at a particular institution.

KOJIMA S

SOURCE INDEX
(AUTHOR INDEX)

KOJIMA S
—HAMA Y — ASPECTS OF THE PSYCHOLOGY OF SPENDING ⑥
JPN PSY RES   24(1):29-38   82   4R
—DOSHISHA UNIV, FAC LETTERS, DEPT PSYCHOL. KYOTO ⑦
602, JAPAN

KOJIMA S   64   STUDY CONSUMER PSYCH
KOJIMA S   72   STUDY CONSUMER PSYCH
⑤ SHINBUN A   72   OBSERVATION ANAL PSY
TAMAKA M   74   PSYCHOL SPENDING ⑧

① author of source item
② coauthor
③ source journal information
④ author's address
⑤ author's bibliography
⑥ title of source item
⑦ number of works cited in author's bibliography
⑧ publication year

Uses:
Locate recent works by an author.

Locate an author's address.

Verify bibliographic information.

B-139

conventional subject index. Nevertheless, citation indexes do seek to link documents according to their content (or at least the perception of their content held by the author of the source work). Although there are limitations to the value of citation indexes they do have some very distinct advantages over more usual indexing techniques, and these are likely to assure citation indexes a place in the information market. The advantages of citation indexes can be enumerated as:

1. There is no need to assign subject terms, and thus there is no intellectual effort required during indexing. The computer merely needs to be fed with the source documents and their citations, and with the appropriate software, will generate the indexes (in printed or machine-readable form). This obviously facilitates the rapid processing of large quantities of documents.

2. A fairly extensive coverage of the literature can be achieved by including only a limited number of source documents. If the key journals in a field are identified, then via the bibliographies of the contributions to these journals a much wider coverage of the literature can be achieved.

3. There are no artificial limits on the length of bibliographies, so no limits are imposed on the depth or exhaustivity of indexing in a citation index.

4. No problems arise in association with word usage. These circumvent many of the problems that must be tackled in subject indexing such as finding the appropriate label for a concept, the emergence of new terms, new meanings for old words, technical and common names and other variations in terminology.

5. Citations can be used across documents irrespective of the language of the source or cited document.

6. Searching can be more precise and direct.

7. A search can be extended over time by cycling, that is, starting with a source document, identifying those documents which it cites, and then identifying those documents which the original cited document cites, and so on. Cycling makes it possible to build up a historical perspective of the development of a subject and the key documents which record those major developments.

8. When compared with KWIC-type title indexes indexing is often more extensive and a greater depth of indexing is achieved. With title indexes the number of index entries is limited by the number of significant terms in the title. With citation indexes the number of index entries is limited by the number of citations given in a document.

9. Interesting perspectives of cross-disciplinary developments can be gathered from citation indexes in a way that would be difficult with traditional indexes which tend to concentrate on a specific discipline for example, physics, chemistry, education.

10. A number of ancillary factors about the development of knowledge can be examined such as the extent of self-citation, the evolution of concepts, extent of citation between documents in different languages, and co-

authorship patterns.

11. The scope of a citation index, especially those published by ISI, is interdisciplinary, and also crosses time barriers in a way that a normal index would not do. For example, in a normal indexing service all the documents listed in the issue for a specific month will have been published in the last year or so. In a citation index, the index may include documents covering several years.

Disadvantages of citation indexes

Given such an impressive array of advantages it may seem surprising that conventional subject indexes to the literature continue to be produced. There are some features of citation indexes which prevent them from completely ousting other indexes. These are:

1. Inconsistency and inaccuracies in citation practices between different documents. Inconsistencies are mostly merely annoying, although it can be difficult to be sure whether a group of citations which look similar all relate to the same document. Inaccuracies can lead to its being impossible to identify the documents to which citations relate. The citation index will reflect any inaccuracies in the citations which are present in the original bibliography.

2. Citation indexes rest upon the assumption that citations represent a link between documents. No distinction is drawn between the citation of a document for serious academic purposes, and the citation for frivolous reasons. Authors can cite another article because it is related to the work in that it makes a contribution in the same area, or because the two pieces of work use the same methodology. Sometimes authors cite another document to lend authority to their own work, or because they wish to demonstrate that they are aware of a document, rather than because they have used the ideas contained in another document.

3. Different types of documents provide citations to varying extents. Trade literature, popular magazines, and newspapers do not abound with citations. Even within the professional journal, different types of paper may by their nature consider citation in varying extents. For example, review articles are expected to be supported by extensive bibliographies, whilst it is unusual for a letter to carry more than the odd citation.

4. The source literature for citation must be defined. Often this will be defined as a set of periodicals. This will mean that monographs may be less well covered by a citation index than might be desired (although they will still feature as cited documents).

The future of citation indexing promises to be interesting. It is important to recognise that citation indexing hinges upon the continuation of documents as separate units, and the perpetuation of the practice of citing other works. Citation indexing would need to be carefully rethought in order to cater for the electronic journal, especially if it becomes necessary to cover both the printed and computer-based journal literature simultaneously.

Chapter 17 Readings

1 Armitage, J.E. and Lynch, M.F., 'Articulation in the generation of subject indexes by computer', *Journal of chemical documentation*, 7(3), 1967, 170–8.

2 Armitage, J.E. and Lynch, M.F., 'Some structural characteristics of articulated subject indexes', *Information storage and retrieval*, 4, 1968, 101–11.

3 Austin, D., *PRECIS: a manual of concept analysis and subject indexing*, Council of the British National Bibliography: London; 1974.

4 Austin, D., 'The development of PRECIS: a theoretical and technical history', *Journal of Documentation*, 30(2), 1974, 47–102.

5 Austin, D. and Digger, J.A., 'PRECIS: the PREserved Context Index System', *Library Resources and Technical Services* 1977, 13–30.

6 Bakewell, K.G.B., 'The PRECIS indexing system', *The Indexer* 9(4), 1975, 160–6.

7 Coates, E.J., *Subject catalogues: headings and structure*, Library Association: London, 1960.

8 Coates, E.J. and Nicholson, I., 'British technology index – a study of the application of computer type-setting to index production', In: Cox, N.S.M. and Grose, M.W., *Organization and handling of bibliographic records by computer* Oriel: Chipping Norton, 1967, 167–78.

9 Costello, J.C., 'Coordinate indexing', In: *Rutgers series on systems for the intellectual organisation of information*, editor S. Artandi. No.7. State University, Graduate School of Library Science: Rutgers, 1966.

10 Cutter, S.A., *Rules for a dictionary catalogue*, 4th edition, Government Printing Office: Washington, DC, 1904.

11 Foskett, A.C., 'SLIC indexing', *Library World* 70(817), 1968, 17–19.

12 Jolley, J.L., 'Punched feature cards', *Journal of Documentation*, 31(3), 1975, 199–215 (Progress in documentation).

13 Kaiser, J., *Systematic indexing*, Pitman: London, 1911.

14 Langridge, D., 'Review of PRECIS', *Journal of Librarianship* 8(3), 1976, 210–12.

15 Mills, J., 'Chain indexing and the classified catalogue', *Library Association Record* 57(4), 1955, 141–8.

16 Peters, H.J., *User reactions to PRECIS indexes*, Liverpool Polytechnic, School of Librarianship and Information Studies: Liverpool, 1981.

17 Ramsden, M.J., *PRECIS: a workbook for students of librarianship*, Bingley: London, 1981.

18 Richmond, P.A., *Introduction to PRECIS for North American usage*,

Libraries Unlimited: Littleton Colorado, 1981.

19 Wellisch, H.H., *The PRECIS index system: principles, applications and prospects . . .*, H.W. Wilson: New York, 1977.

20 Verdier, V., *Final report of the PRECIS/translingual project*, British Library Research and Development Department: London, 1981.

21 Weintraub, D.K., 'An extended review of PRECIS', *Library Resources and Technical Services* 23(2), 1979, 101–15.

22 Wilson, T.D., *An introduction to chain indexing*, Bingley: London, 1971.

Citation indexing

23 Garfield, E., *Citation indexing, its theory and application in science, technology and humanities*, Wiley: New York, 1979.

24 Garfield, E., 'Science Citation Index: a new dimension in indexing', *Science*, 144(3619), 1964, 649–54.

25 Keen, E.M. 'Citation indexes', *Aslib Proceedings* 16(8), 1964, 246.

26 Martyn, J., 'Citation analysis', *Journal of documentation*, 31(4), 1975, 290–7. (Progress in documentation).

27 Martyn, J., 'An examination of citation indexes', *Aslib Proceedings* 17(6), 1965, 184–96.

Part IV   Systems

18 Cataloguing systems – centralised and shared systems

18.1 Introduction

Libraries have long recognised the benefits of co-operating in catalogue production. There seems little point in hundreds of cataloguers in separate locations wading through cataloguing codes and classification schemes in order to create a variety of catalogue records for the same work, unless the local situation requires specific features in respect of cataloguing or classification. Both centralised cataloguing systems and co-operative networks are means of sharing cataloguing effort and cataloguing information. Their objectives are however slightly different, even though in any discussion of computerised cataloguing systems co-operative networks and centralised cataloguing are inextricably linked. Most libraries exploit the fruits of centralised cataloguing in some way, and it is difficult to envisage a co-operative network which does not make use of centrally produced records.

Centralised cataloguing is the cataloguing of documents by some central organisation such as the British Library for the British National Bibliography (BNB), or the Library of Congress. The main purpose of centralised cataloguing is to create a standard and acceptable record that can be inserted into the catalogues of a large number of independent libraries.

In *co-operative cataloguing* a number of otherwise independent libraries share the work of producing a catalogue for their mutual benefit. In particular, a central feature of co-operative cataloguing is the union catalogue, which is intended to permit improved access to and exploitation of the resources of the libraries in the co-operative.

Most co-operative or shared cataloguing ventures today rely to some extent on centrally produced catalogue records.

Apart from participation in a co-operative cataloguing scheme, and the exploitation of centrally produced cataloguing data, libraries have one other possible strategy in the creation of catalogues. This is to opt for local cataloguing, using either a purpose-designed software package or a standard software package. This option is considered in more detail in Chapter 20.

Many large library systems have some contact with shared and centralised cataloguing activities, but may also resort to local cataloguing for the cataloguing of specific kinds of materials. In general, the larger public and academic libraries exploit centralised and shared cataloguing for most of their monograph cataloguing. The situation for the cataloguing of serials varies considerably, and there are notable differences in practice between the United States and the United Kingdom. Nonbook materials are more likely to be catalogued locally, although many shared cataloguing systems, and increasingly, centralised cataloguing systems do cater for nonbook materials. In general, then, there are many options in selecting a system for the production and maintenance of catalogue records.

18.2 The computer and cataloguing systems

Most of the systems introduced in the remainder of this chapter are computer-based. Over the past fifteen years computer-based cataloguing systems have become increasingly prevalent, and no large library can now ignore computerised cataloguing systems. With the advent of micro-computers even much smaller cataloguing operations can effectively be computerised. Nevertheless, it cannot yet be said that all cataloguing is conducted with the use of a computer, and even some major library systems persist with manual cataloguing practices. Figure 18.1 tabulates in summary form many of the attractions of computerised cataloguing systems. It is plain

Figure 18.1 Attractions of computerised cataloguing systems

1. Easy co-operation between systems because machine readable records can be transferred easily from one system to another, files from different sources can be merged.
2. Multiple copies are easy to produce.
3. No filing or other routine catalogue maintenance is required of cataloguers.
4. Different catalogue formats can be chosen for different cata-logue locations, both in terms of different record formats, and different physical forms of catalogues.
5. Extracts of the main catalogue can be produced, to cover for instance, branches or special collections.
6. It is possible to use centralised cataloguing data.
7. In many instances it is cheaper to use a computerised cataloguing system.
8. In computerised systems, the cataloguing subsystem can interface with other systems, such as acquisitions and circulation control systems, and be used as the basic bibliographic file in these systems.

from this table that computerised cataloguing is likely to grow in importance, and that the time has arrived when it is more appropriate to ask why cataloguing is still conducted on a manual basis, rather than to seek to justify the use of computers in cataloguing.

18.3 Centralised cataloguing

Centralised cataloguing should remove duplication in cataloguing effort. In order that this can be achieved and that centralised cataloguing is viable, it is necessary that:

(a) Libraries should catalogue and classify a document in the same way (that is, without centralised cataloguing there would be real duplication of cataloguing decisions). For this to be the case requires some standardisation in cataloguing and classification practices. Generally, the availability of centralised cataloguing records will, if the economic aspects are favourable, encourage uniformity, but a readiness and a trend towards consistency is a prerequisite to the success of centralised cataloguing. If different libraries have very different requirements of catalogues then centralised cataloguing will not prove attractive. Generally libraries have been able to accept uniform bibliographic records, which they will then amend or supplement with other data according to local needs. Typical local data might be locations, loan status, items in special collections. Less standardisation has been achieved with regard to the subject approach to documents, than with the description and the author/title approach.

(b) A number of libraries must acquire the same document. Extensive duplication in fact occurs only in respect of a limited number of documents. Many libraries have special collections of foreign, unpublished or unusual materials which include items unlikely to be acquired by other libraries. It is relatively economic to produce centralised records for documents which many libraries acquire. Thus, for instance, popular fiction that is included in the collections of a large number of public libraries, can easily be handled by a centralised service. It is less obviously effective to aim to generate a centralised cataloguing service which will cover all the materials acquired by libraries in a given country. If some records are required by only a limited number of libraries, it will be difficult to recoup the cost of creating and maintaining these records. Almost inevitably then, many libraries will have acquisitions for which records are not available in a centralised cataloguing service. The relative proportion of material covered and not covered respectively for the new stock of any given library by a centralised cataloguing service will be a significant factor in that library's decision about participation in a system using centralised cataloguing records. So some materials, in particular books, are likely to be covered to varying extents by centralised cataloguing services. Other materials are never covered by centralised cataloguing services. At the present time these include periodical articles, the individual papers in conference proceedings, and other items which might possibly be revealed by analytical cataloguing. The bibliographical control of such items is the province of in-house indexing, analytical cataloguing, and abstracting and indexing services, and associated data bases.

(c) A mechanism exists whereby the central cataloguing agency or agencies can view new documents, preferably prior to publication, or at least very soon after publication. It is essential that the central agency is able to provide records for new documents as soon as a librarian receives the document, otherwise documents will have to wait in cataloguing departments until the record does become available. If there are excessive delays in the record becoming available, and long delays become a common phenomenon, the librarian who is anxious to make new stock available for the user as soon as possible will resort to local cataloguing. Thus excessive delays in the availability of cataloguing records from the central agency will negate much of the value of a central service. Usually a central cataloguing agency is based upon a national library or copyright office, where publishers are required by law to send at least one copy of every book published in that country. Cataloguing-in-Publication can also assist in reducing delays, and this is considered separately below.

18.3.1 Merits of centralised cataloguing

A quick list of the merits of centralised cataloguing is useful in summarising some of the features of these services:

1. Economy of effort, particularly in eliminating unnecessary duplication of cataloguing effort.
2. Superior cataloguing may result, since more consistency and closer adherence to standard codes are likely to emerge with cataloguers who spend all of their time cataloguing, than with a librarian who tackles cataloguing as one of various professional tasks.
3. Uniformity of cataloguing between a number of libraries who are all using centrally produced cataloguing records will help readers and librarians. This advantage must be tempered by the fact that the standard centrally produced record may not always be consistent with local requirements, and local modifications are likely.
4. In some instances the exploitation of centralised cataloguing records contributes to more prompt cataloguing, since less local cataloguing needs to be performed. However, delays in the generation of centralised records can be a considerable nuisance.

18.3.2 Examples of centralised cataloguing services

1. The Library of Congress The Library of Congress started distributing printed catalogue cards as an early centralised cataloguing service. The LC service was the first large-scale service, and the LC remains the centralised cataloguing agency of prime importance to American libraries. The machine-readable cataloguing records which are now generated by the LC, LC MARC are important in both American and British libraries. The cataloguing products, which extend to proofsheets, printed catalogues, MARC tapes, and Cataloguing-in-Publication data, are merely an extension of the cataloguing activities of the LC, and thus records are made available for items in the LC.

The LC continues to offer a catalogue card service. Cards can be ordered in sets for use in an individual library's card catalogue. Alternatively a library may receive proofsheets of every LC catalogue record, and make a selection from these when items arrive. This arrangement is faster than waiting until documents are ordered, and then ordering cards, because the proofsheets are available to a library in respect of every item catalogued by the LC. However, proofsheets are not popular today, because, amongst other factors, it is necessary to file and control proofsheets and this is tedious and time-consuming. Many libraries now make use of commercial services which store the LC cataloguing records on microfiche and from which individual records can easily be retrieved.

The Library of Congress Catalog: A Cumulative Catalog of Books Represented by Library of Congress Printed Cards (now the *National Union Catalog*) was first published in 1942, and represented the first attempt to publish an integrated series of the card records. This publication originally covered the years 1898 to 1942, and two supplements covering the years 1942 to 1947 to 1952 respectively were subsequently issued. The *National Union Catalog* is still published with quarterly updates, and is cumulated annually and quinquennially. Cataloguers use the NUC and other LC catalogues to verify authors and titles and as sources of authoritative catalogue records. Cards may be ordered through the NUC.

In the United States there are processing centres which offer a variety of services based upon LC records. Most provide catalogue cards with books, and some process the material by providing, for example, markings, book pockets and cards.

In 1966 the LC initiated a pilot project to examine the possibility of generating machine-readable cataloguing data, and distributing it to user libraries. The project was known as the MARC (from Machine Readable Cataloguing) project, and the pilot project involved distribution of MARC tapes to sixteen participating libraries. In 1969, the MARC Distribution Service was established to act as the agency for the dissemination of MARC records to subscribing libraries and institutions. Originally the tape related only to English language monographic material currently catalogued by the LC.

The current LC MARC data base contains both records created by the LC staff and those created by co-operating libraries and verified by the LC. Most of the records are for post-1966 publications, but as a result of the RECON Project (retrospective conversion) and the COMARC Project (Cooperative machine readable cataloguing) records for many earlier materials are also present. The data base is made available to other libraries in the form of magnetic tapes.

Important points of difference can be enumerated between BNB and LC MARC data bases. These are that:

1. Being a catalogue of a national library the LC MARC data base has a much wider coverage including a more comprehensive coverage of maps, government publications, and foreign books.
2. The cataloguing practices (for example, the author headings which are established, and the subject headings) reflect American cataloguing practice and American perspectives.

In respect of this second point, the divergence between American cataloguing practice and UK cataloguing practice is less than it once was, and so LC MARC records are likely to be more universally acceptable.

2. The British National Bibliography and BLAISE The British National Bibliography, which is now the responsibility of the British Library Bibliographic Services Division, was established in 1950 under the auspices of the Council of the British National Bibliography. The service was originally based upon the books received by legal deposit in the British Museum, and later upon those received by the Agency for the Copyright Libraries. The British National Bibliography (BNB) is a weekly printed list, with entries classified and arranged by the latest edition of DC (since 1971). Separate author/title indexes, and a monthly subject index (compiled according to PRECIS indexing, see 17) are included. BNB has two four-monthly cumulations per annum, which are superseded by an annual volume, and then triennial cumulations.

BNB was established as a national bibliography, and not primarily as a cataloguing aid. However, its potential in this direction became evident, and in 1966 a catalogue card service was started; this was the beginning of the centralised cataloguing function. Cards could be purchased using the BNB serial number and later using the ISBN. Catalogue cards are available for each item recorded in the weekly BNB, and for Cataloguing-in-Publication (CIP) records prepared from the page proofs of forthcoming titles. Catalogue cards may be ordered individually, or as a complete set of cards, for one year.

344

BLAISE, the British Library Automated Information Service, became operational in 1977. It is related to BNB in that many of the BLAISE user services exploit the UKMARC data base and other data bases generated by the British Library Bibliographic Services Division, such as the British Education Index. BLAISE offers a variety of services bridging the cataloguing and information retrieval functions. Some of these are briefly introduced below:

1. Information Retrieval Services The information retrieval services are split into two components: BLAISE-LINE and BLAISE-LINK. BLAISE-LINE offers access to a number of bibliographic files which are held on a computer in the United Kingdom. Figure 18.2 gives some details of these files. A search of these files may be useful for compiling bibliographies, identifying information verifying references, and in the ordering of photocopies and loans. Access is available from any suitable terminal to BLAISE subscribers. BLAISE-LINK provides access to files in the biomedical and toxicological areas, which are available on the computer of the National Library of Medicine (US). These data bases include MEDLINE, which gives references in all aspects of medicine, psychology, physiology, pharmacology, veterinary science, dentistry and nursing. The CANCERLINE files cover cancer, TOXLINE and RTECS cover toxicity and pollution information respectively, POPLINE covers references on fertility, contraception and demography, and HEALTH is for non-clinical aspects of health care. For the librarian, CATLINE, SERLINE and the NAME AUTHORITY FILE give authoritative records of books and serials held by the National Library of Medicine. Various supporting services are available for the BLAISE-LINE file. AUTOSDI is a current awareness service. Document ordering is available through the Automatic Document Request Service, which provides a link to the British Library Lending Division. OFFSEARCH is a means of running a search overnight on more than one data base, in a cost-effective mode. The BLAISE-LINE and BLAISE-LINK Search Services are available to those who do not have access to a terminal and wish BLAISE to conduct the occasional search on their behalf. Training manuals and support services, such as the Help Desk, are a particular feature of the BLAISE information retrieval services.

2. LOCAS or the Local Catalogue Service was introduced in 1974 to offer a complete cataloguing service from data preparation to catalogue output, for those libraries who would like to benefit from the advantages of centralised computer processing, but who do not wish to manage the computerised processing for themselves. This centralised system offers libraries an extensive range of options in terms of the frequency of catalogue

Figure 18.2 BLAISE-LINE files

AVMARC

Subject coverage: All subject areas.
Information type: Bibliographic records of non-book materials with particular emphasis on audio visual materials used for teaching purposes.
Time span: 1960 to date.
Availability: Online access.
Special features: ● Records are in AACR2 format and can be used for cataloguing. ● Special Physical Description codes describe in detail the materials recorded. These can be used to search for a specific type of a-v material, with particular characteristics.

BRITISH EDUCATION INDEX

Subject coverage: Traditional facets of primary, secondary, tertiary and further education plus adult and continuing education, student counselling, special and vocational education, child psychology, delinquency and truancy, sociological perspectives, teacher training and assessments.
Information type: Bibliographic records of journal articles and conference proceedings.
Time span: 1976 to date.
Availability: Online access.
Updated: Quarterly.
Special features: ● All records are indexed using PRECIS for maximum subject retrieval. PRECIS is the Preserved Context Indexing System developed by the British Library.

HELPIS

Subject coverage: All subject areas.
Information type: Bibliographic records for audio-visual materials including films, videotapes, sound-recordings, tape-slide programmes or slide sets with substantial accompanying booklets and filmstrips. The materials are intended for use in institutions of higher education.
Time span: Currently available materials.
Availability: Online access.
Updated: Monthly.
Special features: ● Of particular interest to universities, polytechnics and colleges planning to use audio-visual materials on their courses. ● UDC classification and PRECIS (Preserved Context Index System) subject headings are assigned to each record and can be used for subject searches. ● Records are in AACR2 format.
Produced by: British Universities Film & Video Council.
Printed publication: The HELPIS file is the online version of two publications: *Higher Education Learning Programmes Information Service Catalogue* and *Audio-Visual Materials for Higher Education*.

LC MARC

Subject coverage: All subjects including fiction.
Information type: Bibliographic records of books.
Time span: 1968 to date.
Availability: Online access.
Updated: Monthly.
Special features: ● Records are in AACR2 format and can be used for cataloguing. ● Details of books soon to be

CONFERENCE PROCEEDINGS INDEX

Subject coverage: All subjects.
Information type: Bibliographic records of proceedings of conferences, symposia, seminars and workshops.
Time span: Comprehensive coverage 1964 to date, but since the file reflects the acquisitions of the British Library Lending Division, material dating back to the 19th century is included.
Availability: Online access.
Updated: Monthly.
Special features: ● The database reflects one of the world's most comprehensive collections of conference proceedings including records identifying monograph chapters, journal features, and parts of reports. ● All conferences can be pinpointed with the minimum of information.

ESTC (EIGHTEENTH CENTURY SHORT TITLE CATALOGUE)

Subject coverage: All subject areas.
Information type: Bibliographic records for all types of printed material including books, lists, advertisements, rules, songs and catalogues published throughout the world during the eighteenth century. The majority of the items are in English but material in other languages such as French, German, Latin and Welsh is also included.
Time span: 1701-1800.
Availability: Online access.
Updated: Fortnightly.
Special features: ● The database is the result of an international project.

published are included. ● Database represents the Library of Congress holdings giving details of English and foreign language material.
Produced by: US Library of Congress.

UK MARC

Subject coverage: All subjects including fiction.
Information type: Bibliographic records of British books and first issues of serial titles.
Time span: 1950 to date.
Availability: Online access.
Updated: Weekly.
Special features: ● Records are in AACR2 format and can be used for cataloguing. ● Library of Congress and PRECIS — Preserved Context Indexing System — subject headings are assigned to each record. ● Details of books soon to be published are included.

UKCTRAIN and MEDTRAIN are small, low cost files which can be used for training and practice.

October 1983

347

production, and the physical form of catalogue. For each participating library LOCAS maintains a MARC-based catalogue file consisting of centrally produced UK and LCMARC records, and locally created records for material which is present in the collection of that library, but for which records are not available in the BL data base. Libraries may add local data, such as class numbers or location information to the records which they select to add to their file. Most LOCAS subscribers are individual libraries who have established a direct relationship with LOCAS. However, LOCAS does support some libraries acting in groups, such as the member libraries of SCOLCAP and the members of the University of London's Cooperative Scheme.

3. Tape Services For organisations with access to computing facilities, BLBSD offers: the Selective Record Service and MARC Exchange Tapes. The Selective Record Service enables libraries to submit requests for individual records from the British Library data bases in machine-readable form. Records are identified by their control number offline, or by a wide range of search keys online. Regular monthly outputs can be supplied, or other arrangements can be made to suit the client. The Exchange Tapes Service enables libraries to build large bibliographic files for in-house use. Weekly tapes of current records, or cumulated back files available as separate year cumulations or at block rates can be supplied.

4. Cataloguing-in-Publication (CIP) CIP is not so much a service, but a feature of UKMARC data bases. It merits a separate mention, and is therefore introduced in this context. The object of CIP is to provide advance information of forthcoming British books. The CIP data is compiled by the BLBSD from preliminary pages of forthcoming works whilst these are still in proof form. The CIP data is then published: in the book itself, in BNB, on BNB cards, and on the UKMARC tapes. Sometimes it will be necessary to upgrade CIP records once the book is published, and this process is undertaken by BLBSD as appropriate. CIP is intended to facilitate the selection and ordering of materials by alerting librarians and others to forthcoming works in advance of their publication.

5. Microprocessor Systems BLAISE offers two packages for offline editing on intelligent terminals. These permit editing and amendment of records offline, and thus reduce online costs, since records are only selected online. BIBDES (Bibliographic Data Entry System) uses an ICL 150L computer and CORTEX runs on a Sirius 128K machine.

These two examples of centralised cataloguing services serve to demonstrate some of the key features of such an agency. Other centralised cataloguing agencies also exist, although their scope, in terms of numbers of users and/or types of services is usually more limited.

18.4 Co-operative networks

Co-operative cataloguing offers an alternative to centralised cataloguing as a means of maintaining a local library catalogue. Some libraries opt to commission a central agency to support their catalogue creation. Others prefer to reduce costs by sharing work with a group of libraries.

Closely associated with co-operative cataloguing is the union catalogue. Indeed, the production of a union catalogue probably rates equally with the economy of cataloguing effort as an objective of co-operative cataloguing ventures. A *union catalogue* then, is;

> a catalogue listing in one sequence the holdings or part of the holdings of two or more libraries.

Usually some indication of the location of the documents catalogued will be given in the catalogue.

18.4.1 Union catalogues

Combined catalogues showing the resources available to a group of libraries have been a feature of library co-operation for many years. Early union catalogues were produced in card or sheaf form, but many union catalogues are now computer-generated, and either printed on microfilm or microfiche. Already some of these catalogues are available in online data bases, and the trend is likely to be markedly towards this form, in order that union catalogues are more widely available to users, and that they better support inter-lending. The value of union catalogues has been well recognised for many years, but computerisation has made a significant difference to the effectiveness with which the objectives of a union catalogue can be achieved. Catalogue maintenance in a large union catalogue based on cards or slips was a nightmare, and it was very labour-intensive to maintain such catalogues at more than one location. It is not surprising that the networks discussed later have all taken advantage of computer processing in some form or another. For an account of the inherent complications of co-operative cataloguing without computers see Needham, Introduction(8).

Whatever their physical form, and however they are maintained, the function of union catalogues remains constant to reveal the total document resources of an area or subject, and thus to aid in satisfying users' requests and in balanced and integrated book selection. It should be noted that a union catalogue will often be a major bibliography in its own right, especially if it covers the resources of a group of major libraries. For many years the British Union Catalogue of periodicals (BUCOP), and its later successor Serials in the British Library are examples which are both union catalogues and major bibliographies.

The immediacy of access to the resources represented in a union catalogue may well be improved in the near future. The readiness with which the catalogue can be accessed is improved by making the catalogue into a data base which can be accessed online by participating libraries and others. However, this does not in itself make the actual resources readily available. Experiments in improved document delivery systems, and the establishment of networks between libraries are under way. Currently, online document request services are possible, but this is not usually a feature of the facilities of any but the largest co-operatives. The normal inter-library loan channels of the telephone and the postal service must still be interposed between the identification of the existence and location of a document, and the receipt of the same document. In the future, the union catalogue will have a central role in library networks where inter-library lending is technologically so straightforward, that boundaries will only exist between libraries in economic terms. Experiments are being conducted by the Birmingham Libraries Cooperative (BCOP) into the use of facsimile transmission for document delivery.

A second objective of union catalogues—to make library resources available when and where they are needed—has not then as yet been fully achieved, but we may look forward to more complete fulfilment of this objective in the near future.

A co-operative grouping may come together to generate a union catalogue. Union catalogues may be compiled to meet differing purposes, and thus can be expected to exhibit a variety of styles. There are a number of characteristics of a union catalogue which need to be established. These are:

1. *Area* Any area covered by a catalogue must be carefully defined. There are local catalogues which are limited in their coverage to the resources of a region or locality. These are useful in showing the reader the resources within easy travelling distance. Many of the networks discussed later are focused on a particular region. The catalogue often forms the basis for co-operation and good relations between the libraries in a region. National catalogues, or those covering the resources of libraries across a wide geographical area may be more difficult to maintain. The *National Union Catalog*, for example, shows only locations of documents in particular libraries.

2. *Material* Limitations may be introduced on the basis of material. For example, most union catalogues concern themselves with monographs. Separate union catalogues may have to be provided for periodicals or music. So the type of material to be covered by a union catalogue may be defined by any of the following parameters:

(a) Form. For example, serials in the British Library covers periodicals in the British Library and around sixteen contributing libraries. The BLCMP Serials catalogue shows serials holdings in BLCMP member libraries.

(b) Subject

(c) Period, for example, the Eighteenth Century Short Title Catalogue.

3. Arrangement The normal arrangement for a union catalogue always used to be an author/title order. This order suffices for a list whose purpose is to identify and locate documents, whose bibliographic details are already known. Subject arrangement would undoubtedly improve the union catalogue as a bibliographic tool, but presents problems in respect of standardisation of subject approach and generally in maintenance. Naturally, with the advent of online public access catalogues, union catalogues will be accessible via a variety of search keys.

4. Description Only minimum detail is necessary for the description of documents in union catalogues. In essence it is only necessary to be able to identify an edition of a work, and for this only author, title, edition and date need necessarily be specified. In practice often more details than this are included, and certainly it is more likely that details in a co-operative cataloguing data base will reflect the cataloguing requirements of the member libraries for their own local catalogues, than any requirements that might be perceived for the union catalogue. An important element of the creation of this joint catalogue record is that member libraries agree to a standard for cataloguing description for the creation of the joint record, even if they make local modifications to records.

The Shared Cataloguing Program (NPAC – National Program for Acquisitions and Cataloguing) was set up by the Association of Research Libraries and the Library of Congress in 1965. A number of libraries receive full sets of Library of Congress cataloguing records in exchange for certain cataloguing information. Cataloguing data is also fed into this system by the British Library. The Shared Cataloguing Program is an essential element in the move towards Universal Bibliographic Control (UBC). IFLA's International Office for Universal Bibliographic Control was established in order to further international control of bibliographic records, and any shared cataloguing programme can make a contribution to this objective.

18.4.2 Examples of co-operative networks

1. OCLC OCLC, the Online Computer Library Centre, was founded in 1967 by a group of Ohio college libraries. In its early years it benefited from a variety of grants to support activities and developments, but since 1971, OCLC has been supported by membership fees and grants for specific research and development projects. Now OCLC has around 3000 members, most of them in North America, but some in other parts of the world. OCLC is based upon extensive bibliographic data bases which have been and continue to be built and shared by OCLC members. Although essentially a co-operative scheme, with a central data base, OCLC also offers a local processing option. The two options then are:

(a) Centralised option Libraries may have direct access to the files held on a computer in Ohio. The central file is the Online Union Catalogue, which contains almost 10 million bibliographic records, from all members. About one-third of the new records are contributed by LC, the National Library of Medicine, the National Agricultural Library and the United States Government Printing Office. This union catalogue contains MARC records for monographs, serials, audio-visual, maps, manuscripts, sound recordings and scores. Records may be searched on ISBN and other standard numbers, and also on search keys derived from names and titles.

In cataloguing, wherever possible, records from the Online Union Catalogue are utilised. If original cataloguing is necessary the LC Name Authority File is available to help in establishing headings. New records are available to other OCLC users as soon as they are entered. Catalogue output is available as COM, cards, magnetic tapes, and accessions lists.

The Acquisitions System integrates data from the Online Union Catalogue with local order and fund data, thus improving order processing and providing current accounting information. The OCLC data base is searched for the appropriate record, and if this is present this may be used in initiating the order. If this is not available, a record can be created on a form online. The receipt of materials and invoices and suppliers' reports are recorded in acquisitions records. The Acquisitions System uses a Name-Address Directory as its source of address information for orders.

The Serials Control System handles check-in, claiming and union listing of serial publications. There is online access to current, detailed copy-specific holdings and location information in the individual library and from union list groups. The CONSER (Conversion of Serials) project built up a large serials data base.

The Interlibrary Loan System increases resource sharing by providing effective loan processing. This system is used both in the United States and between the United Kingdom and European countries and the United States. The intending borrower merely specifies a search key for the item he wishes to borrow, and the system provides a bibliographic description, and permits the requester to specify up to five potential lending libraries, and the system transmits the requests to these libraries one at a time.

(b) Local Library System LS/2000 OCLC is developing a local library system that will eventually include circulation control and online catalogues. The local system is designed to be flexible enough to meet the needs of a single library or those of a library cluster. OCLC's local system will permit

libraries to automate in stages. Eventually the LS/2000 will support circulation and cataloguing and provide online public access catalogues, administrative control, and serials check-in. The library can define its own authority files, indexes, bibliographic and patron record contents and other features. It is thus possible to design a local system tailored to the needs of the individual library within the range of options available with LS/2000.

OCLC Europe supports a nationwide telecommunications network in the United Kingdom and Ireland to provide users with dedicated access to the OCLC data bases and associated service in the US. The OCLC Europe network is connected to the OCLC computer system in the US by a dedicated link via an undersea cable.

2. LASER The London and South Eastern Library Region (LASER) is an organisation for library co-operation within Greater London, and various counties in the South East of England. LASER operates an interlending service which is based upon its union catalogue. A transport scheme is operated for interlending in London and the South East, and various bibliographic services are offered based on LASER's minicomputer.

There are currently 1.23 million records on the LASER minicomputer system, representing the 40 million volumes held in member libraries. The LASER minicomputer system is in union catalogue form, and includes UKMARC records as well as LCMARC records for books acquired by LASER libraries, and records generated by LASER member libraries. Records can be accessed by author, title and book number. A microfiche version of the LASER data base, the LASER Union Catalogue on Microfiche shows records to the end of 1982 in author order. A selective record service and a card service is available to member libraries for records relating to their collections.

3. BLCMP BLCMP (originally Birmingham Libraries Cooperative Mechanisation Project) is a co-operative venture which embraces both network and stand-alone services, and batch and online services. Formed in 1969, the first operational system was implemented in 1972-3. Today, BLCMP offers services to nearly fifty member libraries, including public libraries, university libraries, polytechnic libraries and others. The shared systems are run on an IBM 4341 computer housed at BLCMP. The shared online system 'BOSS' utilises a private telecommunications network.

BLCMP maintains extensive data bases of MARC records. All UKMARC data is available, LCMARC from 1972 and BLCMP member libraries Extra MARC cataloguing. The data base contains a large number of audo-visual items, music and serials. Online interactive searching can be performed on author/title acronyms and traditional control number searching is possible and the only means of access on the offline batch system.

353

The Cataloguing Systems were the first to be developed. The first systems were batch mode and batch mode catalogue record processing is still available. BOSS (BLCMP On Line Support Service) provides a fully integrated online acquisitions and cataloguing system. The online cataloguing system allows users to search for, edit and create records. Tailored formats are provided on the screen for the input and amendment of records. Records are of two types: general bibliographic records which contain the base bibliographic data, and local records relating to local information of particular interest to an individual library. An extensive Name Authority File is maintained. BLCMP produces union and individual library catalogues, and these last are available in a range of formats. The union catalogues are on microfiche. An online public access facility is being developed.

The Acquisitions and Ordering System provides facilities for the ordering and receipt of library materials. Records of items on order or recently received are created, consulted and amended online. The acquisitions systems is presently only available to subscribers to BOSS, but will be offered as a stand alone option at a later date. Prior to creation of an order record, the user may search to discover whether an item is already in stock, and to ascertain its bibliographic details. BLCMP data bases include CIP data, and will be enhanced to cover data from suppliers' data bases. Any record may be used for inclusion in an order, and tailored input formats facilitate the creation of orders. Various other facilities are available, such as printed orders, chasing, and maintenance of records. The order can be retrieved for receipt details to be added when the document arrives.

BLCMP's Circulation System, CIRCO, can be extensively tailored to meet local requirements. CIRCO operates as a stand alone circulation package but may also be linked to BLCMP's centralised cataloguing and acquisitions services. BLCMP's stand alone systems run on Data General Eclipse computers, a range covering both micros and mainframes. CIRCO incorporates all the usual functions associated with the issue, return and reservation of library materials. Data-capture units are light pens, and such units can be made available at various locations in the library for public consultation. Enquiries can be made to discover the status of particular records. Access is available by author/title key and classmark, as well as by control number and charging number.

Other facilities include the possibility of generating: current accessions lists, subject indexes, selected sequences, Regional Library Bureaux notifications and printed accessions registers.

4. SWALCAP SWALCAP is a non-profit making organisation based at the University of Bristol. Established in 1969, SWALCAP has been financially self-sufficient since 1979. The aim of SWALCAP is to provide integrated computer services for library housekeeping purposes, and to keep these services up to date. Its primary function is to provide a centre for software and hardware expertise for its members, and in order to achieve this, it has its own computer centre.

SWALCAP supports a network arrangement of remote terminals and minicomputers linked to the central computer via private lines. All online facilities are available from all terminals. Access to individual transactions is made via a menu which lists each application as detailed: circulation, direct data entry, print files, terminal system control, cataloguing.

The MkII circulation system is an enhanced version of a system which was originally the core of the SWALCAP services. The service centres on an online short title catalogue and an online registration file. For libraries with catalogue records in MARC format the short title catalogue can be created automatically from this data base. Some terminals will be linked to telepens for issue, return and renew functions. Enquiries as to the status of items may be input through any terminal. Management information is available for loan statistics.

The cataloguing service has been in use since 1978. From 1983 a MkII cataloguing and acquisitions system has been in operation. In this Mk II system all records in the data base will be available online and are accessible by control number, author/title, or title and author acronym keys. A link between the MARC records in the catalogue system and the circulation system permits the records in the short title catalogue to be displayed in full. Online editing and amendment of catalogue records, and a variety of modes of output is available for member libraries. There are nineteen member libraries.

5. *Other cooperatives* There are other networks which support the sharing of cataloguing data. SCOLCAP is based on the National Library of Scotland and is financed by the Scottish Education Department, and through subscriptions from around twenty member libraries. A union file currently contains 832,000 general records, and associated local records. The services being developed are an integrated online cataloguing and acquisition system with a link to BLAISE for data required by members but not found in the local data bases.

There are also other cataloguing co-operatives in the United Kingdom. For example, NEMROC (Newcastle Media Resources Organisation Committee) provides a forum for libraries in the region of Newcastle with good collections of audio-visual materials to pool their ideas. SHEMROC is a similar grouping for the Sheffield area.

WLN (Washington Library Network) is composed of libraries in the states of Washington and Alaska in the United States, and is expanding to cover other states and libraries in Canada. WLN was first established in 1967 when the Washington State Library took responsibility for developing the network. After a pilot trial in 1972 in which ten libraries participated, an online system was developed in 1975. The system now functions as three inter-related subsystems: the bibliographic (implemented in 1977); acquisitions (implemented in 1978); and batch retrospective conversion (developed in 1980). The bibliographic subsystem is the part which supports cataloguing activities such as data base maintenance, online searching, and the generation of online and COM union catalogues, bibliographies and so on.

RLIN (Research Libraries Information Network) is a system used by the Research Libraries Group (RLG), a group dedicated to resolving common problems in collection development, management, access and preservation. RLIN provides RLG members, about twenty-five research libraries, with an online catalogue, and acquisitions and inter-library loan subsystems. The software is known as BALLOTS, which is an online system offering rather more online information retrieval facilities than OCLC and other cataloguing agencies.

The Library of Congress has assumed the role of network co-ordinator in the United States. This was initiated formally by the calling of the first meeting of the Network Advisory Committee in 1976. Since the early 1970s the LC has engaged in various activities which have in some way supported the work of the co-operative. The LC began to establish a core bibliographic data base in the early 1970s. Within LC, there have been several automation projects designed to facilitate access to this data base. These include MUMS (Multiple Use MARC System) in connection with online interrogation and correction of MARC data; APIF (Automated Process Information File) which makes it possible to determine whether an item is in stock and to speed up and improve processing techniques; and SCORPIO (Subject Content Oriented Retriever for Processing Information Online), a general purpose retrieval system designed for use with MARC data bases. The LC has also participated in two co-operative programs for the conversion of printed records to machine-readable form: COMARC for monographs, and CONSER for serials records.

Naturally there are also co-operative networks outside the UK and the US. One very significant co-operative UTLAS (University of Toronto Library Automation System) has been operating with computer-based products since 1973. The network includes around two hundred institutions, and more than six hundred libraries receive products or services from the system. Although many of the members are in Canada there are now users in the United States and Japan. Using the CATalogue Support System (CATSS) libraries may derive, edit or input cataloguing data to create individually structured files. The data base include over ten million records. From 1978, CATSS has offered an authority file to enable clients to create and maintain authorised forms of names, uniform titles and subject headings.

LIBRIS (Library Information System) is a major library automation project in Sweden. It includes a cataloguing module. BUMS is the name of the system developed by Bibliotekstjanst, the Swedish Libraries' Central Service Organisation.

6. *UKLDS* The UKLDS is more of a data base and a set of software for the support of a data base, than a cataloguing co-operative. Nevertheless, in the sense that the UKLDS is a co-operative cataloguing venture it has a place in this section. The UKLDS or the UK Library Database System is a proposal from the Cooperative Automation Group (CAG) which was first disseminated in a discussion paper published in 1982. CAG's membership consists basically of representatives from each of the British library co-operative, BLCMP, LASER, SCOLCAP, SWALCAP, and from BL Bibliographic Services Division, and Aslib, the Library Association, SCONUL (the Standing Conference of National and University Libraries) and COPOL (the Council of Polytechnic Libraries).

Initially at least, the proposal is for the establishment of a centralised data base, and the software to support the establishment and communication with the data base, which will support shared cataloguing requirements. This data base would allow the co-operatives to pool all Extra-MARC records created by the members of the co-operatives, and would thus eventually become a very substantial bibliographic data base. A proposed input standard for records in the UKLDS for monographs has been published in 1983. This standard is compatible with AACR2 and the UK MARC format. Input standards for various other media are currently being developed, since there is some concern that much of the value of the data base may be negated if it does not seek to cover all materials which libraries might acquire. At present, there are only preliminary discussions concerning subject access to the data base, and in respect of the inclusion of holdings data. Either or both these facilities would enhance the value of the data base beyond merely providing catalogue records to either a UK union catalogue, or a data base for information retrieval.

Although many of the co-operatives were established originally to create a union catalogue, and make possible the sharing of library resources, it should be evident from the above examples that the co-operatives have played a much more extensive role in recent years, and are set to continue in their expanded role. This expanded role emerged from the fact that the catalogue data base is the central record of the resources of a region. Other library housekeeping systems rely upon the catalogue data base. Co-operatives have then been instrumental in the development and introduction of new technology in libraries. In this area members of co-operatives have benefited greatly from the exchange of information, the mutual solving of system problems, and the general pooling of expertise. It is these features which have led the co-operatives to develop integrated housekeeping systems, and which have led co-operative members to select these systems rather than those of the commercial software vendor. Often, the facilities offered by a co-operative may not be as sophisticated as those available from software vendors, but the support of a group of libraries is valued. Whether, in the future, the co-operatives will be able to fund appropriate developments at a sufficiently rapid rate remains an unanswered question.

Chapter 18 Readings

A. Cataloguing networks

1 Bakewell, K.G.B., 'The UK library networks and the Co-operative Automation Group', *Aslib Proceedings* 34 (6/7), 1982, 301–9.
2 'General support for a UK library database system' *Library Association Record*, 85(5), 1983, 180–2.
3 Hewitt, J.A. 'The impact of OCLC', *American Libraries*, 1976, 268–75.
4 Holmes, P.L., 'The British Library Automated Information Services', *Online Review* 3(3), 1979, 265–274.
5 *Independent versus co-operative systems:* proceedings of a seminar held at the School of Librarianship and Information Studies, Newcastle upon Tyne Polytechnic, 22 September 1982, editors M. Watson *et al.*, Library Association, University College & Research Section, Northern Group: Newcastle upon Tyne, 1983.
6 Kilgour, F.G., 'Shared cataloguing at OCLC', *Online Review*, 3(3), 1979, 275–279
7 'Library cooperatives and LOCAS: ten years of growth', *Vine*, (28), 1979, 37–48.
8 Martin, S.K., *Library networks, 1978–1979*, Knowledge Industry Publications: White Plains, New York, 1978.
9 *OCLC: a national library network*, ed A.M. Allison and A. Allan, Mansell: London, 1979.
10 Plaister, J.M., *Computing in LASER: regional libraries cooperation*, Library Association: London, 1982. (Case studies in library automation).
11 Plotnik, A., 'OCLC for you – and ME?!' *American Libraries*, 7, 1976, 258–67.
12 Rowley, J., 'National database: near useless monolith or hope for the future?', *Library Association Record*, 85(9), 1983, 307–8.
13 Seal, A.W., *Automated cataloguing in the UK*, University Library, 1980; Bath, BLRDD Report 5545.
14 Stevens, N.D., 'Library networks and resource sharing in the United States', *Journal of the American Society for Information Science*, 31(6), 1980, 405–11.

B. Cataloguing-in-publication

13 *Cataloguing-in-publication: what is happening?* Proceedings of a one-day seminar held at the Library Association on 21 October 1981. Library Association Cataloguing & Indexing Group, 1982. (*Catalogue and Index* (63/64), 1981/1982).

14 'Cataloguing-in-source', *Library Journal*, 85(8), 1960, 1535–37.

15 'Cataloguing in/at source', *Library Resources and Technical Services*, 15(1), 1971, 6–27.

16 CIP International Meeting, Washington, DC, 13–17 September, 1976, *Library of Congress Information Bulletin* 35(46), 1976, 701–2.

17 Green, S. 'The Cataloguing-in-publication project: a background note', *Vine*, 28, 1979, 27–30.

18 Gosling, W.A. and Perkins, L.L. 'Cataloguing-in-publication' *Unesco Bulletin for Libraries*, 28(6), 1974, 305–7.

19 Ranganathan, S.R., 'Pre-natal classification and cataloguing on its way', *Annals of Library Science*, 6(4), 1959, 113–25.

20 Swindley, L.R., *Cataloguing-in-publication: an international survey*, Unesco: Paris, 1975. (COM. 75/WS/32)

21 Wingate, H.W., 'Cataloguing-in-publication: problems and prospects', *Library Resources and Technical Services*, 16(4), 1972, 423–32.

19.1 Introduction

Online information retrieval services, which permit users scattered in a number of locations in the world to search data bases held on a computer which may be many miles distant from the user and his terminal, started to develop in the late 1960s and the early 1970s. There are now over 2000 data bases extending across science, technology, business, social science and the humanities, mounted on a number of computers spread at various locations throughout the world. Users are able to use terminals many miles distant to search the computer data base of their choice, with the support of a telecommunications network to link terminal to computer. This can be summarised as:

Terminal_____Telecommunications network _____Computer

The telecommunications facilities necessary for online searching will be considered in section 19.2 and the hosts responsible for mounting data bases on computers will be examined in section 19.3. All that remains to be mentioned here is the terminal. Terminals for use in online searching may be printer or Visual Display Units, and may often contain both components. Some systems call for dedicated and specially designed terminals. LEXIS, the legal data base and its companion NEXIS fall into this category. A microcomputer or word processor as a terminal will need an inexpensive software package in order to convert the machine into a form that makes it suitable for external communication. Otherwise, microcomputers, word processors and other intelligent terminals have distinct advantages as they can, if so designed, be used to store search strategies and results of searches.

19.2 Telecommunications

In order that computers which are many miles distant from each other be able to communicate, or that a terminal be able to send messages to a computer, there has to be a medium for the communication of such messages. Communication is usually achieved primarily through a telecommunications network. There are two components of such access: the national and international networks, and the telephone.

19.2.1 National and international networks

There are national and international telecommunications networks which have been designed for transmitting information to and from computers, rather than transmitting people's voices. Most of these networks rely upon a technique known as packet switching. In packet switching the message is split up in order to be sent through the network in short fixed length packets. Each packet includes the address of the final destination, and the packets travel separately, perhaps taking different routes through the network. This means that a large number of messages can be combined together along the same line, giving economies of scale.

Notable telecommunications networks are Tymnet and Telenet, which are predominantly North American, but also have nodes in Europe and other parts of the world. These two provide access to nearly all major American hosts. Access to Tymnet and Telenet from Europe is possible via agreements with the national Post, Telephone and Telegraph authorities (PTTs). In the United Kingdom the International Packet Switch Stream (IPSS) enables searchers to access computers in North America. IPSS links to Tymnet, Telenet, Uninet and Autonet.

Access to hosts in Europe is facilitated by EURONET. A number of European hosts, including BLAISE, INFOLINE, DIMDI and DATA-STAR are accessible through EURONET. EURONET also provides links to other European networks, such as the Scandinavian network, SCANNET. Hosts in Europe can also be contacted through the European part of the IPSS network. Hosts within the United Kingdom may be accessed by a UK user via British Telecom's national network for data access, Packet Switch Stream (PSS). PSS has nodes in many major cities; users pay ordinary call charges to the nearest node, plus a charge for the use of PSS. Provided there is a node within a local call distance, this arrangement is reasonably priced. However, since most hosts are in South East England, access can be expensive from other parts of the UK. Thus some hosts, for example BLAISE, have installed their own networks with local dial-up nodes in various large cities. Normally there is no charge for the use of these networks.

Other hosts also have their own networks. Dialog provides DIALNET as a link between California and London. SDC has a line from the USA to its computer in Woking. ESA-IRS has ESANET which has a node in London. Most computer bureaux which host the factual data bases have their own world-wide networks. These private networks are generally cheaper than public networks.

19.2.2 Telephones

To get into these national and international networks which are suitable for long-distance communication, a telephone link must be used to access the closest node. It is possible to use dial-up access via the public switched telephone network. A leased line connection is useful for heavy users, since it offers higher speeds of transmission, and permits the use of local storage devices. The terminal must be linked to the telephone line via either an acoustic coupler or a modem.

A modem is permanently wired, and converts digital messages which the terminal and computer understand into analogue messages capable of being transmitted down telephone lines. Acoustic couplers serve a similar purpose except that they are not permanently wired; the handset is placed in the acoustic coupler to achieve a connection once a telephone line has been opened.

19.3 Online hosts

Online system hosts, sometimes known as online system suppliers, online service vendors and online service spinners are responsible for mounting data bases upon a computer and making the arrangements necessary for such data bases to be searchable from a large number of remote user terminals. In this section we are primarily concerned with hosts that make large bibliographic data bases publicly available. Some data base producers are also vendors. For example, LEXIS and NEXIS are both produced and mounted by Mead Data Central.

MEDLINE, produced by the US National Library of Medicine, is mounted by the National Library of Medicine. However, many major data bases are available through what are known as supermarket hosts. Such hosts purchase or license data bases from producers and convert data on tapes to a uniform format with standardised bibliographic element names so that the basic commands and search techniques apply across all data bases offered by a specific vendor. Hosts also offer various support services such as manuals, search aids and training facilities.

Most supermarket hosts offer a range of ten to fifty data bases. In total there are now over 1500 data bases available on science, technology, business, social sciences and humanities subjects. For more details of the range of data bases see 19.7. In order to have access to the data bases offered by a specific host it is necessary to sign on as a user. Most information services will start by signing with two, three or four main hosts, and learn these systems, and become familiar with these data bases before progressing to other systems and other data bases. Once a user is registered, a password will be issued which provides access to all or most of the data bases offered by the host as and when the user wishes. Many of the major data bases are available through more than one host. It becomes necessary to select both the most appropriate data base for any given search, and also the most appropriate host. These issues will be considered later, but first some of the major hosts are introduced.

SDC ORBIT

The Systems Development Corporation's (SDC) search service runs ORBIT from a computer in Santa Monica, California. ORBIT has been operational since 1972, and has around seventy data bases mounted. ORBIT is the exclusive vendor for around half of its data bases. Many of the SDC files are scientific and technical. Several of the exclusive data bases cover petroleum and fossil fuels. These include APILIT from the American Petroleum Institute which covers magazines, journals, papers and reports. APIPAT, also from API, covers refining patents from various countries. TULSA is the equivalent of the printed Petroleum Abstracts. Other data bases include several offering access to US government information such as CRECORD, the index of the Congressional record, and FEDREG, the Federal Register. Also available are other assorted data bases, including ACCOUNTANTS (index), SPORT (printed equivalent is Sport and Recreation Index), and WPI (World Patents Index covering the patent specifications issued by patent offices in major industrial nations).

SDC ORBIT also offers certain special services. These include an SDI (Selective Dissemination of Information) service and the facilities for users to establish and maintain their own private data bases. Electronic Maildrop is an online document ordering feature, where documents can be ordered from various suppliers. The Data Base Index is an online data base of basic index terms used in any of the SDC data bases and helps users to determine which files are most likely to supply information on a given subject. Training programmes, search aids and various publications all support the SDC ORBIT services.

DIALOG

DIALOG information retrieval services is run by Lockheed Information Systems from a computer in Palo Alto in California. Over one hundred data bases are available, of which around half could be broadly categorised as scientific and technical. Large scientific and technical files include CA SEARCH, SCISEARCH and BIOSIS PREVIEWS. However, the scope of the data bases is wide, and extends to the arts, social sciences, public affairs, current events and business. Included are ART MODERN (printed equivalent–Art Bibliographies Modern), AMERICA: HISTORY AND LIFE, and MANAGEMENT CONTENTS. Most of the data bases are bibliographic in nature, but DIALOG does offer some statistical and directory files. Amongst these are the Encyclopaedia of Associations, EIS INDUSTRIAL PLANTS and Predicasts and International Time Series and Forecasts.

SDI is available on a number of data bases. DIALORDER is an online ordering service; document requests are supplied by one of twenty-two suppliers. The DIALOG Private File Service allows organisations online access to their private files, and permits subscribers to build and maintain their own files. Various search aids and training facilities are offered.

BRS

Bibliograpic Retrieval Services Inc (BRS) is run from Scotia, New York. A relative newcomer to the marketplace, having commenced operation in 1977, BRS is a small host offering access to around thirty data bases. Its policy is to acquire data bases that are heavily used, and although no attempt has been made to acquire exclusive rights to data bases, nine of its data bases are not available from any other source. These nine are either in medicine or serials. BRS offers MEDLINE, and also ALCOHOL USE/ABUSE, DRUG INFO and other medical data bases not available through other supermarket hosts. BRS also has two serials files. These are the National Agricultural Library's NAL SERIALS, and MARC SERIALS which lists serials catalogued by the Library of Congress. Another interesting data base is BOOKS-INFO, a file of bibliographic data on books in print, from Brodart Inc. Other data bases are ERIC, MANAGEMENT CONTENTS, SOCIAL SCISEARCH, CA SEARCH and INSPEC. Some large files are only online for the most recent three to five year portions.

BRS offers an SDI service. Also available is a cross data base for multi-file searching (BRS/CROSS), online accounting, private data base services and an online catalogue service. Prices tend to be lower than those on SDC and DIALOG, and this has obvious attractions. The range of data bases has attracted a number of academic libraries.

ESA-IRS

The European Space Agency's (ESA) Information Retrieval Service (IRS) was first established in the form of the European Space Research Organisation's Space Documentation Service (ESRO SDS) in 1965. Based at Frascati in Italy, ESA-IRS was one of the first organisations to offer online search facilities. Data bases originally focused upon space research and technology. Now ESA-IRS offers access to thirty-five data bases, mostly in science and technology. ESA-IRS has back-up services in various European countries; the service offering such facilities in the United Kingdom is IRS-DIALTECH.

INFOLINE

Pergamon-INFOLINE came into being in its present form in 1980 when it was taken over by Pergamon. Based in London, Pergamon-INFOLINE offers around twenty to thirty data bases of various types and sizes. Data bases include: CA SEARCH and COMPENDEX, both large scientific data bases. Smaller bibliographic data bases include: WORLD TEXTILES, ZINC, LEAD & CADMIUM ABSTRACTS, and RAPRA ABSTRACTS. Directory data bases include: DUN & BRADSTREET'S KEY BRITISH ENTERPRISES, FINE CHEMICALS DIRECTORY, and the DIRECTORY OF COMPANIES.

BLAISE

BLAISE is another United Kingdom host. It services are considered in Chapter 18.

DATA STAR

DATA STAR, offered by Radio-Suisse, mounts various data bases including: business data bases, for example ABI/INFORM, NYTS, PREDICASTS, MANAGEMENT CONTENTS, FINANCIAL TIMES COMPANY INFORMATION; biomedical data bases, for example, BIOSIS PREVIEWS, MEDLINE, EXCERPTA MEDICA: chemical data bases, for example, CHEMICAL ABSTRACTS, and CHEMICAL ENGINEERING ABSTRACTS; and technical data bases for example, NTIS, INSPEC and COMPENDEX. Altogether between twenty and thirty data bases are offered.

BELINDIS

BELINDIS, the Belgian Information and Dissemination Service is offered by the Data Processing Centre of the Belgian Ministry of Economic Affairs. Around ten data bases are offered, with notable data bases being EAI (Economics Abstracts International), CREDOC-BLEX (Belgian legislation) and INIS (International Nuclear Information System). These reflect the general coverage which is particularly in the areas of law and legislation, economics and energy.

ECHO

ECHO is the European Commission's own host service. Since 1980 it has offered access to data bases and data banks either wholly or partially sponsored by the Commission of the European Communities. Data bases are mainly of a European nature, including information on research organisations and a multi-lingual terminology data bank to User Guidance files.

Other European hosts include DIMDI, the German Service, and Telesystèmes-Questel based in France. Both these hosts offers around thirty-five data bases each. There are now over twenty online hosts connected to EURONET, offering altogether access to around 150 data bases. All the major European hosts mentioned above are linked into EURONET.

Hosts for non-bibliographical data bases

Non-bibliographical data bases include numeric, textual-numeric, properties and full text data bases. Non-bibliographic data bases are offered by many more suppliers than bibliographical data bases, and are particularly used for businesses and industry to extract information in the fields of business, economics, trade and commerce. Such hosts are more likely to be accessed by end-users such as economists and managers, than information workers. Frequently numeric data bases and the hosts which support them permit some computation and manipulation of the retrieved data.

The most significant suppliers of non-bibliographical data bases are:

1. Automatic Data Processing Inc (ADP), which offers a number of financial and economic data bases with the aid of their TSAM (Time Series Analysis and Modelling) on the DATALYST service. Included are the UK-Macro-CSO (Central Statistical Office), and the International Financial Statistics Databases.

2. IP Sharp, which makes available a number of public data bases including the UK CSO, the International Monetary Fund and the US Consumer and Wholesale Price Indexes, via the MAGIC software which allows for the manipulation of time series and non-time series data.

3. GEISCO is a US service offering information on mineral resources in the USA, and over 95 other countries. Included are the BI/DATA data bases which contain almost 20,000 time series covering the economics of one hundred different countries. MAP (Management Analysis and Projection System) is available for manipulating the data.

4. Business International Inc. is another US service covering economic and marketing activities in over seventy countries.

5. Data Resources Inc., again US-based, covers data bases in economics, finance, energy and weather.

6. SIA in the United Kingdom covers information on travel and transport, economics in EEC countries, construction of nuclear power stations, and financial information.

19.4 Hosts – points for comparison

Data base hosts must be compared and contrasted in order that a sound selection of host may be made for any specific search. Obviously, the overall objective is to retrieve as many relevant documents, and as few irrelevant documents in the minimum time and at the least cost and user inconvenience. Although hosts offer similar services, and the pressures of the marketplace mean that any vital facility must be offered by all of the major hosts, there are differences between the services offered by the different hosts. Apart from the different data bases available from the different hosts, there may be differences in the way in which any given data base can be searched under various hosts. For some data bases the selection of the data base will determine the hosts, but on other occasions other factors must also be considered. Specifically, then, hosts may vary in respect of:

1. The data base offered As already explored, the numbers of data bases offered by any specific host will vary, as can the subject coverage and language of the available data bases. Also, different hosts may have different time spans of any given data base available for online searching.

2. Search facilities The elements of records that can be searched may differ from one host to another. Certainly the field formats may vary and the fields names may be different. See Chapters 5 and 6. Some systems offer more extensive facilities with regards to contextual or proximity searching, and truncation. For non-bibliographic data bases various special facilities may be required.

3. Command languages Command languages are an essential feature of the search facilities of any given host. Figure 19.1 summarises and compares some differences between different hosts. A command language is the language with which the search proceeds; the commands are the instructions that the searcher can issue to the computer. Different hosts have different command languages depending upon their search software. Command languages are considered in a little more detail in 19.6.

4. Formats for records Various formats are available for viewing the details of retrieved references. Sometimes it is possible for the searcher to select the elements that he requires, but in searching other hosts only a few standard formats are available.

5. Additional facilities Many hosts offer other facilities in addition to the basic online search facility. Often SDI or document delivery services are available. These may become increasingly important as hosts seek to match the needs of users more closely.

Figure 19.1 A comparison of some common commands from various online hosts

CAS ONLINE Commands— Comparison Chart

COMMAND FUNCTION	CAS ONLINE	DIALOG	SDC	BRS	ESA/IRS
Prompt	=>	?	USER:	¬	?
Change files	FILE	FILE BEGIN	FILE	..CHANGE/	.FILE BEGIN
Execute a search	SEARCH	SELECT SELECT STEPS COMBINE	(FIND)	..SEARCH	SELECT COMBINE
Precedence of Boolean operators	1. AND .NOT 2. OR	1. NOT 2. AND 3. OR	1. AND 2. NOT 3. OR	1. AND 2. NOT 3. OR	1. NOT 2. AND 3. OR
Look at inverted index	EXPAND	EXPAND	NEIGHBOR	ROOT	EXPAND
Specify level of postings detail	SET POSTINGS	-------	AUDIT	..SET DETAIL	------
Restrict search	RANGE	LIMIT	(date ranging)	..LIMIT	LIMIT
Save information for later use	SAVE	END/SAVE	STORE	..SAVE	END/SAVE KEEP

	DELETE (name)	.RECALL (name) .RELEASE	PURGE (name)	..PURGE PS (name)	.RECALL (name) .RELEASE
Remove saved items from storage	DELETE (name)	.RECALL (name) .RELEASE	PURGE (name)	..PURGE PS (name)	.RECALL (name) .RELEASE
Look at answers online	DISPLAY	TYPE	PRINT	..PRINT	TYPE
Print answers offline	PRINT	PRINT	PRINT OFFLINE	..PRINTOFF	PRINT
Cancel offline print order	DELETE (print no.)	PR-(set no.)	(Done within PRINT command)	..PURGE (print no.)	PR-(print no.)
Order original document	ORDER	ORDERITEM	ORDER	MSGS	ORDER
View session history	DISPLAY HISTORY	DISPLAY SETS	HISTORY	..DISPLAY	DISPLAY SETS
Restart session	DELETE HISTORY	BEGIN	RESTART	..PURGE	BEGIN
Send message to vendor	SEND	- - - - - -	COMMENT	MSGS (address BERS)	MESSAGE
End the online session	LOGOFF	LOGOFF	STOP	..OFF	LOGOFF

6. *Support services* Most hosts offer some support and training services. Help desks, training courses, manuals, newsletters and other search aids can influence the effectiveness of a searcher. Good training and careful instruction can often lead to a searcher being effective with even the most complex searching systems and data bases. The availability of such support services must be considered, but availability is not the only factor. Support services must be effective, accessible (for example, training courses in the searcher's own locality), and reasonably cheap.

7. *Time availability* Most hosts are not available twenty-four hours a day, seven days of the week. Some down time is necessary for maintenance and updating of the files. Hosts are available for a variable number of hours in the day, and a variable number of days in the week. For example, DATA-STAR is available on Mondays from 10.00 to 18.30, and on Tuesdays to Fridays from 8.00 to 18.30 (Central European Time). Times should be sought which coincide with the user's requirements.

8. *Cost* The cost of searching a specific data base for a given search can be difficult to assess, but is obviously an important aspect of the searching process. There will be special rates for additional services such as SDI or document delivery. Normally, charges will comprise data base connect charges, and print charges per reference. Telecommunications charges will also add to the cost of a search. The data base connect charges sometimes include data base royalty charges, but for other hosts these will be charged separately. Print charges are usually charged per reference retrieved, with online and offline prints often attracting different tariffs, and different record formats being charged at different rates. But matters are not as straightforward as merely analysing the direct costs. If extensive use is likely to be made of a particular data base discount charges are available by contracting to buy a predetermined number of connect hours per year.

9. *Experience* The searcher's experience with a specific host may be an important factor in determining his search effectiveness. Thus, from the searcher's point of view it is important not only to assess the specific features of the host, but also to examine his own skills.

19.5 The future for online hosts

Until recently supermarket hosts have been predominant in the market. These have their own specialised, and often unique command languages, and have been oriented to specialist searchers. The most effective searchers are those who have both system experience and some familiarity with the subject area in which they are searching. These hosts are often searched by information intermediaries who have acquired specialist searching skills. One trend for the future is likely to be the development of hosts which cover more specialist subject areas, and which are designed for interaction with the end user. Already such specialist hosts are common in the non-bibliographic data base sector, and these hosts can be expected to become more numerous. The differences in approach will include:

1. Catering directly for the needs of the end user and planning for interaction with the end user.
2. Exploration of different formats for information, so that the information is in a form compatible with the end use.
3. Close contacts will need to be maintained with clients in order to monitor their needs.
4. Factual information, in the form of statistics, and full text will become more central.
5. Language of documents and data bases will need to be tailored to each community; geographical constraints may be introduced, so that a data base can be searched in a 'French' command language in France, and in a 'German' command language in Germany.
6. The reputation of the information and its authority will be more exposed to examination.
7. Further developments will depend to a considerable extent upon the prices that the market is prepared to pay for information products.

A parallel development which is likely to support proliferation of specialist hosts is the establishment of STN International. STN International is a host arrangement being spearheaded by Chemical Abstracts Services. The American Chemical Society will share resources with other data base producers, permitting other data base producers either to mount files on the ACS computer in Ohio or to acquire the ACS software under the condition that the host makes its computer accessible via an international network. This is viewed as a mechanism for data base producers to become hosts, and to share the cost and risk of participating in an international host service. The arrangements should also negotiate resistance to perceived 'American dominance', erode price differentials between Europe and the US, and permit each country to support its own online services.

A variety of nodes, with important files available at all nodes, and mutual back-up between nodes will be linked to form an international network. The network will, it is planned, eventually cover scientific, technical and some commercial literature. Primary literature, secondary literature, numerical and factual data will all be represented. The network will support data base building, display, document ordering and online retrieval.

Alongside this network approach there are an increasing number of data base producers who are mounting their own data bases. This is likely to be particularly important for directory-type data bases and other full text data bases, such as electronic journals.

Against this proliferation of hosts there is a distinct awareness amongst users of the need for rationalisation. Some users hope that market forces will force some of the smaller hosts out of the marketplace, but with cheaper telecommunications and computing technology this seems something of a vain hope.

19.6 Command languages

A command language is the set of commands or instructions that the searcher uses to instruct the computer to perform certain operations. Negus has identified fourteen basic functions for which commands must be present in any online command language. This set of commands forms the basis for the EURONET Common Command Language, which is available for searching on some of the European hosts. These same functions are also seen to be important in framing the International Standard for Command Languages

These command functions are:

CONNECT	to provide for logging on
BASE	to identify the data base to be searched
FIND	to input a search term
DISPLAY	to display a list of alphabetically linked terms
RELATE	to display logically related terms
SHOW	to print references online
PRINT	to print references offline
FORMAT	to specify the format to be displayed
DELETE	to delete search terms or print requests
SAVE	to save a search formulation for later use on the same or another data base on the same system
OWN	to use a system's own command when the general system, in this case EURONET, does not cater for a specialised function available on a particular system
STOP	to end the session and logoff
MORE	to request the system to display more information, for instance to continue the alphabetical display of terms.
HELP	to obtain guidance online when in difficulty.

As can be seen in Figure 19.1 which compares the commands for several hosts there is no standard command language. The different command languages are associated with the different retrieval software used by the different hosts. As far as users are concerned, standardisation of command languages is highly desirable. The need to become familiar with different command languages for different hosts is a considerable barrier to effective retrieval. In particular, when one command means one thing in one system and something else in another system this is likely to lead to confusion. Hosts are less keen to standardise, although the EURONET Common Command Language has been adopted by various hosts, and there is some recognition of the potential benefits to the user of greater standardisation.

19.7 Data bases

The array of data bases available through one or other of the online hosts is rapidly expanding. By the early 1980s one estimate put the number of publicly availably files at five hundred.

As mentioned earlier in Chapter 5, there are two different types of data bases: bibliographic data bases, and non-bibliographic data bases. The bibliographic files allow the searcher to retrieve references to work that has appeared in documents such as journal articles, conference papers, books, dissertations, patents and technical reports. The subject areas which such data bases cover may range from relatively narrow subjects, to interdisciplinary areas. The number of non-bibliographical data bases which have been created is a matter for open speculation. Certainly there are a number of such data bases which are publicly available. The majority, however, are private. Many private data bases and data banks are consistently supported and updated by individuals and organisations on microcomputers, minicomputers and mainframes. Here we are concerned only with publicly available data bases. In this realm, there are data banks covering, for instance, business statistics and government series, chemical dictionaries and directory files. In some subject fields, notably business, there may be both bibliographic and non-bibliographic data bases covering different aspects of the topic.

Data bases can be produced by three types of organisation:

government bodies, for example, CHILD ABUSE AND NEGLECT from the Children's Bureau of the National Center on Child Abuse and Neglect (US), and AGRICOLA from the US National Agricultural Library, and others.

professional societies, for example, INSPEC from the Institution of Electrical Engineers (UK), WORLD ALUMINIUM ABSTRACTS, from the American Society for Metals, and MLA Bibliography from the Modern Language Association.

Figure 19.2 Some types of data bases with examples

Type	Example	Producer	Printed equivalent/ comments
Chemistry	CA SEARCH	American Chemical Society	Chemical Abstracts/ very large
	RAPRA ABSTRACTS	Rubber & Plastics Research Association	RAPRA Abstracts/ small, specialised
Biology, Medicine, Toxicology	MEDLINE	National Library of Medicine	Index Medicus/ very large
	BIOSIS PREVIEWS	Biosciences Information Service	Biological Abstracts
	EXCERPTA MEDICA	Excerpta Medica	Various, for example Anatomy, Anthropology
	VETDOC	Derwent Publications Ltd	VETDOC Abstract Journal/ veterinary science and medicine
	TOXLINE	National Library of Medicine	toxicology
Energy and Environment	TULSA	University of Tulsa	Petroleum Abstracts/petroleum exploration and production
	ENERGYLINE, ENVIROLINE	Environment Information Center Inc.	Energy Information Abstracts/— Environment Abstracts/—
	SURFACE COATINGS ABSTRACTS	Paint Research Association of Great Britain	World Surface Coatings Abstracts/—
Engineering and Physics	COMPENDEX	Engineering Index Inc.	Engineering Index/—
	ISMEC	Cambridge Scientific Abstracts	ISMEC Bulletin/ mechanical engineering
	SAE ABSTRACTS	Society of Automotive Engineers Inc.	SAE Abstracts/ vehicle related technology

	Institution of Electrical Engineers	Science Abstracts/ physics, electronics and electrical engineering, computer technology
INSPEC		
Agriculture, Food, Pulp & Paper, Textiles		
CAB ABSTRACTS	Commonwealth Agricultural Bureaux	Various e.g. Agricultural Engineering Abstracts/—
AGRICOLA	US National Agricultural Library, and so on	Bibliography of Agriculture/—
FSTA	International Food Information Service	Food Science and Technology Abstracts/—
Geology, Geophysics,		
OCEANIC ABSTRACTS	Cambridge Scientific Abstracts	Oceanic Abstracts/—
Meteorology, Water Resources		
CANADA WATER	Inland Waterways Directorate, Environment Canada	—/—
Multi-disciplinary		
PASCAL	Centre National de la Récherche Scientifique	Bulletin Signalétique/—
Scientific/Technical		
NTIS	National Technical Information Service	Government Reports Announcements and Index/—
COMPREHENSIVE DISSERTATION INDEX	University Microfilms International	Dissertation Abstracts International and so on./—
Patents		
WPI	Derwent Publications	World Patents Index
CLAIMS	IFI/Plenum	
US PATENTS	US Patent Office	
INPADOC	International Patent Documentation Center, Vienna	

Continued

Figure 19.2 Continued

Type	Example	Producer	Printed equivalent/Comments
Scientific and Technical	CIS data bases, for example	National Institute of Health and the Environmental Protection Agency Chemical Information System	
Non-bibliographic Sources	MASS SPECTROMETRY SEARCH SYSTEM, X-RAY SINGLE CRYSTAL SEARCH SYSTEM, MATHEMATICAL MODELLING SYSTEM		
	ELECTRONICS COMPONENTS IRS		
	DATABANK		
	LABORATORY ANIMAL DATABASE	Battelle Laboratories	
	MARTINDALE ON-LINE	Pharmaceutical Society of Great Britain	Drugs and their uses and effects —a directory
Legal data bases	LEXIS	Mead Data Central	Full text— Legal information
	WESTLAW	West Publishers	
	EURO???	European Law Centre	Full text of case law and legislation of UK, EEC and Western Europe.
Business, News and Government	NEXIS	Mead Data Central	Full text— news
	NNI	Information Access Corp.	National Newspaper Index
	PREDICAST'S FEDERAL INDEX		
	ABI/INFORM	Data Courier Inc	

	Database	Host	Description
Social Sciences	ECONOMICS ABSTRACTS INTERNATIONAL	Learned Information Ltd.	
	PROMT	Predicasts Inc.	Market abstracts
	DRI	Data Resources Inc.	
	EXSTAT	Extel Statistical Services with Automatic Data Processing Corp.	
	CURRENCY	I P Sharp	
	KOMPASS-FRANCE	Kompass; Société pour l'informatique	Manufacturing companies and so on, in France
	KEY BRITISH ENTERPRISES	Dun & Bradstreet	British business
	SOCIAL SCISEARCH	Institute for Scientific Information	Social Sciences Citation Index
	SOCIOLOGICAL ABSTRACTS		Sociological Abstracts
	PSYCHLOGICAL ABSTRACTS		Psychological Abstracts
	EXCEPTIONAL CHILD EDUCATIONAL RESOURCES	National Information Center for Special Education Materials	
Humanities	RLIM ABSTRACTS		Music
	ART MODERN		
	HISTORICAL ABSTRACTS		Historical Abstracts

commercial organisations, for example, SCISEARCH and SOCIAL SCISEARCH, from the Institute for Scientific Information, and PROMPT, and so on from Predicasts.

Figure 19.2 will repay full consideration. It is more than a list of data bases. It demonstrates than some, but not all data bases have a printed equivalent, and identifies some examples of the various types of data bases.

The future will most likely see continued growth and diversification in the number of data bases. This will make it yet more difficult for the information worker and the end user to keep up to date with the full range of data bases, and the facilities offered by the various hosts.

19.8 A checklist of features to consider in comparing and evaluating data bases

As earlier sections, and Figure 19.2 amply demonstrate, there is a great deal of choice with regards to data bases. No two data bases are identical. Indeed there are usually only a limited number of data bases covering any given subject field or type of literature. However, even if two data bases appear to have a similar coverage they can usually be found to differ in some other respect, and in general the appropriate selection of data base is important for effective retrieval. In order to make such a selection it is necessary to become familiar with the range of data bases that any specific librarian or information worker might be asked to consult so that searching can proceed effectively. Such familiarity can be cultivated with experience, and will consider the following features of data bases. Despite the plethora of data bases, the searcher will frequently find that there is no ideal data base for a specific search and may well need to consult two or more data bases before a search is complete. Some of the factors to consider in the selection of data bases are:

1. Coverage – does the data base provide access to the appropriate subject field?
   —is the data base comprehensive?
   —to what extent does the coverage of the data base overlap with other data bases in similar subjects?
2. What is the currency of the file and the frequency of updates (for example, monthly, daily)?
3. How easy is the data base to use, and has the user experience of searching this data base, and is s/he therefore likely to achieve effective retrieval?
4. Output, both on screen and in hard copy. What are the options for the record content? Is there an abstract as part of the record? Is there a full text record available on the data base?

5. Indexing language – is it controlled or natural language, or both? What is the extent and specificity of indexing, and so on? Are all of these factors appropriate to the desired retrieval performance in this specific instance?

6. Cost.

7. Documentation, and search aids available to support searching on the data bases, such as classification schedules, printed or machine-viewable thesauri, and so on.

8. Any biases which might adversely affect search results (for example, emphasis on US or European published material)

9. Length of data base available online, or its starting date.

10. The host through whom the data base is available and its facilities (see 19.3).

Chapter 19 Readings

1 Bourne, C.P., 'Online systems: history, technology and economics', *Journal of the American Society for Information Science*, 31(3), 1980, 155–60.

2 'Butterworths launch LEXIS in UK', *Program* 14(3), 1980, 138–9.

3 Cronin, B., 'Databanks', *Aslib Proceedings* 33(6), 1981, 243–50.

4 Cuadra Associates, *Directory of Online Databases*, Cuadra Associates, Inc.: Santa Monica, Ca, 1979 onwards.

5 Deunette, J.B., *UK online search services*, 2nd edition, Aslib: London, 1982.

6 Deunette, J.B. and Dibb, L.C., *Online databanks*, Aslib: London, 1983.

7 Dunning, A.J. and Schur, H., 'EURONET training workshop, 1976', *Aslib Proceedings*, 29(9), 1977, 326–33.

8 East, H., 'UK abstracting and indexing services—some trends' *Aslib Proceedings*, 31(10), 1979, 460–70.

9 *EUSIDIC database guide*, Learned Information: Oxford, 1980.

10 Foster, A., 'External databases: an overview', *Aslib Proceedings*, 35(9), 1983, 346–53.

11 Gray, J.C., 'Euronet', *Aslib Proceedings*, 28(10), 1976, 338–40.

12 Hall, J. and Brown, M.J., *Online bibliographic databases*, 3rd edition, Aslib: London, 1983.

13 Henry, W.M. *et al.*, *Online searchings: an introduction*, Butterworth: London, 1980.

14 Hoover, R.E., 'A comparison of three commercial online vendors', *Online*, 3(1), 1979, 12–21.

15 Houghton, B. and Convey, J., *Online information retrieval systems: an introductory manual*. Bingley: London, 1977.

16 Houghton, B. and Convey, J., *Online information retrieval systems: an introductory manual to principles and practices*, 2nd edition, Bingley: London, 1984.

17 King, J., *Searching international databases: a comparative evaluation of their performance in toxicology*, British Library: London, 1983. (Library and Information Research report 3).

18 Mahon, B., 'Euronet DIANE—the European on-line information network', *Program*, 14(2), 1980, 69–75 (Special issue on networks).

19 Meadows, C.T. and Cochrane, P., *Basis of online searching*, Wiley: New York, 1981.

20 Negus, A.E., 'Development of the Euronet/DIANE common command language' in *Proceedings 3rd International Online Information Meeting, London, December 1979*, Learned Information: Oxford, 1979, 95–8.

21 *Proceedings of the International Online Information Meetings, 1st–7th, 1977–1983*, London, Learned Information: Oxford, 1977–1983.

22 Wanger, J. and Landau, R.N., 'Non-bibliographic online database services', *Journal of the American Society for Information Science*, 31(3), 1980, 171–80.

Note: Directories of data bases frequently contain useful introductory or explanatory items on the subject.

In-house information retrieval and cataloguing systems

20.1 Introduction

Information retrieval systems were first developed in the late 1960s and early 1970s in special libraries and information units which sought to exploit the advantages of computer processing in the maintenance of local indexes, data bases and current awareness services. Many of the early systems were perceived as replacements for manual techniques, including, for example, the preparation of card indexes, the maintenance of post-co-ordinate indexes on cards, abstracts and other current awareness bulletins. These systems offered a more cost-effective approach to the control of information, often permitting greater quantities of information to be sifted and directed to the appropriate end user, than would have been possible with manual systems. Many of the early systems ran on mainframe computers, in batch mode. Now, systems are available to run on all types of computers and all sizes, and most systems operate primarily in online mode. However, it continues to be the case that one of the great advantages of such systems is the opportunity to input data once, and then to reformat it to produce a range of products each tailored to a specific need.

When computers were first harnessed for information retrieval and cataloguing applications, the information retrieval systems, and some of the cataloguing systems developed in different environments. In the libraries which were engaged in large-scale cataloguing co-operation was central to developments, as outlined in Chapter 18. These cataloguing co-operatives developed software which would support cataloguing jointly. Probably the importance of being able not only to share the development costs of the software, but also being able to share the data base which comprised catalogue records, that is a union catalogue data base, determined the developments in this area. Thus the networks discussed in Chapter 18 emerged as computer-based systems. In information retrieval applications it was more usual for one organisation to carry most of the burden of development of the system, and then to market it to others. Thus, user groups subsequently emerged, as others adopted systems, but were not usually responsible for the original design of the software package. These user groups, once established, were however, often important influences in the further development of systems.

Thus there have been different influences in the development of cataloguing and information retrieval software packages, respectively. These two are nevertheless treated in this one chapter together, because in some respects there is convergence of systems. Cataloguing modules appear in packages originally designed for information retrieval, and also in packages whose primary purpose is library housekeeping. No detailed mention is made of the modules included in such packages which are not concerned with cataloguing, such as modules for circulation control, acquisitions and ordering and serials control. These topics are considered to be beyond the scope of this text. Many software packages which support information retrieval can be used to develop catalogue data bases, since in essence there need be little difference between a cataloguing data base and other information retrieval data bases. In addition, various software packages include a cataloguing module which permits catalogue data to be entered in a MARC format, and thus it is possible for libraries to create catalogue data bases which are compatible with other MARC-based catalogue data bases, such as those which are the products of centralised and co-operative cataloguing ventures. For larger libraries, with large quantities of new acquisitions, records for which may exist in other MARC data bases, this can be an important facility.

20.2 Software packages – some definitions

The introduction has attempted to explain the link between information retrieval and cataloguing in local systems, but before we proceed to examine these systems further it is perhaps worthwhile to review some definitions.

Software is the programs or lists of instructions which are necessary to enable a computer system to conduct specific tasks. A *software package* is a set of programs intended to achieve a specific objective, or designed to instruct the computer to execute a set of tasks in order to organise information in a pre-assigned manner. Many packages are available for purchase or lease, but there are also strictly in-house packages and packages developed by specific software houses under contract from one organisation.

Library and information workers are primarily concerned with software packages for text retrieval or information retrieval. In addition to the special purpose information retrieval packages, there are also a number of general purpose packages which offer some information retrieval functions. The different types of software can be identified as:

1. *Basic software*

Often referred to as utilities, basic software packages are available for performing basic operations such as data entry and validation, sorting and merging files and editing data. A data entry and validation package typically allows the user to define a form to be displayed on a VDU, and by using a cursor, or other prompts, enables data to be entered in this format. Some simple checks on the data entered may be possible, extending, for instance, to ensuring that there are no alphabetic characters in a field which is supposed to be comprised entirely of numeric characters. Sort packages are designed to sort a specified file of records into order according to a particular field or key. There are many different algorithms available for sorting, and this leads to a variety of packages. Some sort programs also include a merge function. Editing packages are likely to contain commands to insert, delete, print and replace specific lines of text, and can also 'find and substitute' specific strings of characters. More sophisticated editors may offer full screen editing facilities, and automatic input and output.

2. *Word processing software*

Word processing software available for use on mainframe computers, microcomputers and word processors was originally designed for application where it is convenient to be able to store a text, then recall this text, and re-use it with minor modifications, at a later date. Typical applications are standard letters, where for instance it may only be necessary to alter an address and the item ordered by the addressee. Otherwise the same letter can be re-used by reprinting from the word processor. Libraries and information units can use word processing software in the preparation and updating of manuals, library guides, and so on, and in the generation of forms, compilation of lists and the production of catalogue cards. Word processing packages must be able to permit the user to manipulate text, as is necessary in alignment of margins, insertion and deletion of paragraphs, lines or words, back-up files, number pages, arrange for text to appear in the centre of the page and underline. In addition, some word processing software has the ability to merge files, arrange records in a file according to some order (for example, alphabetical by name) and search for specific character strings within small files. These are the rudimentary elements of an information retrieval system.

3. *Data base management systems*

Data base management systems may offer some facilities which are also evident in information retrieval software, as outlined under 4. Although there is some discussion as to the nature of a Data Base Management System (DBMS), in general they aim to:

allow applications programs to be written independently of the DBMS control program;

support applications programs being written in a high level language
create and maintain a data base through utility programs
allow data to be re-organised to accommodate growth, shrinkage and so on
provide data security and access safeguards
cope with system failure and generate restart procedures.

DBMSs are essentially programming frameworks, and can offer good storage and retrieval, but often are intended for programmers to interact with, and thus may need a programmer in order to make them usable to libraries. Some DBMS systems (for example, MicroQUERY and Cardbox) have 'query language' auxiliary systems which make them more amenable to a non-programmer.

4. *Text retrieval packages*

Although each of the types of software introduced in 1, 2 and 3 above can be used for information retrieval, there are also special purpose in-house information retrieval packages which have been written specifically for the type of text retrieval applications to be found in special libraries and information units. These packages do not seem to have a clear label, but may be referred to as free text of full text packages, or as in-house information retrieval systems. None of these labels is entirely accurate, in that some packages which one would want to include in this category do not match one or other of these labels. Nevertheless, these are the terms used in the literature. When comparing such packages and DBMS Ashford (1984) has made the following distinctions:

the software is normally self-contained and can be set up with a minimum of involvement of computer specialist staff;
records in this software are independent, of variable length and are composed mostly of natural language texts;
access is by content rather than structural position, although most systems provide some sort of structural option for holding fixed format data;
the primary access is through an inverse file (concordance or lexicon) of text terms drawn from the records as they are placed on the data base.

Thus, a predominant feature of such software packages is the user related interfaces, which permit a non-programmer to comprehend and interrogate the data stored. This type of software will be considered at more length later in the chapter.

5. *Software associated with searching external online information retrieval systems*

Obviously software supports the searching on external online information retrieval systems. Increasingly, there are two other categories of software on the marketplace. There are software packages, mainly for use on microcomputers, for supporting online interaction with an external database, which permit the storage of search profiles locally, and the development and editing of search profiles, and search outputs locally. Userlink Systems Ltd have developed various systems of this type. Also available from the online hosts themselves are private file facilities, whereby the users can exploit the software used by the large hosts, on the host's computer, in order to maintain their own files.

6. *In-house library housekeeping*

A variety of the software packages which are available will support library housekeeping routines, as discussed earlier. Packages may support some or all of the following:

cataloguing
acquisitions and ordering
serials control
circulation control

and may also offer a range of management information. Oriel and Geac are considered as examples of this category in 20.8.

20.3 Why use a commercial package?

Discussion so far has concentrated on software packages. This tends to imply that the selection of an already existing package is a sensible choice in many instances. Obviously it is possible to write your own software package, or to commission someone to do this for you. In general, provided that there is a package available which meets most of the requirements of the unit concerned it is advisable to choose a software package from those available. Why?

1. Packages are used by many clients of the developer, and this very fact can lead to many benefits. First, the investment cost is spread over many users. For example, a competent, robust, efficient free text storage and retrieval system represents at least five man years of programming work (at £20,000 per year or more) and the larger systems could be considerably more expensive to develop. Such systems are available in the market for between £10,000 and £30,000.
2. Since a software package is to be sold it must be visible on the marketplace. This means that it must be well documented, with for example user manuals, test data and guidance on setting up systems. Also, the

supplier with a number of clients has enough maintenance income to justify the establishment of a sound maintenance service.

3. Packages which have been used will be thoroughly tested in various applications, and any weaknesses corrected.

4. Various desirable features will be incorporated into a package which may not occur to the new user as being of importance. These might include security passwords, backup, restart and recovery programs and integrity checking, resumption after interruptions, skilled and novice level assistance, among other features.

20.4 Hardware options

Before we embark upon more extensive consideration of the software packages and their use in information retrieval, it is worth reviewing the options for computer hardware. This section goes no further than the exploration of ideas which are important for the appropriate support of software packages. There are three sizes of computer: mainframes, minicomputers and microcomputers upon which software packages for information retrieval may be mounted. Figure 20.1 makes some basic comparisons.

1. *Mainframe computers*

Mainframe computers are rarely dedicated to the library's own sole application, unless the library concerned happens to be a national library, offering online access to its data bases to a wide audience. Mainframes may be the mainframe computer of the parent organisation of the library, that is the local authority computer for the public library, the research establishment computer for the library of a research establishment, and so on. In other cases, access to mainframes may be via a computer bureau. Computer bureaux are organisations which sell computer time and other computing and associated facilities, on a commercial basis. They offer the client access to the sophisticated facilities of some of the largest computers, and the possibility of building very large data bases. Some libraries may be attracted by other aspects of a bureaux service. Bureaux can be useful for:

access to shared data bases (as, in say, union catalogues)

access to a specific desired software package, which would demand too much hardware for the library to contemplate its own installation

professional systems expertise and support

proving trials, and the deferment of commitments until a suitable size of data base has been accumulated in the computer system.

Figure 20.1 Hardware options

		Data volumes in store		
		Small (up to 0.5 million characters)	Medium (0.5 to 50 million) characters)	Large (over 50 million characters)
Amount of processing	Small	(Don't bother with a computer) Word processor	Conventional or microform publishing	
	Medium	Microcomputer or shared system	Typically minicomputer	Minicomputer or mainframe
	Intensive	'Super' word processor or minicomputer or shared system	Minicomputer or 'Super' minicomputer	Mainframe or 'Super' minicomputer

Reproduced from: Williams, H.L. **Computerised Systems in Library and Information Services: Proceedings of a Conference of the Aslib Biological and Agricultural Sciences Group.** June 1982. Aslib, 1983.

2. *Minicomputers*

Minicomputers are the half-way house. Intermediate in size between mainframes and microcomputers, minicomputers offer considerable computing facilities, and are usually comprised of several microprocessors in a parallel group. Minicomputers can be very flexible in handling a number of varied interactive tasks and usually have highly developed operating systems which can support online users. Minicomputers may be dedicated, and used only to support the library and information department's data bases (and possibly to make them available at a number of locations via appropriately sited terminals). In other applications, minicomputers may be shared by other sectors of an organisation, or exploited on a bureau basis.

3. *Microcomputers*

Microcomputers are cheap, but offer more limited capacity, and generally somewhat less sophisticated retrieval facilities than either of the previous two options. Microcomputers are best at single tasks, having limited addressing capability, and are difficult to program except in relatively high level (and inefficient) programming languages. Microcomputers are likely to be dedicated for library use, and some libraries or information units may have several microcomputers, either linked in a network, or operating separately and supporting distinct functions (for example, circulation recording and current awareness data base). Because microcomputers are often the sole responsibility of the library, the information worker needs to be more concerned with the maintenance of the hardware than might be the case with either mainframe or minicomputers. In some organisations microcomputers will be maintained (that is, mended) by a central computer department, but if this is not the case it may be necessary to take out separate maintenance contracts. In any event, those using the system will need to concern themselves with the general management of the data bases, including such details as: keeping sufficient supplies of floppy discs, updating the data bases, keeping duplicate copies of the data bases, preparation of instruction guides and so on.

20.5 Options for software packages

This section reviews the chief factors that must be taken into account in selecting an appropriate software package. This is followed by some brief comments on a representative, but far from comprehensive, selection of the software packages used for information retrieval and cataloguing.

The most important, and perhaps obvious factor is to establish that the package is compatible with the machine on which it is to be used. Indeed, in some instances, the hardware may be selected to match the selection of software, but where this degree of flexibility is not possible, obviously the machine may constrain the options available considerably. Some packages are portable and are available in different versions. CAIRS is a good example of such a series of systems, which will run on a number of different machines, including both minicomputers and microcomputers of various capacities. The early systems were mainframe, developed in the late 1960s and early 1970s. Hence, many of these systems are now well established in the market, with sound maintenance arrangements, and have been thoroughly tested. Some minicomputer packages came onto the market in the mid-1970s, and the microcomputer packages have in general emerged over the past three to four years. In the microcomputer range, there are two types of package: the cheap single user package, and the more expensive, multi-user package.

In general, the costs of packages vary considerably, but it is usually the case that you get what you pay for. Although there are some notable bargains, in general as one goes up the price range from microcomputer packages at £100 to minicomputer and mainframe packages at £30,000 there are improvements in capacity and retrieval facilities, together with other factors listed below.

The market is relatively volatile and changes are to be expected. However, large systems with many users have an element of built-in inertia, and are likely to be more stable. Smaller microcomputer-based systems are more likely to come and go.

20.6 Checklist of points to consider in opting for a specific system

Against the context of the points that are made above concerning the market for information retrieval software packages, there are obviously a number of factors which must be considered prior to the commitment to a specific software package. These could be grouped into four basic categories:

General

1. Cost.
2. Extent of use of the software by other libraries and information units, and their experiences with the software.
3. Whether the software can produce the required output from the given input in a reasonable time.
4. The producer and the supplier of the software – these may be two different agencies. Plainly it is worth seeking both reputable suppliers and producers, since they have an interest in offering a sound product.

Technical

1. The software must be written in a programming language which is available on the computer being used.
2. The operating system required by the software must be available on the computer system to be used.
3. Is the hardware configuration required by the software available, for example, amount of storage, number and capacity of disc drives, addressable screen cursors etc?
4. Is other software, such as sort programs, edit programs and word processing programs necessary before the software can be used?
5. Are there any limits on the types of data that can be input? For example, are there limits on the total storage capacity of the system, that is, the number of records, and the sizes of records or fields? Are both fixed and variable fields possible?
6. Ease of use – is the software supporting a system which is straightforward to understand and user-friendly?
7. Format in which the software is supplied. Formats could include discs and tapes of varying sizes. Often a variety of formats are available for any

given system, but one format must be suitable for the hardware configuration to be used, and must be specified.

Support

1. What documentation is available? Documentation should include a user manual, an operations manual, and a detailed description of how the software works.
2. Personal support in the form of advice and maintenance facilities will also be important. Training in the use of the software, advice on its implementation, the sharing of expertise through membership of a club of existing users can all be valuable.

Legal factors

1. Is there a warranty?
2. Is the contract satisfactory?

20.7 A checklist of applications of in-house cataloguing and information retrieval systems

Having briefly reviewed the range of software packages available, the applications and uses to which such packages can be put have already been introduced. This section is merely a summary of the applications areas, drawn together in a coherent form. Applications, then, include:

1. Online information retrieval
(a) from in-house data bases, which may be either catalogue or other bibliographic data bases, but which are usually, in this sphere of activity, bibliographic in some sense.
(b) from external data bases, where local software packages are used on in-house microcomputers in order to support the interaction with the external data bases. These packages permit more efficient searching and the reformatting of search results into, say, reading lists and bibliographies.
2. Printed catalogues and indexes, lists and bibliographies may all be extracted from the in-house data base. Using the one data base as a basis for different selections of records, or fields in records, or different arrangements of records, may offer a whole range of products. Some packages specialise in the printing of indexes, current awareness bulletins and other products, and offer a wide range of layouts, typefaces and so on.
3. Printed current awareness bulletins and selective dissemination of information services may be produced from similar facilities to those in (2) above, except that here the announcement will relate only to newly added items.

4. Online current awareness services, such as selective dissemination of information or news bulletins. To be effective this requires that users have access to terminals on a regular basis, but includes the possibility of libraries with an organisational computer and terminals scattered throughout an organisation, making ideas available on a current awareness basis.

Clearly, in order to achieve the products above, it is necessary for the software package to be able to support those activities involved in the generation and maintenance of the database.

Some software packages will also include facilities for:

1. Circulation control, that is maintaining records of books on loan, and borrowers.
2. Acquisitions, that is maintaining records of materials on order, and financial data concerning expenditure, as well as details about suppliers.
3. Serials control, that is serials circulation control, and serials ordering and acquisition control.
4. Management data, that is, numbers of items borrowed, funds expended in various directions, current awareness notifications followed up (that is, items borrowed after announcement).

20.8 Some systems

MicroQUERY

MicroQUERY is a general purpose information retrieval package for use on the RML 380Z, with dual disc drive. Available from the Advisory Unit for Computer based Education, Hatfield, the package is a cheap product which has been marketed extensively for use in schools in the United Kingdom. It is a fair example of what is possible with a small microcomputer, and a relatively limited software package. Written to the Hertfordshire Command Standard, MicroQUERY consists of the following programs:

QUERY – for interrogation, allows specific questions to be framed with the aid of commands and logical links between terms in fields. For example:

QUERY AGE LT 16 AND CBIRTH IDENT'NORFOLK'

would permit records where the value in the AGE field was less than 16 and the text of the CBIRTH (County of Birth) field read NORFOLK, in a data base where the records had fields AGE and CBIRTH, to be retrieved. Searching is relatively slow because the software package does not use an inverted file, but rather examines each record in turn to see whether it matches the search criteria.

QEDIT – enables the establishment, editing and updating of data files to proceed. Relatively small files can be successfully handled and there are constraints on field size (seventy characters maximum). The software was not essentially designed for bibliographic data bases, but does support these adequately.

QSORT – permits the user to sort the results of a search into alphabetical or numerical order.

QCLASS – produces tables or histograms from numeric data.

QLABEL – allows the printing of labels, for example address labels.

The cost of the package is around £50.

Cardbox

Cardbox, distributed by Caxton Software Publishing Company, London, is a small data base management system that simulates a stack of index cards. Various formats are available, but one feature of the system is that records can be displayed in card format. The basic features of the system are shown in Figure 20.2. The system has to be customised to suit any specific application so that it suits the commands of the microcomputer with which it is being used. Cardbox is typical of many data base management systems in that it allows the creation of data bases composed of records, which are in turn composed of fields. It is recommended for a variety of applications, amongst which are records of suppliers, staff, record collections, books, journal extracts, club membership, household possessions and so on, and is likely to find users in both the home and business worlds. In contrast to many data base management systems, Cardbox has a carefully refined user interface. For example, when setting up the format for records in a data base, the user can draw a form on the screen, complete with headings for each field, and then, as data is entered it goes into the form. The same data can be displayed in various formats by using multiple-format files, and there is a print format which is separate from the screen display format (for printing labels and so on). Searching can be performed on the whole record, or only on specified fields. Searching proceeds in levels or stages, with one set of documents being retrieved according to one criterion, and then this set is shifted according to the next criterion to be applied. Cardbox reads data from, and writes it to disc during parts of the search process; this can lead to delays, but on the other hand, expands the size of data base that the system can handle. Cardbox is also available in an upgraded version Cardbox-Plus, and both cost less than £300 each.

STATUS

STATUS has been developed by the Computer Science and Systems Division at AERE Harwell to provide an easily installed system, with which users can interact in plain language. The package is available as a separate package for running on the purchaser's own computer, or it can be used on

392

Figure 20.2 Main features of Cardbox

A. A Screen Showing the Format of Records

SOFTWARE FACTSHEET

Product: CARDBOX   Type: Card Index
Retail Price: £155   Machine: CP/11 MP/11
File Size: CP/M 8MB MP/M 16MB   Records: 65,500 maximum
Record Size: 1484 ch maximum   Fields: 26 maximum
Field Size: 1484 ch maximum   Index Limits: None

Notes: Allows complex searching using up to 99 separate criteria.
       Widely available from distributors in USA, UK and Australia.

Published by Caxton Software Ltd of London. 01-379-650

B. Functions and Main Menu Options

Functions		Main Menu Options	
Select	keep all cards which match the selection criteria	Create/Edit	Format File
		Create/Use	Data File
		Copy/Erase	Files
Exclude	throw away all cards which match the criteria	Analyse	Reports on file and index use and effi-
Include	bring back cards which match the criteria		ciency when planning changes
Mask	use before Select and Exclude to match both indexed and non-indexed words	Repair	Reports on the condition of a file, recommends action and provides appropriate functions
Back	'undo' the last selection		
Clear	'undo' all the selections		
History	display your last 18 selections	**CAPACITIES**	
Delete	delete the current record	Maximum file size-8Mb with CP/M, 16Mb with MP/M	
Read	load records from a disk file	Maximum number of records-just over 65500	
Write	create a file on disk containing the current selection	Maximum record size-1404 characters	
Format	view your records in a different format	Maximum number of fields-26	
Print	print all or part of the current selection in the required format	Maximum field size-1404 characters	
		Maximum number of indexed words/field-no limit	
Quit	return to the main menu	Maximum number of indexed words/file-no limit	
		Maximum number of search levels -99	

a bureau basis. The system has been implemented on a wide range of computer equipment, including: ICL 2900 series, IBM 303, DEC, VAX, PRIME 300 and 400 etc., BURROUGHS B6700 UNIVAC 1108, and others.

STATUS is implemented as an integrated suite of FORTRAN modules designed for portability and flexibility in adaptation to various user environments. A STATUS data base contains two major components:

1. The text file which is a stream of text as inserted by the user containing a minimal number of control characters which indicate the internal structure of the text. Any kind of textual data can be accommodated including text and structured tabular data. Input is structured into four levels:

ARTICLE is the fundamental level, equivalent to a record. ARTICLEs may be of any length.

CHAPTER is a sequence of articles. Searches may be restricted to a given chapter or series of chapters.

PARAGRAPH is a subunit of an article.

WORD is a character string bounded by spaces or other chosen characters.

2. The concordance is a structured list of the vocabulary used in the text, containing pointer references to all occurrences of the words within the text file. This is created when the data base is generated or updated. It permits efficient searching without scanning the full text file sequentially. The user may input a list of 'common words not to be concorded'.

A STATUS data base can be created from any suitable terminal. The user is led through a dialogue which prompts him to specify the parameters of the data base to be created, such as its name, special characters and numerals to be allowed in the concordance, the common word list, an estimate of data base size and name sections and keyed fields. The text is checked by the system, then added to an amendment list and the text data base and concordance are created by a specific update command. The data base may be modified by adding single articles, or a batch of articles, or by amending existing articles, or deleting existing articles. The system permits sophisticated searching of data bases. The simplest question contains a single search term, for example, Q harwell? will find all articles containing the word 'harwell'. More complex questions may make use of both Boolean logic operators ('+', ',' and '−' representing 'and', 'or' and 'not' respectively). Thus

Q accident + seat belt? finds all articles which contain both the word accident and the phrase seat belt.

Contextual logic is also available permitting terms to be required to appear within a specified number of words of one another, or within named sections. Macros and synonyms may be used to assist with complicated searches, the storage of personal profiles (for say current awareness profiles), and retrieval in data bases where information may be contained in more than one language or under special codings.

Special security facilities are available. Various user aids support the user in the use of the system. Application areas include: personnel records, catalogues of products and suppliers, directories, technical reports and records, marketing research information, plan and asset registers, current awareness services, mailing lists, accident and incident records, building and construction standards, clinical and health records, committee minutes and records, and so on. There are currently many users in Europe and over a hundred users worldwide, and around fifty of these are members of the STATUS Users Group. Associated software has been developed, and this includes the STATUS Report Generator, the STATUS Data Preparation Aid, and the STATUS Thesaurus Processor. The software currently costs between £12,500 and £25,000 and has been on the market around eight years. An annual maintenance charge of 10 per cent of the purchase price can be paid for support and maintenance of the system.

CAIRS

CAIRS is a suite of programs from Leatherhead Food Research Association. Amongst the systems marketed by CAIRS Marketing are mainframe, minicomputer and microcomputer-based systems. The first CAIRS systems were marketed in the mid-1970s. Various of the packages will run on TEXAS Instruments business series 300, 600, 800, Perkin Elmer 3200 series, IBM-PC and the ACT Sirius, and the software is written in RTL 2.

Data entry is primarily through online interactive use of formatted screens, although batch entry is also possible. The maximum record size, and field sizes are large for the larger systems, but can be more restricted for the Micro-CAIRS systems. For example, with a microcomputer with a Winchester disc unit with a minimum capacity of five mgbytes, several thousand records, each of 250 characters maximum length, could be handled on one disc. All fields are variable length, and the number of index keys assigned is limited only by the disc storage space. Amendment and editing of records is via the same formatted screen as used in data entry.

Each field of a record is treated separately for indexing purposes, and the user defines which type shall operate on any field. The thesaurus is held as a separate file, and a user-defined stop list with preferred terms for synonym control may be used. In addition, total vocabulary control with the thesaurus as a Go-list may be selected for both automatic and manually assigned keywords. Searching facilities include Boolean logic, with nesting to as many levels as required. Right hand truncation is possible, and data base range limitation is available. Restriction of individual search terms to specific fields is also possible. The thesaurus and the index may be viewed, and the output format from a search is under the user's control: any fields in any order may be displayed. Various other support facilities are available, such as Help and MENU facilities, and some word processing features. Any useful search profile can be stored permanently, and SDI profiles can be run in batches. Printed indexes can be provided to user defined formats, and stand alone sub-data bases can be created. Security features can be used to restrict access to certain functions and files within the data base. Help desk and user groups are also offered.

Prices range from £1400 to £26,000. To examine the Micro-CAIRS options, MS/A costs £14000, MS/B £3500 and MS/C £5000. A microcomputer with its disc drive capable of supporting the system will cost from £6000 upwards. Support and maintenance contracts of various types are available from between £150 and £1000 per annum. Figure 20.3 demonstrates the different features available with different versions of the system.

ORIEL Metalogue

Metalogue is available from Oriel Computer Services, Chipping Norton, Oxfordshire. It is essentially a package for the creation of catalogues and catalogue data bases. The software package is a flexible system which permits systems to be tailored to individual user's requirements. Within a restriction of total record size of maximum of 30,000 characters, an intending user is free to format the records in his system. The system is available on an ACT Sirius 1 microcomputer and other 16 bit microcomputers; with up to ten mgbytes of disc storage, total hardware and software costs start at around £6000.

System commands and displayed messages can be changed by the librarian to suit local requirements. Authority records can be constructed. Any number of index sequences can be defined. Screen displays can be printed for further references. A wide range of output formats can be defined, selected, ordered and generated including printed catalogues, catalogue cards and so on.

In due course the following features will also be available:

1. information retrieval style search facilities
2. order/accessioning modules
3. periodical control
4. networking of microcomputers to allow system expansion
5. MARC compatible input and display
6. links to the circulation control system.

Figure 20.3 Features of CAIRS

A. Micro-CAIRS

MICRO-CAIRS SOFTWARE FEATURES	:	MICRO-CAIRS PACKAGE		
	:	MS/A	MS/B	MS/C
Database setup and screen generation	:	•	•	•
Data entry on-line - formatted screens	:	•	•	•
Data editing on-line	:	•	•	•
Indexing - free text, automatic, tagged,	:	•	•	•
manual, number and relational	:	•	•	•
Indexing - as above with thesaurus	:		•	•
Index on-line view	:	•	•	•
Index listing	:		•	•
Index editing (automatic)	:	•	•	•
Thesaurus entry and editing on-line	:		•	•
Thesaurus - STOP/GO vocabulary control,	:		•	•
synonym control, search aid, BT, NT,	:		•	•
RT, and Macro Team	:		•	•
Thesaurus on-line view	:		•	•
Thesaurus listing	:		•	•
Search system (using index) FIND	:	•	•	•
Search system (using index) SINV	:			•
Search system (serial on text) SSER	:		•	•
Boolean AND, OR, NOT operators	:	•	•	•
Truncation, right hand on index	:	•	•	•
Truncation, left and right hand on text	:		•	•
$>$, $<$ and = number searching on text	:		•	•
Set creation	:			•
Stored search profiles	:			•
SDI production	:			•
Output format - user controlled	:	•	•	•
Field output - user controlled	:	•	•	•
Device for output - user controlled	:			•
Field synonyms	:		•	•
Field decode systems	:			•
Sorting records on output	:			•
Catalogue and printed index production	:			•
Listing by accession number	:	•	•	•
Listing by database	:	•	•	•
Listing by file code/ security code	:		•	•
Help system - standard facility	:	•	•	•
Help system - user controlled	:		•	•
Menu system - user controlled	:		•	•

Continued

Figure 20.3 Continued

MICRO-CAIRS SOFTWARE FEATURES	:	MICRO-CAIRS PACKAGE		
	:	MS/A	MS/B	MS/C
News facility - user controlled	:		•	•
Database security	:	•	•	•
Record security	:	•	•	•
Field security	:	•	•	•
Task security - user controlled	:			•
Libraries per database	:	1	3	8

B. Mainframe/Mini CAIRS

Functional comparison of software packages . . .

Function	CAIRS Software Package (Mainframe/mini)				
	C-A	C-B	C-C	C-D	C-E
No of libraries/database	1	3	5	8	16
No of security files/library	2	5	5	10	26
Multi user software (max users)	3	5	5	16	N/A
Database/screen design software	N	N	Y	Y	Y
Tailored input screen structure	Y	Y	Y	Y	Y
Data entry on-line (screen based)	Y	Y	Y	Y	Y
Data entry - batch	N	N	S	S	S
Data editing on-line	Y	Y	Y	Y	Y
Data editing - batch	N	N	S	S	S
Document preparation system	N	N	S	S	S
Free text indexing	Y	Y	Y	Y	Y
Full field indexing	Y	Y	Y	Y	Y
Automatic indexing	Y	Y	Y	Y	Y
Tagged Indexing	N	N	Y	Y	Y
Manual Indexing	Y	Y	Y	Y	Y
Manual Indexing - relational	Y	Y	Y	Y	Y
Number indexing	N	Y	Y	Y	Y
Index on-line view	Y	Y	Y	Y	Y
Index listing	N	Y	Y	Y	Y
On-line thesaurus Stop/Go control	N	Y	Y	Y	Y
Preferred term	N	Y	Y	Y	Y

Continued

Figure 20.3 Continued

	CAIRS Software Package (Mainframe/mini)				
Function	C-A	C-B	C-C	C-D	C-E
BT/NT/MT/RT	N	N	Y	Y	Y
Search aid	N	Y	Y	Y	Y
Auto BT/NT/MT profile expansion	N	N	Y	Y	Y
Profile explosion on screen	N	N	N	N	Y
Auto posting on indexing	N	Y	Y	Y	Y
Thesaurus on-line view	N	Y	Y	Y	Y
Thesaurus listing system	N	Y	Y	Y	Y
Thesaurus editing system	N	Y	Y	Y	Y
Stored search profiles	N	N	Y	Y	Y
Current awareness/SDI systems	N	N	Y	Y	Y
Bulletin/Journal generation	N	N	Y	Y	Y
Search systems (FIND)	Y	Y	Y	Y	Y
Search systems (SINV)	N	N	Y	Y	Y
Search systems - serial (SSER)	N	Y	Y	Y	Y
Boolean AND/OR/NOT searching	Y	Y	Y	Y	Y
Term truncation on searching	Y	Y	Y	Y	Y
Truncation left and right on text	N	Y	Y	Y	Y
Range searching numbers (index)	N	Y	Y	Y	Y
Range searching numbers (text)	N	Y	Y	Y	Y
Set creation and storage	Y	Y	Y	Y	Y
Scan set allocation on-line	Y	Y	Y	Y	Y
Output (user controlled) formats	N	N	Y	Y	Y
fields ouput	N	N	Y	Y	Y
field order	N	N	Y	Y	Y
Output devices (user controlled)	N	N	N	N	Y
Output - sorting	N	N	Y	Y	Y
Catalogue/printed index production	N	N	N	Y	Y
Library loan function	S	S	S	S	S
Library circulation function	S	S	S	S	S
Listing by accession number	Y	Y	Y	Y	Y
Searching by accession number	Y	Y	Y	Y	Y
Listing by file code	N	Y	Y	Y	Y
Listing by security file	N	Y	Y	Y	Y
Listing holdings file	N	Y	Y	Y	Y
Text replacement/validation tables	N	N	N	Y	Y
Standard Help pages	Y	Y	Y	Y	Y
User definable Help/Menu pages	N	N	N	Y	Y
Menu driven system	N	N	N	Y	Y
News page	N	N	N	Y	Y
Accounting/charging systems	N	N	N	N	Y

Continued

Figure 20.3 Continued

Function	CAIRS Software Package (Mainframe/mini)				
	C-A	C-B	C-C	C-D	C-E
Accession number modification	Y	Y	Y	Y	Y
Database/file/record security	Y	Y	Y	Y	Y
Field synonyms	N	N	Y	Y	Y
Field headings - user control	N	N	N	Y	Y
Task security - user controlled	N	N	Y	Y	Y
User group control/definition	N	N	N	Y	Y
User password control	Y	Y	Y	Y	Y
Word processing flags and controls	N	N	Y	Y	Y
View system status	N	Y	Y	Y	Y
View file status	Y	Y	Y	Y	Y

ASSASSIN

ASSASSIN was originally developed by the Agricultural Division of ICI plc, in the late 1960s in order to provide a more effective means of generating their local indexes and current awareness services. The package is now available on a lease or bureau basis, and costs around £30,000 for a ten-year lease. There are around thirty users, mainly in the United Kingdom and Europe. Now in its sixth version, ASSASSIN 6, ASSASSIN runs on a range of IBM, DEC and ICL machines, and is written in ANSI Cobol.

Data can be input online through interactive edit programs, and also online using a word processor. Batch input is also possible. Each document may contain up to four million characters, and may be divided into up to nine sections, and each section may be divided into up to ninety-nine subsections. The data base can be divided into up to 9999 subfiles, and searching can be limited to specific subfiles, or combinations of subfiles. Indexing may follow different strategies for different files, and sections of a document in any one file can be treated differently, for example, not indexed, all words indexed, only marked words used for indexing. Stopwords may be used, as may options on index structure, noting synonyms, alternative spellings, and broader and narrower terms.

Searching can be performed with the Boolean logic operators. Searches can be limited by subfile, date and security level, and right hand truncation is available. Other features of searching are: character string searching of the text, numeric range searching, and word proximity searching. There is novice and expert mode assistance available during searching, and it is possible to add private notes to a public document. All sets created in a search session can be displayed, and the end results can be displayed in one of various pre-set formats, or in a format set by the end user.

SDI can be generated in either a printed form, or made available for online viewing. Various printed products can be provided including: printed KWOC indexes, whose coverage may be restricted by date, subfile, security and type of word, printed alphabetic listing of index terms, and a printed listing of index terms and their related terms.

INFO-TEXT

INFO-TEXT Text Management and Document Retrieval System is available from Henco Software Inc, Waltham, Mass., USA, and was developed by DORIC computer systems. The range of systems can be acquired for between about £8000 and £20,000, and has been available only since 1983. The package will run on various PRIME and DEC VAX machines, starting with the PRIME 2250 and the DEC VAX 11/730 upwards. INFO-TEXT is a complete programming language, which has been designed for the use of non-programmers, but nevertheless has full programming functionality. The system accesses existing host files, and can be interfaced easily to other packages.

Online input is possible. The package is also capable of linking to any existing ASCII data and treating it as its own. Fixed length field data can occupy up to 4096 characters in a suitable record, and any number of fields can be specified within this limit. Variable length fields can be of any length, and there can be up to 450 of these in a record. The user specifies the level of indexing for each item. A stopword list is maintained for each data base, and stopwords are recorded in the dictionary of all indexed terms. This dictionary is online at all times for enquiry and holds details of the terms, and their occurrences.

Searching facilities involve all the normal possibilities, such as use of Boolean logic operators, truncation, range searching, and contextual searching. Following an enquiry, data can be displayed printed, saved or copied, in a variety of formats, so that printed indexes and so on may be generated.

SCIMATE

SCIMATE is a micro-computer based package which is oriented towards downloading from and interaction with the data bases available on the major hosts. SCIMATE is available from ISI, Philadelphia, USA, and will operate on a number of microcomputers, under the operating system CP/M. Information may be input online or via word processors, paper tape and optical character recognition, or online from a host data base. The package will handle up to 1900 characters per record, and up to 1900 characters per field, with up to twenty fields per record. In order to support interaction with external hosts, autodialling log-on and off-load from major hosts using a universal search language is possible. Edited hits may be moved into the user file as required. The files thus created may be string searched, or searched with full Boolean logic. Search profiles can be stored for SDI searching. Stored files can be printed in various formats and arrangements.

GEAC Computer Corporation Ltd

GEAC Computer Corporation Ltd is a general supplier of computer systems based in Canada, and with subsidiary companies in the United Kingdom and the United States. The Library Information Systems Division specialises in integrated library systems. These systems have been installed in a number of libraries in the United States, Canada, the United Kingdom and Europe. Amongst the libraries using GEAC systems are public, university and polytechnic libraries. Some examples of users are: Preston Polytechnic, Somerset County Library, Hull University, PBC Limburg Bibliothèque Nationale, University of Waterloo, Regina Public Library, Smithsonian Institution, New York University and Pasadena Public Library.

The GEAC system includes the following modules: Loans, fines, reservations, public access system, catalogue, networking, statistical information, acquisition, local community information service. At intervals GEAC releases new software which is intended to update the system. Modules can be acquired individually or as a total package. A facility which extends beyond library housekeeping permits the viewing of outside data bases. Information for the whole system is immediately updated as data is processed through the work stations. The system will handle all types of library stock and there are no limits on its capacity.

The system runs on a GEAC computer, to which are linked work stations. These VDUs have full alphanumeric keyboards, with special function keys and rotating screens. Light pens can be used to read in data from bar codes on borrowers' cards, books, records, audio-visual materials.

The catalogue subsystem provides a public online catalogue which offers bibliographic information which can be accessed by author, title, class or any control number. In addition the system offers keyword and Boolean searching. The VDU gives step by step instructions for those not familiar with search procedures. The inputting of catalogue records is supported by the possibility of authority control, compatibility with the MARC format, and the availability of the full ALA character set. If so desired, the module permits catalogue data bases to be linked to national or co-operative cataloguing data bases, in order to extend the bibliographic data base, and to facilitate the processing of catalogue records.

Chapter 20 Readings

1 Ashford, J.H., 'Software cost: making or buying it', *Program,* 10(1), 1976, 1–6.

2 Ashford, J.H., 'Storage and retrieval of bibliographic records: a comparison of database management system (DBMS) and free text approacher', *Program,* 18(1), 1984, 16–45.

3 Ashford, J.H. and Matkin, D., *Studies in the application of free text package systems,* Library Association: London, 1982. (Case studies in library automation) .

4 Aston, M., 'Information technology – here and now benefits', *Aslib Proceedings,* 35(1), 1983, 52–8.

5 Boss, R.W., *The library manager's guide to automation,* Knowledge Industry Publications: White Plains, N.Y., 1979.

6 Burton, P.F., *Microcomputer applications in libraries and information retrieval: a directory of users,* Library, Leith Nautical College: Edinburgh, 1981.

7 *Computerised systems in library and information services,* ed. H.L. Williams, Aslib: London, 1983.

8 Dewe, A., *An annotated bibliography of automation in libraries, 1975-1978,* Aslib: London, 1980.

9 Hawes, D.F.W. and Botten, D.A., *Library automation at the Polytechnic of the South Bank,* Library Association: London, 1983. (Case studies in library automation).

10 Lancaster, F.W., *Clinic on library applications of data processing, 1978. Problems and failures in library automation,* University of Illinois: Urbana-Champaign, 1979.

11 Lewis, D.E. and Robinson, M.E., 'Computer-based cataloguing at Loughborough University of Technology 1968-1982: a review', *Program,* 17(2), 1983, 52–7.

12 Lundeen, G., 'Microcomputers in personal information systems', *Special Libraries,* 72(2), 1981, 127–37.

13 Marcus, R.S. and Reintjes, J., 'A translating computer interface for end-user operation of heterogeneous retrieval systems. 1: Design; 2: Evaluations', *Journal of the American Society for Information Science,* 32(4), 1981, 287–317.

14 Matthews, J.R., *Choosing an automated library system: a planning guide,* American Library Association: Chicago, 1980.

15 *Microcomputers in libraries,* eds C.C. Chen and S.E. Bressler, Neal-Schuman: New York, 1982.

16 *Minis, micros and terminals,* ed. A. Gilchrist, Heyden: London, 1981.

17 Petrie, J.H. and Cowie, J., 'A microcomputer based terminal for assisting on-line information retrieval', *Journal of Information Science,* 4(1), 1982, 61–4.

18 'Program: special issue on software packages for information retrieval', *Program,* 16(3), 1982.

19 Purton, A.C., 'Microcomputers for home indexing: a report and guide', *The Indexer,* 13(1), 1982, 27–37.

20 Rowat, M.J., 'Microcomputers in libraries and information departments', *Aslib Proceedings,* 34(1), 1982, 26–37.

21 Rowley, J.E., *Computers for libraries,* Bingley: London, 1980.

22 Rowley, J.E., *Mechanised in-house information systems,* Bingley: London, 1979.

23 Royan, B., 'Minicomputers in cataloguing', *Program,* 10(2), 1976, 37–46.

24 Tagg, W.T.R., *Computer software: supplying it and finding it,* British Library: London, 1983. (Library and Information Research Report 10).

25 Tedd, L.A., *Case studies in computer-based bibliographic information services,* British Library: London, 1979. (BLRDD Report 5463).

26 Tedd, L.A., *Introduction to computer-based library systems,* Heyden: London, 1977, 2nd edition, 1984.

27 Tedd, L.A., 'Software for microcomputers in libraries and information units', *Electronic Library,* 1(1), 1983, 31–48.

28 Wilson, C.W.J., *Directory of operational computer applications in United Kingdom libraries and information units,* Aslib: London, 1977.

Part V   User perspectives

21 Filing and order in indexes and catalogues

21.1 Introduction

Earlier sections have considered in some detail the headings and search keys to be used in catalogues and indexes. In any situation where a number of such headings are to be displayed one after another, some well-recognised filing order must be adopted for arranging headings with respect to one another. Thus in printed, card and microform catalogues and indexes the filing order is important in assisting the user in the location of a specific heading which may be inter-mixed with other headings. In computer based systems, displays of headings, index terms or search keys are sometimes encountered, and here it is also useful to work with a defined filing order, but such an order is less essential as online searching of computer data bases is normally supported by facilities which make scanning through sequences easier than it would be in printed lists. If no filing order is recognised, the only way in which appropriate headings and their associated records can be retrieved is by scanning the entire file.

Since most headings in catalogues or indexes comprise primarily numbers (usually Arabic numerals) and letters of the Roman alphabet it is these characters that must mostly be organised, and for which a filing order must be defined. All the careful work of a cataloguer or indexer is to no avail, if a heading having been assigned to a record, and a record prepared, the record is not filed in the expected place, in accordance with its heading. A user needs to know, for instance, whether a work by John McMillan can be found before or after one by Eli Marner. Equally, a set of subject headings such as:

Faith
Faith, Confessions of
Faith healing
Faithfulness

could be filed in a number of possible orders, and the adopted order needs to be declared. The arrangement of headings into an overall sequence is important, and an order which is erratic, unpredictable, or with which the user is not familiar can lead to poor retrieval in any printed, card or microfilm index or catalogue.

Although filing has been traditionally regarded as part of the catalogue or index creation process, and its status in this respect was more than obvious in large card catalogues, filing orders today are more important for the searcher than the indexer. Prior to computerisation of the production of catalogues and indexes considerable clerical effort was expended in filing index and catalogue cards. One of the biggest and most evident advantages of computer production of catalogues and indexes is the elimination of the need for filing. The computer, once instructed on the desired filing order, is eminently suitable for filing, achieving a level of consistency which was a remote dream in the days of human filers. Increasingly, information workers do not need to know how to file a given heading, but rather to predict where a sought heading is like to have been filed in a sequence. Thus familiarity with normal filing orders becomes an important factor in complete and speedy retrieval from almost all printed sources.

With the onus on the searcher to achieve familiarity with filing orders, there are other factors that need to be considered.

The most common order is alphabetically by letters of the Roman alphabet arranged in their normal order. Other possible orders may be numerical, chronological (by periods of time), geographical (grouping places within a country or region together) or classified (according to a classification scheme, and ordered in keeping with the notation of the classification scheme). It is important to recognise that some of these orders will be more self-evident than others. Even alphabetical order presents its problems, some of which are discussed in succeeding sections. However, for some audiences, even the straight 'a to z' sequence of alphabetical order may present serious difficulties. Schoolchildren, students, and others whose native language is written in a non-Roman script may find alphabetical order according to Roman characters an almost insurmountable hurdle in the use of catalogues and indexes. Consider, for example, that in order to arrange a set of words alphabetically it is necessary to consider each letter of each word in turn, before the words can be correctly placed in alphabetical order. So, although, as we shall see, alphabetical and to some extent numerical order are common, it should be recognised that some people will have difficulty with these orders, and as much help and assistance should be given within the catalogue or index, and outside it as is reasonably possible.

For classified catalogues, or shelf arrangement of non-fiction according to a classification scheme, it is necessary to establish a filing order for the symbols used in the notation of a classification scheme. For further details on this see the Chapters on Classification, 13 and 14. The filing order for notation in classification schemes is normally given in the text of the scheme, so the comments that follow relate primarily to alphabetical indexing.

In computer-based information retrieval systems the importance of filing orders varies considerably. The characters to be arranged may vary, but many of the access points used in such systems are basically alphabetical in nature. In systems where documents can be retrieved according to search keys on a string search basis few problems arise. Order is not important since any specific string of characters can be located directly. Sometimes displays of alphabetically close terms may be used in a search in order to review all the possible variations on a key word (for example, to note in a natural language index that documents may be indexed under any of: photogenic, photograph, photographic, photographs, photography and so on.) Here, unusual orders may result in search terms which might have been helpful being overlooked.

In menu-based information retrieval systems alphabetical order may be important, especially if the menu asks a user to identify the alphabetical range within which he expects a term to fall. Thus, a user will have difficulty in locating Allen and Unwin, if this is filed under G. Allen and Unwin, or George Allen and Unwin. Whichever of these headings is chosen will necessitate the user initiating a search to search different parts of the sequence.

21.2 Filing codes

Just as in the establishment of headings for use in catalogues and indexes a code was deemed useful in the maintenance of consistency between catalogues and cataloguers, so a code is a wise precaution in any search for standard filing orders. The object of such consistency is to improve the coincidence between the order expected by the user and that actually encountered in the index or catalogue.

Apparently, an 'a to z' sequence offers little possibility of confusion. However, reflect that every character or form of heading which might feature in a catalogue or index must have a uniquely defined place in a sequence. For example, does London, Jack file before or after London Bridge, and where will a title such as 'All the 9's' file? Filing codes are primarily concerned with guidance on interfiling difficult cases into a basically alphabetical order.

Unfortunately, libraries and other agencies engaged in filing entries in printed indexes and catalogues do not adhere to one filing code. Even when a specific filing code is adopted local deviations from the code are to be expected. Given the diversity of filing practices, it is at least as important to recognise the most common filing dilemmas, and to review some of the possible solutions, as to learn the provisions of one code thoroughly. However a quick review of the major codes will help to provide a context for later discussions. No attempt is made here to provide a full comparative study, but should a reader desire such a study there is a very interesting account in Hunter and Bakewell (See Chapter 1 n.6).

Cutter's Rules for a Dictionary Catalog contains rules for filing in a dictionary catalogue. Later cataloguing codes have tended to regard filing as a separate issue, and hereafter, special codes for filing are evident.

ALA (American Library Association) Rules for Filing Catalog Cards (1942) was essentially a summary of various acceptable methods of filing as practised in American libraries at the time of its compilation. The nature of the compilation of the code led to rather little consensus, and many alternative rules, which together made the code rather confusing. The second edition of the *ALA Rules for Filing Catalog Cards* was issued in 1968, and aimed to take account of developments in cataloguing rules and practice. This edition aimed more directly to recommend straight alphabetical order, keeping the exceptions to a minimum. An abridged edition of the ALA 1968 Code was also published. Both were extensively used both in America, and in more restricted contexts in the United Kingdom.

ALA Filing Rules (1980) supersedes both the first and second editions of the *ALA Rules for Filing Catalog Cards*. These rules follow a general trend in filing practices in endorsing the 'file-as-is' principle outlined below. These rules aim to be more widely applicable than their predecessors. They are intended to be applicable to many types of bibliographic displays and thus could be a significant influence upon filing practices. The introduction to this code certainly repays reading, and contains sensible advice, not so much on recommended filing orders, but on how to make a filing order amenable to the public.

BS (British Standard) 1749: Recommendations for alphabetical arrangement and the filing order of numerals and symbols was originally published in 1951 as a specification for 'alphabetical arrangement'. An intermediate standard was published in 1969 as 'Specification for alphabetical arrangement and the filing order of numerals and symbols'. The 1983 revision consolidates much British filing practice. This standard is designed to take account of computerised filing and covers alphabetical arrangement in lists of all kinds, including bibliographies, catalogues, directories and indexes. BS1749 takes into account the International Standards Organisation Standard – ISO7154: 'Documentation – Bibliographic filing principles', which is in course of preparation.

The Filing Rules for the Dictionary Catalogue of the Library of Congress were first published in 1956 and have been influential in American filing practice, and have contributed to the development of the ALA rules. These LC rules were revised in 1971 in order to provide a set of rules which was amenable to computer filing. This code was used in the Library of Congress in a number of its computer-produced files and catalogues and superseded in 1980 by the *Library of Congress Filing Rules*. These are more elaborate than the ALA rules, with twice the number of rules, and exhibit a tendency to adhere to traditional classified arrangements (which is in keeping with stability in Library of Congress catalogues).

The British equivalent to the LC rules are the *BLAISE Filing Rules*. Publishing in 1980, these rules summarise British Library filing practice as embodied in its various MARC data bases. These rules were drafted according to principles developed by the International Standards Organisation, and have their origins in the report of a Working Party on Computer Filing set up by the Library Association Cataloguing and Indexing Group. Other computerised cataloguing networks also have filing rules and conventions.

21.3 Problems and principles in filing

The emphasis in this section will be on the major filing problems and their potential solutions, rather than any type of systematic review of the different solutions offered by specific codes. A fully comparative account of recommendations for filing orders is likely to prove confusing until the reader has attained some familiarity with the general problems, and the solutions offered by one code. It is however important to note that the solutions to problems do vary between codes.

21.3.1 *Basic orders*

There are two basic orders that can be adopted for alphabetical sequences of headings. These are word-by-word, or letter-by-letter. Figure 21.1 shows one set of headings arranged according to these two orders. Word-by-word filing files one word at a time, and exhausts all headings containing a specific word before proceeding to longer words with the first word as part of them. Thus Child will always file before Children. One way of indicating the requirement to adhere to word-by-word filing is to instruct a filer to file a space before any letter. Letter-by-letter filing takes no account of spaces, and requires the filer to file in alphabetical order merely in response to the letters in the headings to be filed.

Subjects which are closely associated and have similar names may be

Figure 21.1 Basic alphabetical filing orders

Word-by-word filing	Letter-by-letter filing
Child abuse	Child abuse
Child artists	Child artists
Child neglect	Childbirth
Child psychology	Childnapping
Child welfare	Child neglect
Childbirth	Child psychology
Childnapping	Children
Children	Children and civil rights
Children and civil rights	Children in poetry
Children in poetry	Children's books
Children today	Children's hospitals
Children's books	Children's plays
Children's hospitals	Children today
Children's plays	Child welfare

grouped by word-by-word filing. Inadvertent variations in authors' names may also be grouped by this approach. Letter-by-letter filing, on the other hand, groups variations of the same word. For example, there will be no difference in filing position between on-line, on line, and online. Word-by-word filing is generally used in catalogues and bibliographies, but some dictionaries, directories, and encyclopaedias use letter-by-letter filing.

21.3.2 *The file-as-is principle*

Modern codes have moved towards the file-as-is principle. This means that headings are filed exactly according to the characters in the heading in the order in which they are presented. Some earlier codes would have filed some headings, such as those composed of numerals and abbreviations in a form which might be regarded as their standard form, but which was not necessarily the form in which they appeared in the heading. In some earlier codes, for example, abbreviations and numerals were filed as if they were spelt out. The file-as-is principle, if applied to Mc would lead to this being filed as Mc, and not as Mac, and Mc would thus appear at a different place in the sequence to that occupied by Mac. The same goes for other common abbreviations such as St and Saint.

The file-as-is principle makes for relatively simple computer filing procedures, and this has undoubtedly been one of the reasons for its growing popularity. Although a computer can be instructed to file Mc as Mac whenever Mc occurs, the instructions to the computer will be simpler if it is not necessary to list a number of such specific cases, but rather to rely upon a blanket instruction to file the characters as they are found in the text of the heading. Filing according to the file-as-is principle can be helpful to the user. The user who knows the common form of the name for which he is searching, will find retrieval straightforward. Thus with the file-as-is principle, the user who seeks MIT or MS London, but who is ignorant of the expansion of the abbreviations in these headings, will be happier to be able to find these headings filed under their abbreviated form, than under a spelt-out version or complete version. Had the heading been filed according to its full form, the user knowing only abbreviations would be unable to retrieve a heading unless appropriate references were provided from the abbreviated form. Another important limitation to any set of filing rules that require spelling-out is that they must either specify at some length how abbreviations or numerals are to be spelt out for purposes of filing, or accept that variations may arise in the way in which specific headings can be expanded. Whilst indexers may be expected to familiarise themselves with spelling out procedures, searchers are rarely likely to be fully conversant with these.

One reason why headings have not always been filed as they appear, is that this approach splits sequences of similar names written in a different form. Thus, if filed as they appear, St Joan and Saint Joan will be separated from each other by Sin, Slavery, Soils, Soldiers, Sonata and Space, to list only a few of the intermediate words in an alphabetical sequence. Of course, in a catalogue or index where the headings are closely controlled, St Joan and Saint Joan would be unlikely to appear. One form would be chosen and used on all appropriate occasions. If such consistency in the establishment of headings exists, this removes or minimises many filing dilemmas. The cataloguer can also alert the user to unexpected filing orders by the judicious use of references. In a filing sequence where natural language terms or titles are being filed it can be more difficult to avoid inconsistencies in the form of heading.

The file-as-is principle means that collocation of similar headings is provided by the consistent use of uniform headings, and does not rely upon inspired filing. This shifts the responsibility for headings and their arrangement into the arena of cataloguers and indexers.

21.3.3 *Some other filing problems*

1. *Sequencing different characters* It is necessary to define the filing value of all characters that might be found in headings in a catalogue or index. BS 1749 defines the preferred filing order of characters as:

(a) spaces, dashes, hyphens, diagonal slashes, all of which have equal filing value.
(b) ampersands

(c) Arabic numerals and Roman numerals arranged in numeric order interfiled

(d) Roman alphabet letters arranged according to the English alphabet.

(e) Other alphabet letters arranged in their commonly accepted order within each alphabet.

This basic order is similar to those recommended in the ALA and LC rules.

2. *Numerals* can either be filed as recommended in BS 1749 or filed as if spelled out. Earlier rules, as discussed in 21.3.2 tended to prefer the numerals to be filed as if spelt out, but this required the codes to specify the nature of spelling out. For example, does 1984 read as nineteen-eighty-four, or as one thousand nine hundred and eighty-four, or as one nine eight four? The filing of numerals also presents other problems which are nicely treated in the ALA rules. These include guidance on how to file:

punctuation, for example, The 5,000 fingers of Dr T,
decimals, for examples, 1.0 für Dich
fractions, for example, 3/4 for 3
non-Arabic notation, for example, Louis IX
superscript and subscript numerals, for example 1^3 is 1, and
dates.

3. *Diacritical marks* such as umlauts, accents, disaereses may either be ignored, or be assigned a filing value. For example, ü may either be filed as u or as ue.

4. *Punctuation, signs and symbols* Punctuation and other signs and symbols must be considered. Normally, that is, in both the ALA rules and BS 1749, punctuation is ignored except where specially mentioned, and where a filing value has been defined for a specific piece of punctuation.

5. *Initial articles* It is well-established practice to ignore initial articles when they occur as the initial word of a title or subject heading, so that unwieldy sequences do not evolve under such words. Thus 'an', 'the', 'a' and 'der' and 'la' will be ignored in filing headings where these are the initial words. In order to be able to execute an instruction that requires that such initial articles should be ignored, it is necessary to be able to recognise initial articles in many languages; this applies whether the filer is human or a computer. Initial articles associated with name headings are sometimes ignored, but on other occasions are used in filing. Often cataloguing codes require that such initial articles should not be included in headings unless they are essential for identification. Thus AACR2 allows 'The Club', but prefers 'Library Association' and not 'The Library Association'. Here it

would be sensible to include the initial article in filing if a deliberate decision has been made to include it in a heading.

6. *Abbreviations and single letters* Abbreviations present problems in filing primarily because different forms of abbreviation may have been established for the same name. A catalogue may include entries under both MEDLARS and M.E.D.L.A.R.S, and under SDC, S.D.C. and Systems Development Corporation. The instinctive reaction is to attempt to frame filing rules which will result in all of these variants filing together. A number of options exist for the filing of abbreviations and acronyms. Abbreviations may be filed as spelt out, but it is more common these days to: file initials as separate one letter words, for example, B.B.C. comprises three one-letter words; and to file acronyms as one complete word, for example, BLAISE is one word.

This is a satisfactory distinction provided it is possible to fit every set of initials or abbreviations into either 'initials' or and 'acronyms'. Such a categorisation may depend rather arbitrarily upon whether stops have been used between letters or not.

7. *Subject entries* Subject headings beginning with the same word may be interfiled in different ways according to the filing value accorded to inverted headings, phrase headings and subdivided headings. Frequently the filing value accorded to a subdivided heading may be different from that for inverted headings, and this may lead to deviations from the strict and most obvious alphabetical sequence. Figure 21.2 demonstrates this.

21.3.4 *Arrangement of different kinds of headings beginning with the same word*

Headings may arise as author, title and subject, and all types of heading may commence with the same word. 'Black', 'Rose', 'London' to give but a few examples could all be entry words in any of the three main types of headings. The problem is whether to opt for strict alphabetical order or whether the user would find it helpful to have types of entries with the same entry word grouped, so that for example, all subject entries are found together, and all personal name entries are kept in a separate subsequence. Many catalogues do seek to achieve some type of grouping of types of entries. However, once a decision has been made to group similar types of entries other difficulties emerge in defining the categories. Amongst both subject and author (or name) entries there will be different types of entries. Name entries, for example, may include personal names, corporate names, and geographical names and their subdivisions or qualifiers. Figure 21.3 shows an extract for BS 1749, which whilst outlining a preferred order for entries of mixed types, also demonstrates the type of entries that may be encountered.

415

Figure 21.2 Filing orders for subject headings

Crime
Crime, sex
Crime—United States
Crime and narcotics
Crime prevention
Crime syndicates
Crime victims
Crimean War
Crimes
Crimes, military
Crimes, political
Crimes against public safety
Crimes against the person
Crimes without victims
Criminal assault
Criminal investigation
Criminal justice, administration of
Criminal law
Criminal procedure
Criminal psychology
Criminals
Criminals - drug use
Criminology

21.4 Arrangement of entries with the same heading

It is quite common under some headings to have a number of entries and references listed. A prolific author may be responsible for a number of books. A particular subject heading may be assigned to several books which discuss the same subject. Any given subject heading may be associated with both entries and references. The preferred sequence of these multiple entries, all with the same heading, needs to be established. First, it is normal to distinguish between references and added entries, and then to group references at the beginning of the sequence associated with a given heading. Next, it is necessary to order the works for which entries are made under a specific subject or author heading. Often, the title will be used for this purpose, but on occasions when the title is not appropriate for use as a filing element, a chronological order of entries for documents according to the date of publication of the document may be preferred.

The comments in this chapter should illustrate that filing is not as

Figure 21.3 Extract from BS 1749—showing arrangement of different kinds of heading beginning with the same word

Rose   (an author)
  See also entries under her real name, Sharples, E.
Rose. The gypsy's warning
Rose - Prophecies
Rose, 1086-1145
Rose VI, Queen of Thule
Rose, Princess
Rose (family)   (surname)
Rose,
Rose, Andrew
Rose, Andrew. The frozen lake
Rose, Andrew. The frozen lake - Criticism
Rose, Andrew - Homes and haunts
Rose, William
Rose   (geographical name)
Rose - Art galleries
Rose - Sports
Rose. City Council. Minutes of meetings
Rose. City Council - Reorganization
Rose. Recreation Department - History
Rose (France) - History   (geographical name)
Rose (France). Conseil municipal (corporate name)
Rose   (a general work on the flower)
Rose - Culture and growth
Rose - Pruning
The Rose: glory of the garden
The Rose: glory of the garden - Criticism
Rose: how to grow it
Rose and District Rose Society
Rose Cathedral
Rose for ever
The rose revived

S. Maria de la Salute
Saint-Amant, Marc Antoine Girard de
Saint-Exupéry, Antoine de
Saint George and the dragon
Sainte-Beuve, Charles Augustin
San Joaquin
Sankt Aposteln (Cologne)
Santa Barbara
São Paolo

straightforward as it first appears. Familiarity with filing orders cannot be assumed. Further, although there is now reasonable agreement as to how to compile catalogues, and which headings to use, there is less unanimity concerning the arrangement of catalogues and indexes. Perhaps one of the main strengths of online access to a computer data base is that problems of arrangement become less significant if string searching is available.

Chapter 21 Readings

1 American Library Association, *ALA rules for filing catalog cards*, ed. P.A. Seely, 2nd edition, ALA: Chicago, 1968.
2 American Library Association, *ALA filing rules*, Filing Committee, Resources and Technical Services Division, ALA: Chicago, 1980.
3 Ayres, F., 'It's not as easy as ABC', *Catalogue and Index* (54), 1979, 1–3, 8.
4 BLCMP. *Code of filing rules*, Birmingham Libraries Co-operative Mechanisation Project, BLCMP: Birmingham, 1971.
5 British Library, Filing Rules Committee, *BLAISE filing rules*, BLAISE: London, 1980.
6 British Standards Institution, *Specification for alphabetical arrangement and the filing order of numerals and symbols*, BSI: London, 1969. (BS 1749)
7 British Standards Institution, *Recommendations for alphabetical arrangement and for filing order of numerals and symbols*, BSI: London, 1983. (Revision of BS 1749)
8 Hines, T.C. and Harris, J.L., *Computer filing of index, bibliographic and catalog entries*, Bro-Dart Foundation: Newark, N.J., 1966.
9 Library Association, 'Catalog and Indexing Group. Working Party on Filing Rules. Filing by computer', *Catalogue and Index* (27), 1972. (Complete issue)
10 Library of Congress, *Library of Congress filing rules*, prepared by J.C. Rather and S.C. Biebel, Processing Services. Library of Congress: Washington, DC, 1980.

22   Document arrangement and guiding

22.1 General principles

Documents in libraries or resource centres must be physically stored. Normally these documents are organised in a way that facilitates retrieval. With closed access collections the choice of arrangement may present only limited problems, since the librarian will act as an intermediary between the stock and the user. Thus, complex and irrational arrangements can be tolerated, since only relatively experienced staff need to be able to locate items. Open access environments, where the public are expected to locate documents for themselves, are different. Documents must be arranged or physically stored in an order which is self-explanatory, and which preferably coincides with the way in which the public normally seek to retrieve a document. For example, if the users of the library in a College of Education normally ask for slides sets by subject, and serials by title, then subject labels (such as classification numbers) and titles are, respectively, serious contenders for arrangement of the documents concerned. Some type of sympathetic arrangement is not only important for the location of specific documents, but assists users in browsing. A helpful arrangement supports browsing by grouping documents which have some characteristic in common, for example, author, subject, age.

Shelf arrangement and supportive guiding are important in information retrieval. For small collections document arrangement may be the only retrieval device available, particularly in bookshops, small public libraries and small specialist collections. Even where a catalogue or index to a collection is available, users do not always consult these tools, and may prefer to locate either individual documents, or documents with specific characteristics by inspection of the stock. In larger collections it may seem more difficult to browse effectively, but even where browsing a complete collection is a daunting prospect, subsets of the collection may be examined by browsing. Hence, although document arrangement, often in the form of shelf arrangement, may be a very unsophisticated information retrieval device it is probably the most widely used such device, and thus deserves special attention. Equally, shelf arrangement is easy to overlook as an information retrieval device. Special attention has to be devoted to the creation of an index or catalogue and its maintenance but the maintenance of orderly shelf arrangement is often considered an unimportant chore.

Why is shelf arrangement popular in information retrieval? Shelf arrangement fails to permit a document to be represented at more than one place in a sequence (unless there are multiple copies), and thus does not allow any given document to be approached from various different angles, or with requirements specified in terms of different characteristics. It may be that, apart from the simple pleasure of browsing, documents arranged on shelves, filing cabinets and so on, may be more easily examined in terms of characteristics of documents which are rarely reflected in catalogue or index records. The physical format of a document (for example, a book, filmstrip, poster), the quality of production, the design of the cover, the apparent age of the document are all factors which can be ascertained on examining the actual document, but which are unlikely to be fully evident from a catalogue.

22.2 Characteristics for shelf arrangement

The document or shelf arrangement in a library or information materials collection is unlikely to follow one sequence for all types of material, and different libraries and user groups may merit different approaches to document arrangement. Two factors determine the type of order which might be adopted in any given application:

1. user convenience
2. library convenience.

Usually, the convenience of the user must be given priority, but on occasions it is necessary to adopt an order or arrangement which supports other library functions (for example, inter-library loan or quick reference) or which leads to the efficient utilisation of space.

There are a number of characteristics which can be used in determining document arrangements, and in any given collection a mixture of these might be applied. Some common characteristics for arranging books are:

author
title
subject
physical form
nature of the information stored in the book
audience level
extent and nature of use of the collection.

Some of the above characteristics are employed in order to differentiate between sequences, whilst others are more appropriate for determining the order within sequences. For example, audience level may be a criterion which is applied in order to divide a collection in a children's library into material suitable for different age groups. The nature of the information, on the other hand, may determine its inclusion in a special collection of statistics or quick reference materials. Titles may be used to determine the alphabetical order of documents, which perhaps have been primarily grouped as being serials or non-serials, or fiction or non-fiction.

Physical form is often used to divide documents according to their physical format. A music library is a good example of an environment where an array of physical forms is available. The library may have music scores, books on music, sound discs and sound tapes, to mention but a few of the possible media. These different media can all be arranged together in one integrated sequence, or separate sequences may be established for books, scores, tapes and discs. An integrated sequence permits book scores and recordings of Beethoven's music to be stored in proximity to one another. Some libraries will find this kind of integrated approach helpful to their clientele, in that it draws items together by their content, irrespective of their physical form. However, integrated stock certainly can present problems in terms of physically housing the items, and keeping an assortment of media in a tidy sequence. Imagine, for example, attempting to interfile maps and charts with books on a specific country. Unless maps were folded it would be almost impossible to file them in an integrated sequence in such a way that they were preserved for a reasonable period of use. Many libraries, then, opt to file different physical forms in separate sequences, and may, for example, rely upon a catalogue to draw attention to the range of media in which a given author or subject might feature.

Apart from separate sequences for completely distinct physical forms (for example, maps, slides, sound discs), sometimes separate sequences are also maintained for different sizes or types of one physical form. The classic and well-known example of such a distinction is that which is frequently found in libraries where books are arranged in separate sequences according to their size, for example, octavo, quarto and folio. Sound recordings will often be divided into discs and cassettes, and then each of these media may be represented by more than one sequence according, for instance, to the size of discs.

Common characteristics on which to base document arrangement are author, or author equivalent, title and subject. To take some common examples, fiction is often organised by author, periodicals by their titles, and non-fiction by subject. These arrangements are compatible with the normal approach of readers to these types of documents, and this to a large extent accounts for the frequency of their occurrence. Fiction is sought for its style and form, which is often characterised by an author's name, whereas non-fiction is sought for the information that it can provide, and information is usually located according to its subject. Serials may be sought by title as part of a specific search for a given part of a periodical, or used for current awareness where each new issue is a means of updating the knowledge gleaned from the first.

Greater difficulties arise when there is no plain arrangement which will suit all users. One such instance is considered in more detail in 22.4.

A number of more unusual arrangements have been tried, but none have met with wide approval. One reason for this is that many of the experimental approaches to shelf arrangement abandon the basic requirement of a shelf arrangement system, which is that each document has a unique place in the sequence, so that not only is browsing possible, but also specific documents can be retrieved. Any shelf arrangement systems which do not permit ready location of specific documents are cumbersome for the user or member of staff seeking a specific document, but on the other hand may eliminate the need to keep documents in a closely defined order.

Reader interest arrangements have been tried in public libraries. These are really a type of arrangement by subject, but the subject categories into which documents are organised are usually broad and do not follow the discipline-oriented approach of many major classification schemes. The categories are usually chosen locally, to be consistent with the interests of library users. In public libraries, these categories are likely to represent major leisure interests.

For example, at Woking, the stock has been split into about thirty sections, such as Health and welfare, War and warfare, retaining the Dewey sequence within each section. Each section has its own bay of shelves. Within each broad subject group Dewey is retained. Thus each group is given a three-letter label, for example, FOO for the Food and drink section. So, the full call-mark for a general book on cookery would be FOO 641.5. This would be used on the book and in the catalogue, to aid in the retrieval of specific documents. Bexley has a different but similar system, which contains 31 broad categories. These include Ancient World, Travel and Exploration, Paranormal and War. Many of the categories are divided into smaller groups. War, for example, is divided into Militaria, War, World War I, World War II, Vehicles and Equipment. Where the subcategory is small the subsequent arrangement is random. Within a large subcategory, books may be arranged in classified order according to Dewey. Again, each category has a three-or four letter code which is used for spine labelling.

A similar approach to arrangement, but one which is less radical than reader interest arrangement, is to rely upon broad categorisation rather than detailed specification. A number of small public and school libraries opt for broad subject categories which follow the main subjects represented in say, DDC and organise the subjects in the same sequence as in DDC. This can easily be achieved by effectively using the second or third summary of DDC as a basis for classification, that is, assigning only two or three digit numbers, depending on the degree of specification required. Thus, for example, all aspects of Music might be classified at the one number 780, and the number 630 used for every document concerned with Farming and Agriculture. Obviously, such categories may be totally adequate to divide up the stock of a small general collection. Compared with reader interest arrangement, this approach based upon one of the major classification schemes has the advantage of being compatible with the approach that users and staff will encounter in larger collections, and may for instance permit all libraries in a public library system to exploit the same classification scheme, regardless of their size. On the other hand, adhering to one of the major schemes carries with it all of the disadvantages of that major scheme. In particular, some would argue that the discipline-oriented approach of such schemes is unsuited to many applications, and that public libraries, for instance, need to take account of the leisure use that they receive.

Service in-depth abandons subject arrangement altogether, and seeks to arrange documents in categories according to their popularity. Arrangements vary, but one possibility is to place more popular books near to the counter, and less popular subjects in more remote areas of the library. Sometimes this is based on locating complete subject areas with respect to their popularity, but it is impossible to treat individual books in this way. Depending on the precise arrangement the objective may be to serve two different types of clientele. For example, books close to the door and the circulation desk may be intended for the user who merely wishes to make a swift selection of items to take away and read elsewhere. Books further into the library may be those judged suitable for detailed study within the library building, and may be stored adjacent to study space.

22.3 Limitations of document arrangement as a retrieval device

Document arrangement labours under some inherent limitations as a document or information retrieval device. These can be briefly enumerated as:

(a) Documents can be arranged in one order only. Any one document may be required by author, title, subject, form or other characteristic, but this one document can only be grouped according to one of these characteristics at any one time. Thus, a non-fiction book which has been placed in a sequence according to its subject content is difficult to locate if only its author is known (without resorting to a catalogue, or scanning the entire collection).

(b) The second limitation follows from the first. Not only can any given document be only placed in one sequence, but that document can only be placed with respect to one category for any given characteristic. Thus a book on 'the history of naval warships' may be sought under history, navy or warships, but can only be placed in a subject sequence according to one of

423

these features, that is with other books on history, or with other books on warships, or with other books on the navy. Equally, a document with several authors can only be arranged in an author sequence according to one author's name.

(c) The document arrangement adopted is often broken, in the sense that documents in libraries are rarely shelved in one single and self-evident sequence. The physical constraints of the library building may lead to sequences continuing on other floors, or sequences being broken by certain subsections being removed from the shelves. Parallel sequences may be established. Consider sequences of reference works, pamphlets, periodicals, outsize material, all shelved possibly according to their subject content. If these are all shelved according to the same subject sequence (for example, the same classification scheme) then these will constitute parallel sequences. The user is presented with much walking around shelves, and altogether a formidable task if he wishes to gather all documents on a given subject.

(d) Only part of a library collection will normally be visible on shelves, in filing cabinets, in map cabinets, and so on. Documents which will not be evident to the browser of shelves, but which nevertheless are available through a library include: documents out on loan, documents which might be obtained by inter-library loan, and any collections which are kept in closed access. Thus the browser may miss valuable items, although some browsers are primarily concerned with only items that are readily and currently available for loan, and will find browsing a perfectly adequate method of gauging the extent of a library collection.

Plainly, catalogues do not suffer from the above four limitations of document arrangement, and indeed are intended to provide the facilities that document arrangement cannot offer. Although document arrangement has limitations, it is important not to forget its popularity, and therefore to attempt to make document arrangement as effective as possible as a document retrieval device. Guiding (as considered in 22.5) is important in enhancing the effectiveness of document arrangement.

22.4 Case study: shelf arrangement and serials

Serials are one of those categories of materials about which there is little consensus as to their preferred order. This derives at least to some extent from the fact that serials are used in different ways. Since a number of different types of sequences have been attempted for serials, it is worth pausing to consider some of the alternatives. The options for the document arrangement of serials are:

1. An integrated sequence, with books and serials on the same subject adjacent to one another, and possibly to other materials on the same subject.

This integrated sequence will usually lead to serials being arranged in classified order according to the same classification scheme used in the sequences for other materials. This approach supports browsing which takes no account of form, but may make it difficult for users to identify serials with specific titles, or to locate the latest issue on a given subject.

2. A semi-integrated sequence, where periodicals are assigned broad class numbers and filed adjacent to the general books on a subject. This arrangement is ideal for well-defined subjects which coincide neatly with the interests of the library user. This approach does tend to lead to small clutches of periodicals on a given subject, for example all periodicals on Mathematics may be filed together, which aids browsing within the subject areas defined by the groups. In an academic library, for instance, students of a given discipline can expect to find all books and serials on their subject grouped together, sometimes in a 'reading room'.

3. Either (1) or (2) above may be used as the basic sequence for bound volumes of periodicals, and current issues of serials (that is, unbound copies) may be separated from the main sequence of books and bound volumes. This sequence of current serials may be arranged according to serial titles, or by subject usually as represented by some classification scheme.

4. Arrange all serials in a separate sequence from that for books and other materials, which is organised in an alphabetical sequence by title.

5. Abstracting and indexing periodicals (which are both tools for access to the periodical literature, and periodicals in themselves) may be interfiled into a common sequence with other serials, or may form a separate sequence. Such a separate sequence can be arranged alphabetically by titles, or by some subject or classified arrangement. Other serials which may be used as reference works such as directories may be located separately in a quick reference sequence.

The options outlined above represent a number of approaches, but the basic choice is between subject arrangement and organisation alphabetically by title. Title and subject coincide with two different approaches to documents. A subject arrangement is tailored to support browsing, and may be especially valuable to the browser who wishes to note new documents in a given subject area. In particular, a subject arrangement for serials is likely to be compatible with browsing for current awareness. A title-based arrangement is helpful to the user seeking a specific title. Often this will be the type of search that ensues when a user has retrieved an interesting reference to a part of a periodical in a reading list, a data base or an abstracting and indexing journal. In this sense, a title-based arrangement is attuned to the requirements of retrospective searching. Inevitably, any serials collection must cater for both current awareness and retrospective use. This dual use may explain the diversity of approaches to serials arrangement.

Figure 22.1 A simple library guide

Cenfac

(Central Facilities Building, Level 3)

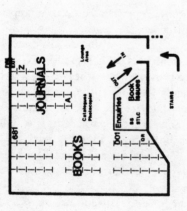

Key

BS	British Standards
QR	Quick Reference
STLC	Short Term Loan Collection

Please note that all material borrowed from Cenfac must be returned there

---

Location of subjects

Cenfac:

All material (books,journals,audio-visual material) in the following subject areas is located in Cenfac:

Computing, Systems	001 – 009
Science, Mathematics	500 – 599 except 526.9 Surveying
History of technology 600 – 609	
Medicine: Scientific aspects	611 – 612
	615 – 616.7
	617 except 617.522 Oral Surgery & 617.8 Otology and Audiology
	619
Engineering and manufactures	620 – 623.9
	629
	660 – 673.9
	678 – 681

F Block:

All other subjects are located in F Block

City of Birmingham Polytechnic

Guide to the Main Library

Address

Main Library
City of Birmingham Polytechnic
Perry Barr
Birmingham B42 2SU

Tel: 021 356 6911, ext 359

Location

The Library is accommodated in two buildings:

F Block	Entrance on level 2 (Levels 1, 2 & 3)
Cenfac	Entrance on level 3 (Central Facilities Building)

Opening hours

Term-time

Monday – Thursday	0930 – 2100 (no books issued after 2030)
Friday	0930 – 1800

Vacation

Monday – Thursday	0930 – 1700
Friday	0930 – 1600

Enquiries

The Enquiry Desks on level 2, F Block and level 3, Cenfac are staffed at all times by professional librarians.

Please ask if you need any assistance

F Block

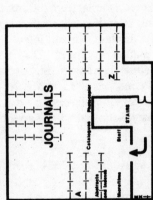

Level 1   Journals

JOURNALS

Catalogues   Photocopier
Staff
STAIRS
Abstracts and Indexes
Microfilms
A

Level 2   Main service area, and books classified at 010-329

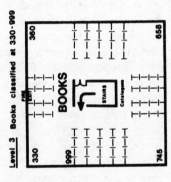

BOOKS

329
010
EDC
Q R
STAIRS
Enquiries
STLC
Book Issue
IN
OUT
STAFF
CATALOGUES
Lounge Area
P
CM
SEMINAR ROOM
(from level 2 walkway) ENTRANCE

Key
CM   Change Machine
EDC   European Documentation Centre
ILL   Inter-library Loans and Reservations
QR   Quick Reference
STLC   Short Term Loan Collection
P   Photocopier

Level 3   Books classified at 330-999

BOOKS

330
999
360
745
658
Lift
STAIRS
Catalogues

STAFF

Assistant Polytechnic Librarian (Reader Services)
Jennifer Beardwood, BSc, MInfSc, ALA

SUBJECT LIBRARIANS

Rose O'Driscoll, MLS, ALA
Senior Tutor Librarian
   Librarianship

Norman Ashfield, BA, ALA
   Bibliography

Bob Bluck, BA, M.Phil, Cert Ed, Dip Lib
   Foreign Languages

Hilary Boucher, MLS, ALA
   Law

Andrew Heron, BA, ALA
   Electrical Engineering

Alison Keyworth, B Lib, ALA
   Educational Development

Brian Lantz, MA, ALA
   Computer Studies
   Mathematics & Statistics

Sharon McIntosh, ALA
   Speech Therapy

Helen Mackin, BA, Dip Lib, ALA
   Health Sciences

Michael Shoolbred, BA, ALA, Cert Ed
   Construction & Surveying
   Mechanical & Production Engineering

Ruth Showler, ALA
   Architecture
   Planning & Landscape

Jane Thomas, BA, ALA
   European Documentation Centre
   Government & Economics

Judith Vernon, ALA
   Accounting & Finance
   Business & Management Studies

Jean Wood, ALA
   Sociology & Applied Social Studies

427

22.5 Guiding

Complete books have been written on the subject of library guiding. It is not possible here to do much more than examine some of the options, and to focus attention briefly on this important aspect which supports the effective use of a library's collection. These few points should be considered in the context of an examination of library guiding in practice. The student is strongly recommended to examine the guiding provided in any libraries to which he has access.

22.5.1 Guides to shelf arrangement

The following possibilities are available for document arrangement guiding:

1. Displays which take a theme approach, for example wild flowers, vintage cars, railways, and gather together material from different places in the library, can be useful in drawing attention to specific aspects of a library's resources. If done effectively, displays can add interest and even excitement to the process of information discovery. Displays do not necessarily offer a systematic key to document arrangement, but they should make certain carefully selected documents easier to locate. Since many displays are changed from time to time (for example, once a week, or once a month) various sections of the stock may be brought to the attention of the library's public over a period of time.

2. Publications, such as book lists, and published lists of specific subject areas present in the stock of a library may assist the user to identify those parts of the stock which might be of particular interest to him. Such lists may be general, just giving an overall outline of the subjects present in the stock of the library, and diagrammatic or coded guides to the whereabouts of the documents on those subjects. Alternatively lists may be mini-bibliographies listing key works in given subject areas.

3. Guiding located in the library A number of possible types of guiding may be evident in libraries. Perhaps some of the more common forms are:

(1) Diagrammatic presentations of the layout of the collection conveniently placed, for example, near the entrance (see, for example, Figure 22.1). These will show major parts of the library building and the location of particular parts of the library's stock. Many devices, such as colours, coding and keys can be used to convey information on such a diagram. Obviously it is important to aim to give as clear a diagram as possible, but some libraries find that it is difficult to convey all the necessary information in a simple manner, merely because the collection is large, or housed in various separate

buildings and wings, and the shelving sequence is complex. Some diagrammatic representations of the layout of the library may unfortunately be daunting.

(2) Large guides to banks of shelving, typically placed on the end of the stack, but possibly also hung overhead or displayed in some other manner close to a bank of shelves. Such guides would show the subjects, and possibly their classification numbers to be located in certain bank of shelves.

(3) Guides to individual sets of books on a specific shelf. Most shelving systems allow for some means of labelling shelves in order to signal the content of books on those shelves. Such labels may pertain to a complete set of shelves, and be attached to the top of a set of shelves, or they may label just one shelf at a time.

Obviously all guiding, whether of the more fixed kind discussed above, or in the form of publications and leaflets, must be pleasantly presented. Good guiding must be carefully designed, possibly by a professional graphic designer, but certainly by someone with a sense of design. The resultant guiding must be clear, by being both easy to read and easy to make sense of. Perhaps it is obvious that guiding must also be accurate, clean and tidy. Guiding is important in conveying an image of the library. It is easy to install appropriate guiding at a given point in time. What is possibly less easy is to making sure that the guiding stays clean, neat and accurate. Regular overhaul of guiding is important, especially for the new user who may rely heavily upon it.

22.5.2 Guides to catalogues and indexes

Some users will have more general experience than others in using catalogues, indexes, bibliographies and data bases, but even the more experienced users will need instructions in the use of specific tools. There may be conflicts between the needs of new and mature users, in the type of instruction that each would appreciate, and certainly more can be assumed in instructions addressed to the experienced information searcher than in instructions for the novice. Nevertheless, the compiler of any information retrieval tool should seek as a minimum to explain the idiosyncracies of that particular tool, and to provide guiding which assists in the examination of various parts of the tool for retrieval.

Internally, in many printed sources, headings are important. Earlier chapters have considered the nature of these headings at some length. Here it is important to emphasise the presentation of such headings.

Headings in card, microfiches or printed catalogues and indexes must be clearly identifiable and facilitate ready scanning. Most computer-based information retrieval systems have some type of 'help' facility. Often a 'help' command calls up information pertaining either to the general use of the system, or to the specific feature in the system with which the user is experiencing trouble. In printed indexes, especially those published and intended for general use remote from their originators, there must be instructions explaining salient features of the index, and possibly, some instructions which should assist with the searching of the index. These instructions may explain features of the index such as the level of post-co-ordination of the indexing language in use, the level of exhaustivity of indexing, and the filing order adopted for the arrangement of headings.

In card and microfiche catalogues, instructions are equally important, although they are more likely to concern themselves with general information concerning the use of the catalogue, such as the type of information contained in a record, and the search keys or headings by which records can be retrieved. In some public access online catalogues, this assistance may well be embedded in the menu-driven approach which the public access online catalogue provides to records. Each step may be suggested to the user, and all essential information given as the search progresses. Notices may be useful in this context for the user who wishes to familiarise himself with the workings of the catalogue before approaching a terminal. Notices conveying, for example, the essential elements of the catalogue are likely to be especially important in association with microfilm or card catalogues.

Instructions in the use of catalogues or indexes may be disseminated to users as part of a library guide, or a general guide to literature searching in specific fields. For example, in an academic library, guides to literature searching in the various fields of study undertaken by the students in that institution are an effective means of explaining the use of various information retrieval tools. Libraries sometimes also find it useful to prepare leaflets which deal with a particular category of information source which might be of use to various users, for example citation indexes. Probably in most libraries instruction in library use and the use of information retrieval tools needs to be available in a number of different modes, in order that all groups are adequately informed. This is not a text in which the full range of library instruction programmes and education for information searching can be fully explored. The reader is referred to n.11, 12 for a more extensive consideration of this topic. Nevertheless it could be misleading to leave this topic without two further comments. First, most types of instructions and guides so far mentioned have been printed, or embedded into the information tool. It is important to remember the place of personal interaction. In a local collection, the librarian is an important source of expertise on the use of information retrieval tools, and various programmes can be evolved in order to exploit this expertise. With large computer-based data bases it is common to have some type of 'help desk' facility through which personal assistance with special searching problems can be obtained.

The amount of detail and style of guiding must be tailored to the anticipated clientele. Where the potential clientele is uncertain, or will come to the tool with a variety of different skills, this can be difficult. One user might have extensive subject expertise when approaching; for example, a tool covering the literature of biology, another user might be lacking such subject expertise, but be very familiar with the format of the index, and other users might respectively have either no experience of either the subject or indexing, or extensive experience of both. Thus pitching instructions at the right level can be difficult. Indeed, some online vendors opt to allow users different levels of assistance, and the user is able to choose the level of assistance which he feels might be appropriate. In instructions addressed to the complete novice it can be difficult to convey all of the complexities of a tool. It may be important to focus on the central features only. If this appears to be excessively difficult, maybe it is time to question whether the tool is too complex.

In conclusion, it should not be necessary to say that instructions and guiding must be as brief as possible, precise, accurate, clear, pleasantly presented and devoid of jargon.

This brief section can do little more than focus attention on the importance of library guiding, both on shelves and in other document arrangement devices (such as files), and in catalogues, indexes and data bases. An effective means of pursuing the study beyond this point is to observe and evaluate examples of guiding and instructions in tools available to the reader.

Chapter 22 Readings

A. Document arrangement and guiding

1 Apted, S.M., 'General purposive browsing', *Library Association Record*, 73(12), 1971, 228–30.
2 Carey, R.J.P., *Library guiding: a program for exploiting library resources*, Bingley: London, 1974.
3 Donbroski, L., 'Life without Dewey: reader interest arrangement of stock in East Sussex library', *Catalogue and Index* (57), 1980, 3–6
4 Foskett, A.C., 'Shelf classification – or else', *Library journal*, 95(15), 1970, 2771–3.
5 Green, R.J., 'The effectiveness of browsing', *College and Research Libraries* 1977, 313–16.
6 Hyman, R.J., *Access to library collections*, Scarecrow Press: Metuchen, N.J., 1972.
7 Hyman, R.J., *Shelf classification research: past, present – future?* University of Illinois, Graduate School of Library Science: Illinois, 1980. (Occasional papers 146)

8 Pollet, D. and Haskell, P.C., *Sign systems for libraries*, Bowker: New York, 1979.

9 Sawbridge, L. and Favret, L., 'The mechanics and the magic of declassification', *Library Association Record*, 84(11), 1982, 385–6.

10 Sykes, A., 'Categorization, or, how Dewey gains a prefix and loses sanctity', *Library Association Record* 84(11), 1982, 383–4.

B. *User Education*

11 Finn, D. *et al.*, *A teaching manual for tutor-librarians*, Library Association: London, 1978.

12 Fjallbrant, N. and Stevenson, M., *User education in libraries*, Linnet, Bingley: Hamden, Conn., London, 1978.

23 Physical forms of catalogue and index

23.1 Introduction

The physical form of a catalogue or index imposes constraints upon the way in which these various tools may be used. In fact some of the distinctions between the computerised data bases and printed indexes derive from the very different physical forms. Some aspects of the retrieval characteristics which are normally associated with particular physical forms have already been reviewed in earlier chapters. This chapter focuses on the physical characteristics rather than the retrieval features of the various physical forms of catalogue and index.

23.2 Physical forms of catalogue and index

Amongst the physical forms that catalogues and indexes can take are: ultrafiche, microfiche, microfilm, computer book form, conventionally printed book form, looseleaf book form, guard book form, sheaf, card and online terminals. The more important physical forms for the future are those which can most effectively be produced from computerised cataloguing systems; however manual cataloguing and indexing are still performed, and it is too early to dismiss those physical forms associated with non-computerised cataloguing and indexing. It is necessary to evaluate the physical forms when starting a new index or catalogue or when processing methods are changed.

In practice many larger libraries contain indexes in many of the above physical forms, for different applications. The library catalogue of one library alone may be available in different physical forms for different locations (for example, computer book form for branches, and microfiche for a central library), or to cover different periods of time (for example, an early catalogue may be card form, and now superseded for recent stock by an online catalogue). If a user finds it necessary to use a range of information retrieval tools in any given library, his search is likely to bridge tools in many different physical formats. This variety of physical forms presents unhelpful complexities to a user, who may have to contend with computer print-out book form, conventionally printed indexes, microfiche and online indexes and catalogues, in even relatively simple searches.

Some of the more popular forms of catalogue and index are now considered in more detail.

23.3 Requirements of a physical form of catalogue or index

Ten points can be introduced in order to identify a suitable physical form of catalogue, or index:

1. Flexibility to allow easy insertion and withdrawal of records, so that the catalogue can be amended to reflect the current state of a library's stock.
2. Compactness, so that valuable space which could be occupied by other library material is not given over to bulky catalogues.
3. Immediate access when required by users and staff, preferably several users at the same time.
4. Portability, for ease of comparison with other bibliographic listings, and the documents themselves, either within the library or beyond (this feature, portability, can be a mixed blessing – things which can be moved have a habit of disappearing!).
5. Availability of multiple copies for branches, additional locations, and other interested parties.
6. Convenient, cheap and quick to reproduce, so that copies may be supplied as required for branches, other libraries and so on.
7. Quick, easy and accurate to use.
8. Inexpensive to maintain.
9. Compatible with co-operative ventures, specifically in permitting the compilation of union catalogues and international indexes.
10. Usable in conjunction with bibliographies and indexes.

Not surprisingly, no one physical form meets all these criteria. Different criteria are relatively more important in various applications, and the physical form appropriate for any given application must be assessed with the assistance of the ten criteria.

The requirements of a physical form of catalogue can be divided into two categories: those which are primarily in the interests of the catalogue or index maintainer, and those which mostly affect the catalogue user. Those which have to do primarily with maintenance might be numbers 1, 2, 6, 8 and 9, whereas the remainder of the list have a more direct impact on use.

23.4 Cards

Card catalogues or indexes comprise a set of cards often 5×3 inches

(122×72 mm), with each entry on a separate card. Cards are filed in drawers, approximately 1000 cards per drawer, which when stacked together may form a catalogue cabinet. Rods may hold the cards in the drawer and stops may prevent drawers from falling out of the cabinet. Various mechanisms for displaying and holding cards are possible, including revolving drums and platforms. Cards, although often a standard size, may be various sizes, and for some post-co-ordinate indexes may be printed with various codes and grids.

Cards catalogues and indexes were popular before computers were as well established as they are now in library housekeeping and information retrieval. Even today, many computerised cataloguing systems generate cards as one physical form of output from the catalogue data base. For large computer-produced catalogues cards represent considerable filing effort, which can be avoided by opting for one on the other physical forms of catalogue. Where cards are still preferred in large catalogues this is either because staff and/or users express a preference for the card form, or because a decision has been made to retain all records on cards so that one integrated catalogue sequence can be maintained. Cards will remain useful for small local and personal indexes, but other options, in the form of microcomputers and their software are beginning to compete in this application.

Qualities of cards

1. Arguably the strongest point in favour of card catalogues is the ease of insertion and withdrawal of cards. The only problem is the mammoth task of interfiling new cards, especially in catalogues where there are large numbers of new or amended entries.
2. Card catalogues are relatively compact, but take up more space than other more recently introduced forms.
3. Several users may access the catalogue simultaneously, although there is generally only one copy.
4. Card catalogues are not portable, but drawers and individual cards can be removed by staff for checking against stock.
5. Multiple copies can be produced, and have been produced by centralised agencies, but:
6. unless printing in many copies is sought reproduction methods can be a little tedious.
7. Easy to use and familiar as a form to many library users.
8. Reasonably economic to produce and cards wear well.
9. Cards used by co-operative agencies, and in the past for some union catalogues.
10. Records can easily be compared with those in bibliographies and indexes provided cards can be removed.

23.5 Computer book form catalogues and indexes

Computer book form catalogues and indexes are one the products of computer processing of catalogue and index records. The output may be in the form of line printer output, or may be computer typeset and presented in a form more akin to a conventionally printed index.

Line printer output is most common in local indexes and catalogues, and has been widely used for producing catalogues, periodicals lists, subject indexes, indexes to collections of reports, catalogues of special collections, and copies of catalogues for branches. As opposed to more professionally typeset computer book form catalogues and indexes this option is cheap and readily available, but may, unless skilfully exploited and designed, lead to bulky catalogues which are difficult to read.

Many published catalogues, bibliographies and abstracting and indexing services are printed with the aid of computer typesetting. This leads to a nicely presented output, which facilitates reading and scanning. This better quality output becomes economic to produce if a reasonably large number of copies are required, as for instance with published lists.

Book form has always been used for abstracting and indexing publications, and other published indexes and directories, but was generally regarded as too inflexible for library catalogues, especially where the catalogue required regular updating to cater for continuing and gradual expansion of the collection. Conventionally printed book form indexes, often without the intercession of the computer are of course still usual for indexes in printed directories, monographs, conference proceedings, reports and individual periodical titles. In these applications it remains important that the index be in the same physical form as the document that it indexes.

Qualities of computer book form catalogues and indexes

1. Conventionally bound book form catalogues were difficult to amend and update. The application of the computer in processing cataloguing records has made it easier to print a new version of the catalogue or index with new entries interfiled with old. This still necessitates reprocessing of old data each time a new edition is prepared, and the other alternative which is adopted by published tools and some catalogues is to issue new records at intervals (of say one month, or one year) and cumulate entries into one integrated series over a longer period. Various cumulations may be possible, but normally there is no attempt to integrate all records into one sequence.
2. Form is relatively compact and can be conveniently shelved alongside similar tools.
3. It is easy to access: in particular, different users may consult different volumes simultaneously.

4. Portability is reasonable. Copies may be taken anywhere for further study.

5. Printed forms are available in multiple copies, and available in a variety of arrangements and formats, provided that the form has emerged from a computerised cataloguing environment.

6. It is easy to reproduce book form, in different qualities, and formats, and for catalogues of subsets of the complete collection. Reproduction can be very suitable for sale and dissemination.

7. Book form is easy to use, readable, and reckoned to be an acceptable format for many users. Advantages are ease of scanning, and the ability to flick between different sequences (for example, author, subject).

8. Maintenance requires printing of new editions or sections. Costs can be kept within reasonable bounds if a method appropriate to the specific application is chosen.

9. Union catalogues are not often produced in book form, due to the large size of such catalogues, and the resultant bulk of any book form union catalogue.

10. It is easy to carry volumes to compare one printed volume with another, or with the output on a terminal.

23.6 Microform catalogues and indexes

Microform catalogues are a common output from computerised cataloguing systems. They have many advantages, not the least of which is their low per copy cost. Since the early 1970s various forms have been used extensively for catalogues, and other forms have sometimes been used for printed indexes. For published indexes, microform is often offered as an alternative form, and the index is also published in hard copy; this is known as simultaneous publication of microform and hard copy. Some dictionaries, directories and other reference works are also available in microform.

Most microform catalogues and indexes are produced by COM bureaux which specialise in producing such products. There is often a range of options for format, type, size and so on. It is not intended to make a comprehensive review of the various different microforms but the following forms are common for catalogues and indexes:

1. Microfiche, usually 208 or 270 frames per fiche, in a piece of film and with a reduction ratio of 42 or 48:1.

2. Microfilm, in either 35 mm or 16 mm roll film, usually but not always packaged in a cassette.

3. Ultrafiche, an extra-high reduction ratio fiche with a reduction ratio of 150 to 200:1.

The various microforms have slightly different qualities, such as slightly different costs for producing in various numbers of copies. Nevertheless, in the interests of brevity the key features that are common to all types of microform in use as catalogues are reviewed below:

1. Ease of modification and amendment is very similar to that of computer produced book form catalogues. Normally amendment is achieved by issuing a new edition at intervals.

2. Microforms are obviously very compact, and the microforms themselves occupy negligible space. The space requirements of catalogues or indexes in microform arise mainly from the necessity of supplying workspace for users, and a location for readers. A greater number of readers will demand more space, but the number of records in the catalogue or index will have little effect upon the space requirements of the catalogue – even a large stock can be represented on a couple of folders of fiche.

3. Immediate access is possible whenever required, according to the number of readers and catalogue copies available.

4. Microforms are portable, but must be read with the intercession of a reader, and although portable models exist, microform readers, in general, are less portable. Sets of fiche are inclined to become misfiled, and odd fiches may be lost.

5. Multiple copies are easy and inexpensive to produce, although readers must be provided and maintained at various sites where the catalogue or index might be consulted.

6. Generally, the more copies, the cheaper the catalogue is per copy. In this respect microform catalogues are particularly amenable to use in union schemes or published indexes, where it is normal for many copies to be required.

7. Microforms are easy to use, although there were early reservations concerning the fact that users need to become familiar with any specific kind of microform and its reader. Some categories of users may be discouraged or confused by microfilm readers, and some readers are less easy to manage (for example, to switch on, locate the appropriate frame) than others.

8. Microforms are quite a cheap form to reproduce and to issue new editions.

9. Microforms are particularly suited to the provision of many copies of union catalogues.

10. It is possible to use microforms in conjunction with other indexes, but only if a printed index can be brought to the microform reader and compared. Alternatively comparisons can be executed by printing the text on the microfiche on to a paper form, and using this for parallel examinations.

23.7 Online catalogues and indexes

The computer offers a new mode of access to bibliographic data bases, direct interrogation of computer-held data bases via online terminals. An online terminal may comprise either a printer, or a visual display unit with a screen, or both a visual display unit and a printer. Numerous different models are available, ranging from purpose-designed terminals which are specifically suited to word processing, models where communication is via a heat sensitive screen, through to terminals which are effectively modified television sets linked to an outside computer by a telephone line. All these may be encountered in accessing catalogues and other bibliographic data bases.

Online terminals are now well established in information retrieval, and in interaction with catalogue data bases for catalogue maintenance. A development of the past three years is the public access online catalogue. This poses more fundamental design problems than the previous applications of online information retrieval, since it must be carefully designed for public use. A parallel development is public viewdata systems where it will also be necessary to consider public access. Such systems may eventually be extensively used for library catalogues and indexes, which are currently more common in one of the other physical forms.

Online catalogues and indexes – qualities

1. Offer easy and instantaneous amendment of records, without the need to issue new editions.
2. Occupy similar space to a microform reader and associated microforms, provided that the same number of service stations is required (this need not always be the case).
3. Offer immediate access, provided that there are no restraints on the availability of the data base or computer facilities.
4. These have relatively low portability. A terminal which accesses the data base must be linked to the computer system.
5. Offer as many 'copies' as there are terminals linked to the computer systems supporting the data base. This means that in an environment where computer terminals are readily available, access to catalogues can be very straightforward, requiring no additional expenditure and no regular outgoings. Other forms of catalogue and index need to be copied, and, accordingly, expense is incurred.
6. Multiple copies of the catalogue or index in the conventional sense are not required, but the data base can be copied and loaded into various computer systems.
7. Potentially this form offers very quick use, but like microform

catalogues or indexes, will need careful introduction in order to negotiate user resistance.

8. Offer competitive costs, depending on the cost of online access to the data base and charging system. The costs of online access must be compared with similar costs of providing print-out in other forms. The purchase and maintenance of terminals must be compared with similar costs for microform readers, card cabinets and so on.

9. Form offers great possibilities for co-operation, as do any of the computerised cataloguing systems, but the success of co-operation will depend upon the compatibility of different library's systems.

10. It should be relatively easy to check references from bibliographies and other indexes and online data bases. An increased number of access points and free text searching should minimise problems arising from incompatibilities between catalogues and indexes from various sources.

This point-by-point evaluation makes a fairly convincing case for the public access online catalogue. These are becoming increasingly popular, especially in libraries in the United States.

Two major hurdles remain before wider implementation can be expected: the cost of equipment for the installations of terminals in all service points in a library service; and user attitudes and acceptance of this physical form of catalogue and index. This has been negotiated with respect to online information retrieval from large external data bases, and experience garnered in this context suggests that the user/system interface requires careful management.

23.8 Other physical forms of catalogue

The major four categories of physical forms outlined so far account for most of the published indexes and catalogues. Some other forms of card index are mentioned in Chapter 17. Cataloguers have, however, been inventive and there exists a plethora of physical forms in which catalogues are to be found. Most of these forms are variations of some type upon either card or printed book form indexes, but have been deemed to be specifically suitable for the applications in which they are encountered.

Visible indexes, strangely, are normally used for catalogues. There are two types:

(a) those holding cards, with only a certain depth of card visible, so that, for instance, headings can be scanned.

(b) those made up of narrow strips about $\frac{1}{4}$ inch (6 mm) wide which are mounted one below another in a frame. In the finished frame the strips are displayed like the lines on a complete page.

Type (b) is usually found as brief entry periodical catalogues, or subject indexes to classified catalogues, possibly for the main stock of the library. Type (a) is used as periodicals accessions registers, in which it is possible to record details of receipt and so on and sometimes for catalogues of other items, such as filmstrips.

The *guard(book) catalogue* is a book form catalogue with several entries on each page, but each entry inserted by pasting slips on to the stout pages of the book. The British Museum has a large guard book catalogue, and some academic libraries use this form. The form is bulky, and time-consuming to maintain, but does offer a book form catalogue in which entries can be inserted and withdrawn.

The *sheaf catalogue* comprises sets of slips held in small looseleaf binders. Slip sizes are typically 7³⁄₄ by 4 inches (19×10 cm) and each binder holds a few hundred slips. Each slip normally carries a separate entry, so the form is both flexible for insertion and withdrawal, but also in 'book form'. Each of the binders is portable and can be separately studied. Because duplicates can be easily made, sheaf catalogues were popular in applications where multiple copies were desirable, such as union catalogues, but the need to maintain large sheaf catalogues has been largely superseded by the products of computer processing. The slips are cheaper, but less durable than cards.

Chapter 23 Readings

1 *Bath University Comparative catalogue study. Final report,* University Library: Bath, 1975. (BLR & D Report 5240–5248)
2 Borgman, C., 'On-line catalogs in the public library: a study to determine the number of terminals required for public access', in: *Communicating information: proceedings of the 43rd ASIS Annual Meeting, 1980,* vol. 17, Anaheim, California, 1980, ed. A.R. Benenfeld and E.J. Kazlanskas. Knowledge Industry Publications: White Plains, N.Y., 1980, 273–5.
3 Boss, R., 'Turnkey minicomputer systems as on-line catalogs', *Reference Quarterly* 20(1), 1980, 40–4.
4 Brownrigg, E.B. and Lynch, C.A., 'Online catalogs: through a glass darkly', *Information Technology and Libraries,* 2(1), 1983, 104–15.
5 Bryant, P., 'The catalogue', *Journal of Documentation,* 26(2), 1980, 133–53 (Progress in documentation).
6 Butler, B., *Library and patron response to the COM catalog: use and evaluation,* Report of a field study of the Los Angeles Public Library System. Revised edition by B. Butler, M.W. West and B. Aveney, Information Access Corp., 1979.

7 Cherry, S.S., 'The moving finger accesses', *American Libraries*, 1981, 14–16.

8 Doszkocs, T.E., 'CITE NLM: natural-language searching in an on-line catalog', *Information Technology and Libraries*, 2(4), 1983, 364–80.

9 Fayen, E.G., 'The online catalog: improving access to library materials', Knowledge Industry: White Plains, N.Y., 1983.

10 Folcarelli, R.J. *et al.*, *The microform connection*, Bowker: New York: 1982.

11 King, M., 'On costing alternative patterns for com-fiche catalogues', *Program*, 14(4), 1980, 147–60.

12 McSean, T., 'GEAC library systems: a survey of current installations', *Vine* (43), 1982, 25–30.

13 *Microforms and library catalogs: a reader* ed. A.J. Diaz, Mansell: London, 1977.

14 *Microforms in libraries: a reader*, ed. A.J. Diaz, Microform Reviews Inc.: Weston, Conn., 1975.

15 Needham, A., *User reactions to various forms and orders of catalogue*, Bath University Library: Bath, 1974. (Bath University Comparative Catalogue Study. Final Report: paper no. 8).

16 OCLC and Research Libraries Group, *Online public access to library bibliographic databases: developments, issues and priorities, Final report to the Council on Library Resources*, Council on Library Resources, 1980. (ED 195 275)

17 *Prospects for the online catalog: summary report*, RTSD newsletter 7(5/6), 1982, 41–7.

18 Research Libraries Group, *Public online catalogs and research libraries, final report to the Council on Library Resources*, Research Libraries Group, 1982.

19 Rowley, J.E., 'Prospects for public access online catalogues: a review' *Library Review*, 1982, 261–7.

20 Saffady, W., *Computer-Output Microfilm: its library applications*, American Library Association: Chicago, 1978.

21 Salmon, S.R., 'Characteristics of online public catalogs', *Library Resources and Technical Services*, 27(1), 1983, 36–67.

22 Scott, A.D., *Report on UK catalogue use survey: physical forms and guiding*, Brighton Polytechnic School of Librarianship: Brighton, 1973 (Also: Scott, A.D., *Staff catalogue use: physical form*, Brighton Polytechnic School of Librarianship: Brighton, 1973.)

23 Seal, A., *Online public access to library files: a bibliography*, Centre for Catalogue Research: Bath, 1984.

24 Specht, J., 'Patron use of an online circulation system in known-item searching', *Journal of the American Society for Information Science*, 1980, 335–46.

25 Spencer, J.R., *An appraisal of computer output microfilm for library*

catalogues. NRCd: Hatfield, 1974.

26 Stevens, N.D., 'The catalogs of the future: a speculative essay', *Journal of Library Automation*, 13(2), 1980, 88-95.

27 Teague, S.J., *Microform librarianship*, 2nd edition, Butterworth: London, Boston, 1977.

Index

Full text software packages 384

GEAC Computer Corporation Ltd 402
GEISCO 366
General classification schemes 186, 212, 249
General Systems Theory 201
Go-lists in indexing 290-1
Governments and government bodies 148-9, 150-2
Guard(book) catalogues 441
Guiding in libraries 424-5, 428-31

Headings
    author 129-41
        for corporate bodies 142-53
    for files 75
    filing of 407-18
    and nonbook materials 46
    see also Subject headings
Homographs 261-2, 293
Hospitality in notation 204-5
Hosts, online 362-72

Identical names 140
Illustrated texts 133
Indexes
    author 9
    to books 9-10, 11
    to classification schemes 185, 197, 199, 207-8
        BC 244, 246
        Colon Classification 241
        Dewey Decimal Classification 218-20
        Library of Congress 229
        and notation 202
        UDC 235
    errors in 181-2
    exhaustivity in 181
    filing and order in 407-18
    guides to 429-31
    measures of effectiveness 178-80
    physical forms of 433-43
    printed 9-11, 291, 430
        definition 5
        production of 6
        records in 20-8
        v. data bases 15-16, 17
    specificity in 180-1
    see also Subject indexes
Indexing

and searching 176-8
subject indexing 173-6
Indexing journals 11
Indexing languages 168-70, 230, 265-95
    natural 289-93
    subject headings lists 265-71
    thesauri 271-89
    see also Controlled indexing languages; natural indexing languages
Indexing services 436
    periodical article citations 51
    and UNIBID 97
Indexing systems, definition 296
Indicative abstracts 72, 74
Indicative-informative abstracts 72
INFO-TEXT Text Management and Document Retrieval System 401
Information retrieval
    in BLAISE 345
    computer-based systems 429-30
        filing order 409
    and document arrangement 423-6
    in-house systems 381-404
    menu-based systems 191-2, 409, 430
    on-line systems
        external services 360-80
    tools of 3-19
Informative abstracts 71-2, 73
Initial articles, filing of 414-15
INSPEC data base
    searching of 322-3, 327
Integrative levels, theory of 200-1
Interlibrary Loan Systems
    OCLC 352
International Serials Data System (ISDS) 53, 57, 58, 61
International Serials Documentation System (ISDS) 53
International Standards Organisation 52
Inventory catalogues 107
ISBDs (International Standard Bibliographic Descriptions) 30-1, 32, 34-6, 37
    for component parts (ISBD(CP)) 65-6
    ISBD(G) 34-6, 37
    for serials (ISBDs) 58, 61
ISBNs (International Standard Book Numbers) 42, 106
Isolates 194, 195, 197-8
ISSNs (International Standard Serial

Numbers) 42

Joint Code (Anglo-American Code (1908)) 118–19

Kaiser's Systematic Indexing 301
Keyword indexes
  and citation indexes 333
  KWIC 161–2, 163
  KWOC 162
Keywords in document summaries 74

LaFontaine, Henri 230
LASER (London and South Eastern Library Region) 353
Laws
  uniform titles 160
Left hand truncation 326–7
Letter-by-letter 411–12
LEXIS full text data base 78, 360, 362
Library guiding 424–5, 428–31
Library housekeeping
  software for 385
Library of Congress
  centralised cataloguing service 343–4
  and co-operative networks 356
  Filing Rules 411
  List of Subject Headings 266, 268, 300–1
  MARC records 85, 213, 221, 222, 229, 248, 343–4, 348
  MARC(S) file 61, 62
Library of Congress Classification Scheme 188, 202, 212, 223–30
  index 229
  main classes 224–5
  notation 224, 226–9
  revision 229
LIBRIS (Library Information System) 356–7
Literal mnemonics 204
Literary warrant 168, 224
Local cataloguing 339–40, 342
Local library systems
  OCLC 352–3
LOCAS (Local Catalogue Service) 345, 348
London Classification of Business Studies 252, 253
Lubetzky, Seymour
  and Catalogue Code revision 120

Main classes (classification schemes) 186, 200–1
  Bibliographic Classification 242–3, 245, 247
  Broad System of Ordering 255
  Colon Classification 240, 245
  Dewey Decimal Classification 214–15
  discipline-orientated 191
  Library of Congress Classification 224–5
  London Classification of Business Studies 253
  Universal Decimal Classification 231–2
Main entries 20, 27
  conference proceedings 148
  corporate bodies 144–5
  title 155, 156–7
Mainframe computers 386–7
Maps
  and bibliographic description 39, 47, 48–9
  Bogg's and Lewis Map Classification 250, 252
MARC (Machine Readable Cataloguing) 229
  and BLCMP 353
  and DC 213, 221, 222
  and LC 213, 221, 222, 229, 343–4, 348
  record format 85–7
  and software packages 382
Marginal storage cards (edge notch cards) 315–16
Martindale Online 78, 79–80
Menu-based information retrieval systems 191–2, 409, 430
Microcomputers 387–8
Microform catalogues 430, 437–8
MicroQUERY 391–2
Mini-abstracts 72–3
Minicomputers 387
Mixed notation 202
Mnemonics 204
Monographs
  bibliographic description 29–42
  physical description area 40–1
MUMS (Multiple Use MARC system) 356
Music
  British Catalogue of Music Classification 252, 254
  cataloguing 46, 48, 49–51